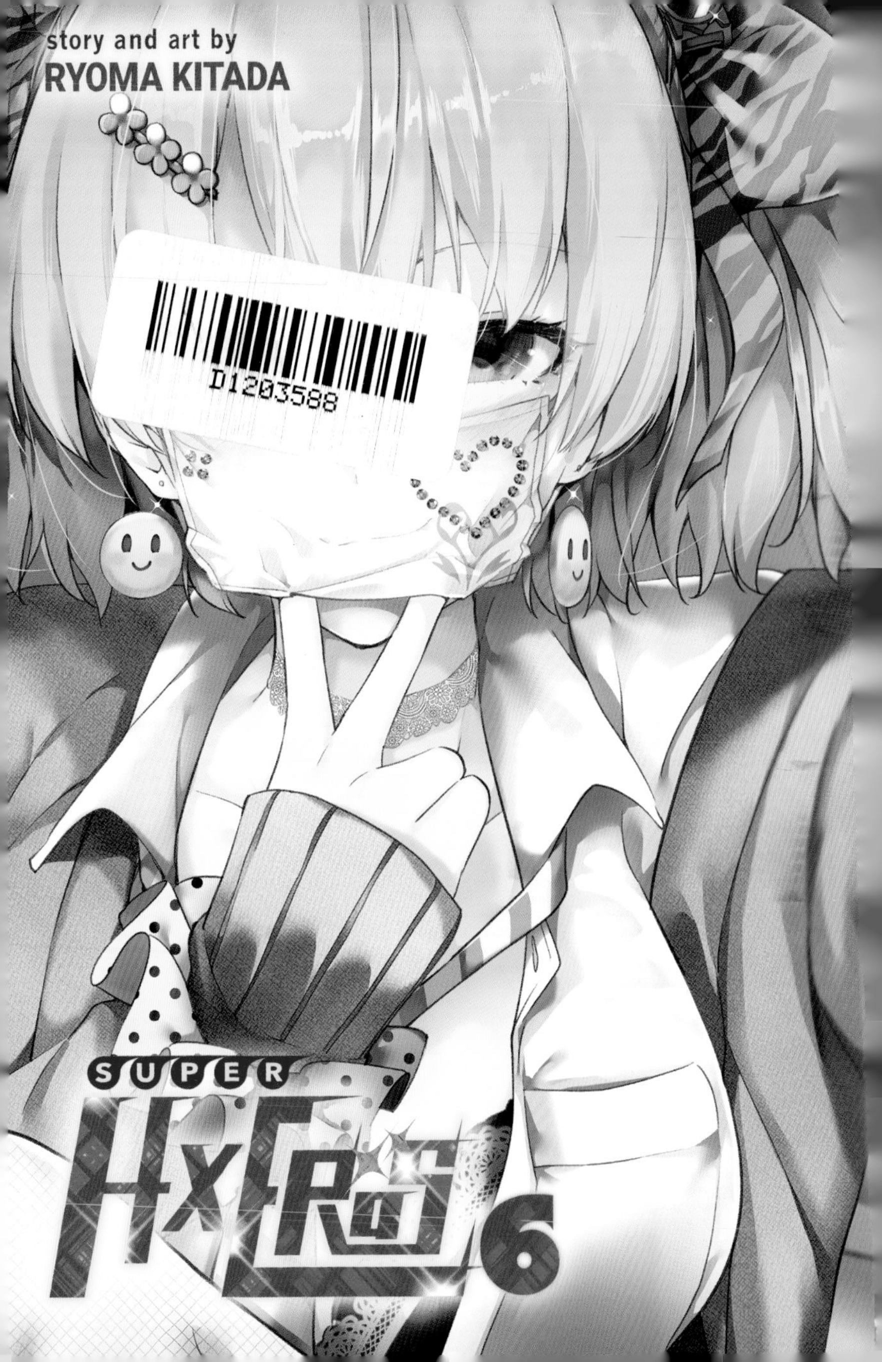
story and art by
RYOMA KITADA
SUPER
HxEROS
6

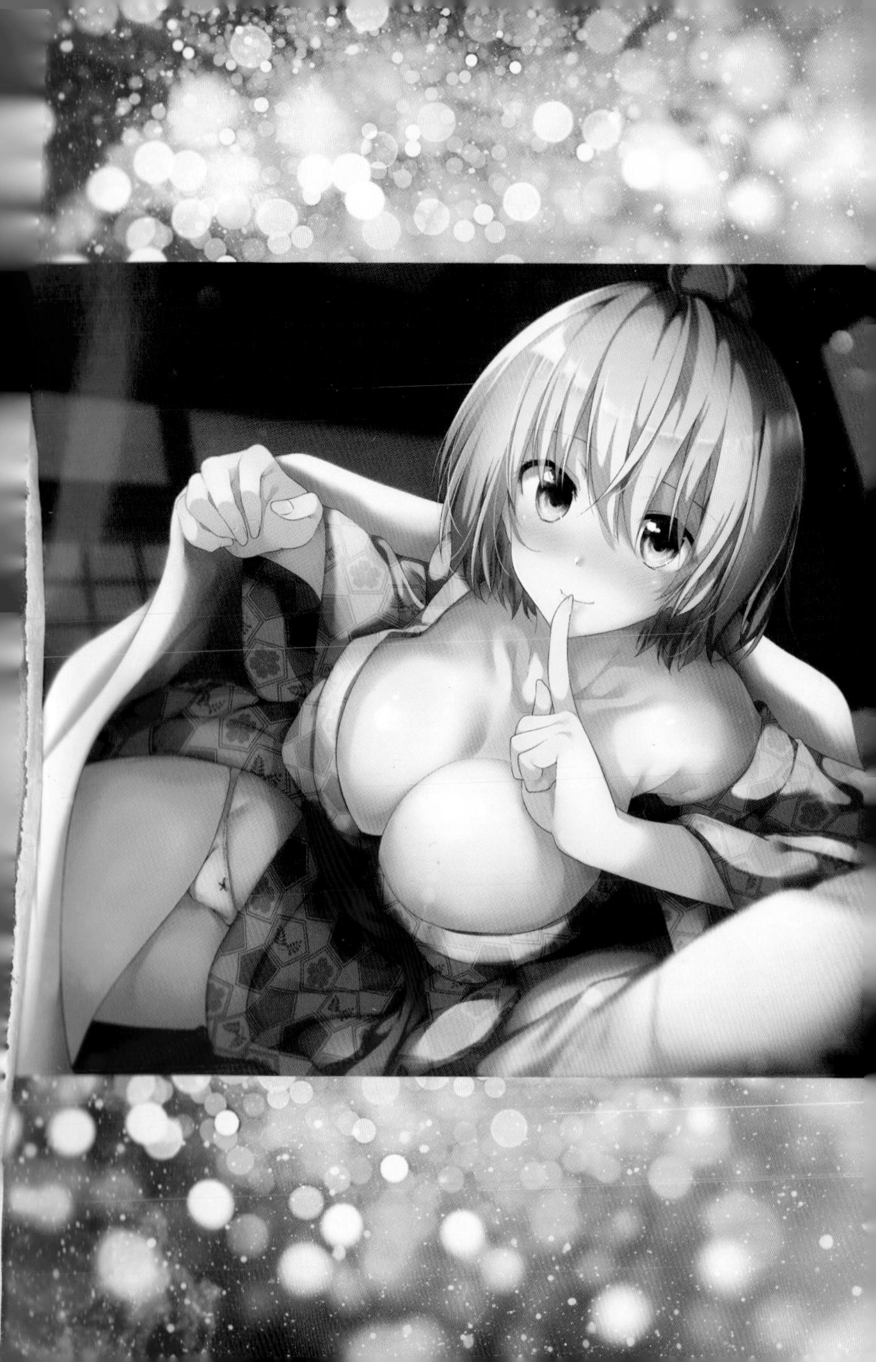

SUPER HxEROS

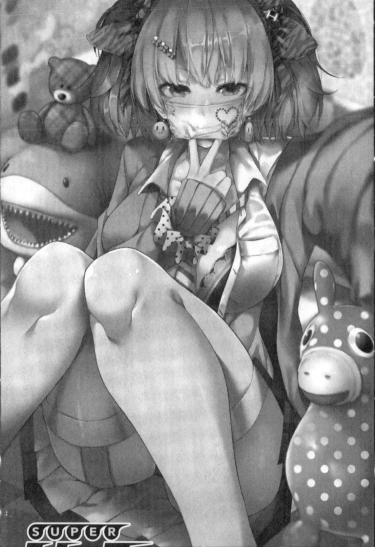

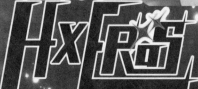

6

RYOMA KITADA

HXEROS Characters

HXEROS: A team of heroes that use the power of eros and H-Energy to fight the alien Kiseichuu.

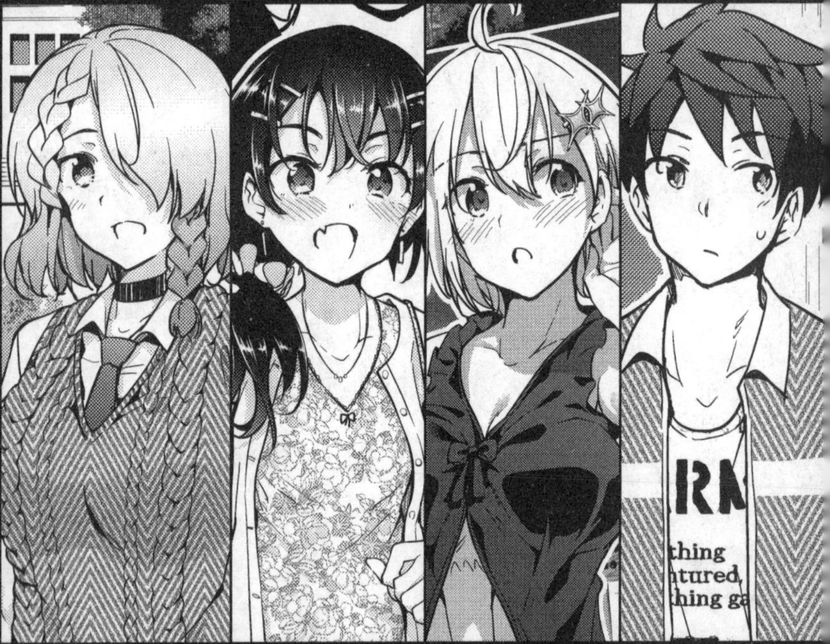

Maihime Shirayuki

HXE White

A sweet, clumsy girl who looks normal on the outside but is a total horndog on the inside.

Momoka Momozono

HXE Pink

Tired of always being in her sister's shadow, she took up the superhero mantle. Has caught onto Retto's feelings for Kirara.

Kirara Hoshino

HXE Yellow

Extremely averse to sex and sexual innuendo due to a traumatic attack in her youth. Haunted by a hallucination of her younger self: Dark Kirara.

Retto Enjo

HXE Red

Became a hero to avenge his childhood friend, Kirara, after a Kiseichuu attack traumatized her as a child. Coincidentally, also in love with her.

Story

The Earth as we know it is in peril: the horrifying Kiseichuu have come to destroy the human race! Thankfully, a team of young men and women have rose to the challenge to fight them off day in, day out. Their name? The SUPER HXEROS.

After being sent on an all-expenses-paid beach vacation, Retto and the gang run into the Tokyo squad and become fast friends. On the way back, Retto notices that Kirara's missing her usual hairclip and goes in search of it. When he brings it back to her, he tells Kirara of the story behind it—that he'd bought it for her back in elementary school to ask her to marry him. Kirara promised him a proper answer, eventually...

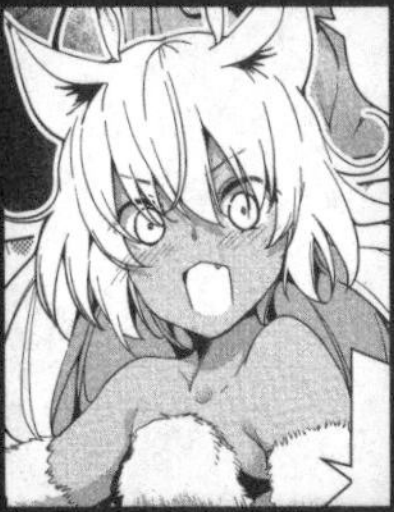

Chacha

Shunned Kiseichuu Princess. Has the ability to amplify H-Energy.

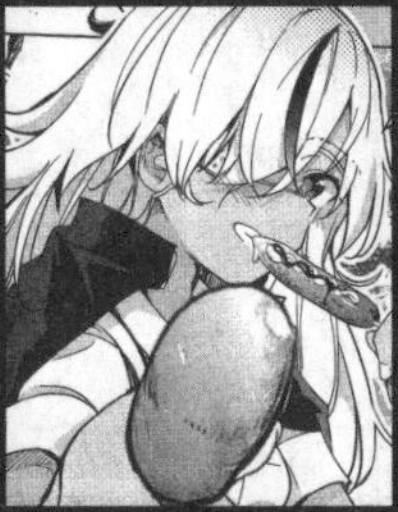

Murasame Shiko

Member of the Tokyo Squad. Wants to make Retto her benefriend.

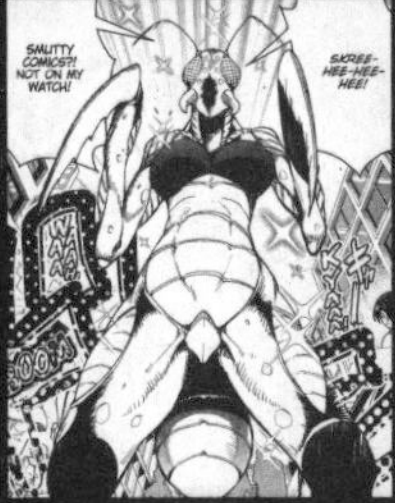
SMUTTY COMICS?! NOT ON MY WATCH!
SKREE-HEE-HEE-HEE!

Kiseichuu

Evil aliens who seek to destroy humanity by draining their H-Energy, the source of human sexual desire.

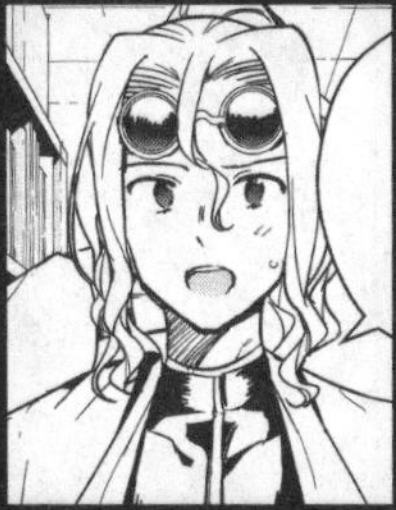

Anno Jou

Leader of the Saitama Squad of the Earth Defense Force. Also Retto's uncle.

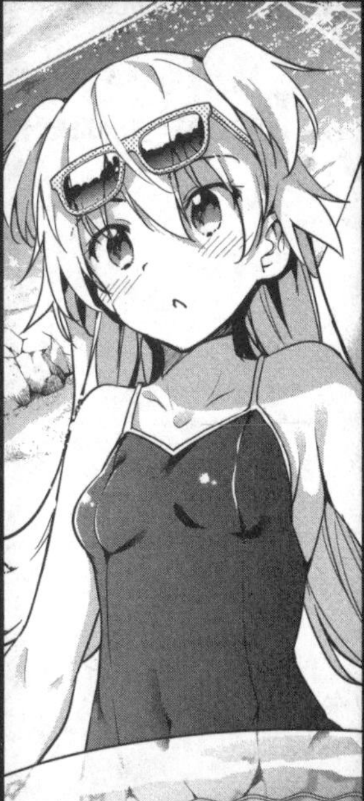

Sora Tenkuji

HXE Blue

Loves to draw hentai manga. In charge of designing the XERO Suits.

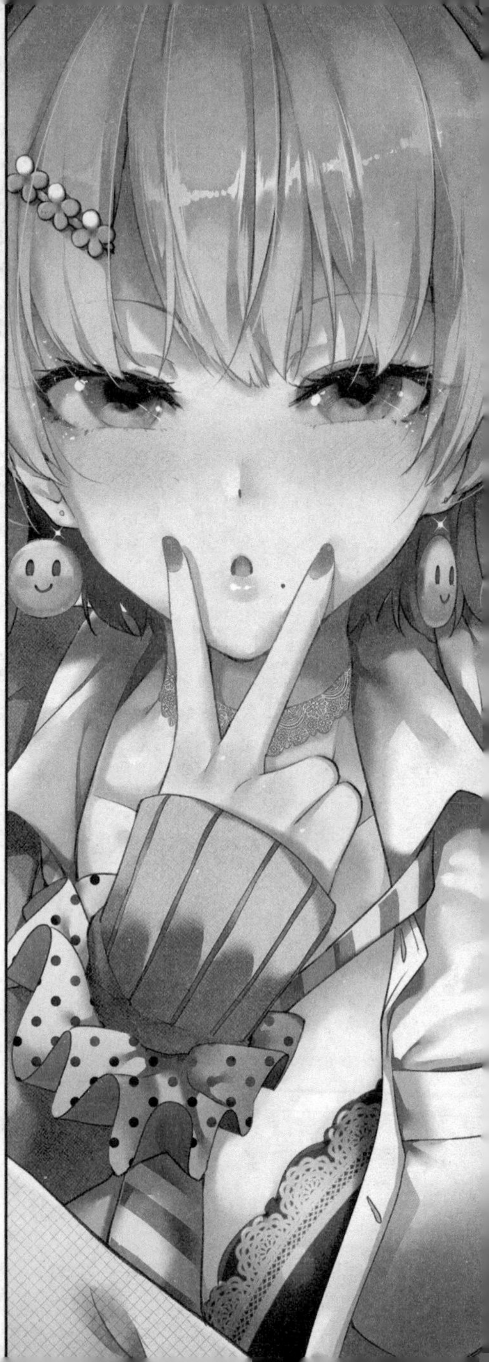

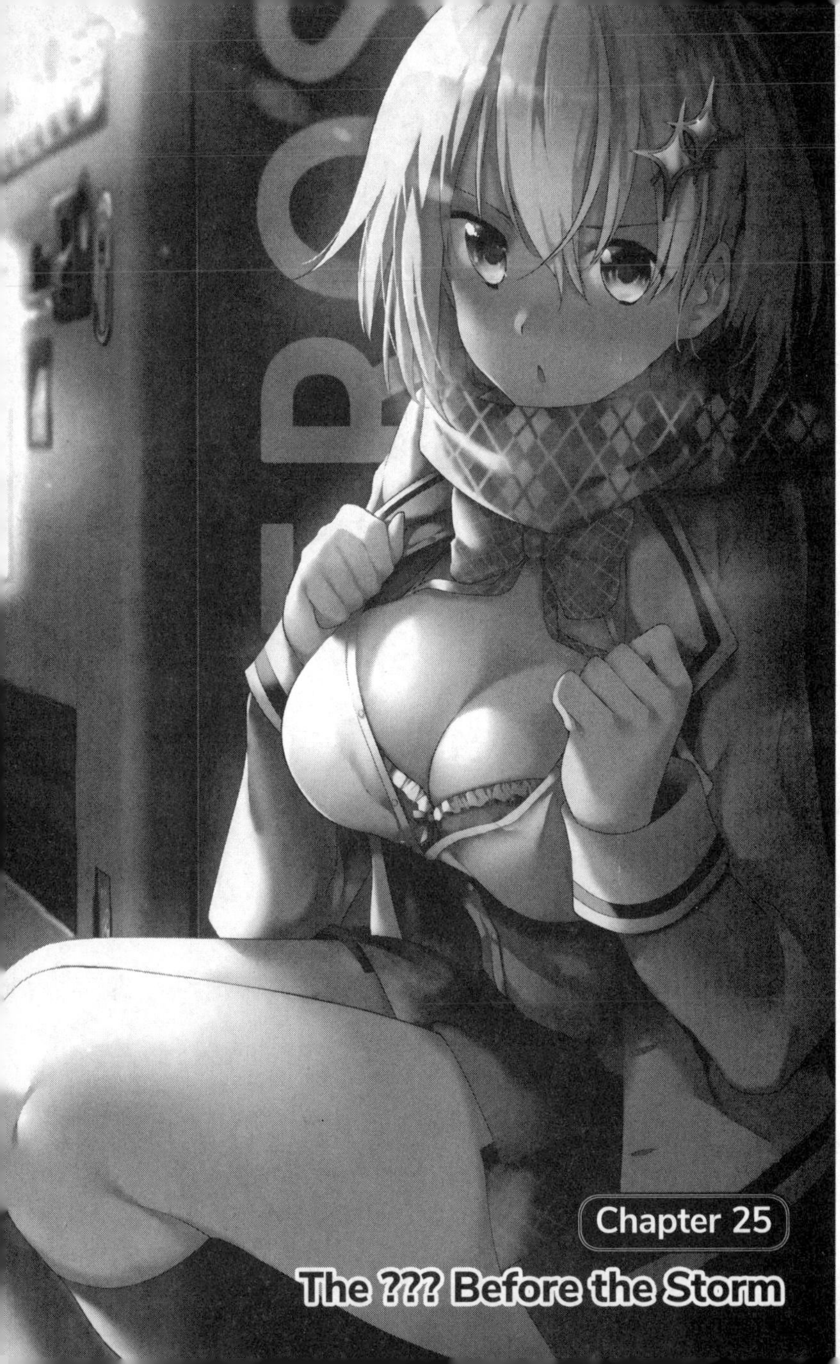

Chapter 25
The ??? Before the Storm

Extra Gallery

SUPER HxEROS

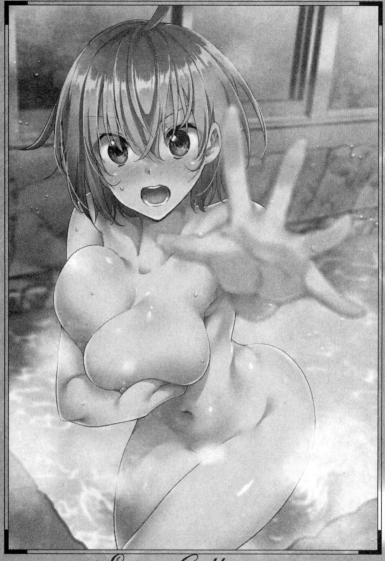

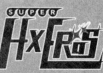

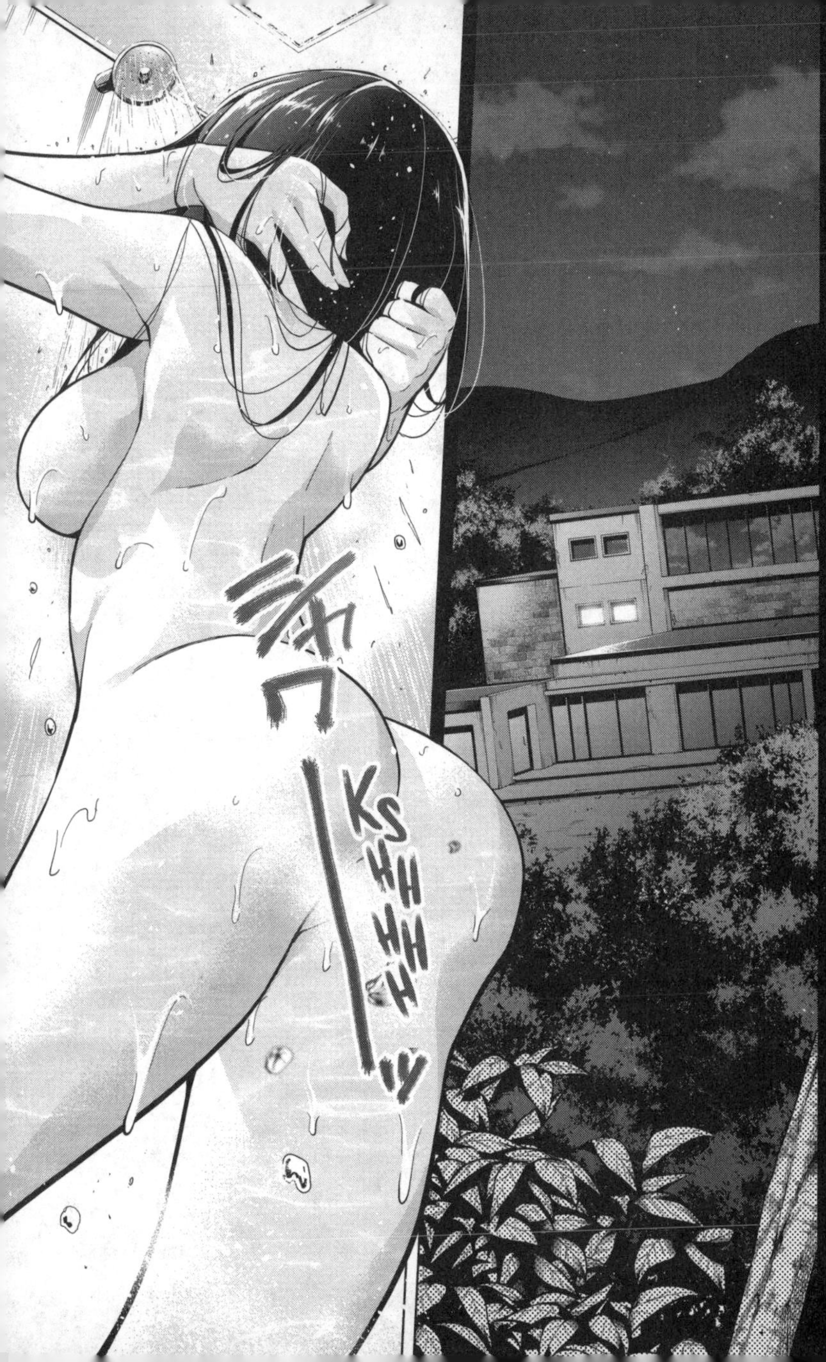
シャワーッ
KSHHHHHH

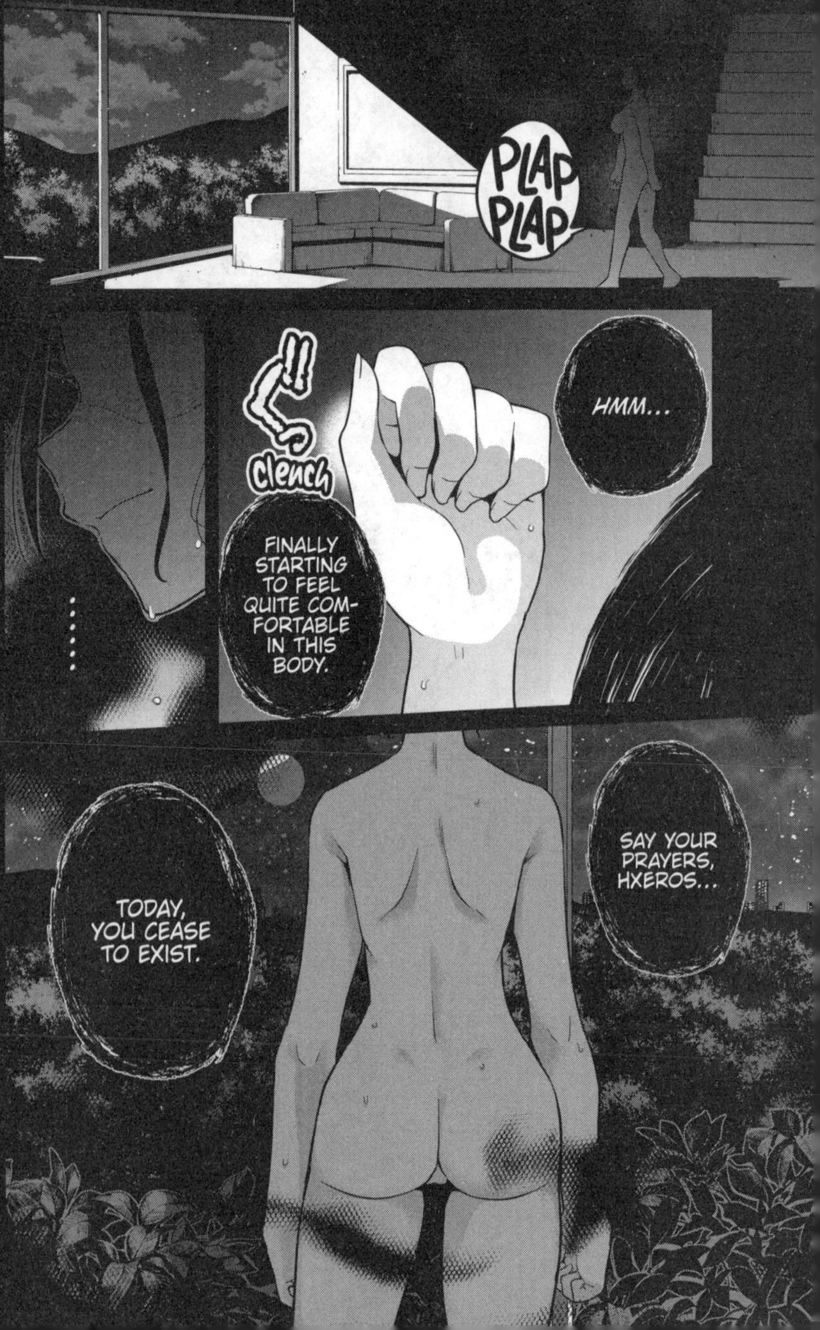
PLAP PLAP
HMM...
CLENCH
FINALLY STARTING TO FEEL QUITE COM-FORTABLE IN THIS BODY.
......
SAY YOUR PRAYERS, HXEROS...
TODAY, YOU CEASE TO EXIST.

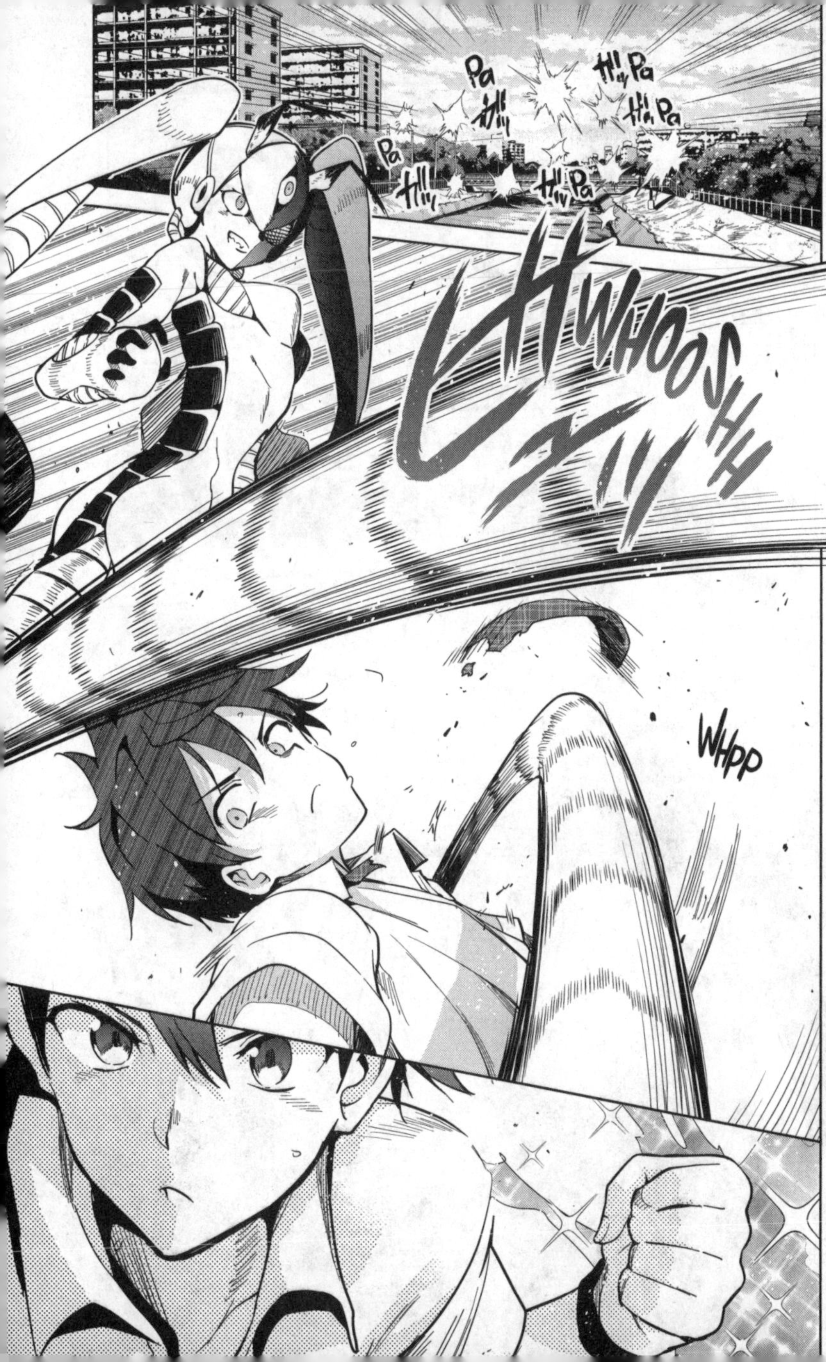
Pa
Pa
Pa
Pa
Pa
Pa
WHOOSHH
WHPP

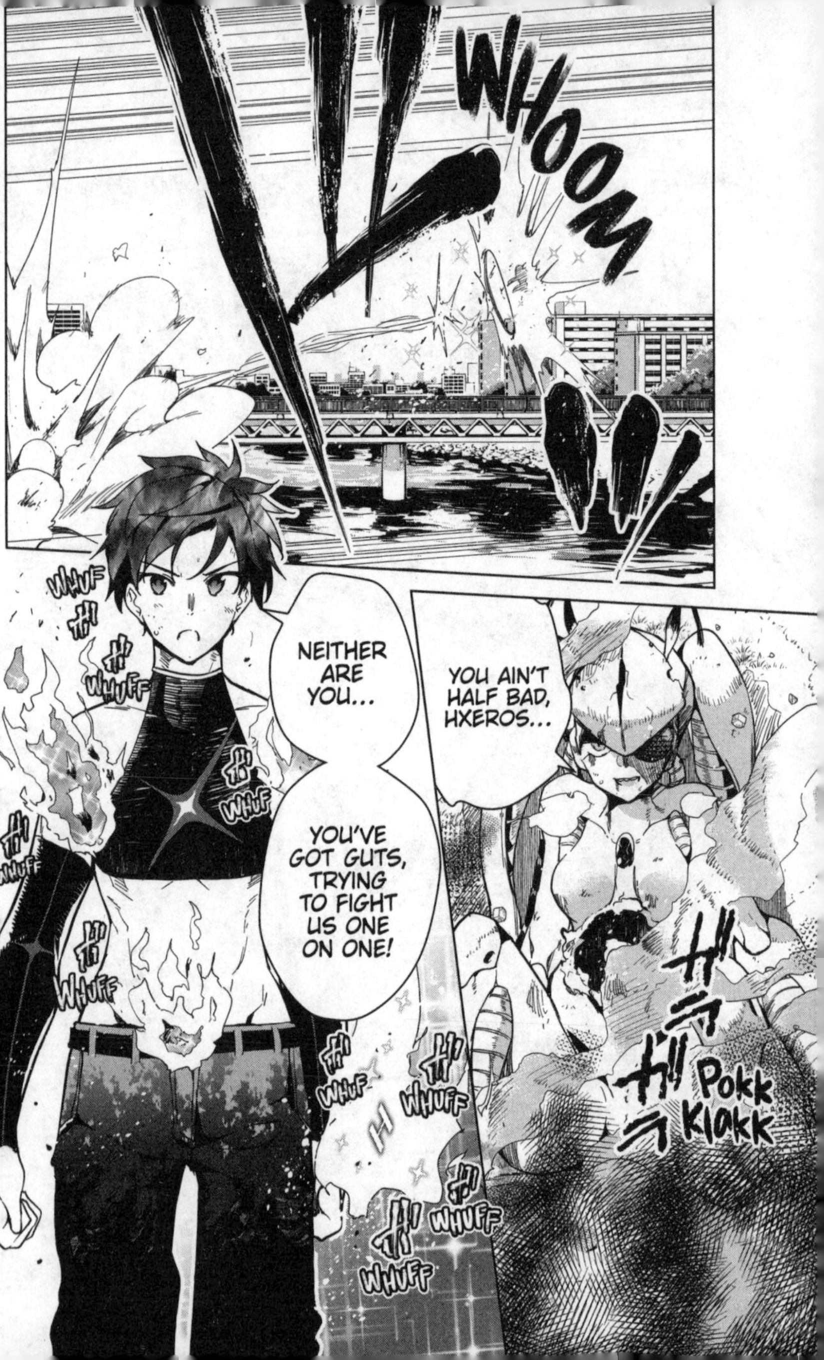
WHOOM
YOU AIN'T HALF BAD, HXEROS...
Pokk
Klakk
NEITHER ARE YOU...
YOU'VE GOT GUTS, TRYING TO FIGHT US ONE ON ONE!
WHUF
WHUFF
WHUF
WHUFF
WHUFF
WHUF
WHUFF
WHUFF
WHUFF

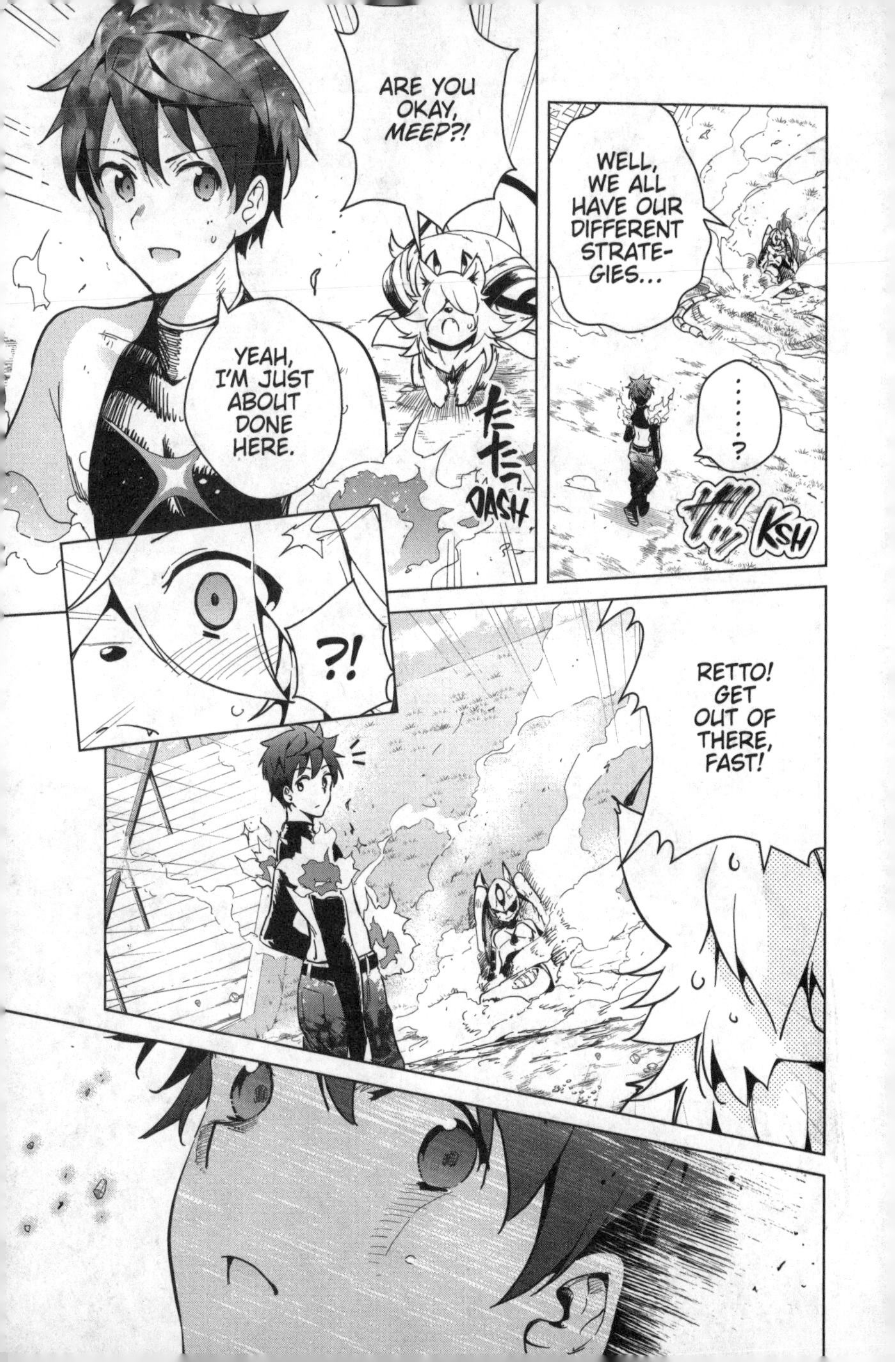
WELL, WE ALL HAVE OUR DIFFERENT STRATE-GIES...
......?
KSH
ARE YOU OKAY, MEEP?!
YEAH, I'M JUST ABOUT DONE HERE.
DASH
RETTO! GET OUT OF THERE, FAST!
?!

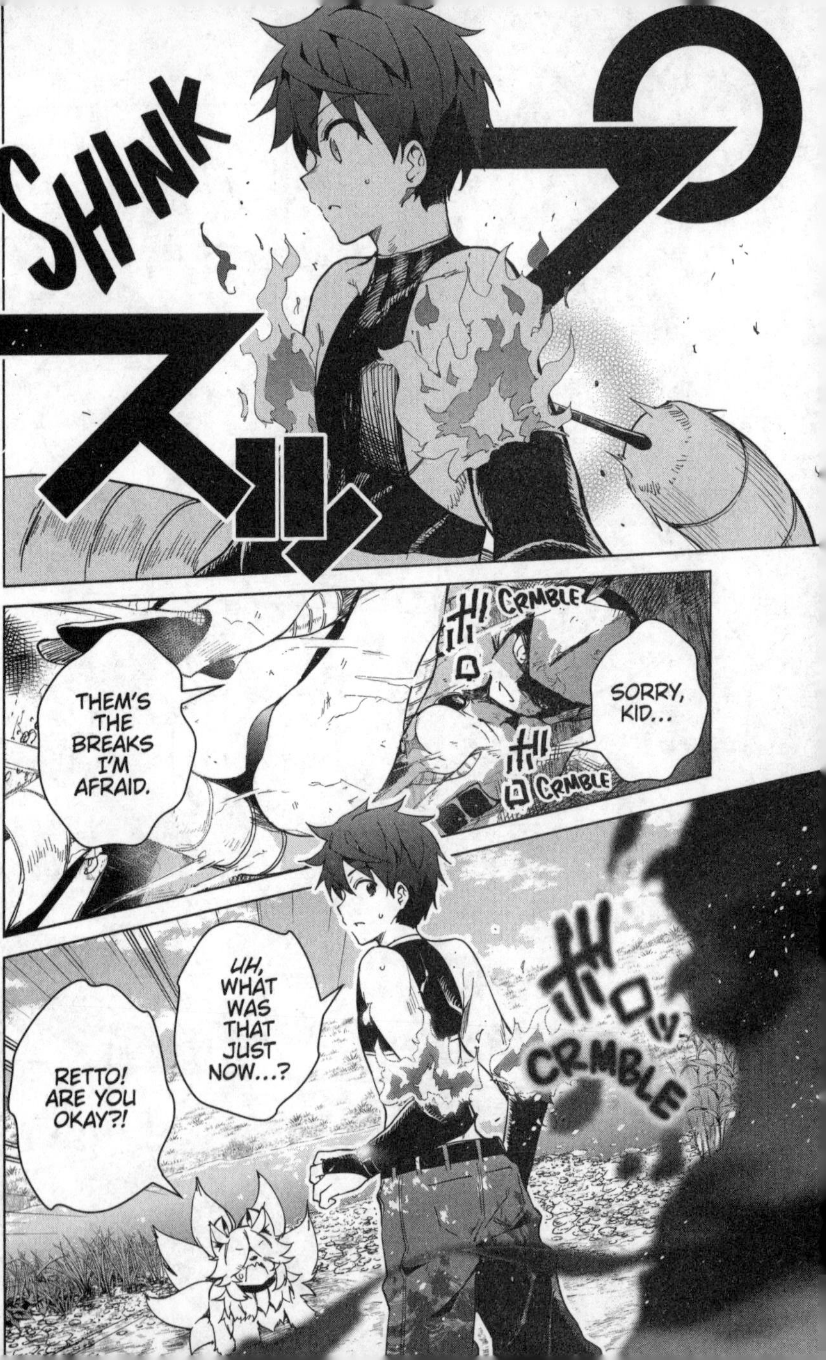
SHINK
CRMBLE
SORRY, KID...
CRMBLE
THEM'S THE BREAKS I'M AFRAID.
CRMBLE
UH, WHAT WAS THAT JUST NOW...?
RETTO! ARE YOU OKAY?!

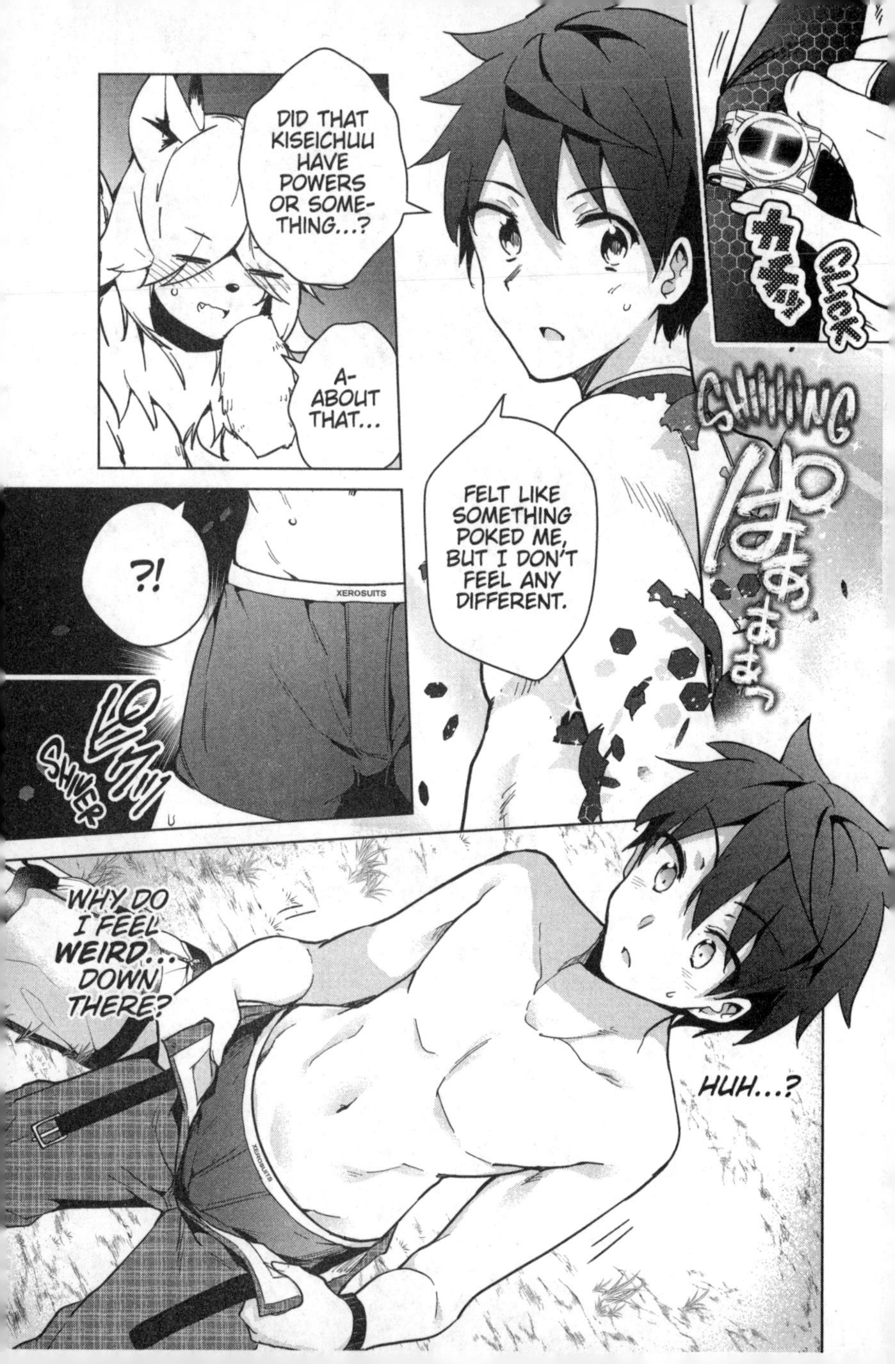
カチッ
CLICK
SHIIIING
ぱぁぁぁ
FELT LIKE SOMETHING POKED ME, BUT I DON'T FEEL ANY DIFFERENT.
DID THAT KISEICHUU HAVE POWERS OR SOME-THING...?
A-ABOUT THAT...
?!
XEROSUITS
SHIVER
HUH...?
WHY DO I FEEL WEIRD... DOWN THERE?
XEROSUITS

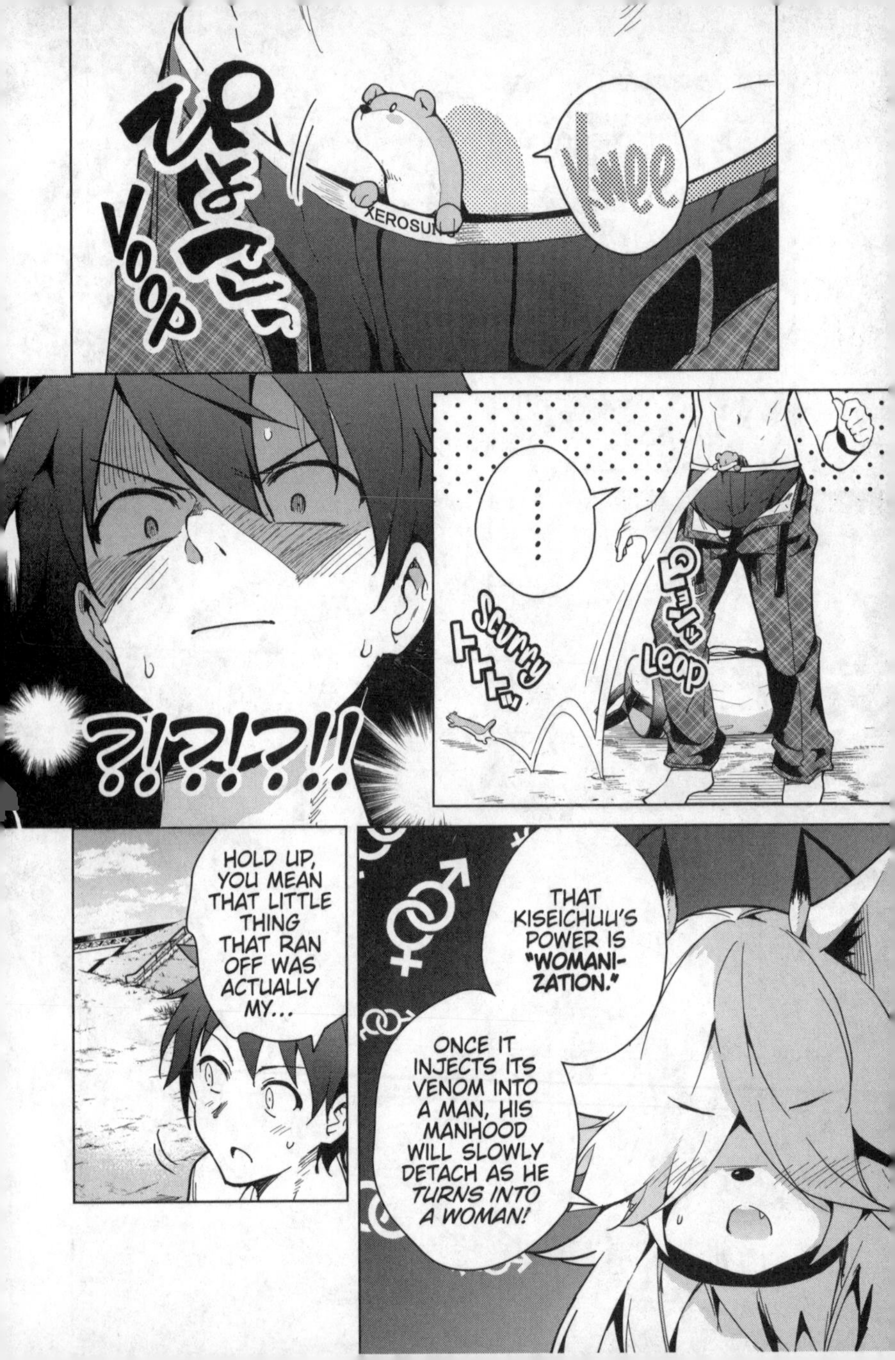
Kwee
XEROSUN
ぴょこ
Voop
……
ぴょっ
Leap
トトトッ
Scurry
?!?!?!!
THAT KISEICHUU'S POWER IS "WOMANIZATION."
ONCE IT INJECTS ITS VENOM INTO A MAN, HIS MANHOOD WILL SLOWLY DETACH AS HE *TURNS INTO A WOMAN!*
HOLD UP, YOU MEAN THAT LITTLE THING THAT RAN OFF WAS ACTUALLY MY...

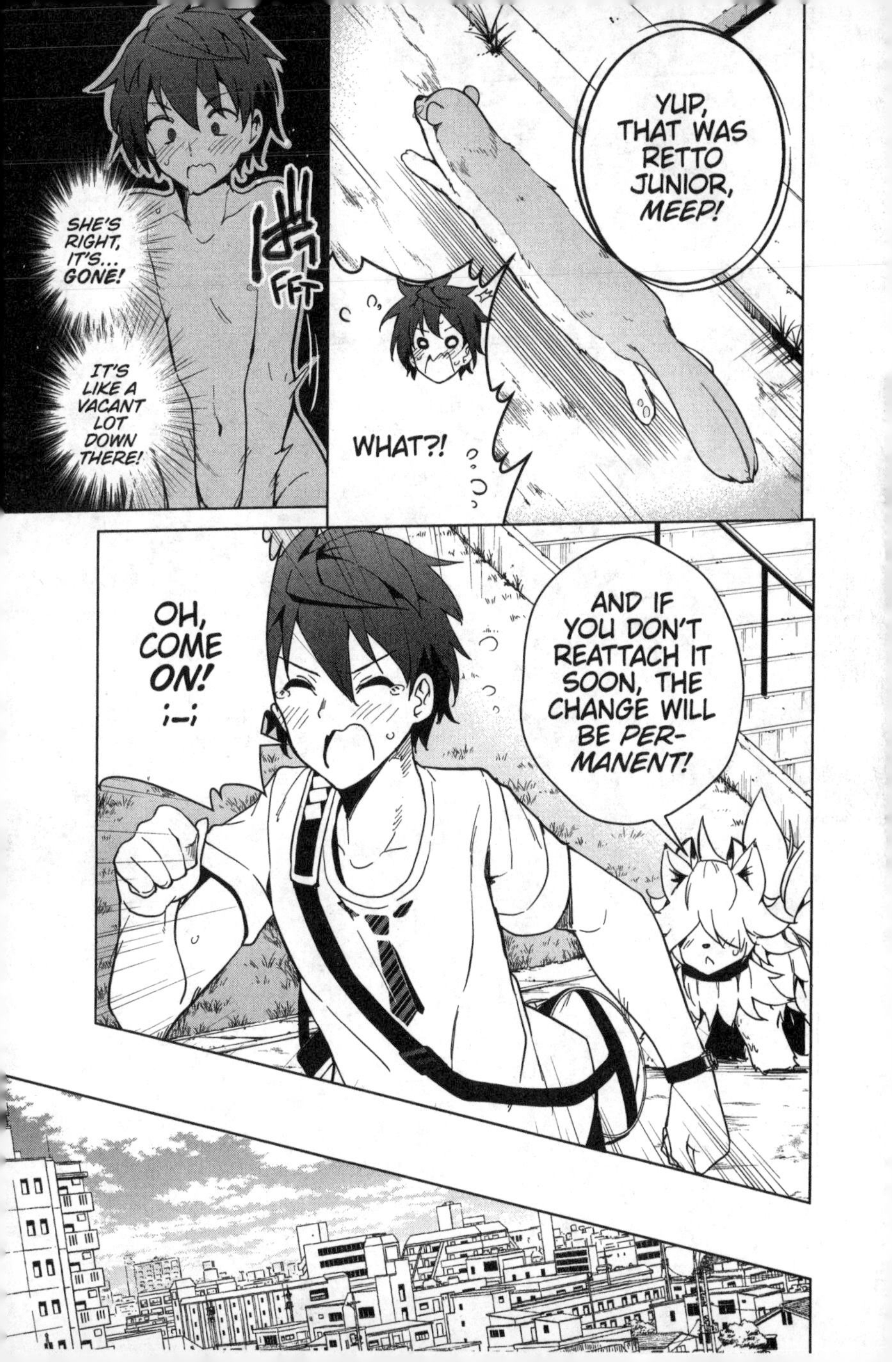
YUP, THAT WAS RETTO JUNIOR, MEEP!
WHAT?!
SHE'S RIGHT, IT'S... GONE!
FFT
IT'S LIKE A VACANT LOT DOWN THERE!
AND IF YOU DON'T REATTACH IT SOON, THE CHANGE WILL BE PER-MANENT!
OH, COME ON! ;_;

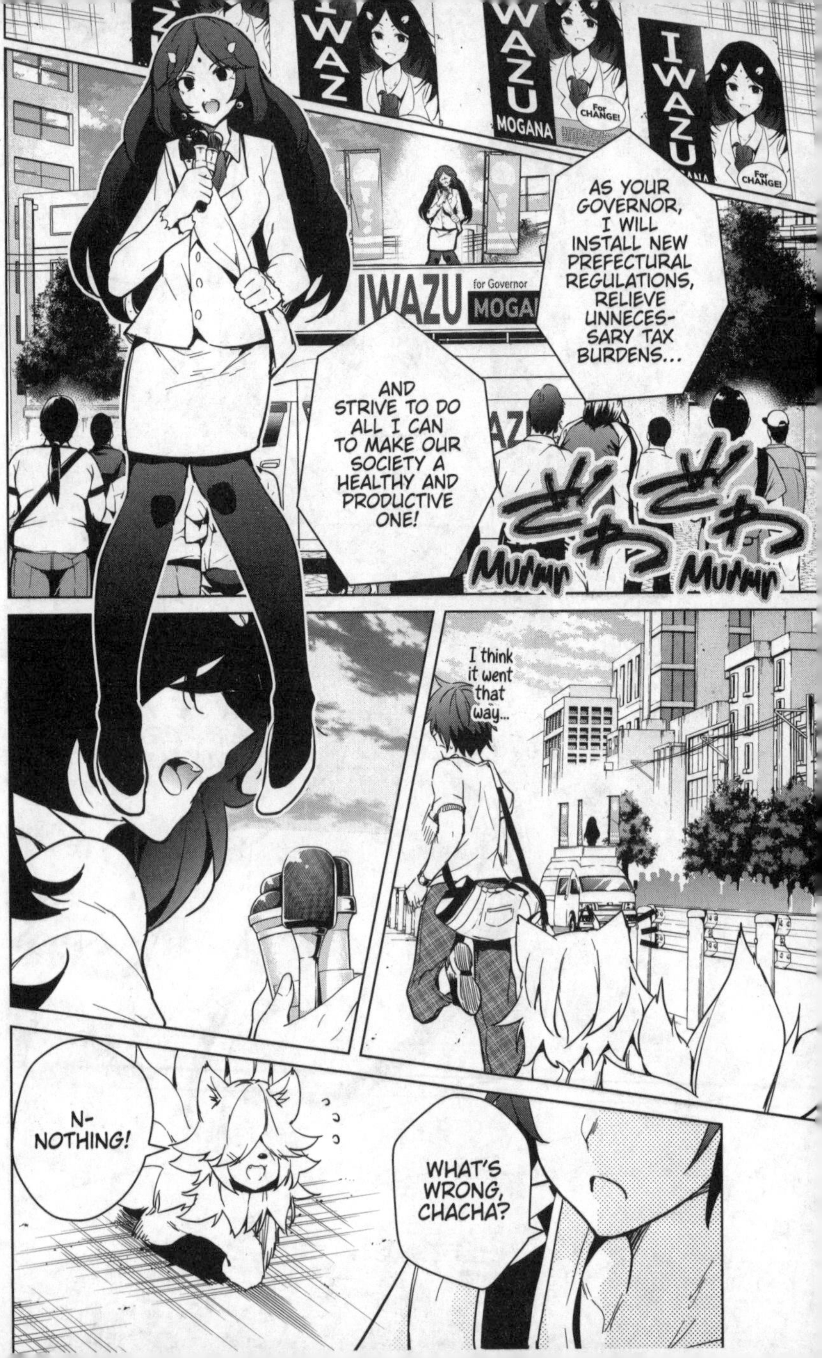
IWAZU
MOGANA
For CHANGE!
IWAZU for Governor
AS YOUR GOVERNOR, I WILL INSTALL NEW PREFECTURAL REGULATIONS, RELIEVE UNNECES-SARY TAX BURDENS...
AND STRIVE TO DO ALL I CAN TO MAKE OUR SOCIETY A HEALTHY AND PRODUCTIVE ONE!
ざわざわ
Murmur Murmur
I think it went that way...
WHAT'S WRONG, CHACHA?
N-NOTHING!

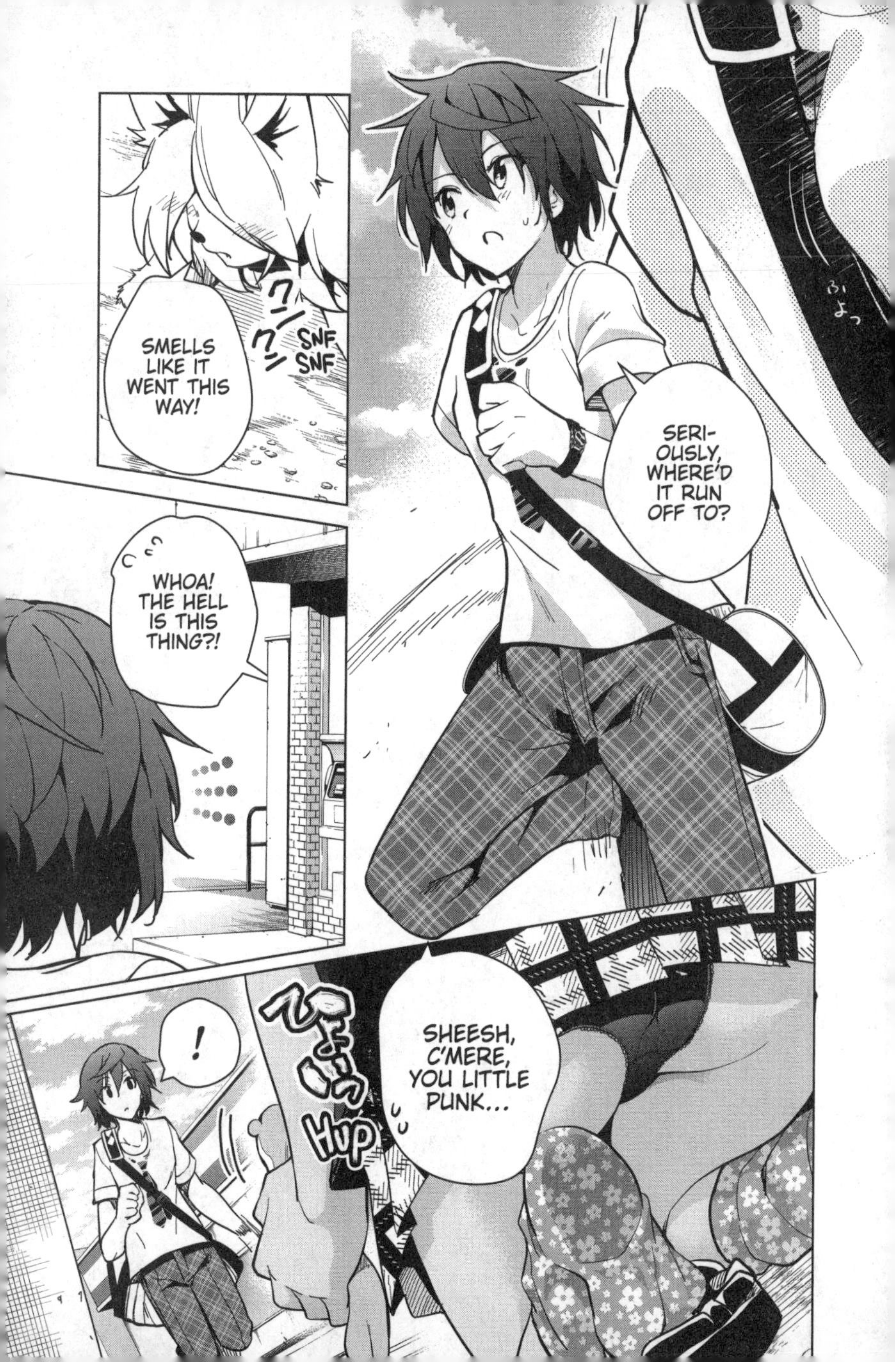
ふよっ
SERI-OUSLY, WHERE'D IT RUN OFF TO?
SMELLS LIKE IT WENT THIS WAY!
SNF SNF
WHOA! THE HELL IS THIS THING?!
SHEESH, C'MERE, YOU LITTLE PUNK...
Hup
!

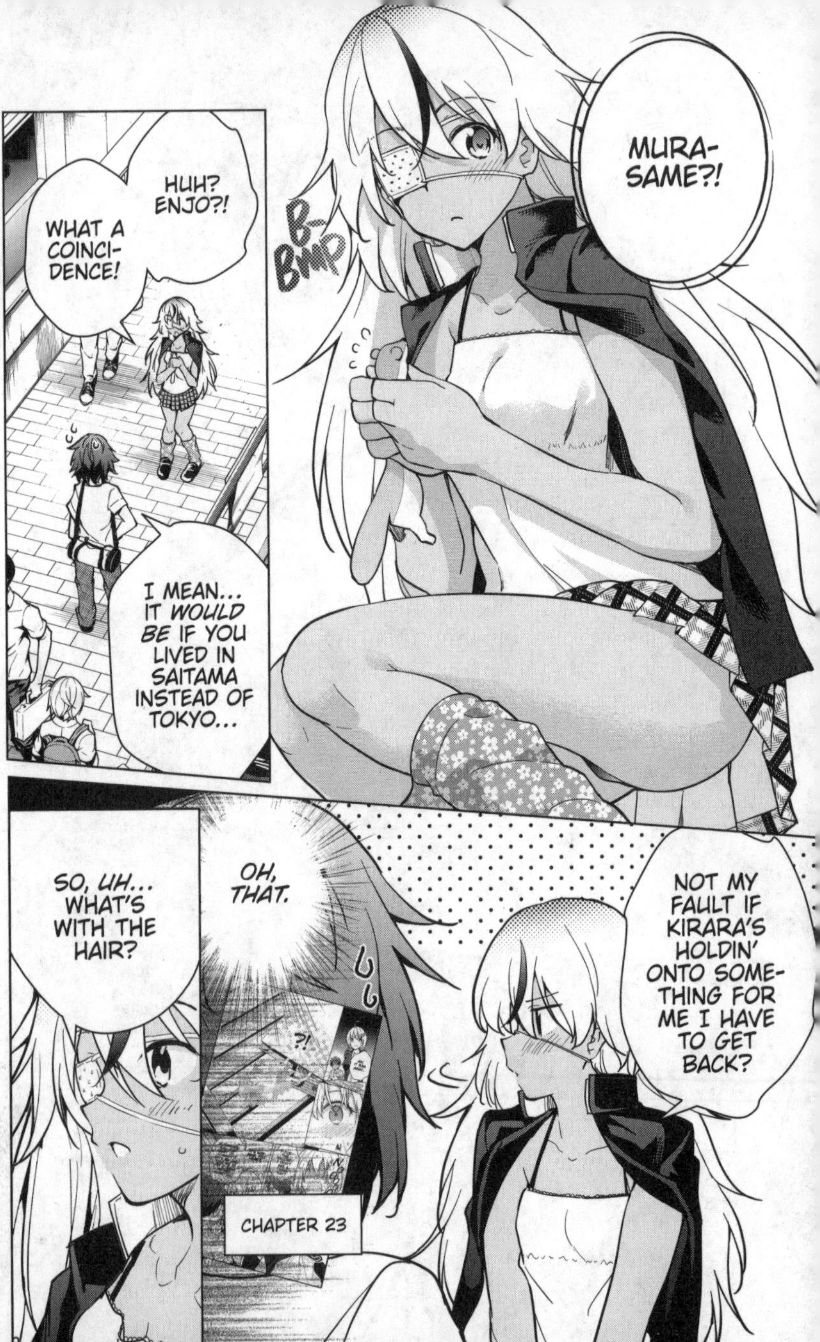
MURA-SAME?!
B-BMP
HUH? ENJO?!
WHAT A COINCI-DENCE!
I MEAN... IT *WOULD* BE IF YOU LIVED IN SAITAMA INSTEAD OF TOKYO...
NOT MY FAULT IF KIRARA'S HOLDIN' ONTO SOME-THING FOR ME I HAVE TO GET BACK?
OH, THAT.
SO, *UH*... WHAT'S WITH THE HAIR?
?!
CHAPTER 23

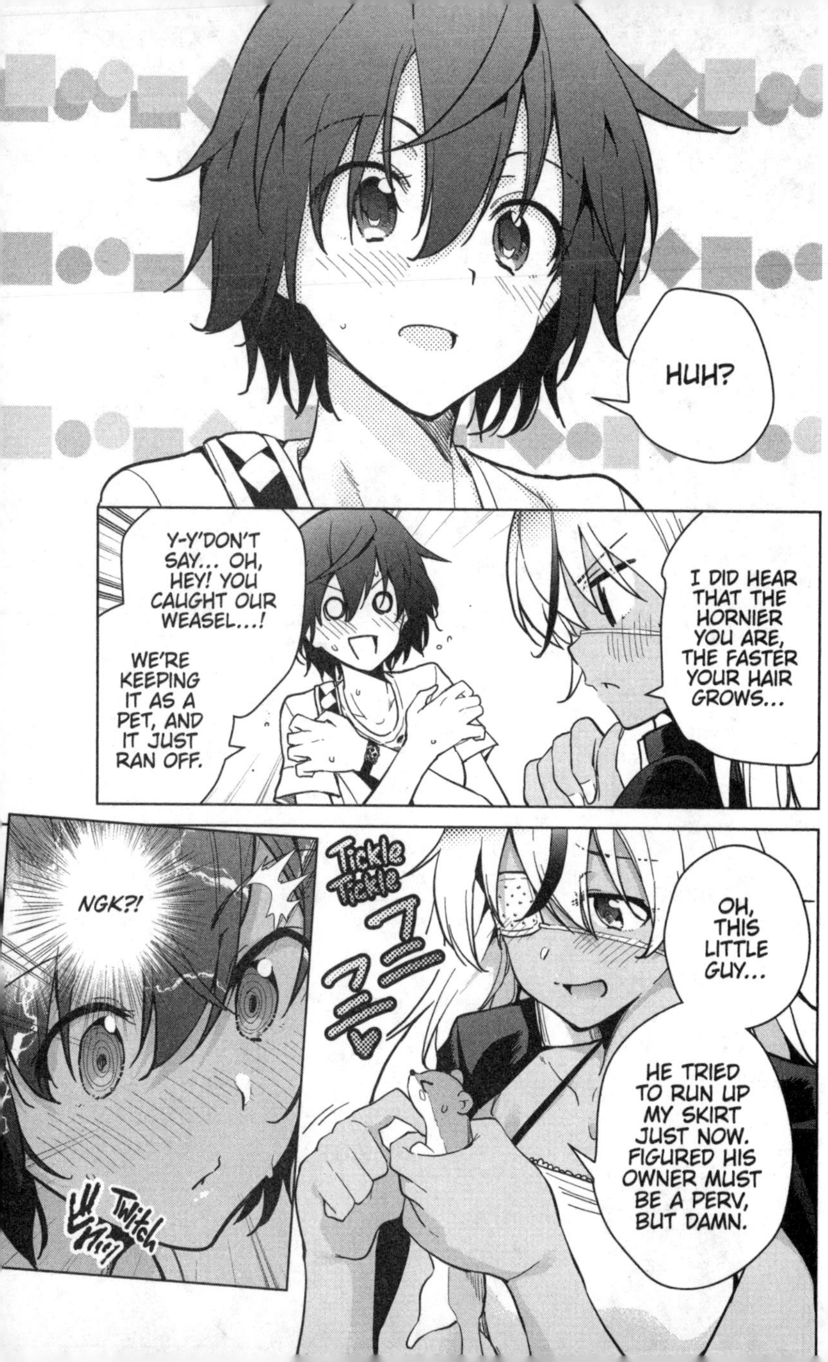
HUH?
I DID HEAR THAT THE HORNIER YOU ARE, THE FASTER YOUR HAIR GROWS...
Y-Y'DON'T SAY... OH, HEY! YOU CAUGHT OUR WEASEL...!
WE'RE KEEPING IT AS A PET, AND IT JUST RAN OFF.
OH, THIS LITTLE GUY...
HE TRIED TO RUN UP MY SKIRT JUST NOW. FIGURED HIS OWNER MUST BE A PERV, BUT DAMN.
Tickle Tickle
NGK?!
Twitch

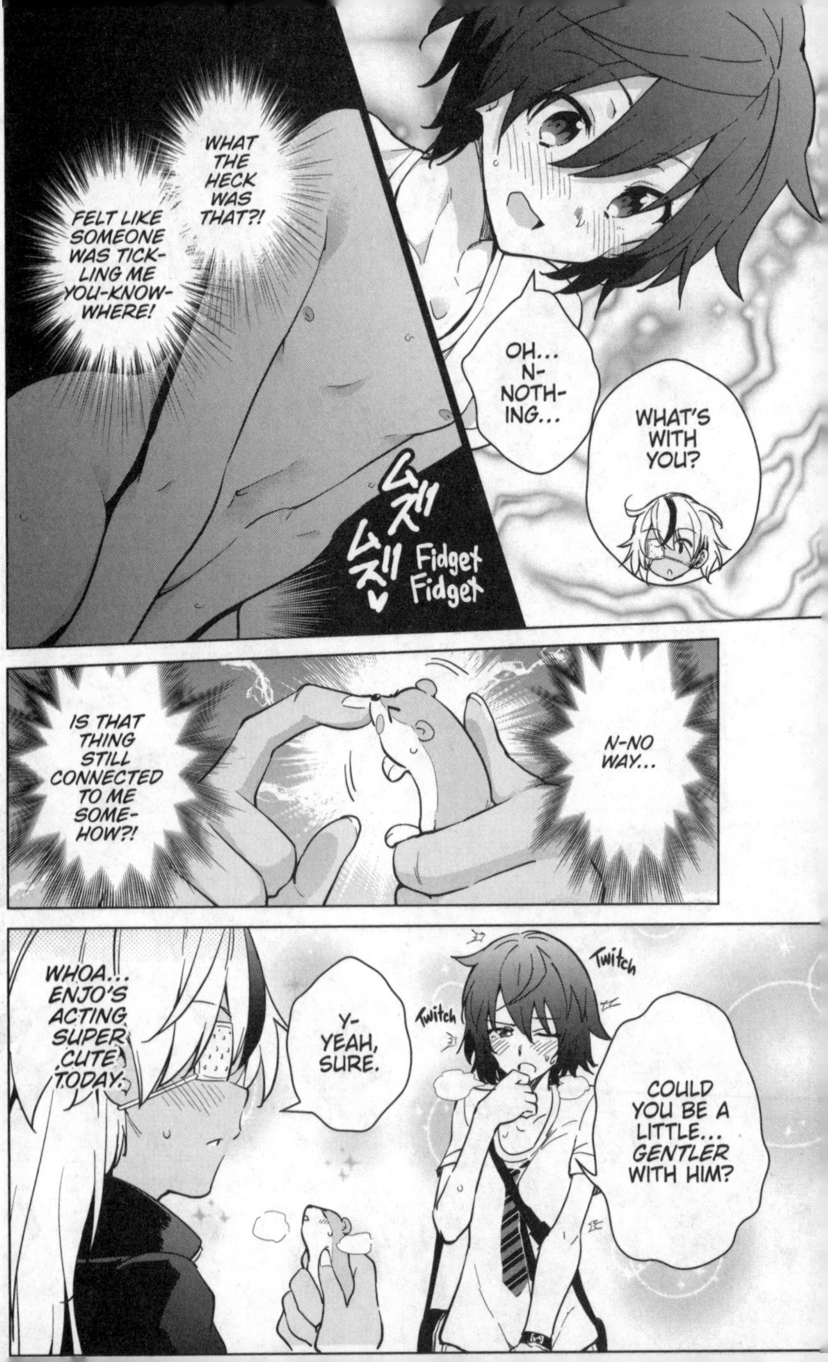
WHAT'S WITH YOU?
OH... N-NOTHING...
Fidget Fidget
WHAT THE HECK WAS THAT?!
FELT LIKE SOMEONE WAS TICKLING ME YOU-KNOW-WHERE!
N-NO WAY...
IS THAT THING STILL CONNECTED TO ME SOMEHOW?!
Twitch
COULD YOU BE A LITTLE... GENTLER WITH HIM?
Twitch
Y-YEAH, SURE.
WHOA... ENJO'S ACTING SUPER CUTE TODAY.

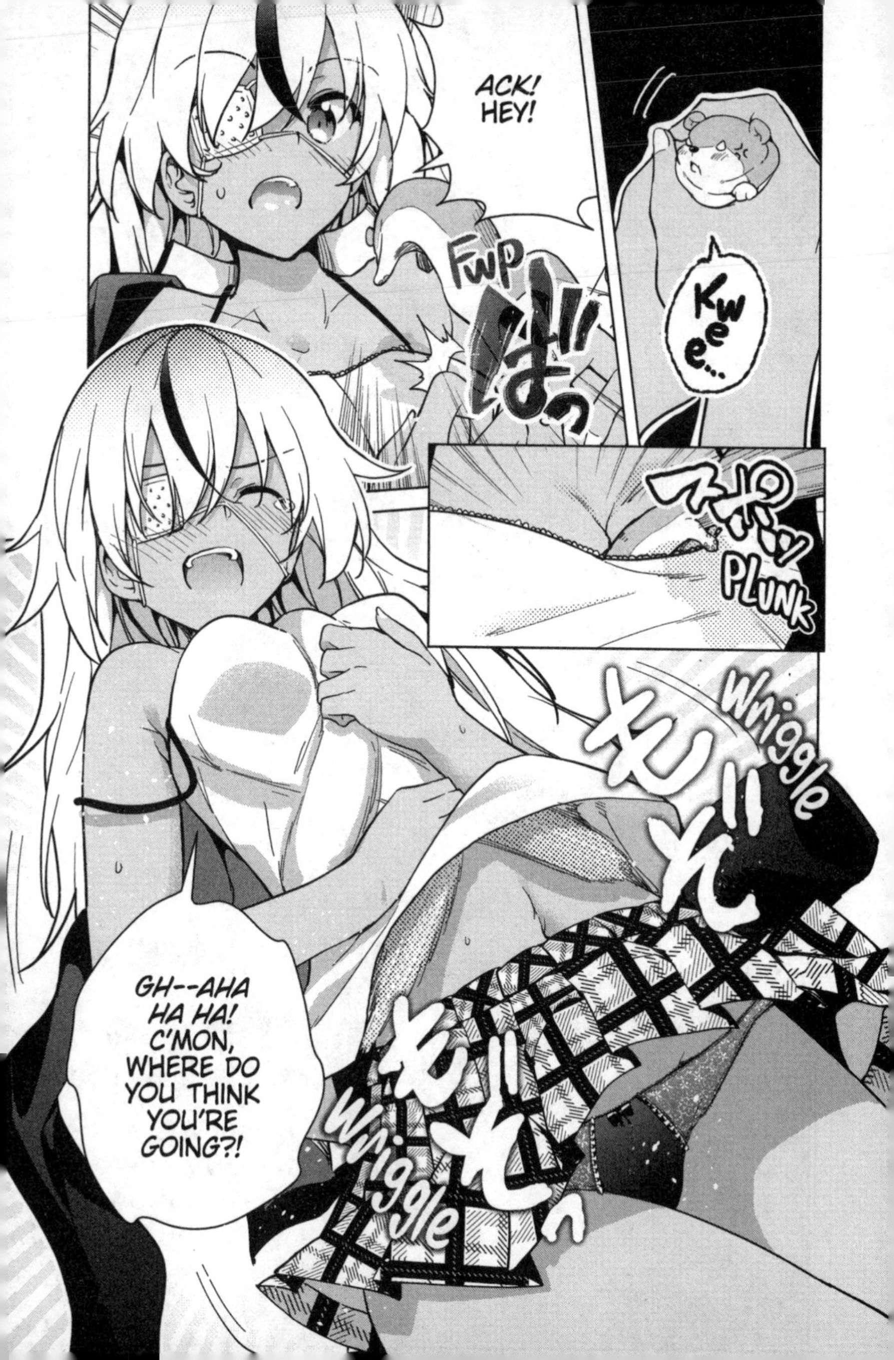
Kwee...
ACK! HEY!
Fwp
ばっ
スポッ
PLUNK
Wriggle
もぞ
もぞ
Wriggle
GH--AHA HA HA! C'MON, WHERE DO YOU THINK YOU'RE GOING?!

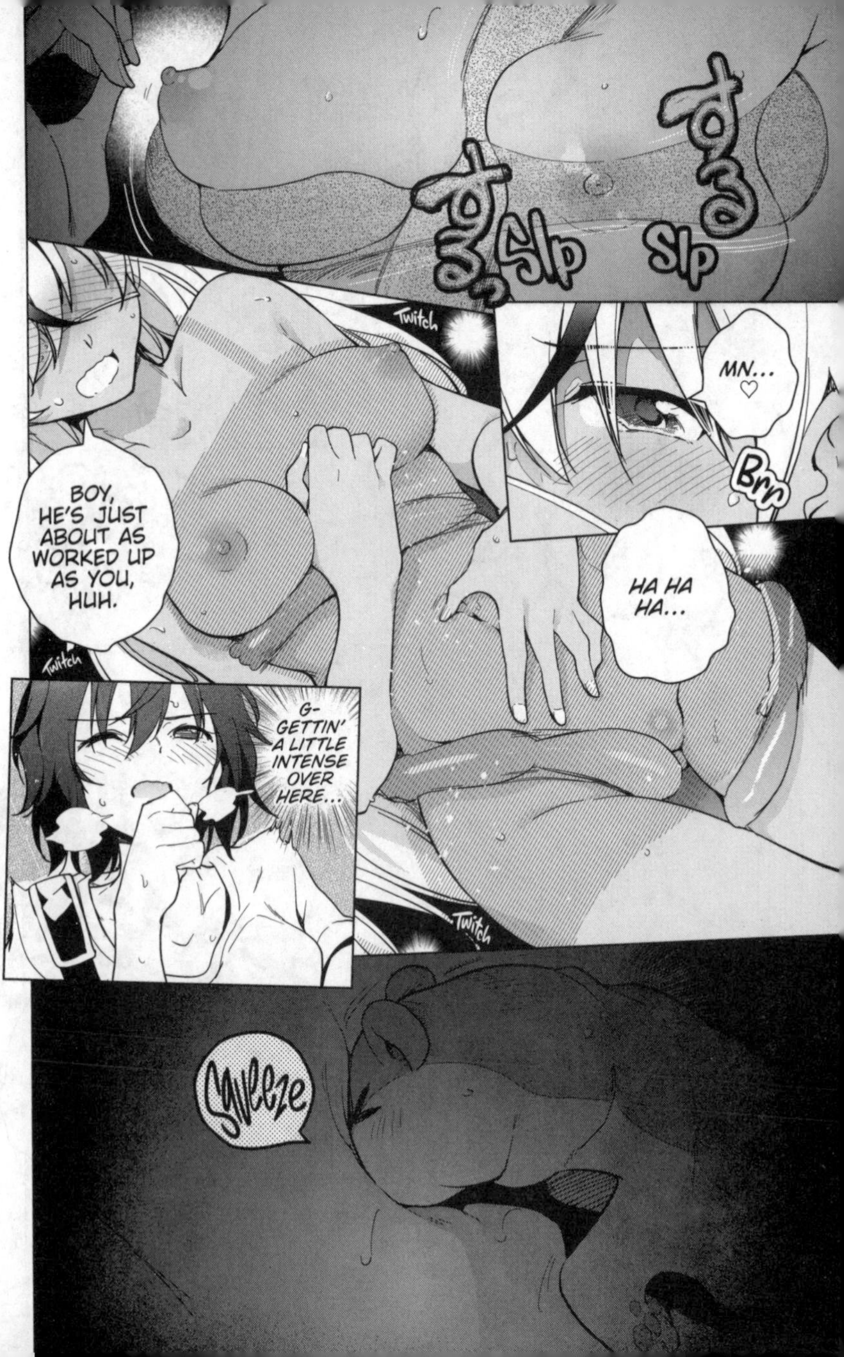
する
Slp
すっ
Slp
MN... ♥
Brr
Twitch
HA HA HA...
BOY, HE'S JUST ABOUT AS WORKED UP AS YOU, HUH.
Twitch
G-GETTIN' A LITTLE INTENSE OVER HERE...
Twitch
Squeeze

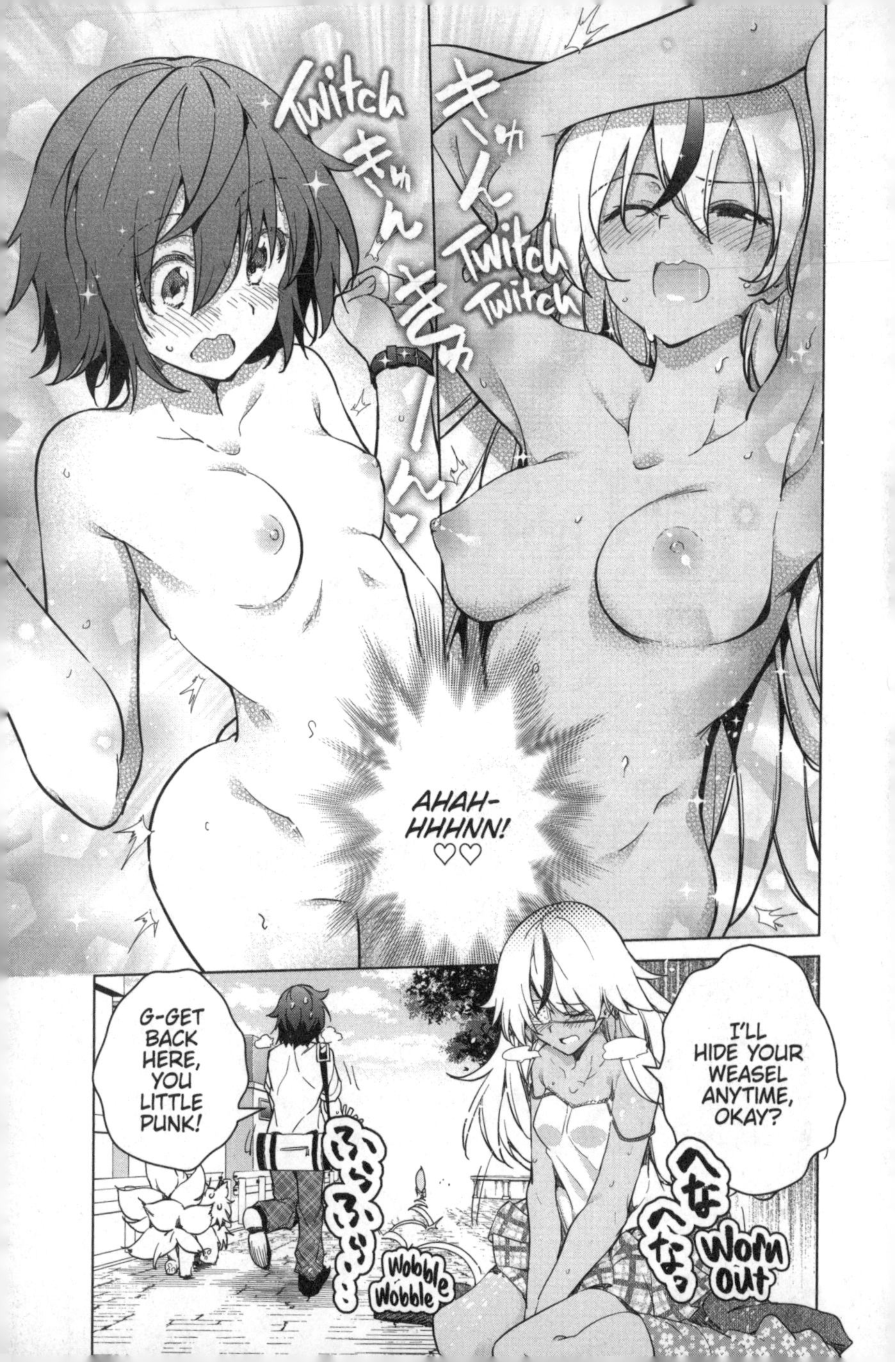
きゅん
Twitch Twitch
Twitch
きゅん
きゅーんっ♥
AHAH-HHHNN! ♡♡
I'LL HIDE YOUR WEASEL ANYTIME, OKAY?
へなへなっ
Worn out
ふらふら
Wobble Wobble
G-GET BACK HERE, YOU LITTLE PUNK!

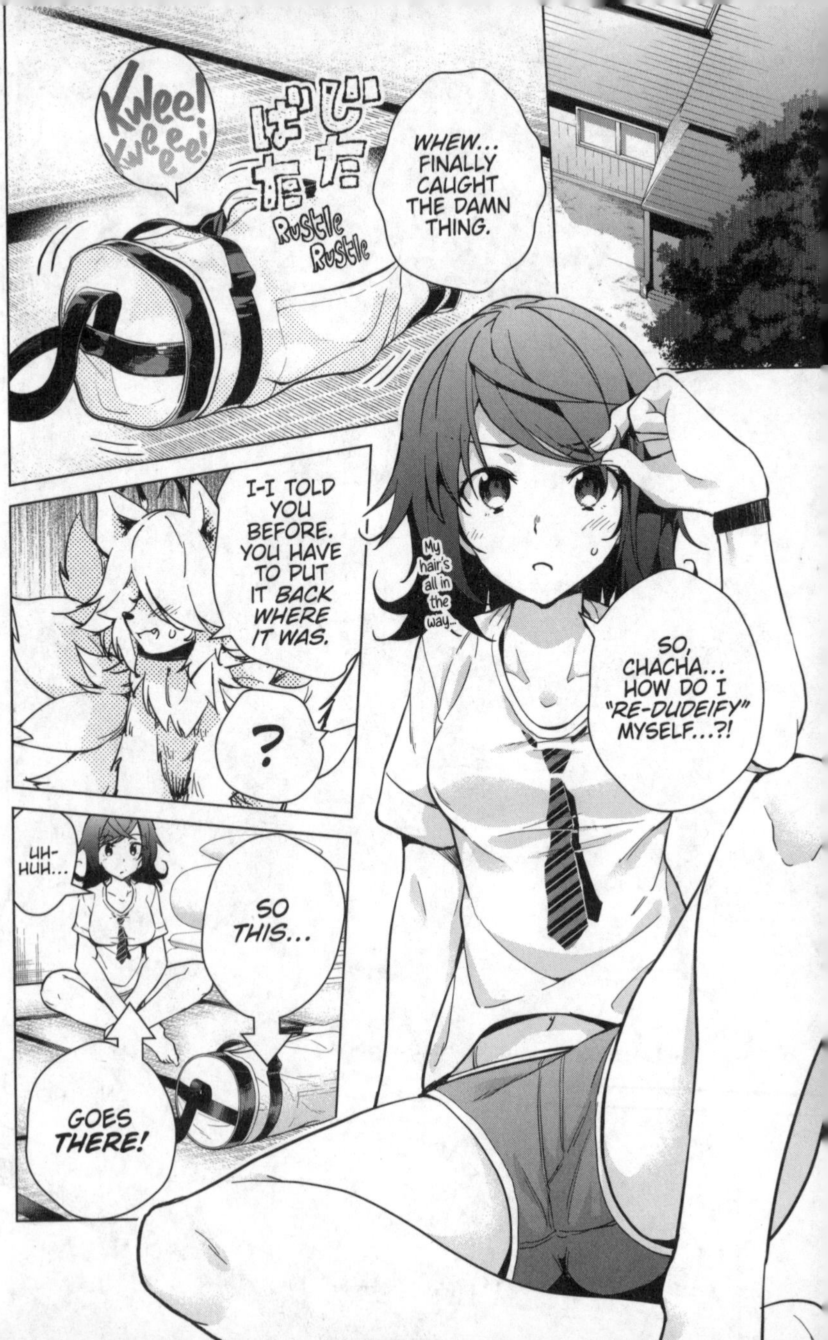
WHEW... FINALLY CAUGHT THE DAMN THING.
Rustle Rustle
Kwee! Kweee!
My hair's all in the way...
SO, CHACHA... HOW DO I "RE-DUDEIFY" MYSELF...?!
I-I TOLD YOU BEFORE. YOU HAVE TO PUT IT BACK WHERE IT WAS.
?
SO THIS...
UH-HUH...
GOES THERE!

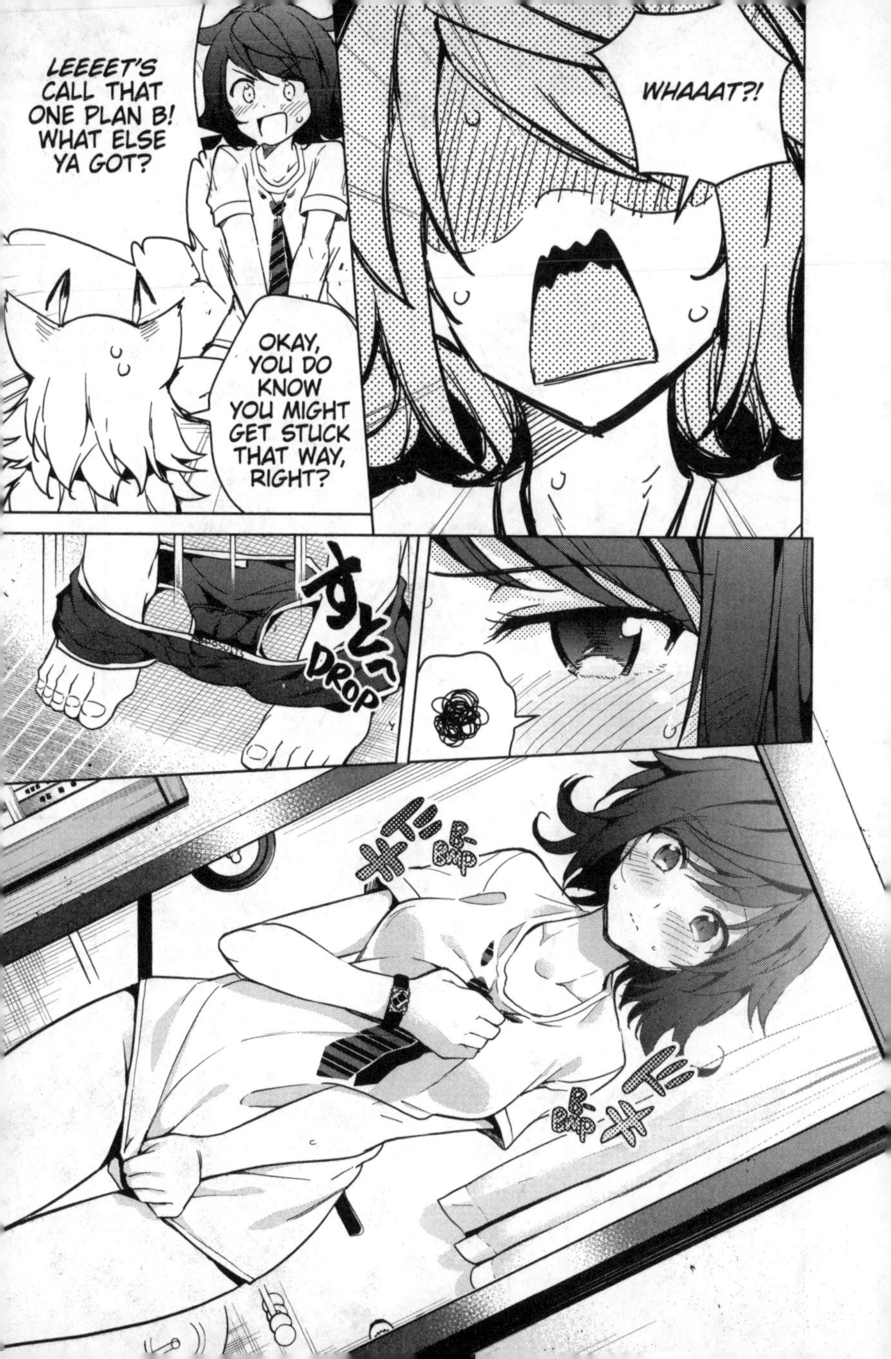
WHAAAT?!
LEEEET'S CALL THAT ONE PLAN B! WHAT ELSE YA GOT?
OKAY, YOU DO KNOW YOU MIGHT GET STUCK THAT WAY, RIGHT?
DROP
B-BMP
B-BMP

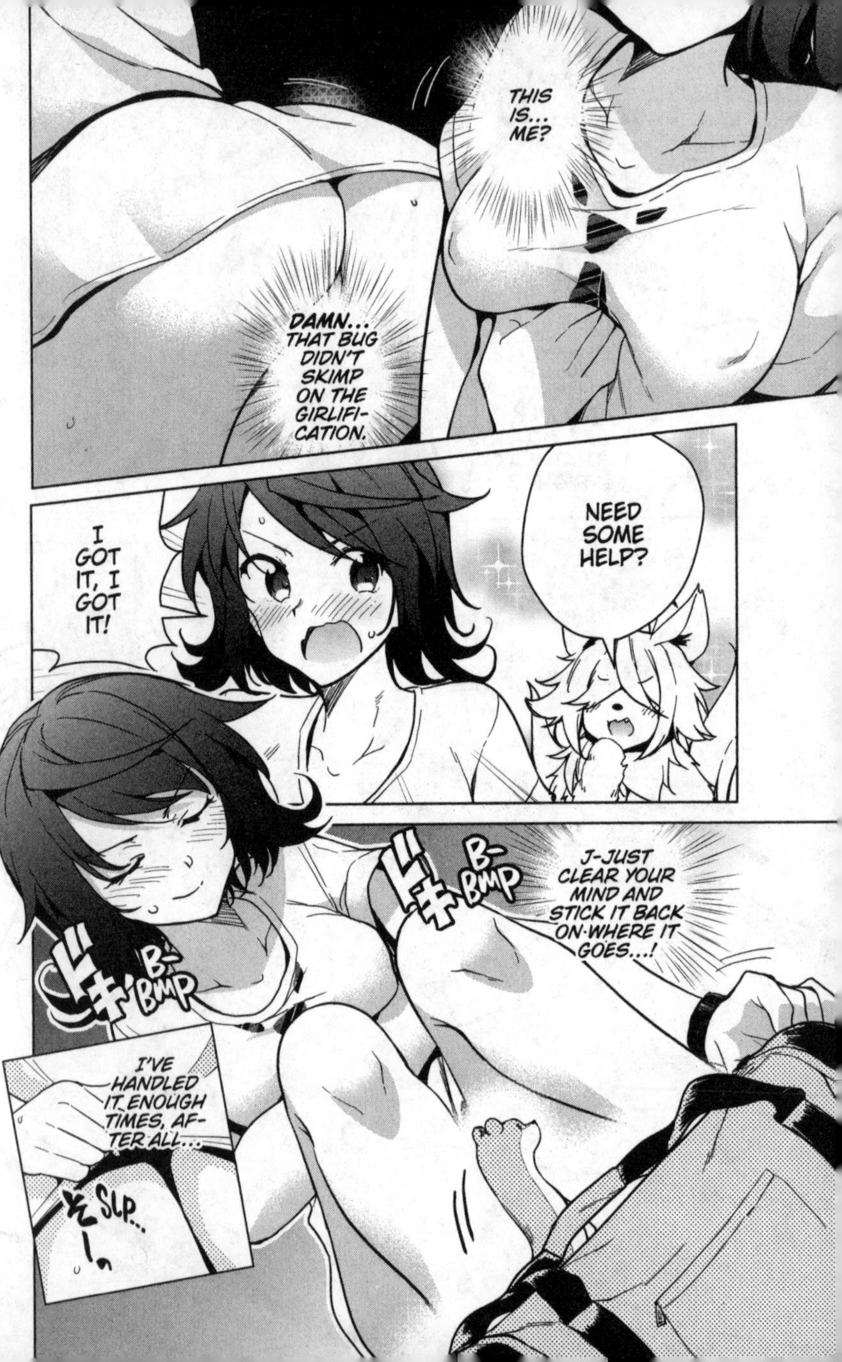
THIS IS... ME?
DAMN... THAT BUG DIDN'T SKIMP ON THE GIRLIFICATION.
NEED SOME HELP?
I GOT IT, I GOT IT!
J-JUST CLEAR YOUR MIND AND STICK IT BACK ON WHERE IT GOES...!
ドキ B-BMP
ドキ B-BMP
I'VE HANDLED IT ENOUGH TIMES, AFTER ALL...
そー SLIP...

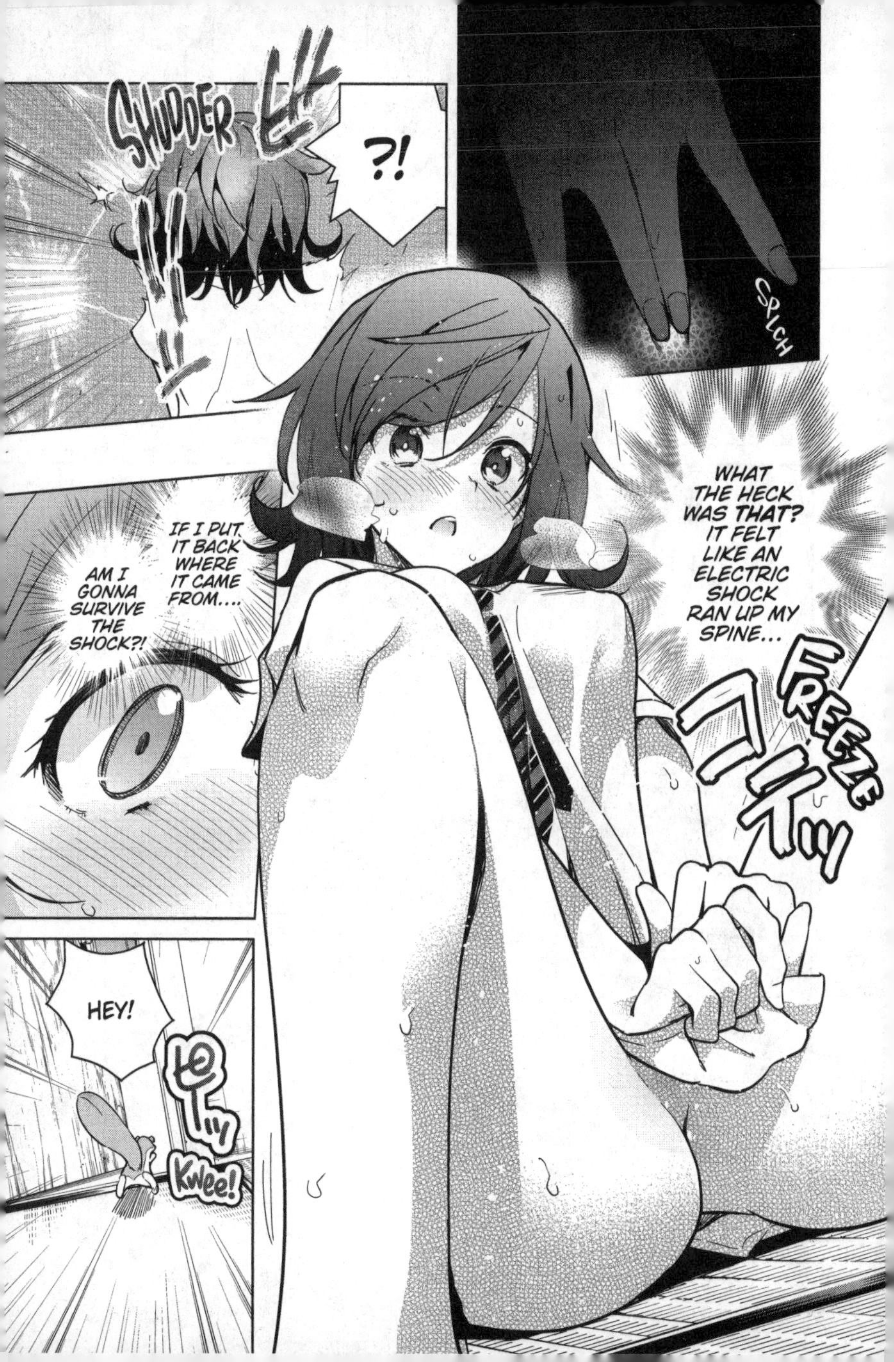
SPLCH
SHUDDER
?!
WHAT THE HECK WAS THAT? IT FELT LIKE AN ELECTRIC SHOCK RAN UP MY SPINE...
FREEZE
IF I PUT IT BACK WHERE IT CAME FROM....
AM I GONNA SURVIVE THE SHOCK?!
HEY!
Kwee!

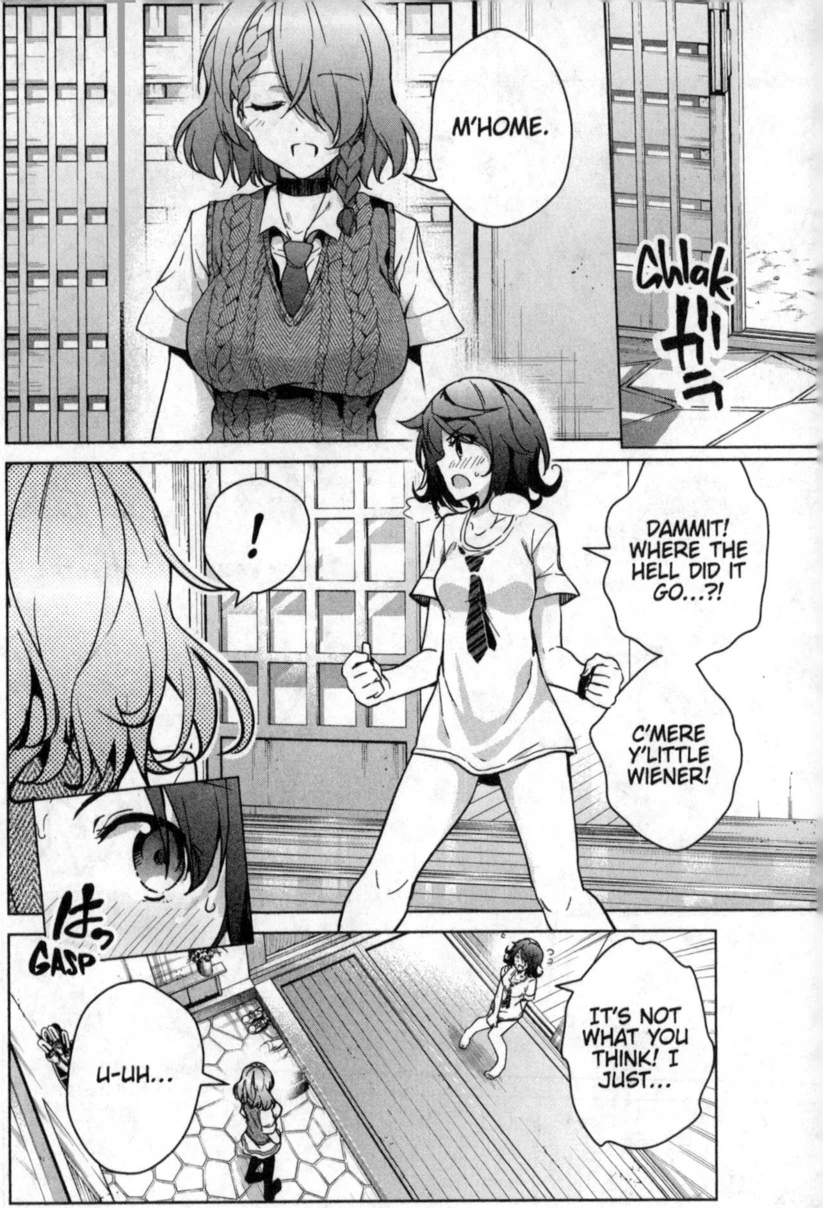

Ghlak
M'HOME.
DAMMIT! WHERE THE HELL DID IT GO...?!
C'MERE Y'LITTLE WIENER!
!
GASP
IT'S NOT WHAT YOU THINK! I JUST...
U-UH...

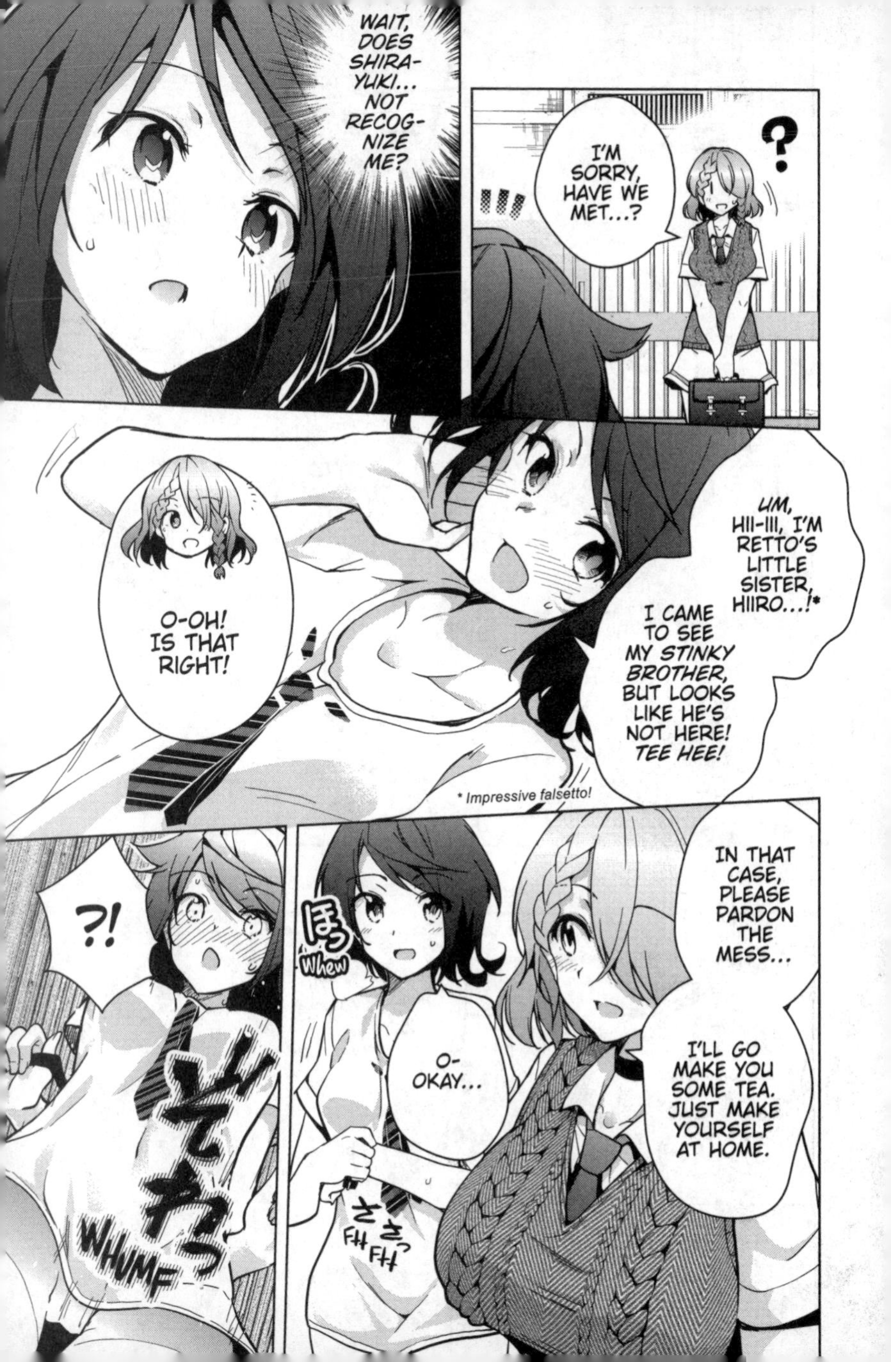
?
!!!
I'M SORRY, HAVE WE MET...?
WAIT, DOES SHIRA-YUKI... NOT RECOG-NIZE ME?
UM, HII-III, I'M RETTO'S LITTLE SISTER, HIIRO...!*
I CAME TO SEE MY *STINKY* BROTHER, BUT LOOKS LIKE HE'S NOT HERE! *TEE HEE!*
O-OH! IS THAT RIGHT!
* Impressive falsetto!
IN THAT CASE, PLEASE PARDON THE MESS...
I'LL GO MAKE YOU SOME TEA. JUST MAKE YOURSELF AT HOME.
O-OKAY...
ほっ
Whew
ささっ
FH FH
?!
WHUMF

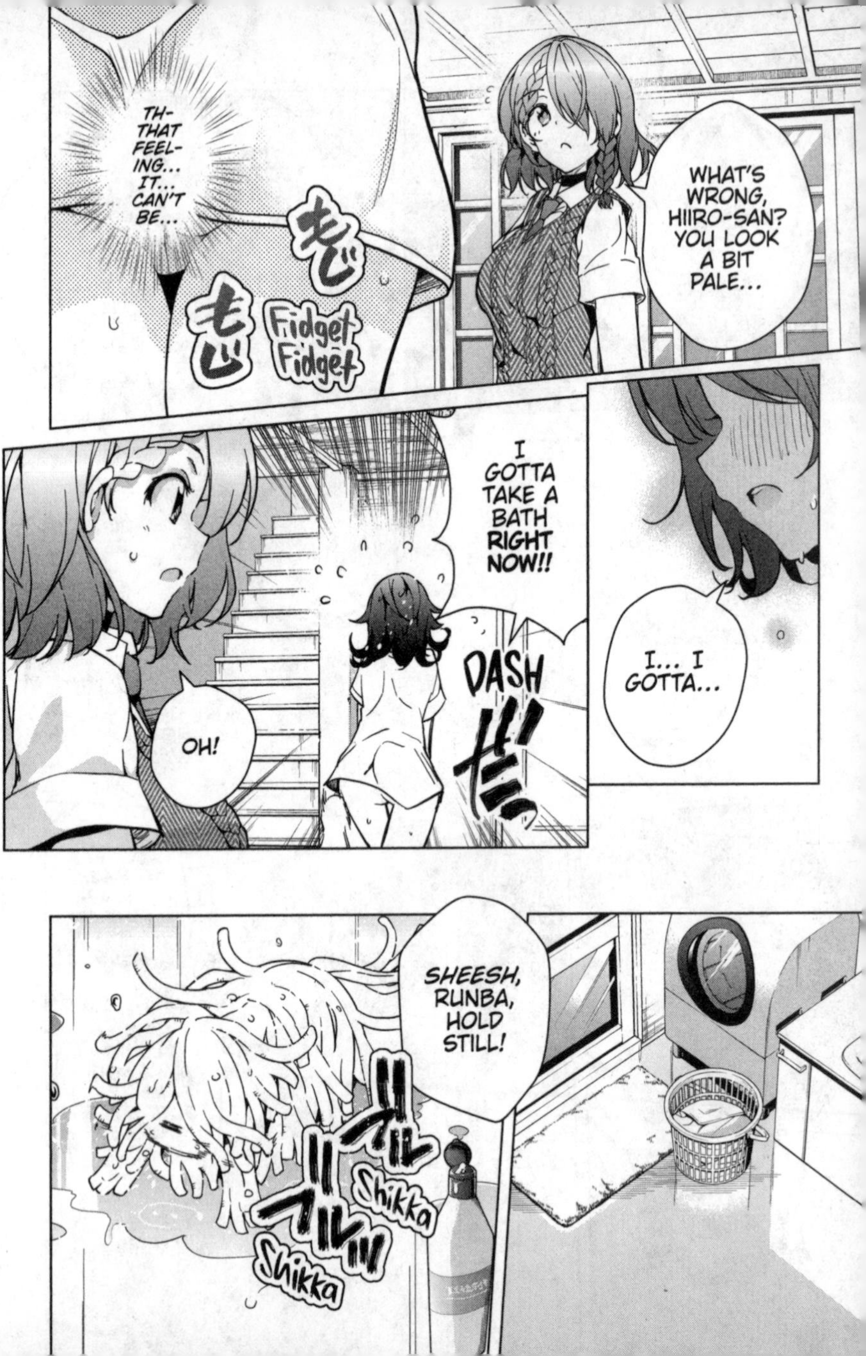
WHAT'S WRONG, HIIRO-SAN? YOU LOOK A BIT PALE...
TH-THAT FEELING... IT... CAN'T BE...
もじもじ
Fidget Fidget
I... I GOTTA...
I GOTTA TAKE A BATH RIGHT NOW!!
DASH
OH!
SHEESH, RUNBA, HOLD STILL!
Shikka
Shikka

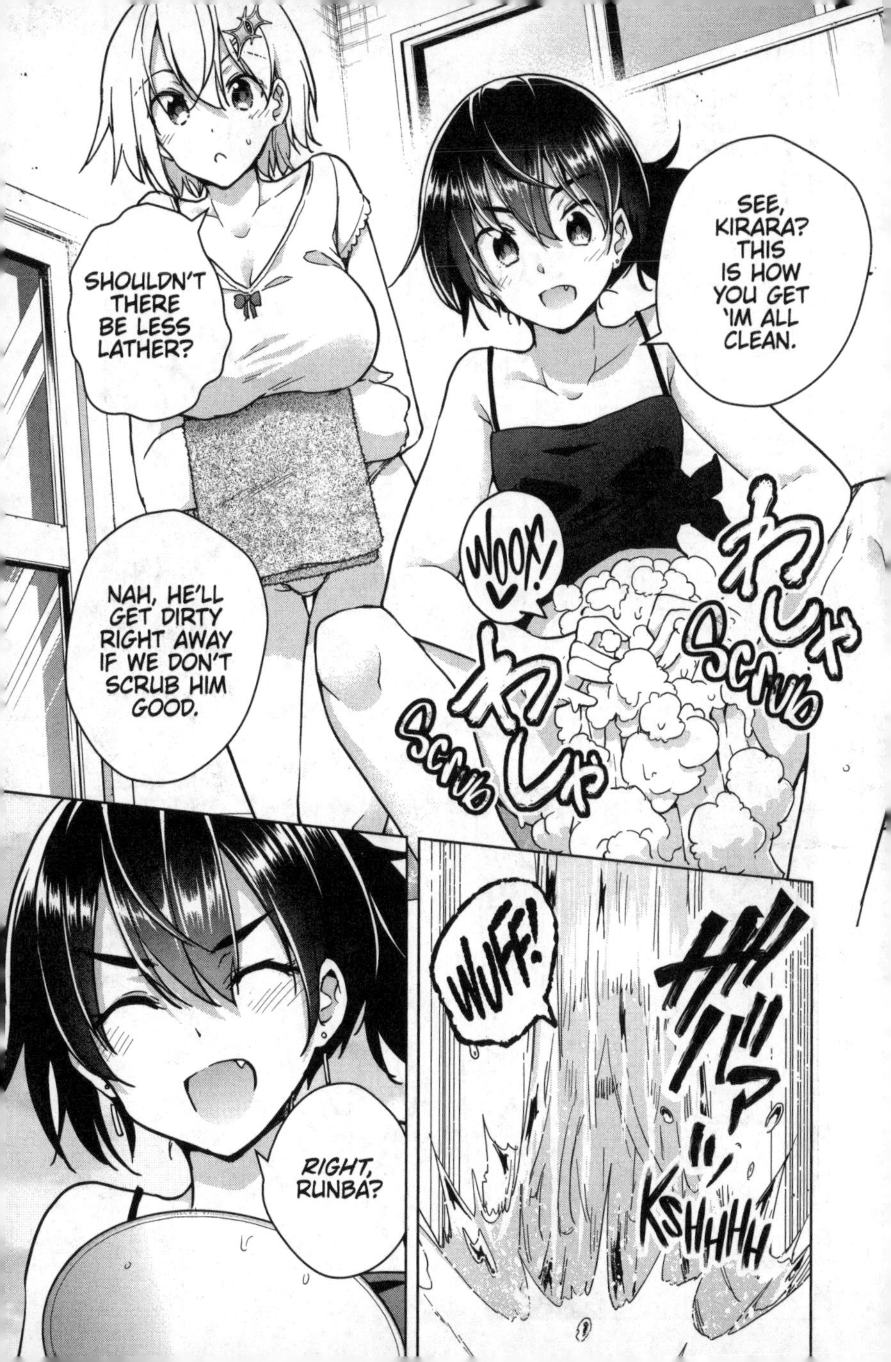

SEE, KIRARA? THIS IS HOW YOU GET 'IM ALL CLEAN.
SHOULDN'T THERE BE LESS LATHER?
わしゃ SCRUB
WOOF! ♥
わしゃ SCRUB
NAH, HE'LL GET DIRTY RIGHT AWAY IF WE DON'T SCRUB HIM GOOD.
WUFF!
ザバァ!! KSHHHH
RIGHT, RUNBA?

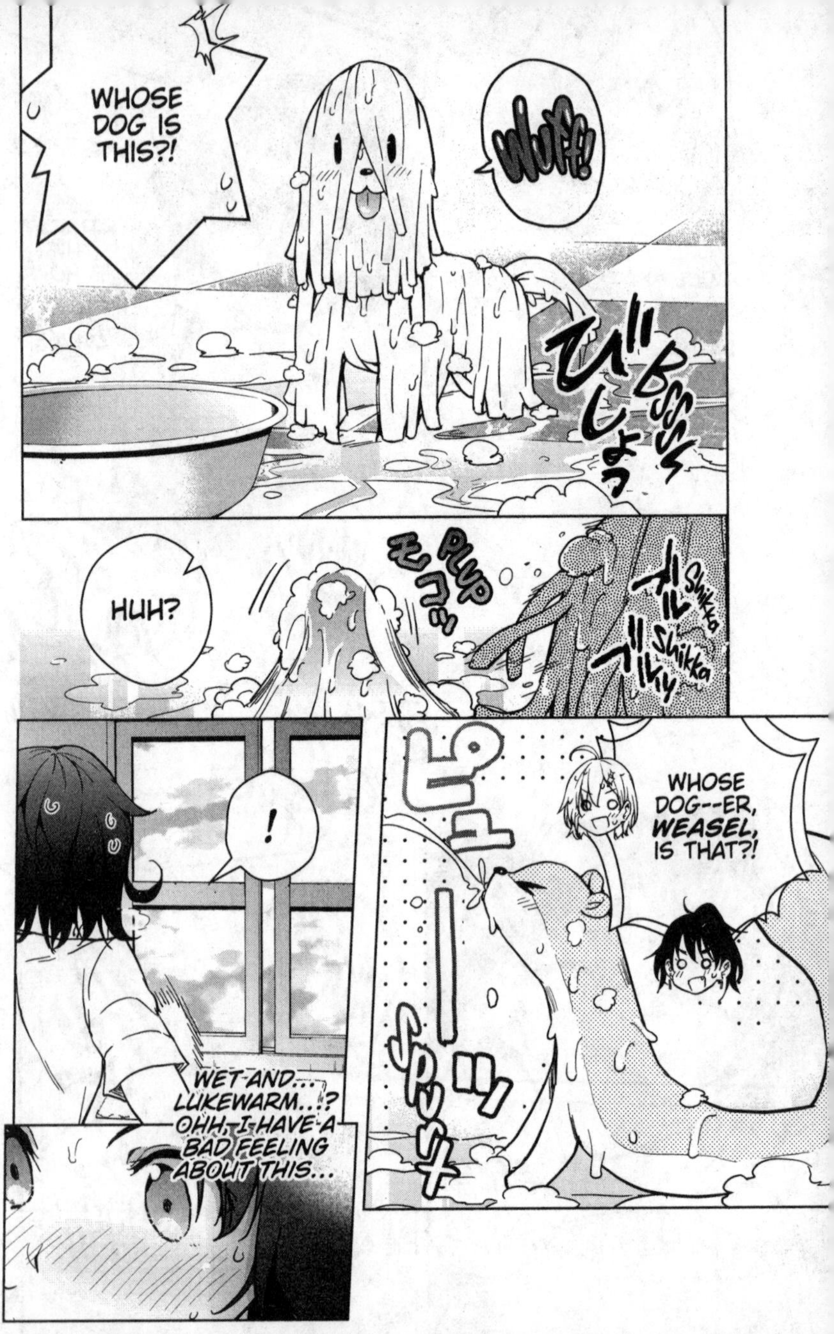
WHOSE DOG IS THIS?!
WUFF!
BSSSH
Shikka Shikka
PLUP
HUH?
WHOSE DOG--ER, WEASEL, IS THAT?!
SPUUT
!
WET AND... LUKEWARM...? OHH, I HAVE A BAD FEELING ABOUT THIS...

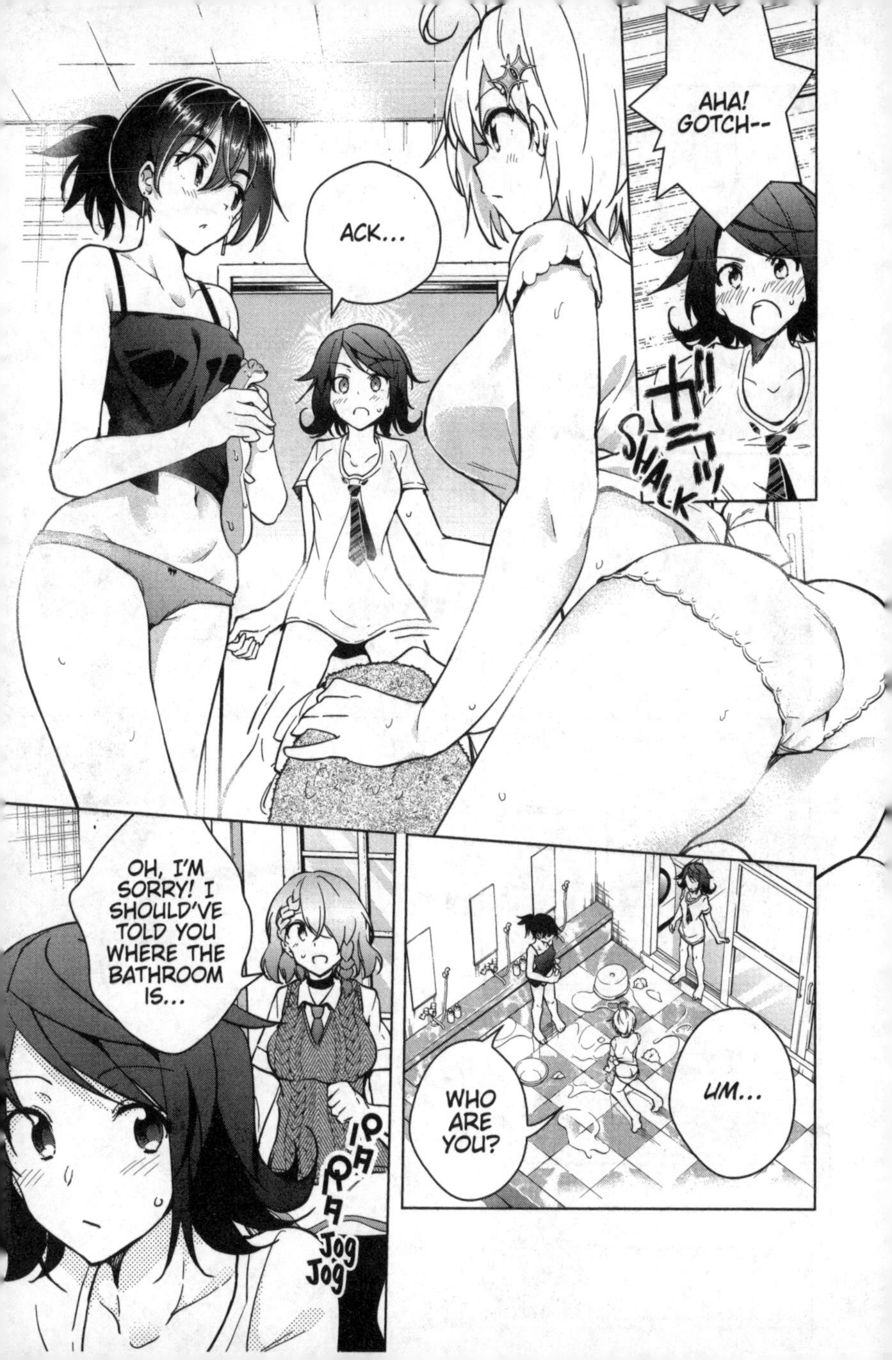
AHA! GOTCH--
ガラッ
SHALK
ACK...
UM...
WHO ARE YOU?
OH, I'M SORRY! I SHOULD'VE TOLD YOU WHERE THE BATHROOM IS...
Jog Jog

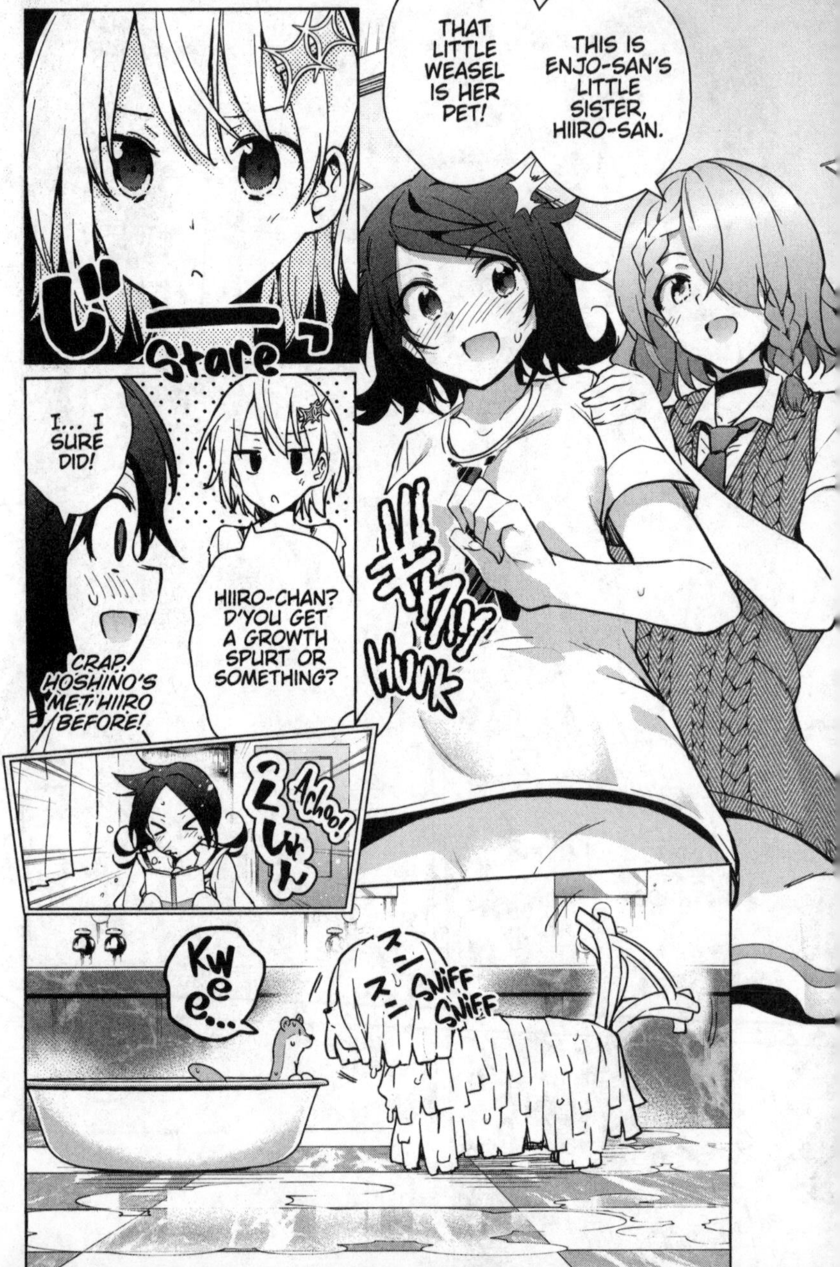
THIS IS ENJO-SAN'S LITTLE SISTER, HIIRO-SAN.
THAT LITTLE WEASEL IS HER PET!
ギクッ
Hunk
じーっ
Stare
HIIRO-CHAN? D'YOU GET A GROWTH SPURT OR SOMETHING?
I... I SURE DID!
CRAP. HOSHINO'S MET HIIRO BEFORE!
くしゅん
Achoo!
スンスン
SNIFF SNIFF
Kwee...

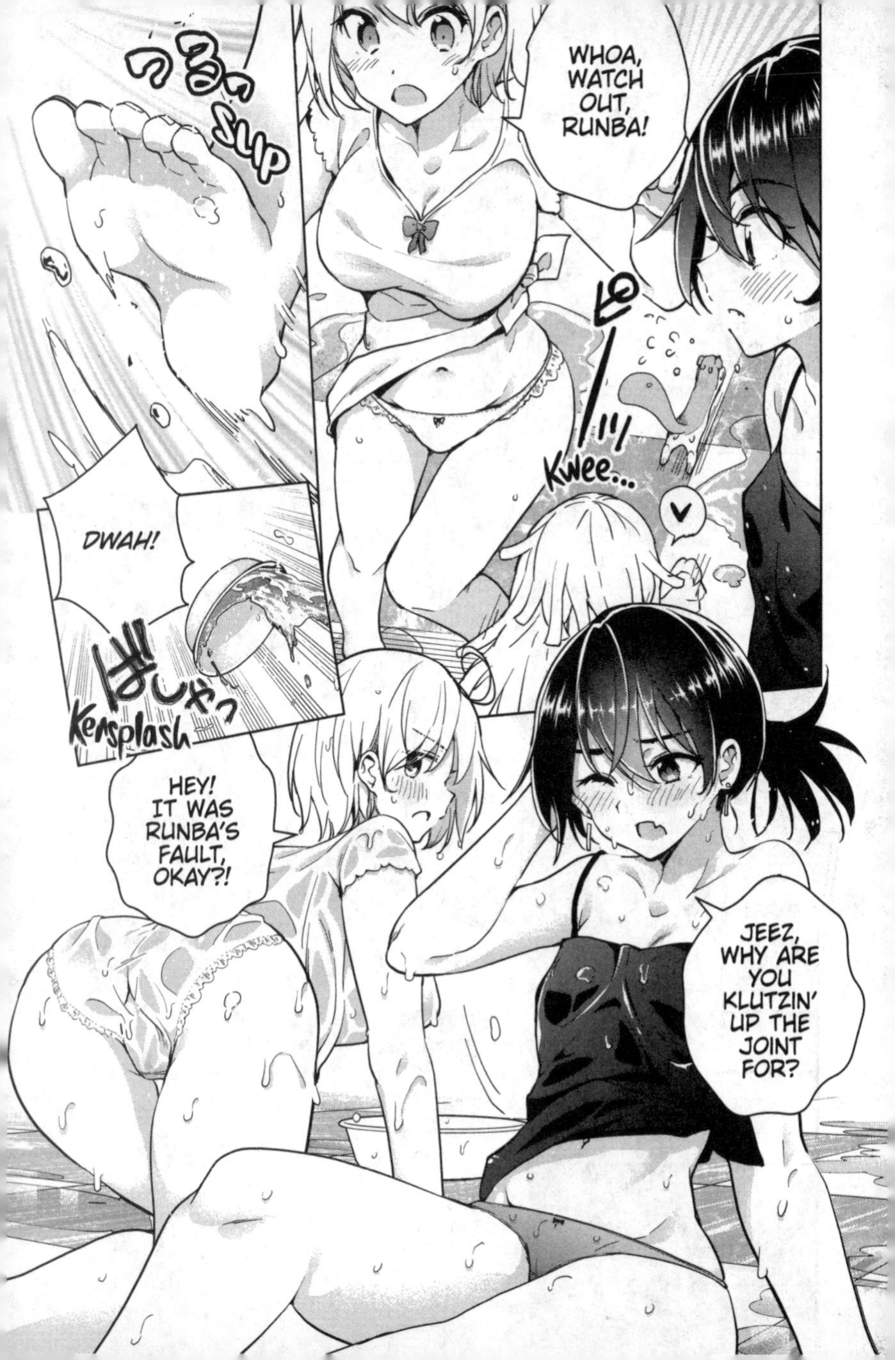
WHOA, WATCH OUT, RUNBA!
Kwee...
つるっ
SLIP
DWAH!
ばしゃっ
Kersplash
JEEZ, WHY ARE YOU KLUTZIN' UP THE JOINT FOR?
HEY! IT WAS RUNBA'S FAULT, OKAY?!

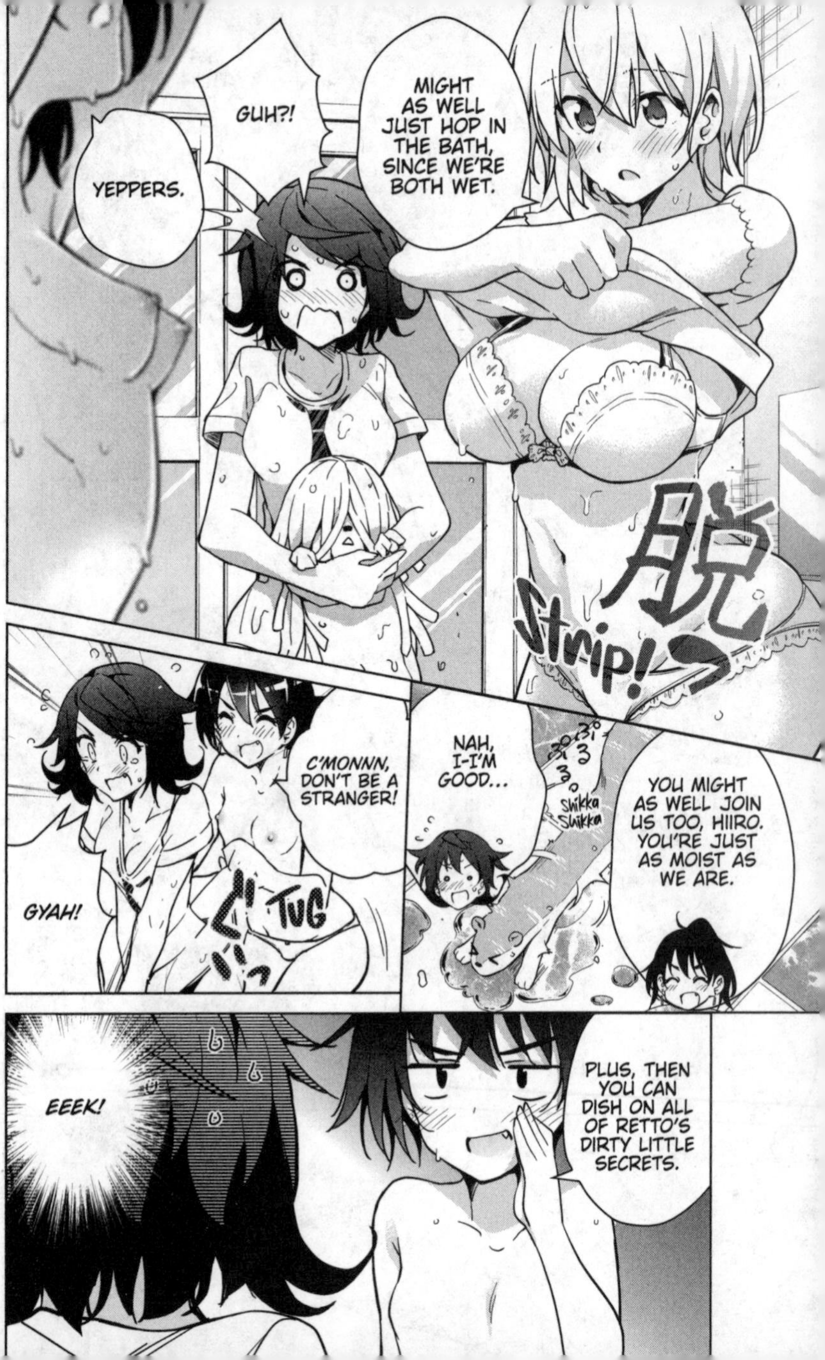
MIGHT AS WELL JUST HOP IN THE BATH, SINCE WE'RE BOTH WET.
GUH?!
YEPPERS.
脱
Strip!
YOU MIGHT AS WELL JOIN US TOO, HIIRO. YOU'RE JUST AS MOIST AS WE ARE.
NAH, I-I'M GOOD...
Shikka Shikka
C'MONNN, DON'T BE A STRANGER!
TUG
GYAH!
PLUS, THEN YOU CAN DISH ON ALL OF RETTO'S DIRTY LITTLE SECRETS.
EEEK!

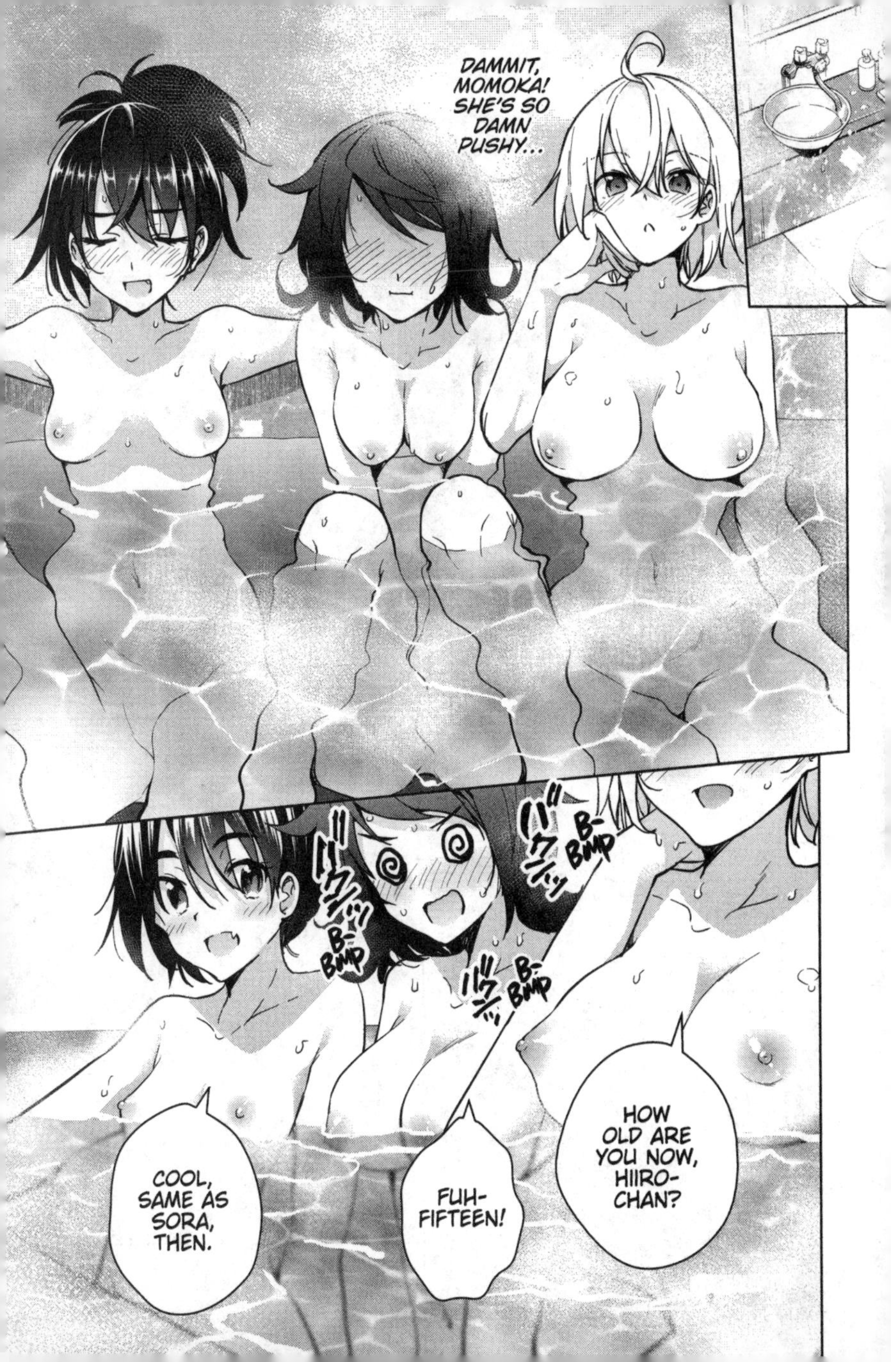
DAMMIT, MOMOKA! SHE'S SO DAMN PUSHY...
B-BMP
B-BMP
B-BMP
HOW OLD ARE YOU NOW, HIIRO-CHAN?
FUH-FIFTEEN!
COOL, SAME AS SORA, THEN.

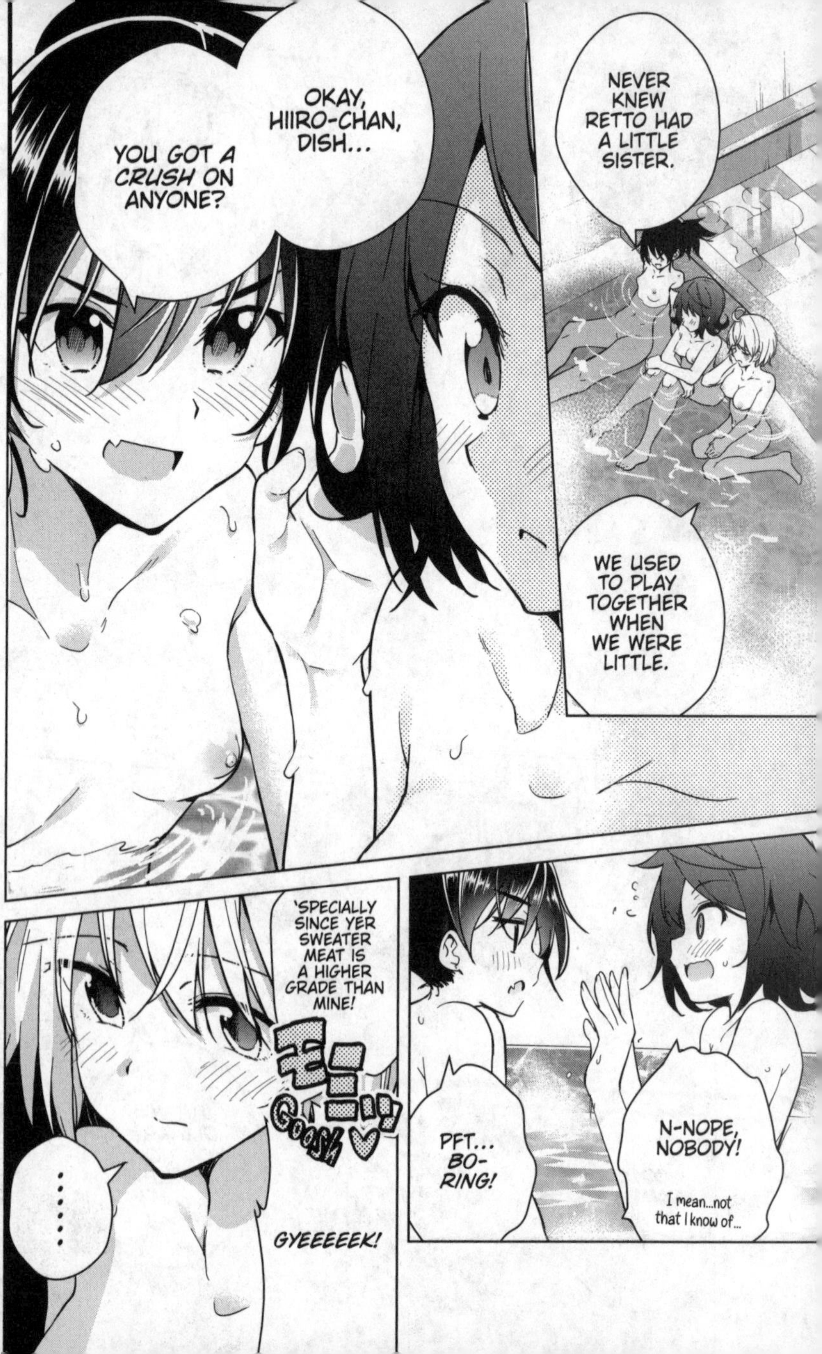
NEVER KNEW RETTO HAD A LITTLE SISTER.
WE USED TO PLAY TOGETHER WHEN WE WERE LITTLE.
OKAY, HIIRO-CHAN, DISH...
YOU GOT A CRUSH ON ANYONE?
N-NOPE, NOBODY!
I mean...not that I know of...
PFT... BO-RING!
'SPECIALLY SINCE YER SWEATER MEAT IS A HIGHER GRADE THAN MINE!
モミッ
Goosh ♥
GYEEEEEK!
......

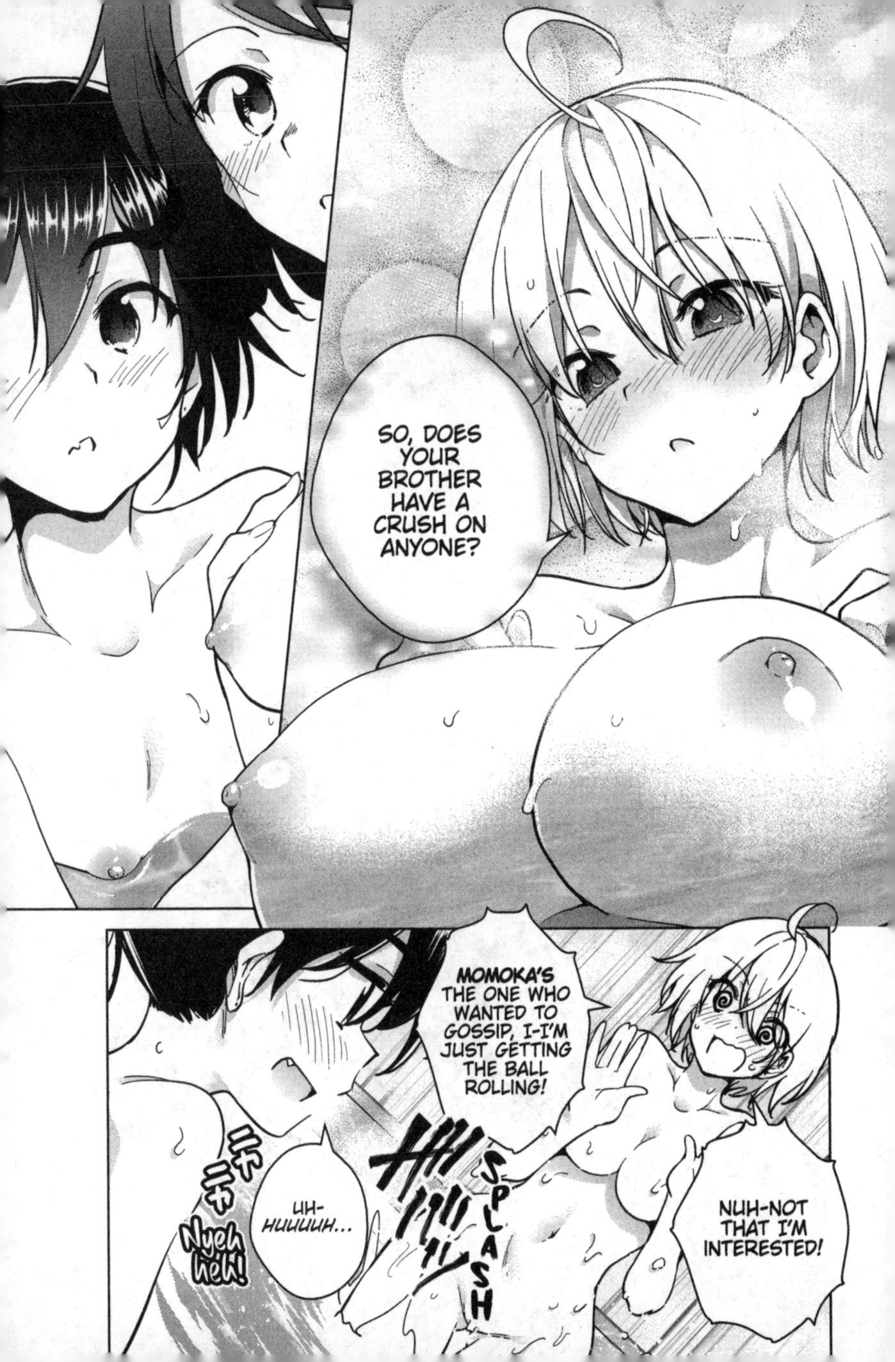
SO, DOES YOUR BROTHER HAVE A CRUSH ON ANYONE?
MOMOKA'S THE ONE WHO WANTED TO GOSSIP, I-I'M JUST GETTING THE BALL ROLLING!
NUH-NOT THAT I'M INTERESTED!
SPLASH
UH-HUUUUH...
ニヤニヤ
Nyeh heh!

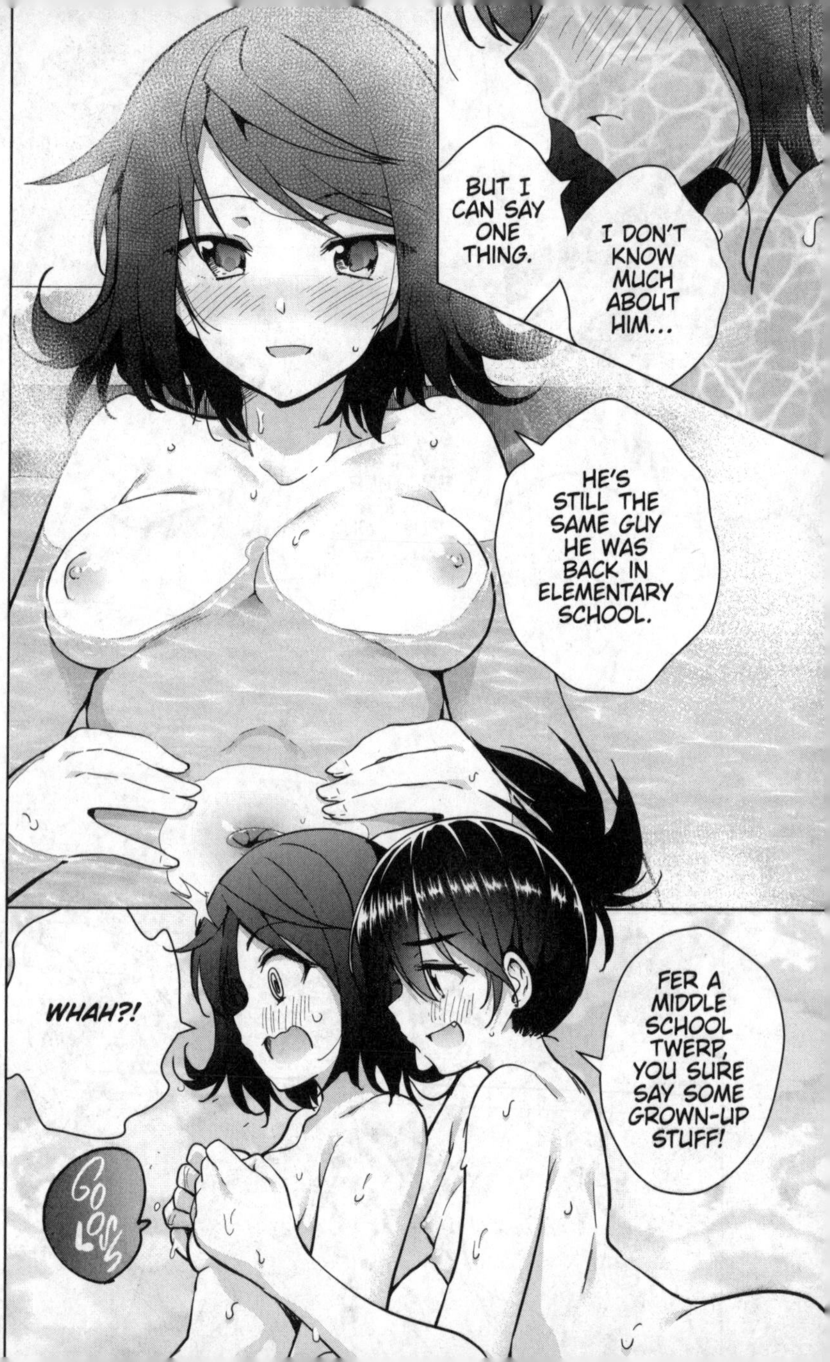
I DON'T KNOW MUCH ABOUT HIM...
BUT I CAN SAY ONE THING.
HE'S STILL THE SAME GUY HE WAS BACK IN ELEMENTARY SCHOOL.
FER A MIDDLE SCHOOL TWERP, YOU SURE SAY SOME GROWN-UP STUFF!
WHAH?!

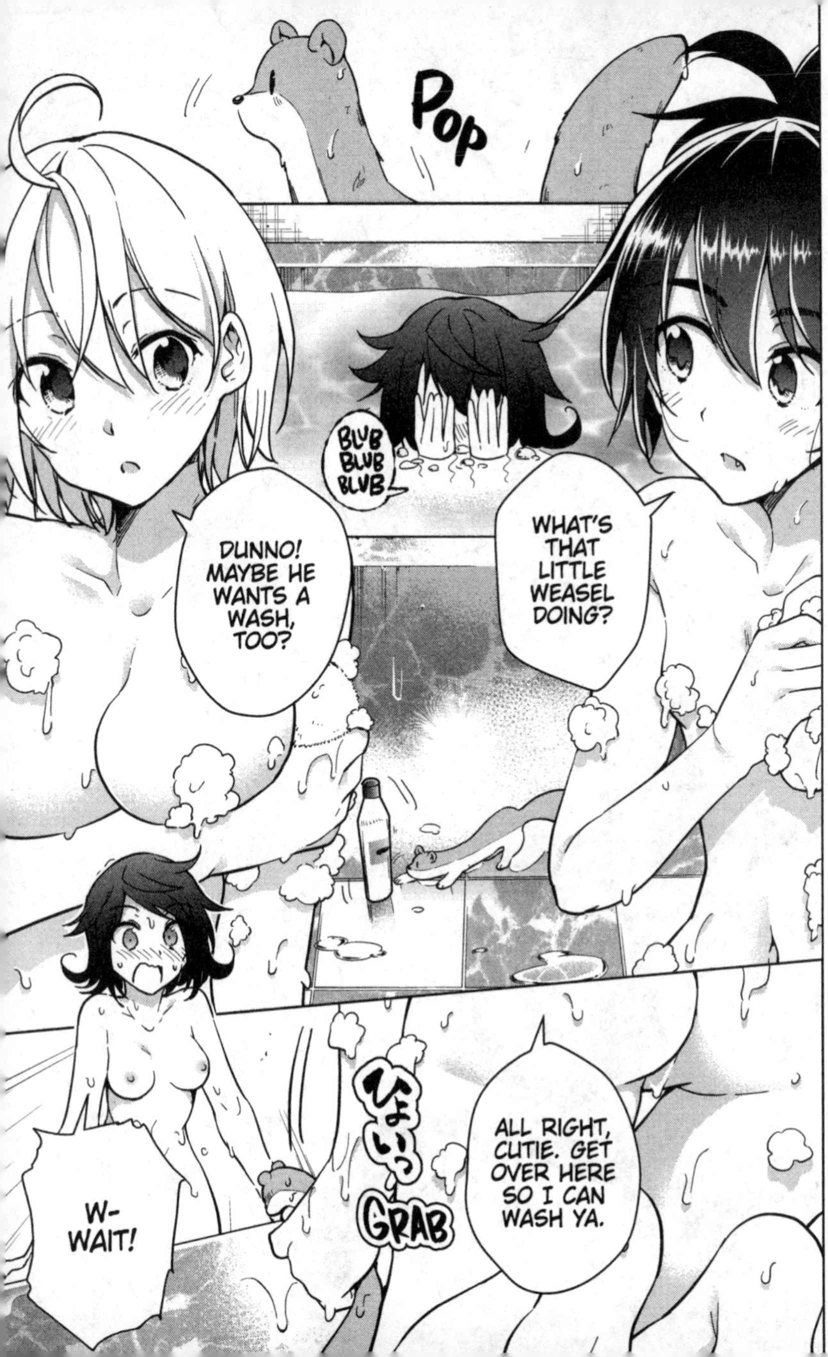
POP
WHAT'S THAT LITTLE WEASEL DOING?
BLUB BLUB BLUB
DUNNO! MAYBE HE WANTS A WASH, TOO?
ALL RIGHT, CUTIE. GET OVER HERE SO I CAN WASH YA.
ひょいっ
GRAB
W-WAIT!

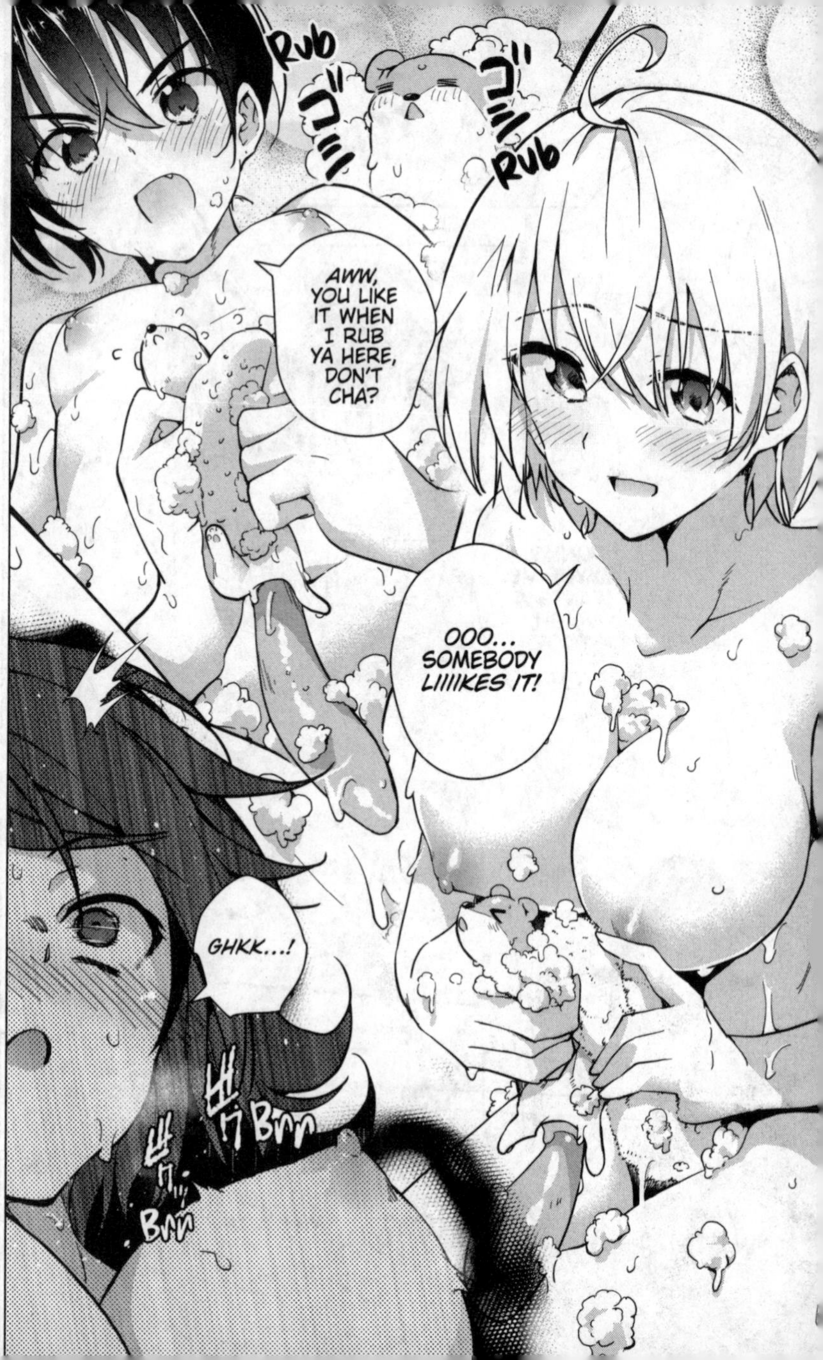
Rub
Rub
AWW, YOU LIKE IT WHEN I RUB YA HERE, DON'T CHA?
OOO... SOMEBODY LIIIIKES IT!
GHKK...!
Brrr
Brrr

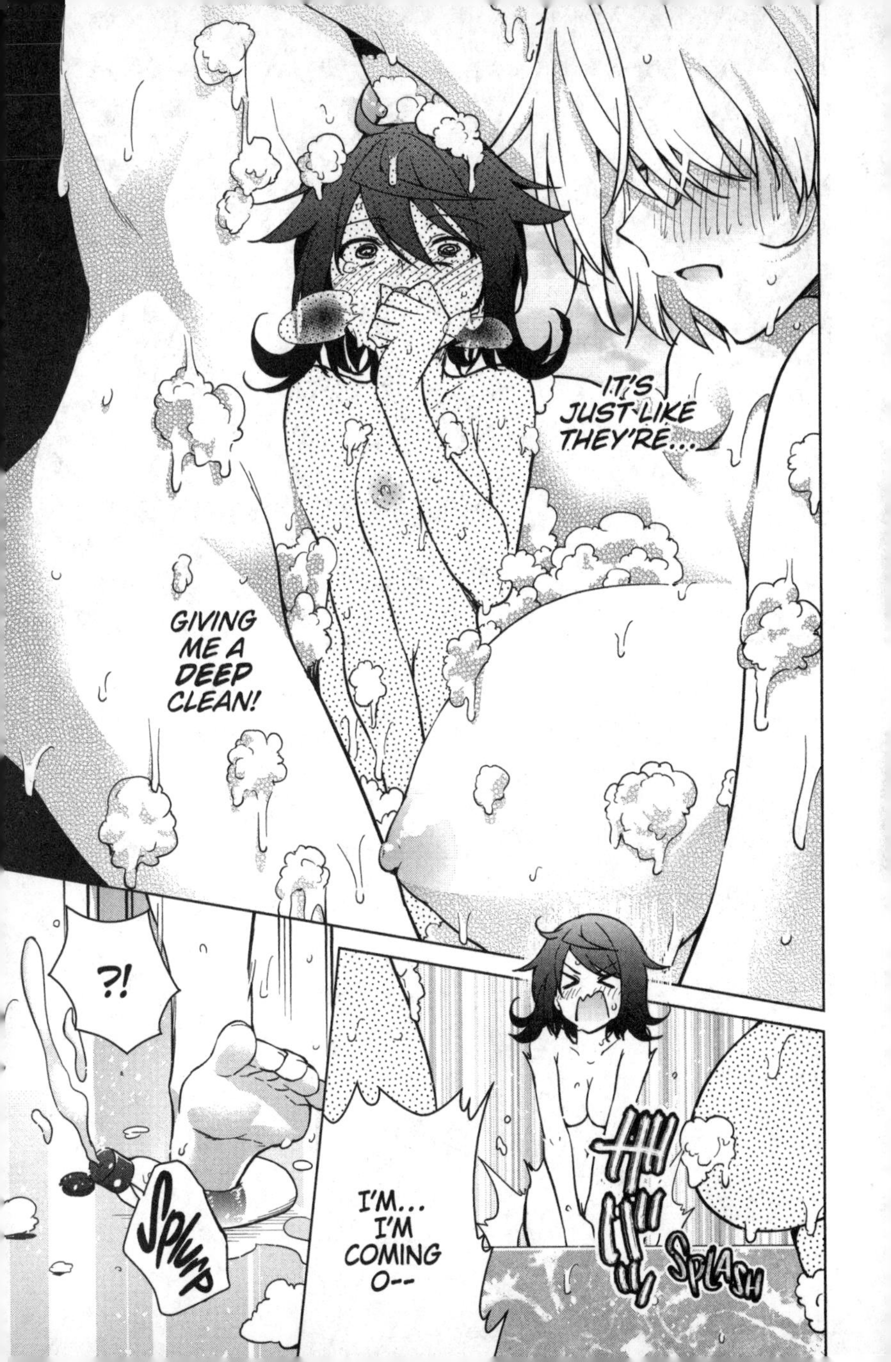
IT'S JUST LIKE THEY'RE...
GIVING ME A DEEP CLEAN!
I'M... I'M COMING O--
SPLASH
?!
Splurp

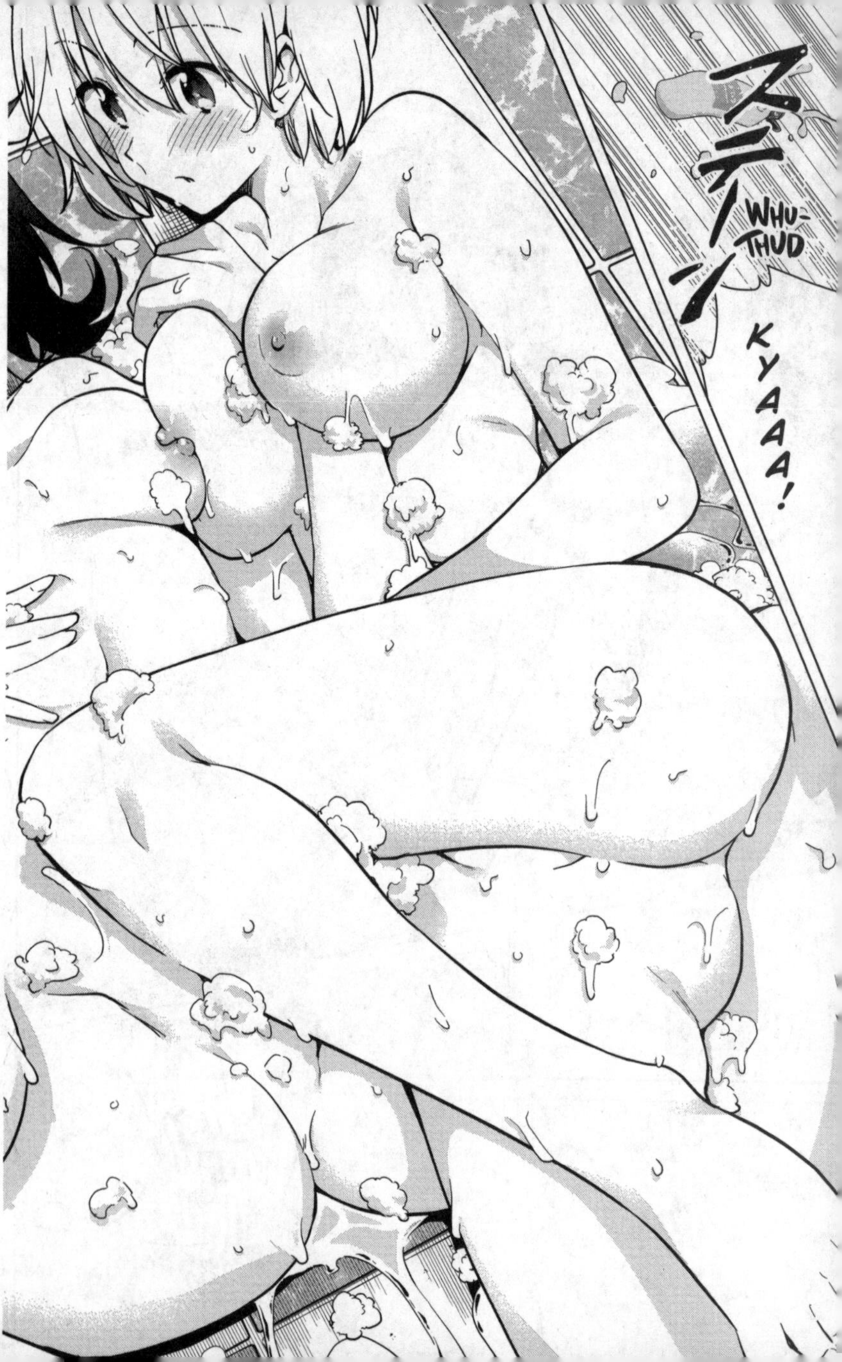
WHU-THUD
KYAAA!

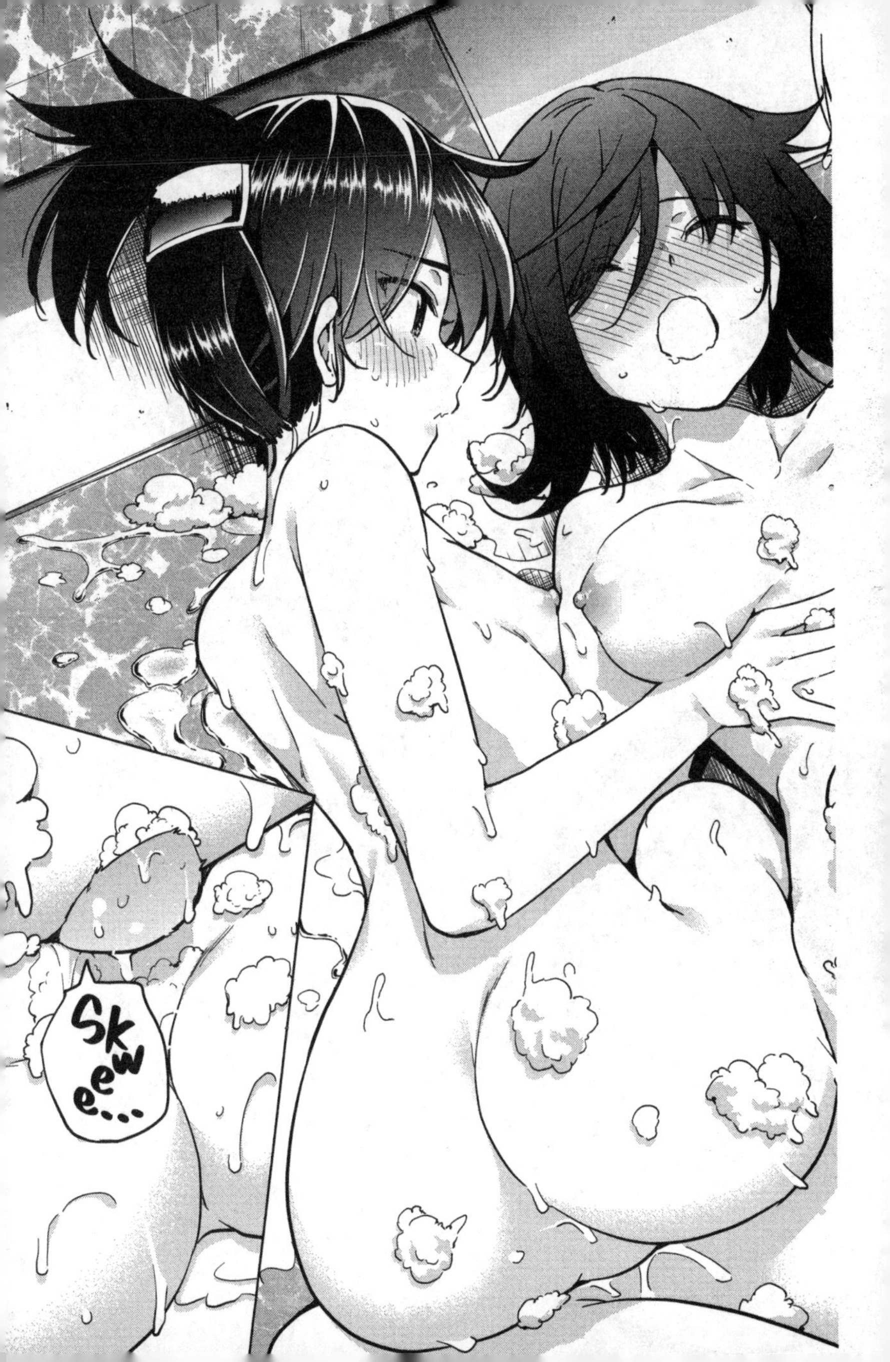
Skwee...

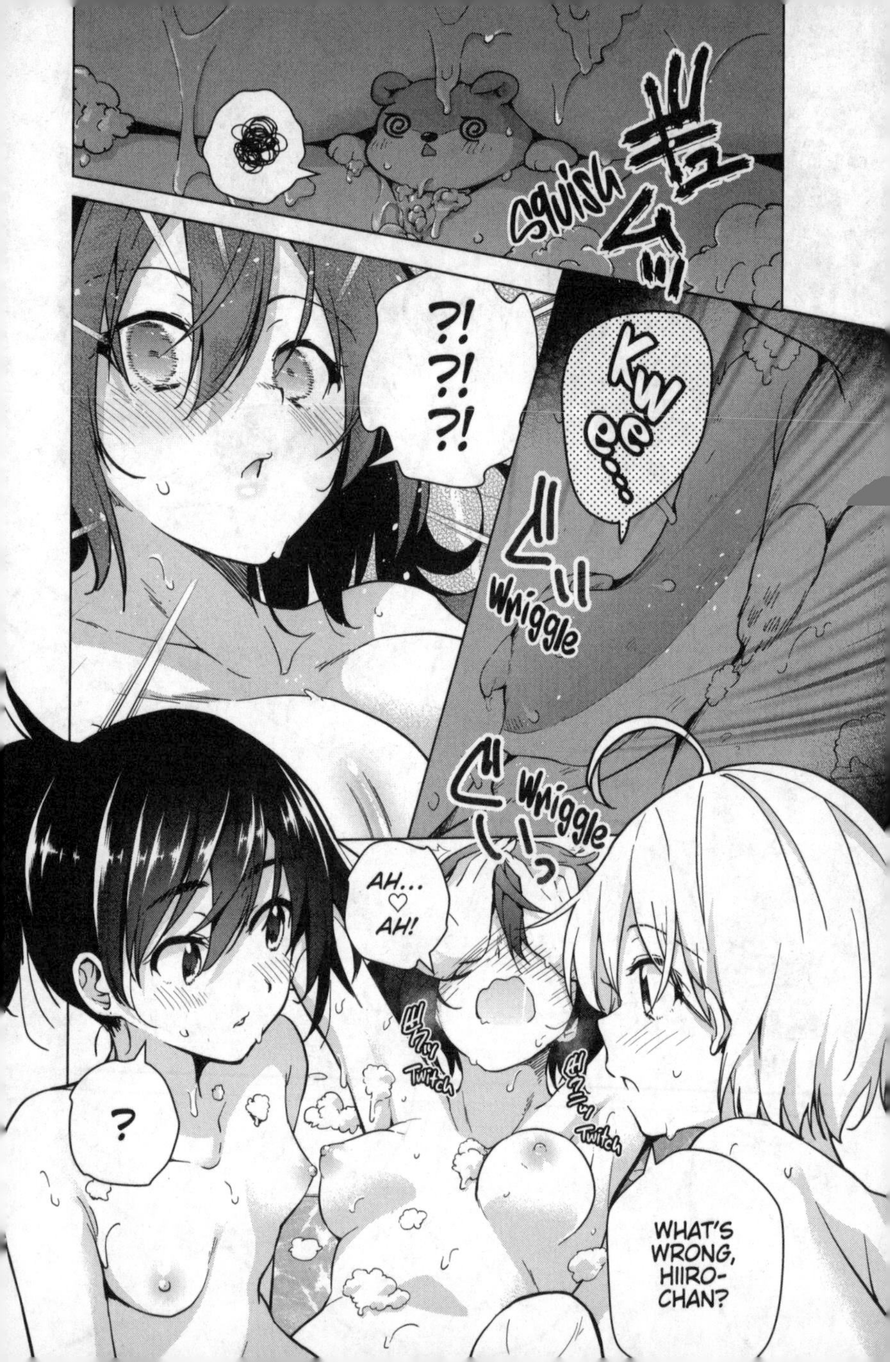

squish
Kwee...
wriggle
?!?!?!
wriggle
AH... ♡ AH!
twitch
twitch
WHAT'S WRONG, HIIRO-CHAN?
?

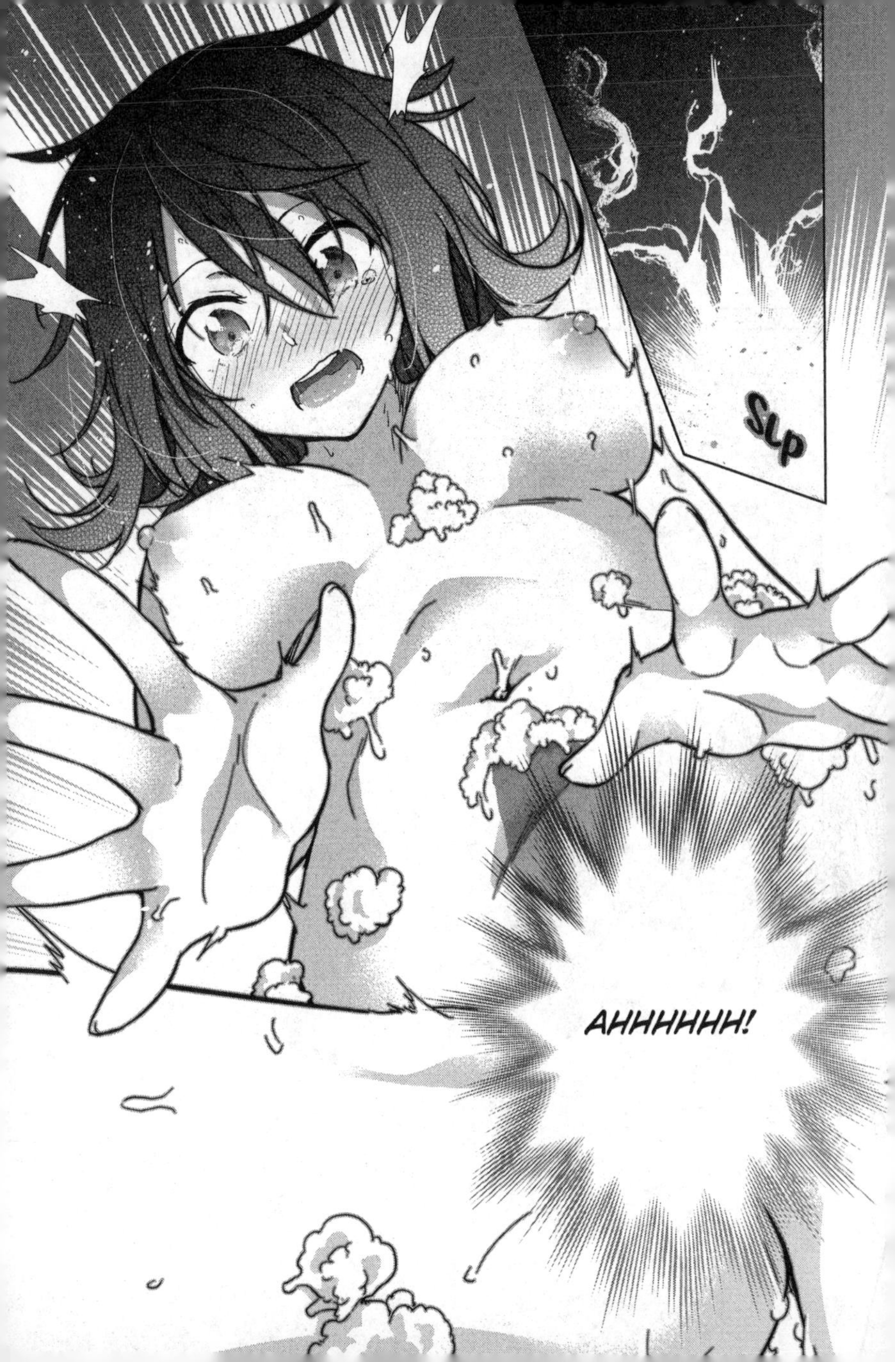
SLP
AHHHHHH!

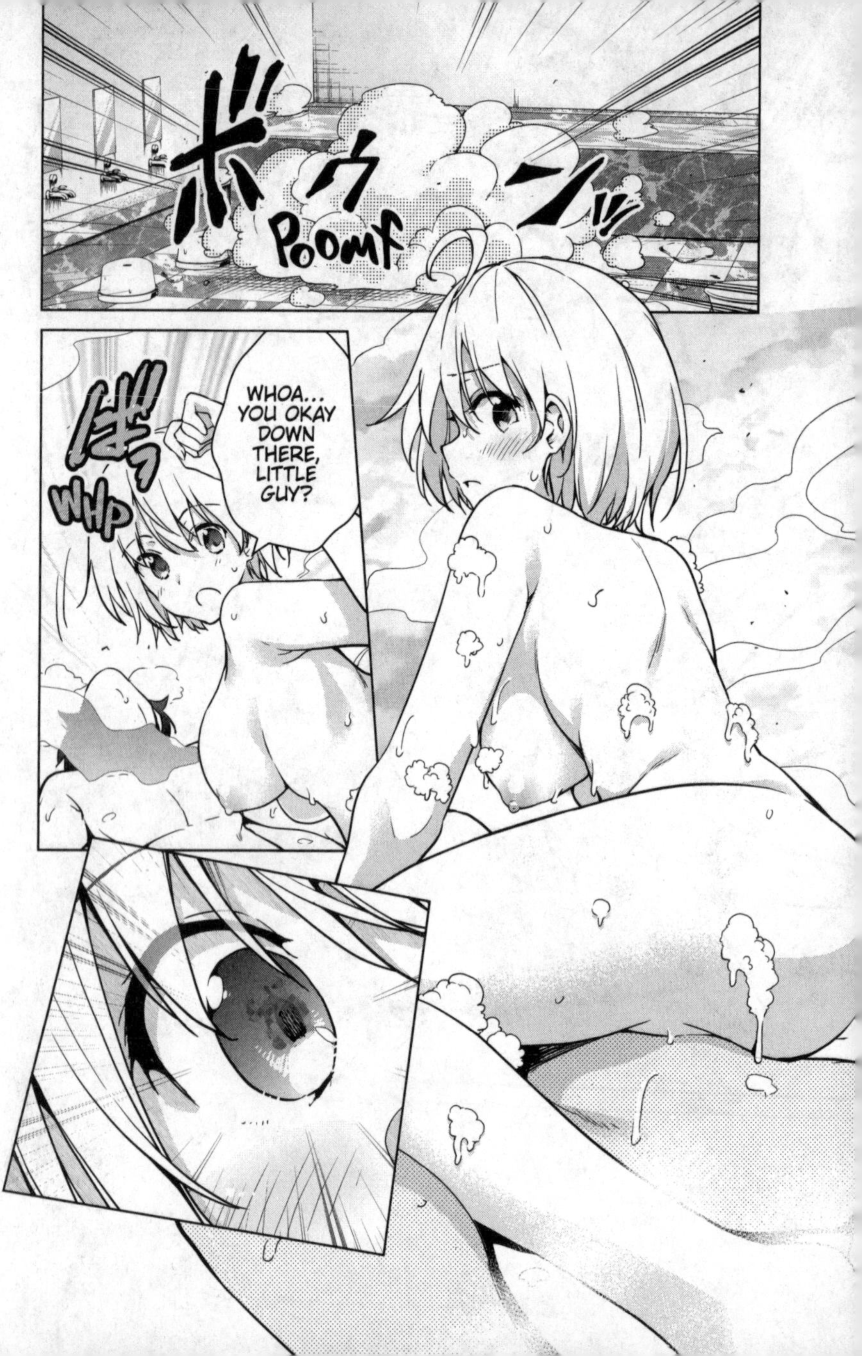
ボウーン!!
POOMF
ぼっ
WHP
WHOA... YOU OKAY DOWN THERE, LITTLE GUY?
...

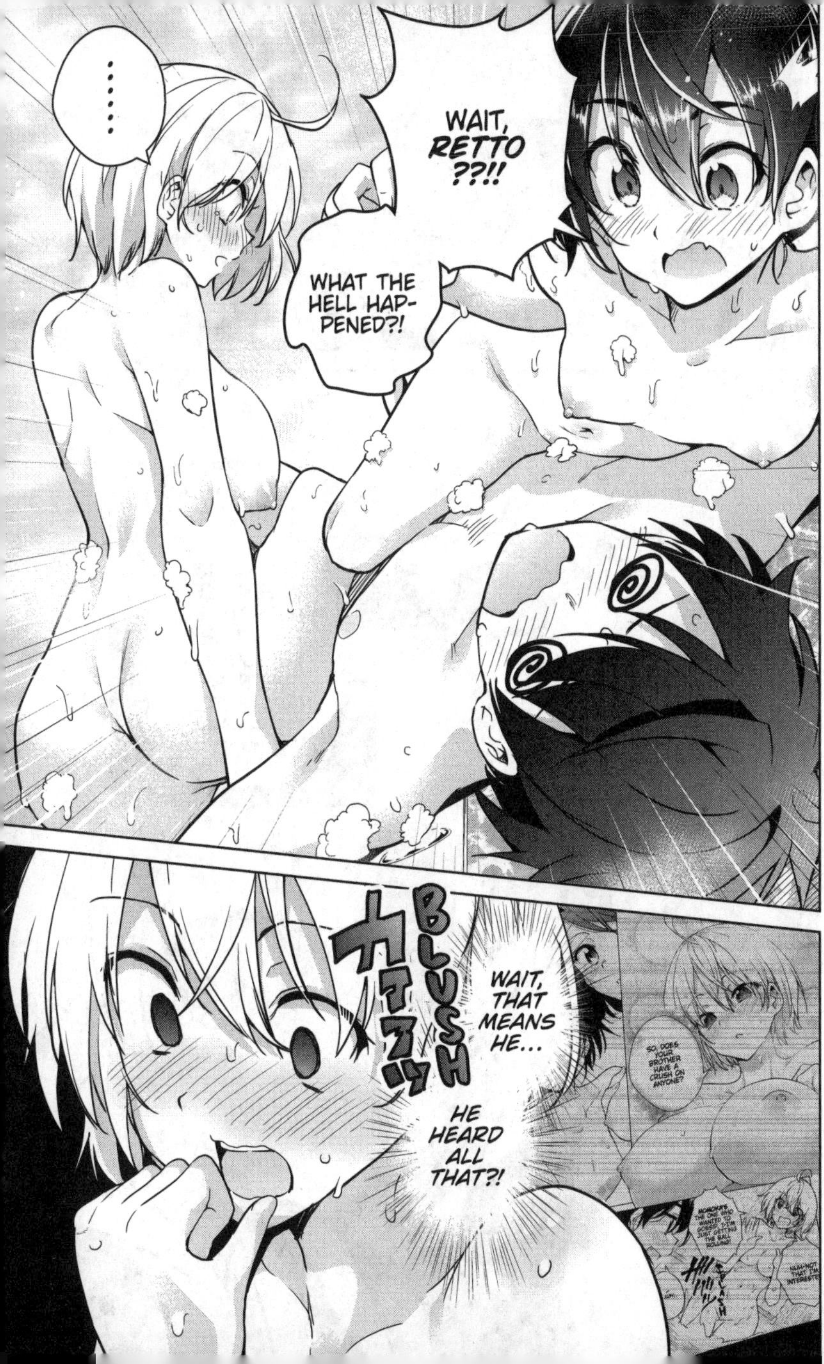
WAIT, RETTO ??!!
WHAT THE HELL HAP-PENED?!
......
SO, DOES YOUR BROTHER HAVE A CRUSH ON ANYONE?
NUH-NOT THAT I'M INTERESTE
MOMOKA'S THE ONE WHO WANTED TO GOSSIP, I-I'M JUST GETTING THE BALL ROLLING!
SPLASH
WAIT, THAT MEANS HE...
BLUSH
HE HEARD ALL THAT?!

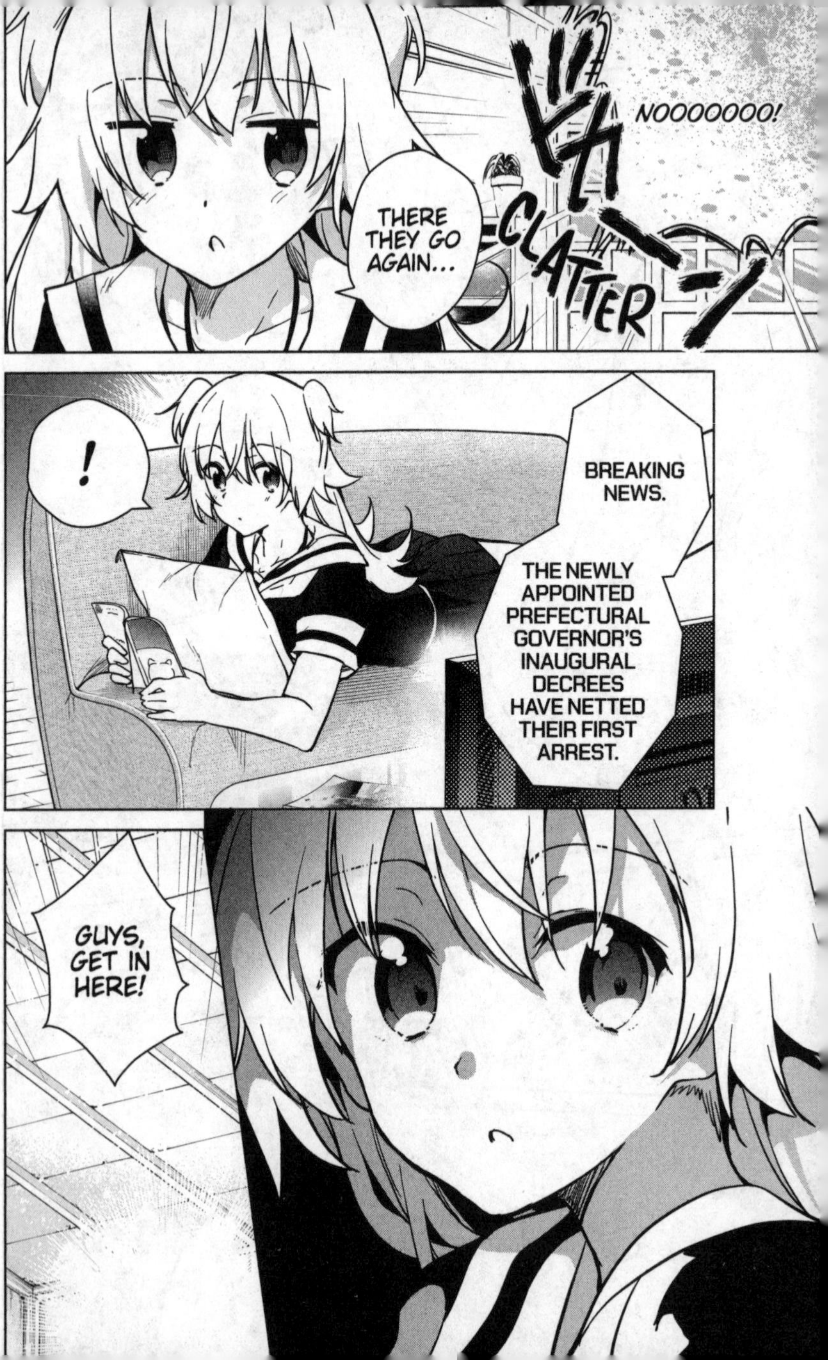
NOOOOOOO!
CLATTER
THERE THEY GO AGAIN...
BREAKING NEWS.
THE NEWLY APPOINTED PREFECTURAL GOVERNOR'S INAUGURAL DECREES HAVE NETTED THEIR FIRST ARREST.
!
GUYS, GET IN HERE!

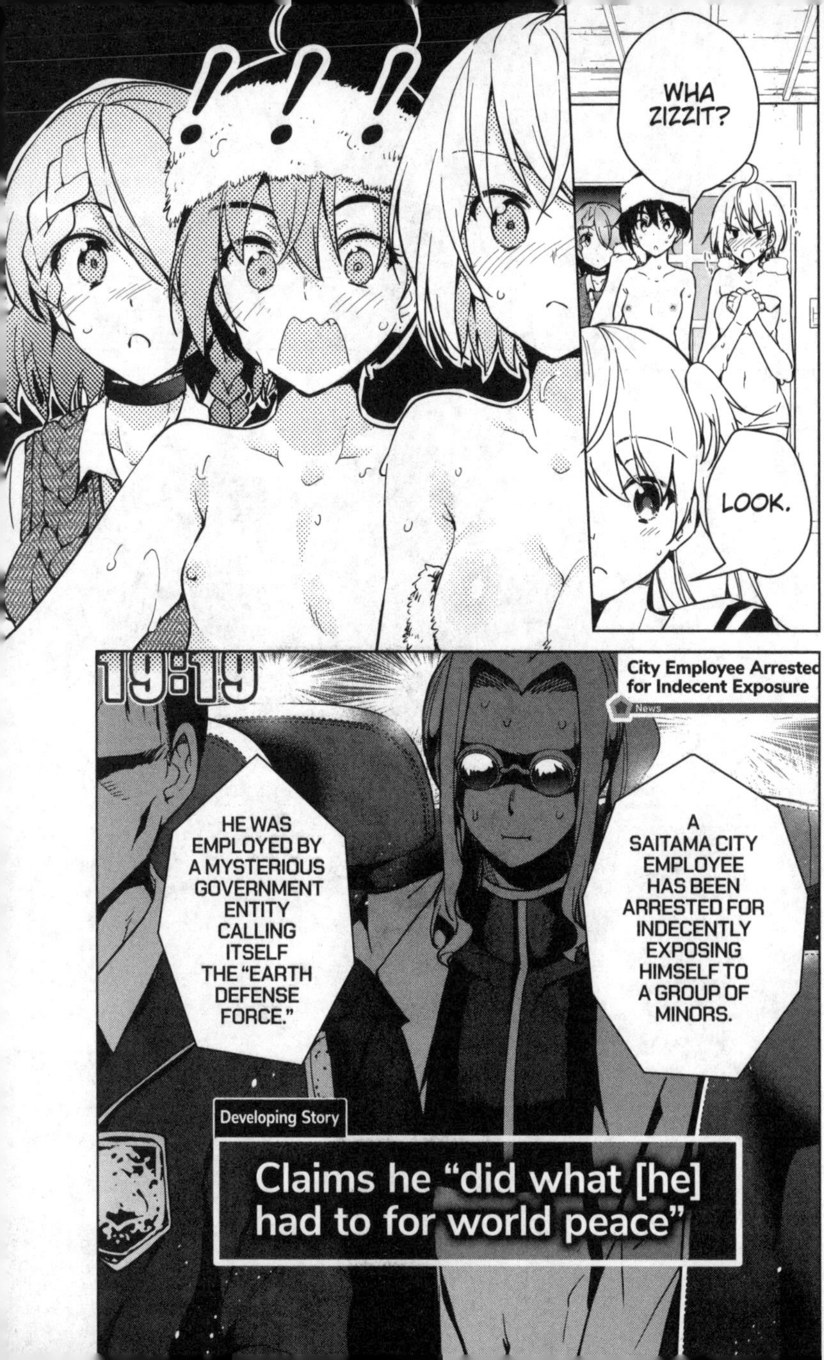
WHA ZIZZIT?
LOOK.
! ! !
19:19
City Employee Arrested for Indecent Exposure
News
A SAITAMA CITY EMPLOYEE HAS BEEN ARRESTED FOR INDECENTLY EXPOSING HIMSELF TO A GROUP OF MINORS.
HE WAS EMPLOYED BY A MYSTERIOUS GOVERNMENT ENTITY CALLING ITSELF THE "EARTH DEFENSE FORCE."
Developing Story
Claims he "did what [he] had to for world peace"

Extra Gallery

SUPER H×EROS

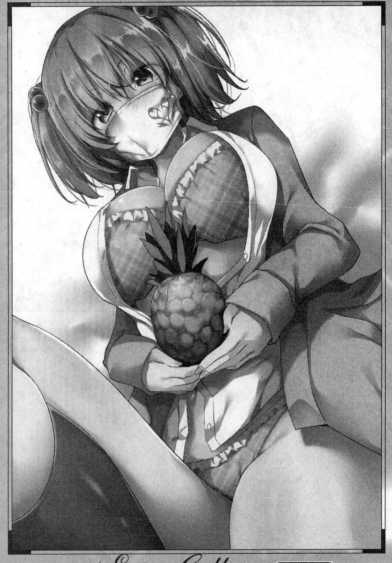

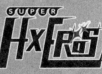

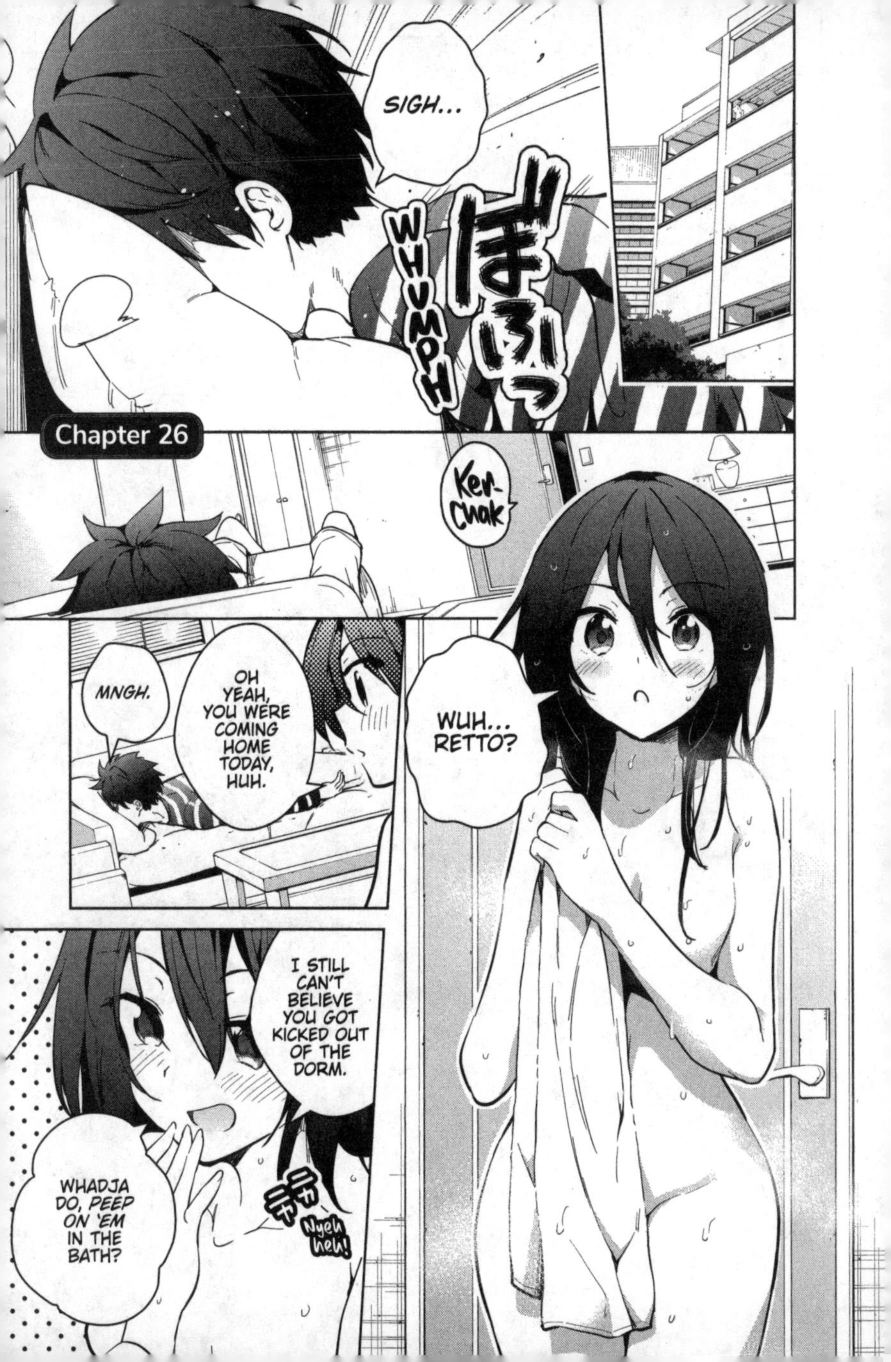
SIGH...
ぼふっ
WHUMPH
Chapter 26
Ker-Chak
WUH... RETTO?
OH YEAH, YOU WERE COMING HOME TODAY, HUH.
MNGH.
I STILL CAN'T BELIEVE YOU GOT KICKED OUT OF THE DORM.
WHADJA DO, PEEP ON 'EM IN THE BATH?
ニヤニヤ
Nyeh heh!

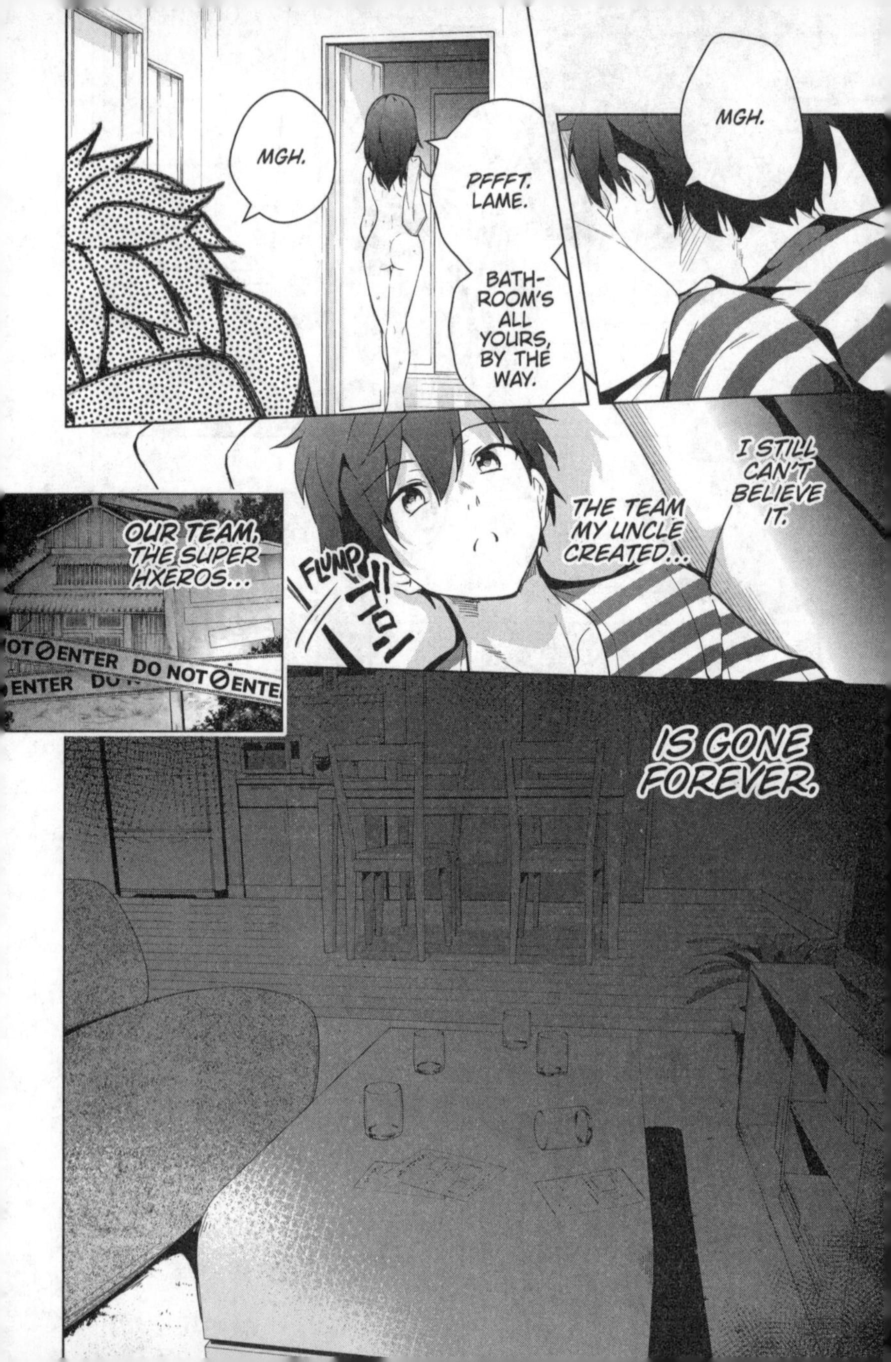
MGH.
PFFFT. LAME.
BATH-ROOM'S ALL YOURS, BY THE WAY.
MGH.
I STILL CAN'T BELIEVE IT.
THE TEAM MY UNCLE CREATED...
FLUMP
OUR TEAM, THE SUPER HXEROS...
IS GONE FOREVER.

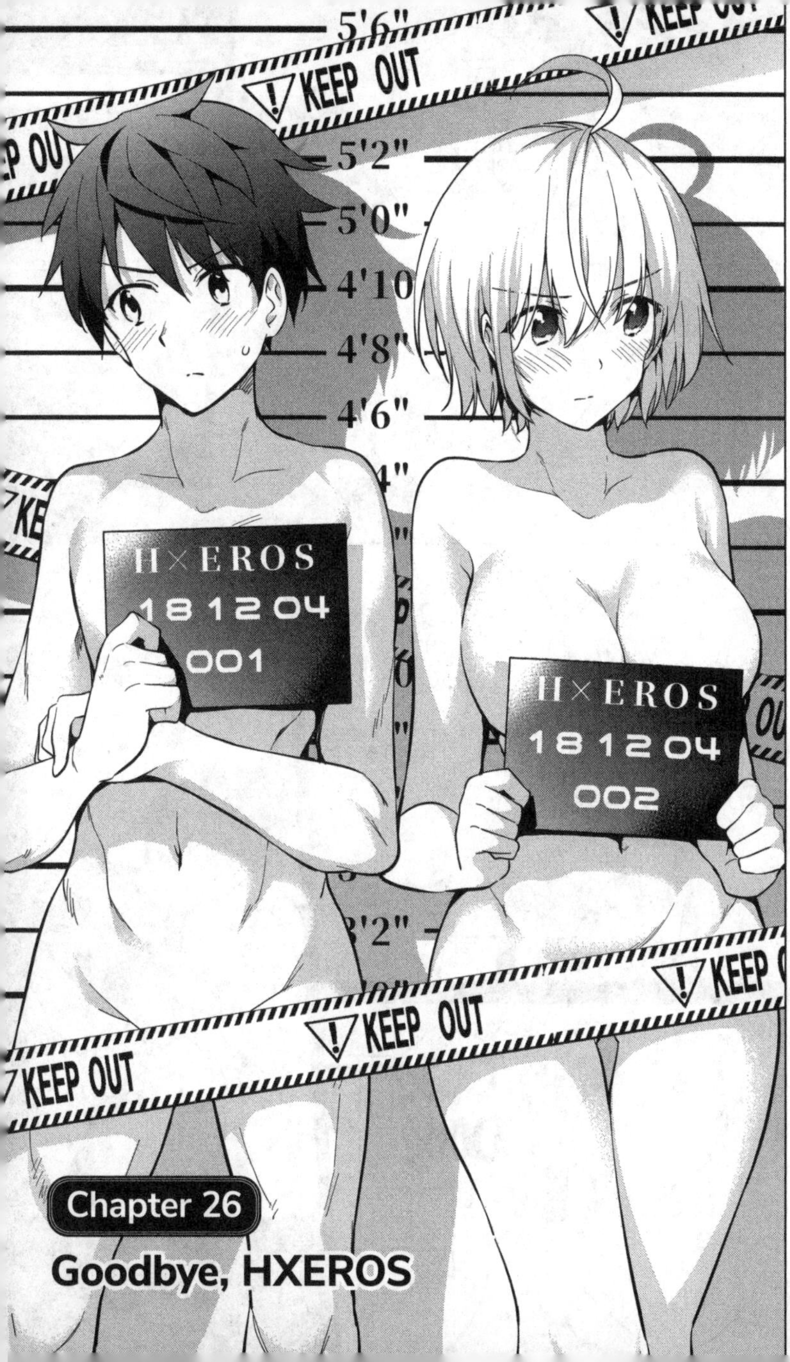
KEEP OUT
H×EROS
181204
001
H×EROS
181204
002

Chapter 26

Goodbye, HXEROS

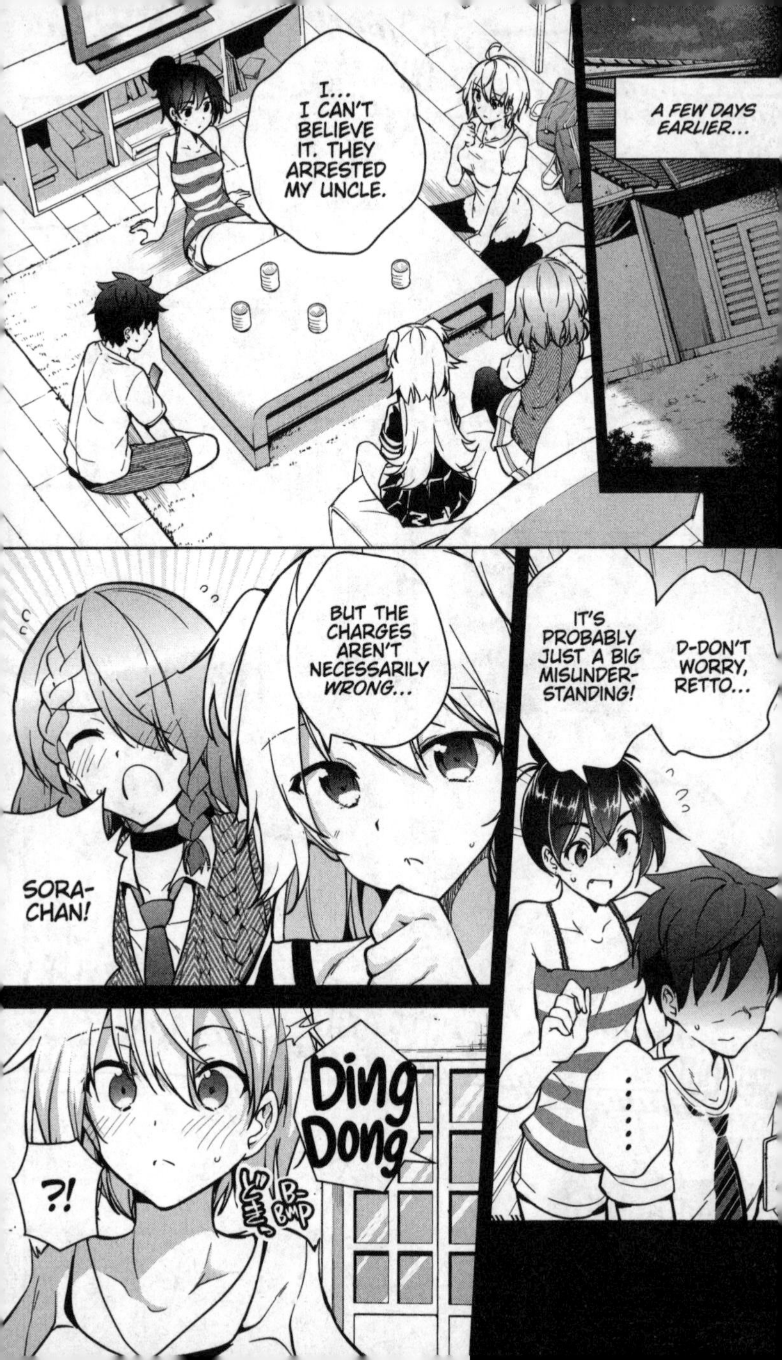

A FEW DAYS EARLIER...
I... I CAN'T BELIEVE IT. THEY ARRESTED MY UNCLE.
D-DON'T WORRY, RETTO...
IT'S PROBABLY JUST A BIG MISUNDERSTANDING!
......
BUT THE CHARGES AREN'T NECESSARILY *WRONG*...
SORA-CHAN!
Ding Dong
B-BMP
?!

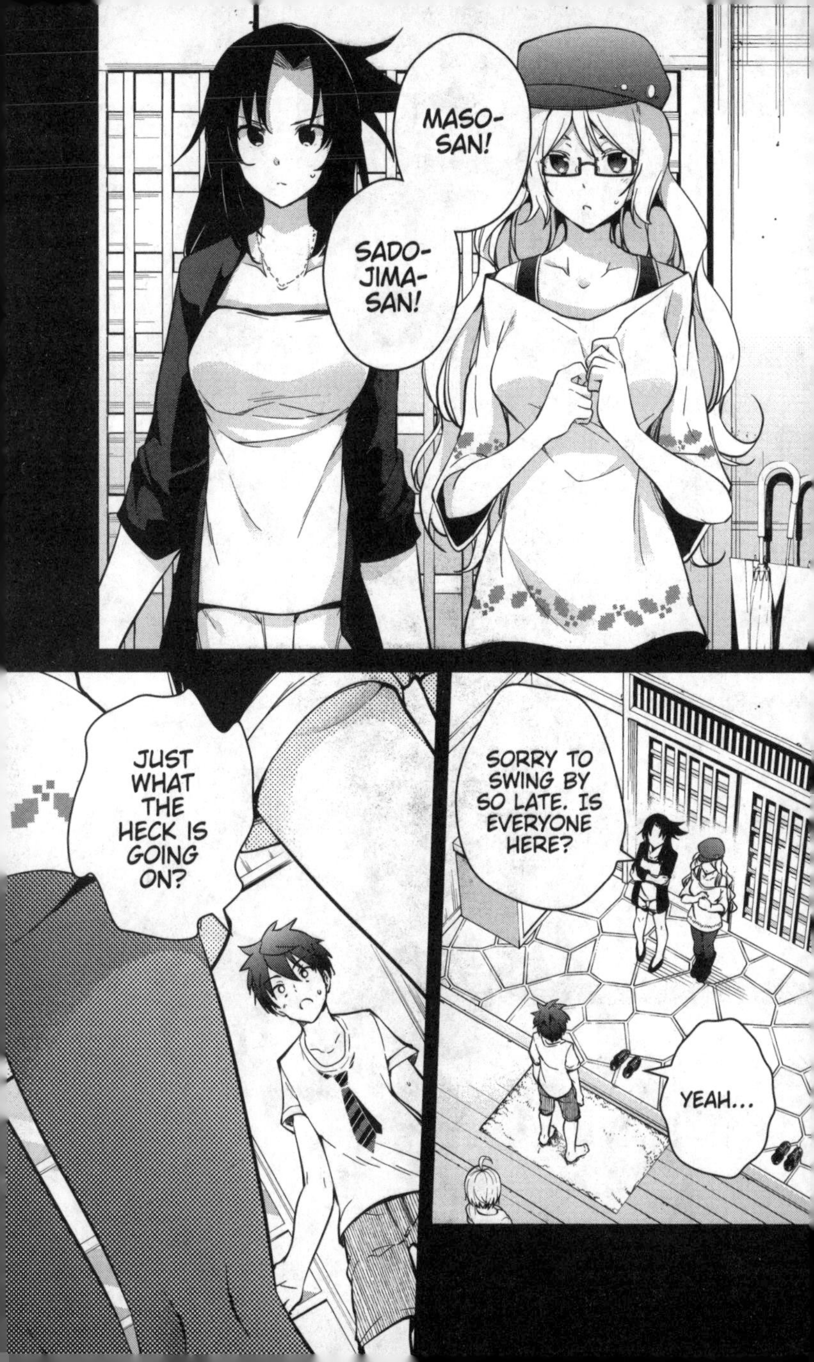
MASO-SAN!
SADO-JIMA-SAN!
SORRY TO SWING BY SO LATE. IS EVERYONE HERE?
YEAH...
JUST WHAT THE HECK IS GOING ON?

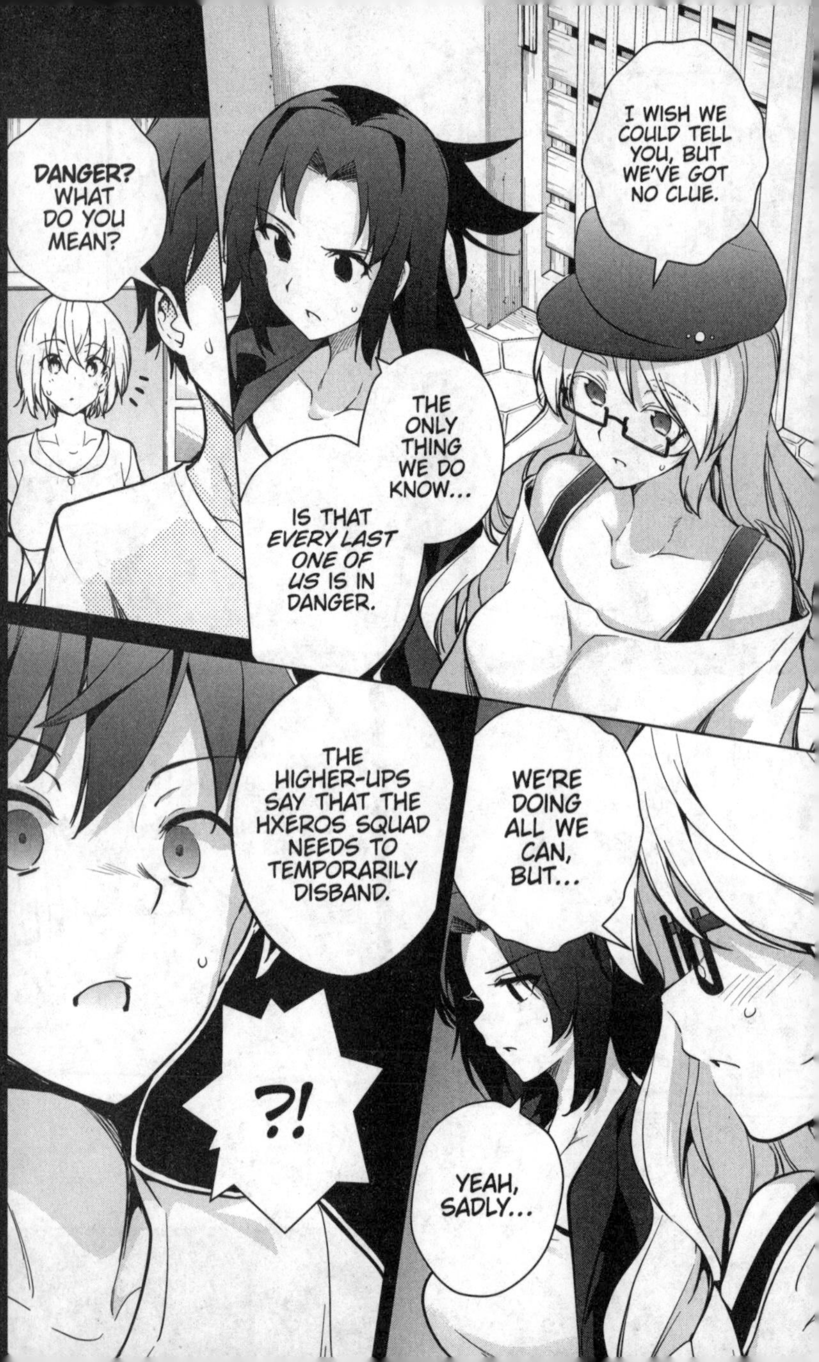
I WISH WE COULD TELL YOU, BUT WE'VE GOT NO CLUE.
THE ONLY THING WE DO KNOW...
IS THAT *EVERY LAST ONE OF US* IS IN DANGER.
DANGER? WHAT DO YOU MEAN?
WE'RE DOING ALL WE CAN, BUT...
YEAH, SADLY...
THE HIGHER-UPS SAY THAT THE HXEROS SQUAD NEEDS TO TEMPORARILY DISBAND.
?!

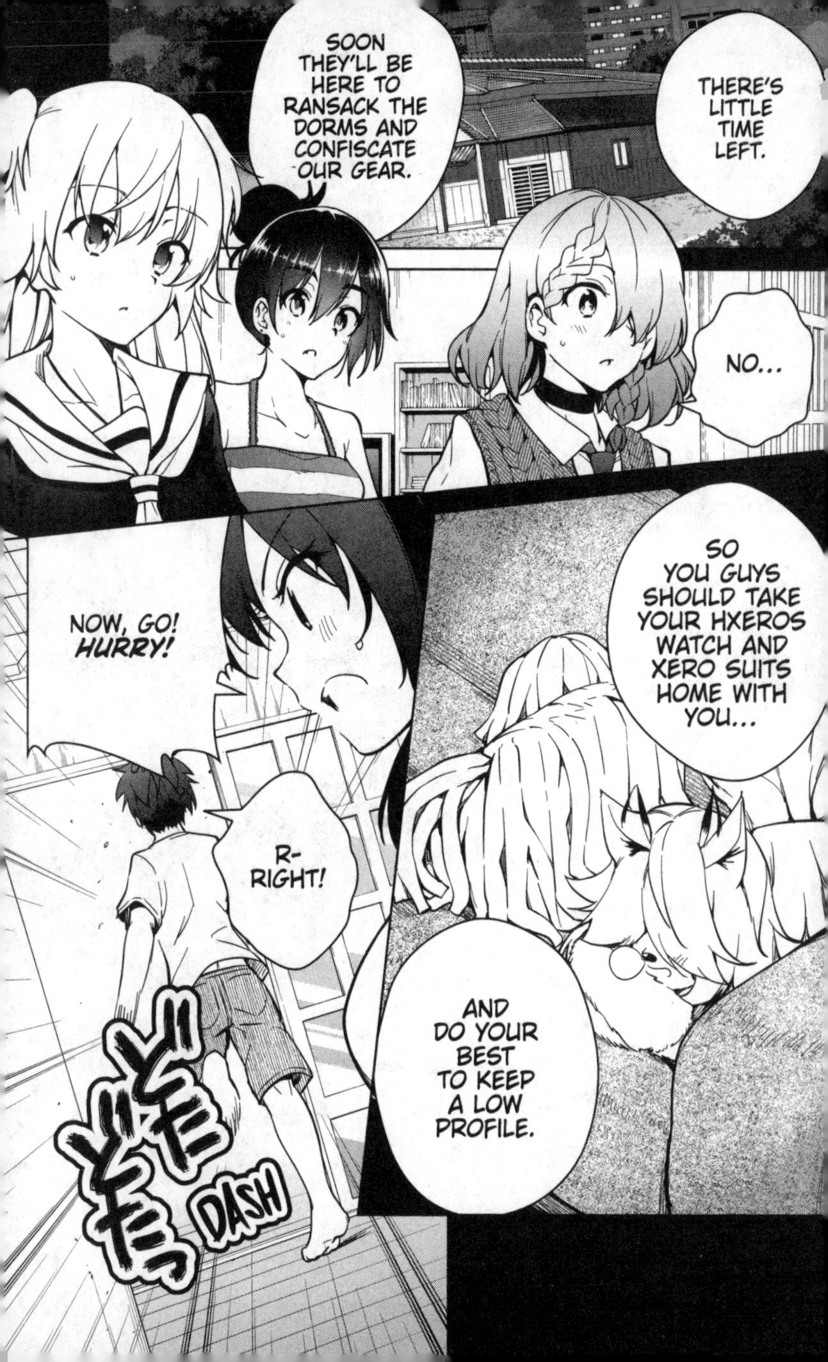

THERE'S LITTLE TIME LEFT.
SOON THEY'LL BE HERE TO RANSACK THE DORMS AND CONFISCATE OUR GEAR.
NO...
SO YOU GUYS SHOULD TAKE YOUR HXEROS WATCH AND XERO SUITS HOME WITH YOU...
AND DO YOUR BEST TO KEEP A LOW PROFILE.
NOW, GO! *HURRY!*
R-RIGHT!
DASH

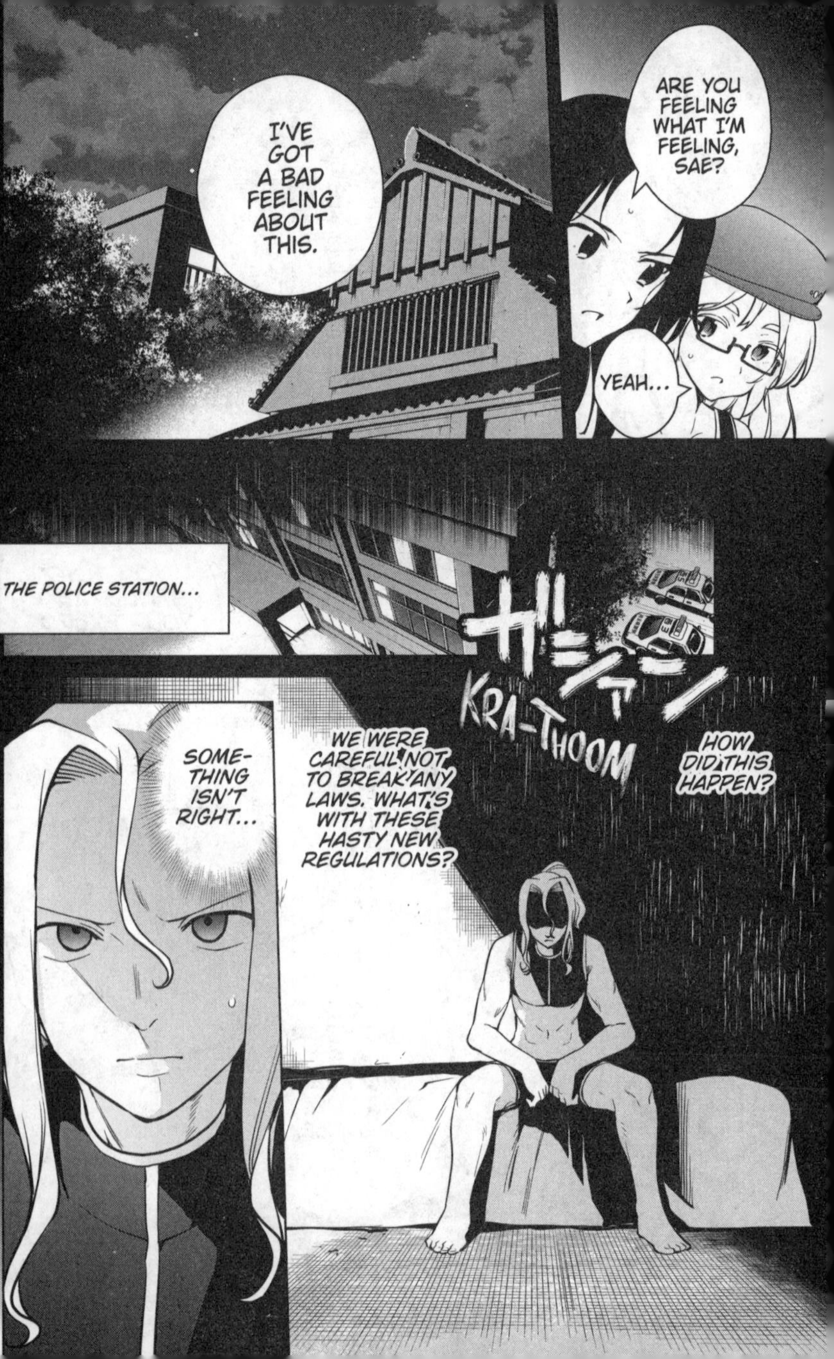

ARE YOU FEELING WHAT I'M FEELING, SAE?
YEAH...
I'VE GOT A BAD FEELING ABOUT THIS.
AT THE POLICE STATION...
KRA-THOOM
HOW DID THIS HAPPEN?
WE WERE CAREFUL NOT TO BREAK ANY LAWS. WHAT'S WITH THESE HASTY NEW REGULATIONS?
SOME-THING ISN'T RIGHT...

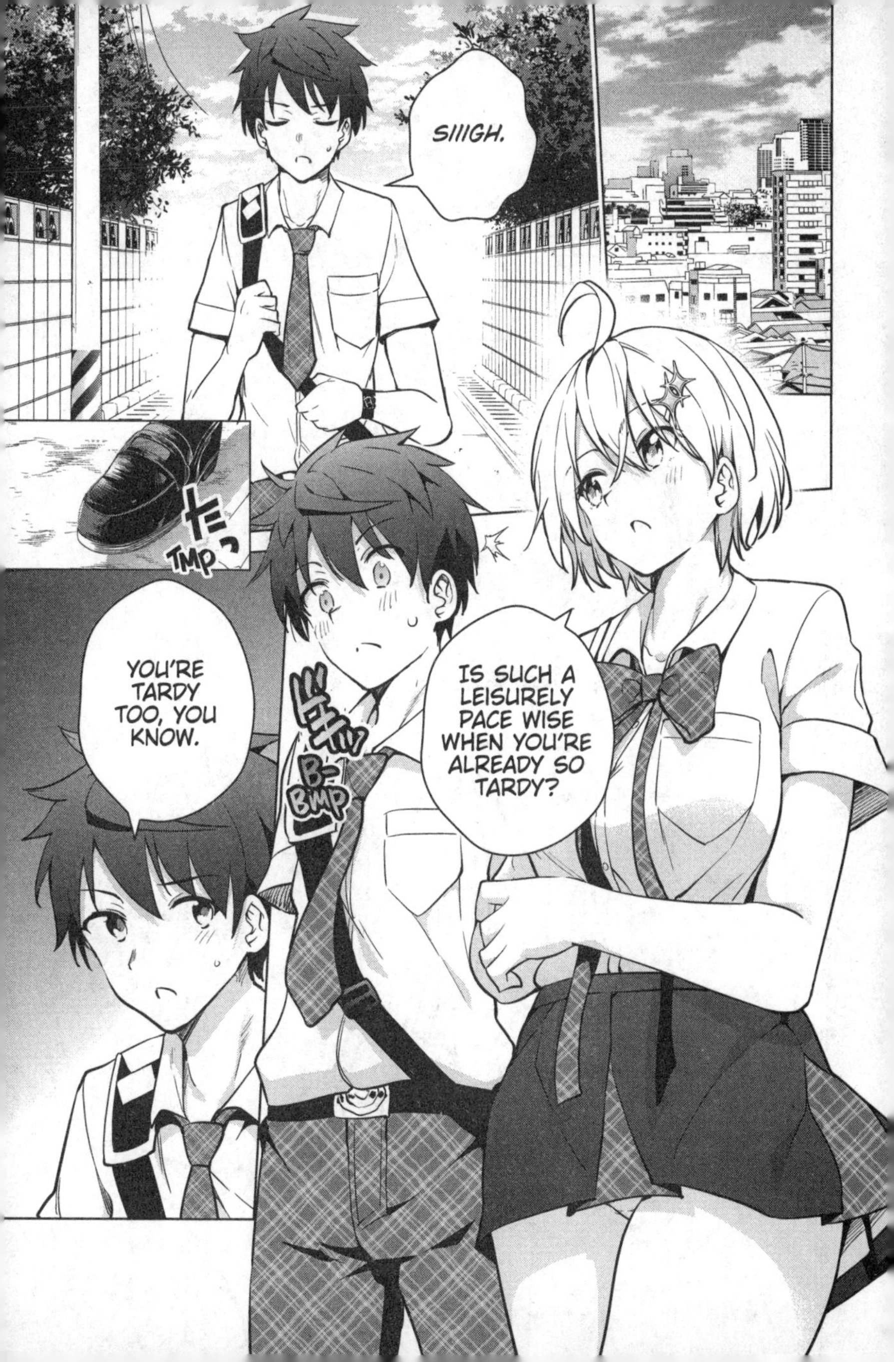
SIIIGH.
B-BMP
IS SUCH A LEISURELY PACE WISE WHEN YOU'RE ALREADY SO TARDY?
TMP
YOU'RE TARDY TOO, YOU KNOW.

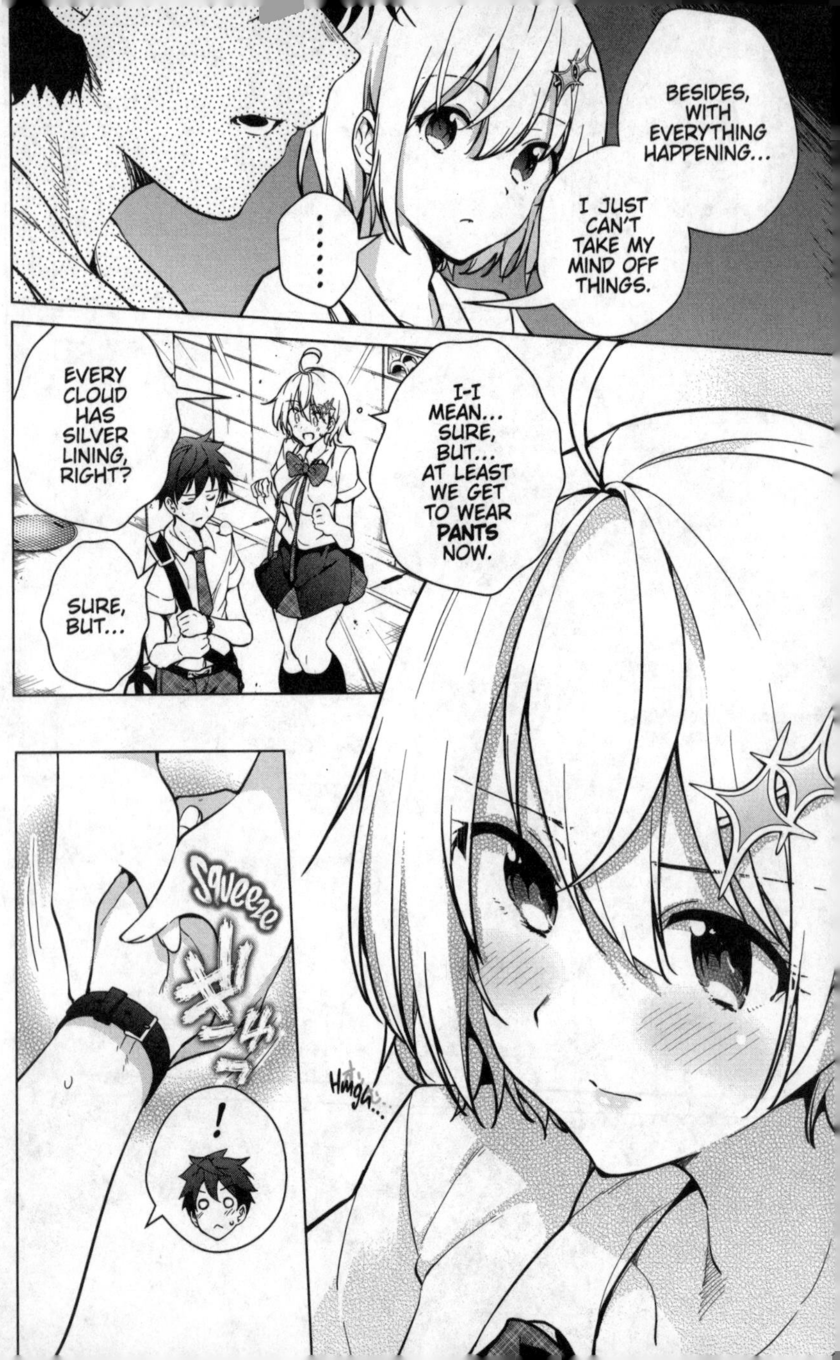
BESIDES, WITH EVERYTHING HAPPENING...
I JUST CAN'T TAKE MY MIND OFF THINGS.
......
I-I MEAN... SURE, BUT... AT LEAST WE GET TO WEAR PANTS NOW.
EVERY CLOUD HAS SILVER LINING, RIGHT?
SURE, BUT...
Hmgu...
Squeeze
!

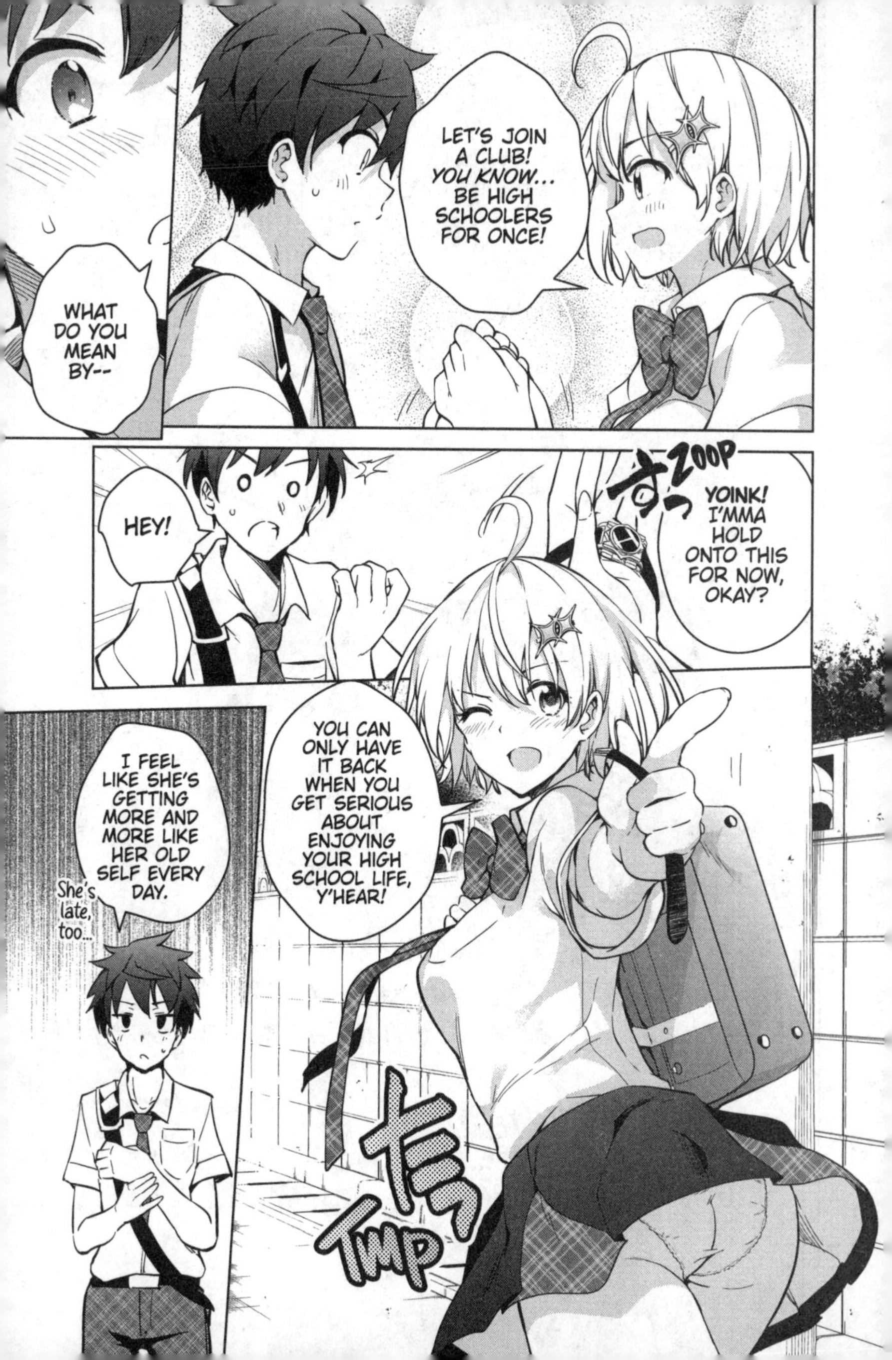
LET'S JOIN A CLUB! YOU KNOW... BE HIGH SCHOOLERS FOR ONCE!
WHAT DO YOU MEAN BY--
ZOOP
YOINK! I'MMA HOLD ONTO THIS FOR NOW, OKAY?
HEY!
YOU CAN ONLY HAVE IT BACK WHEN YOU GET SERIOUS ABOUT ENJOYING YOUR HIGH SCHOOL LIFE, Y'HEAR!
TMP
I FEEL LIKE SHE'S GETTING MORE AND MORE LIKE HER OLD SELF EVERY DAY.
She's late, too...

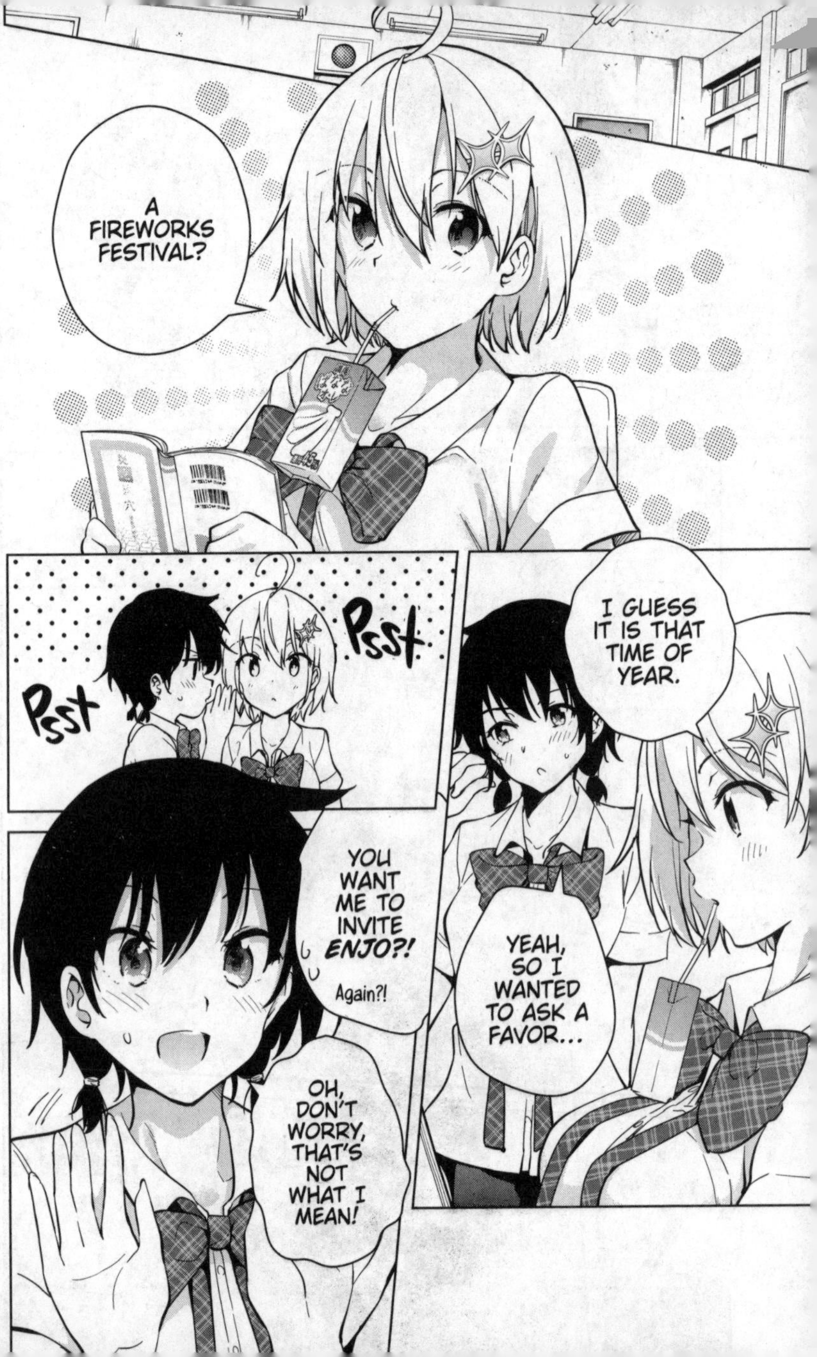
A FIREWORKS FESTIVAL?
I GUESS IT IS THAT TIME OF YEAR.
YEAH, SO I WANTED TO ASK A FAVOR...
Psst
Psst
YOU WANT ME TO INVITE ENJO?!
Again?!
OH, DON'T WORRY, THAT'S NOT WHAT I MEAN!

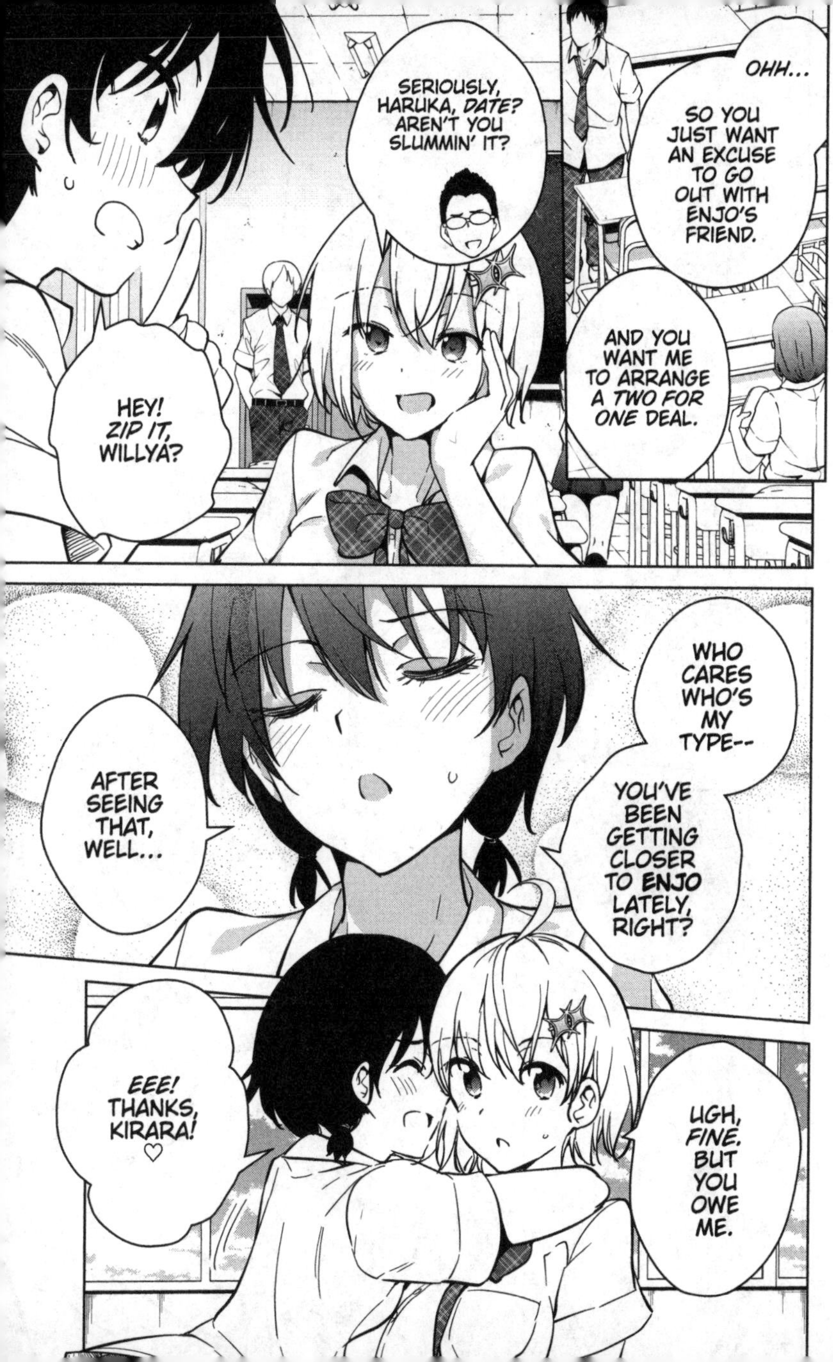
OHH...
SO YOU JUST WANT AN EXCUSE TO GO OUT WITH ENJO'S FRIEND.
AND YOU WANT ME TO ARRANGE A *TWO FOR ONE* DEAL.
SERIOUSLY, HARUKA, *DATE*? AREN'T YOU SLUMMIN' IT?
HEY! *ZIP IT*, WILLYA?
WHO CARES WHO'S MY TYPE--
YOU'VE BEEN GETTING CLOSER TO ENJO LATELY, RIGHT?
AFTER SEEING THAT, WELL...
UGH, *FINE*. BUT YOU OWE ME.
EEE! THANKS, KIRARA! ♡

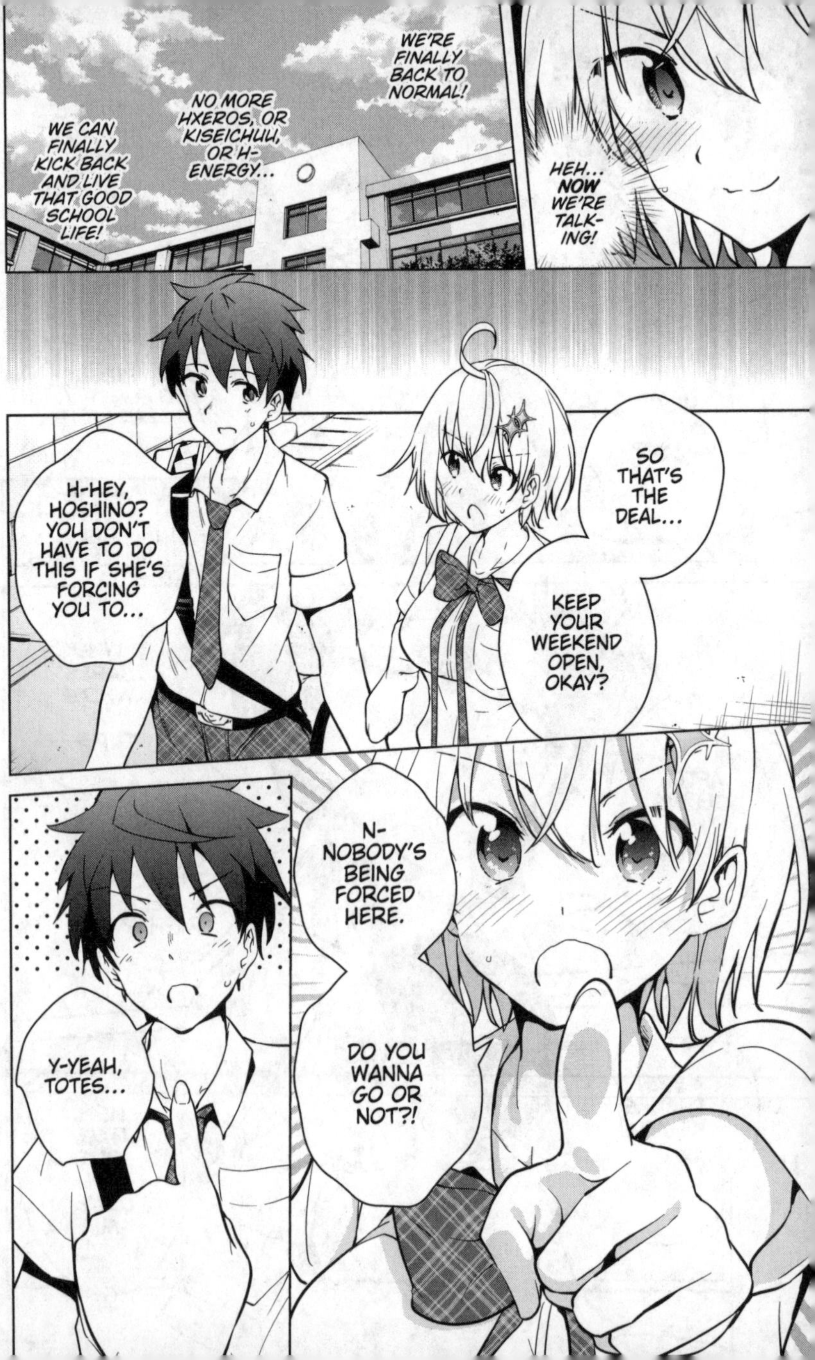
HEH... **NOW** WE'RE TALKING!
WE'RE FINALLY BACK TO NORMAL!
NO MORE HXEROS, OR KISEICHUU, OR H-ENERGY...
WE CAN FINALLY KICK BACK AND LIVE THAT GOOD SCHOOL LIFE!
SO THAT'S THE DEAL...
KEEP YOUR WEEKEND OPEN, OKAY?
H-HEY, HOSHINO? YOU DON'T HAVE TO DO THIS IF SHE'S FORCING YOU TO...
N-NOBODY'S BEING FORCED HERE.
DO YOU WANNA GO OR NOT?!
Y-YEAH, TOTES...

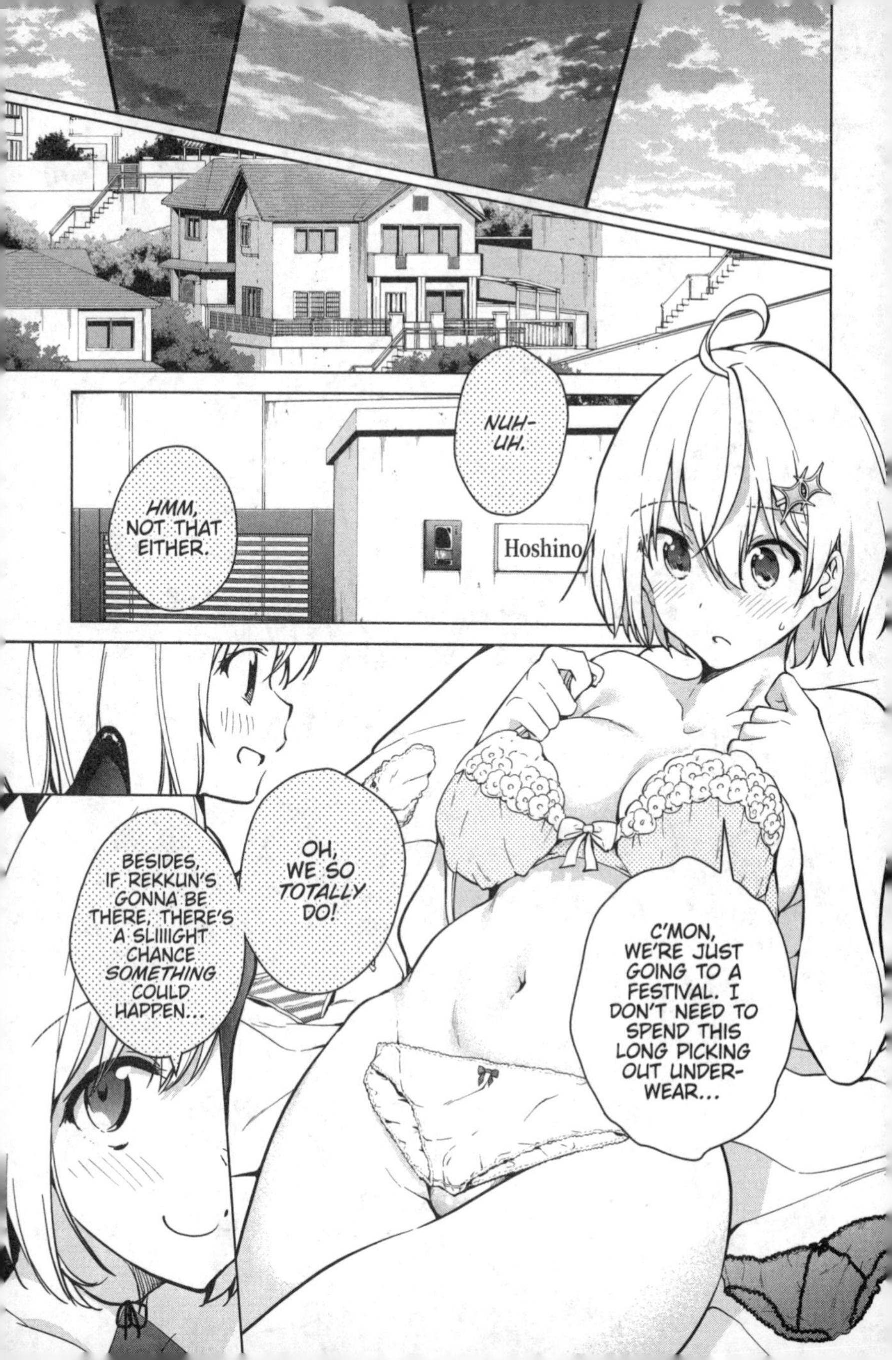
NUH-UH.
HMM, NOT THAT EITHER.
Hoshino
C'MON, WE'RE JUST GOING TO A FESTIVAL. I DON'T NEED TO SPEND THIS LONG PICKING OUT UNDER-WEAR...
OH, WE SO TOTALLY DO!
BESIDES, IF REKKUN'S GONNA BE THERE, THERE'S A SLIIIIGHT CHANCE SOMETHING COULD HAPPEN...

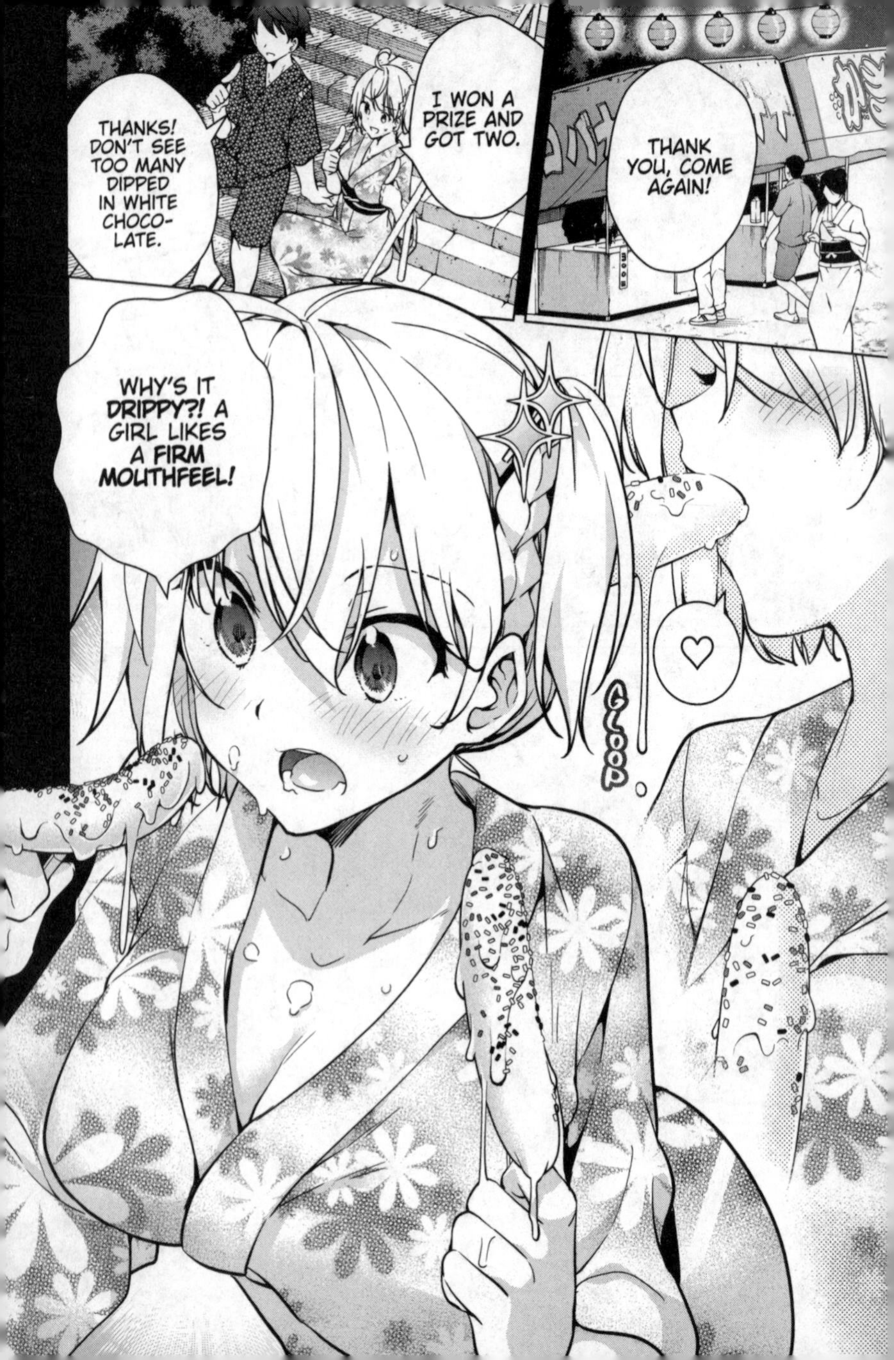
THANK YOU, COME AGAIN!
I WON A PRIZE AND GOT TWO.
THANKS! DON'T SEE TOO MANY DIPPED IN WHITE CHOCOLATE.
WHY'S IT **DRIPPY?!** A GIRL LIKES **A FIRM MOUTHFEEL!**
♡
GLOOP

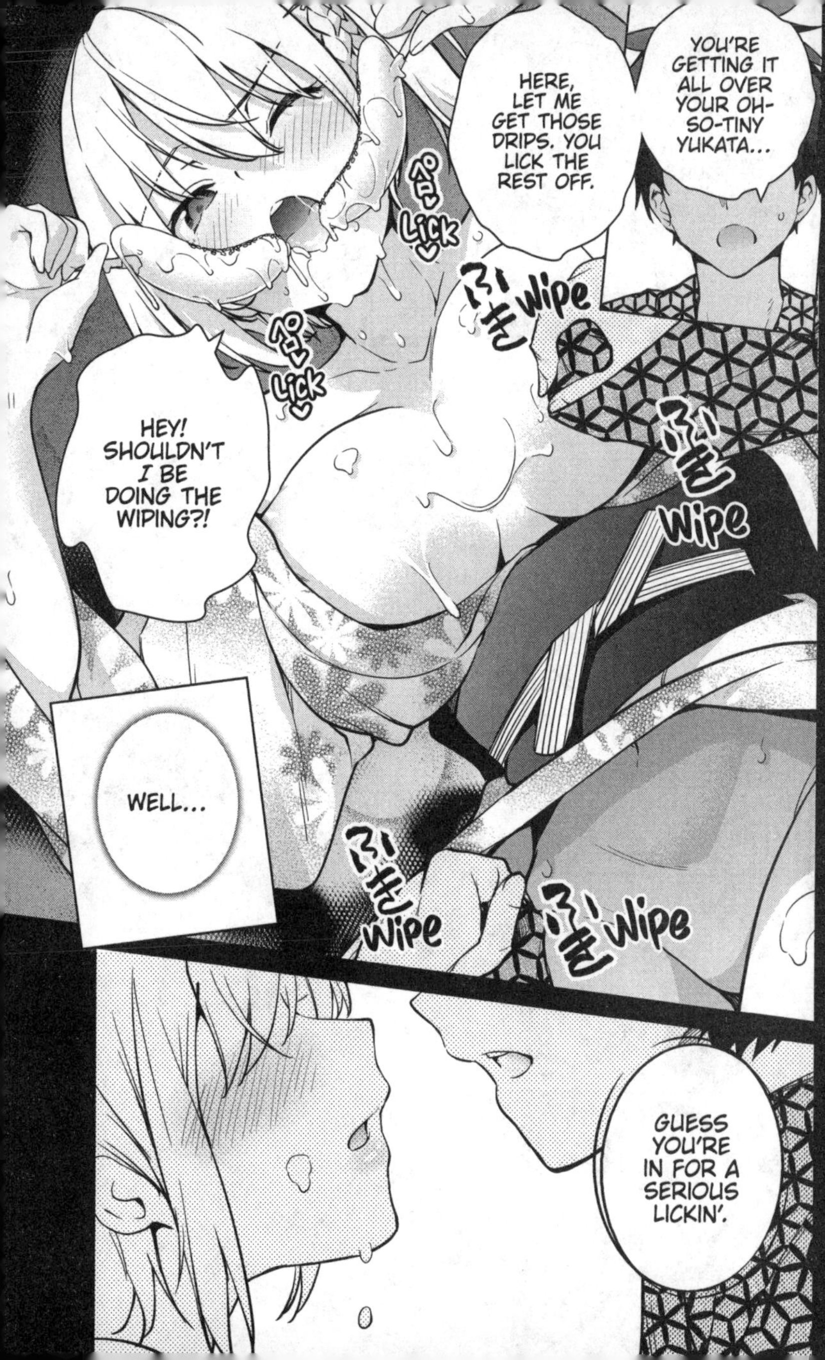
YOU'RE GETTING IT ALL OVER YOUR OH-SO-TINY YUKATA...
HERE, LET ME GET THOSE DRIPS. YOU LICK THE REST OFF.
ペロ Lick
ふき wipe
ペロ Lick
HEY! SHOULDN'T I BE DOING THE WIPING?!
ふき wipe
ふき wipe
ふき wipe
WELL...
GUESS YOU'RE IN FOR A SERIOUS LICKIN'.

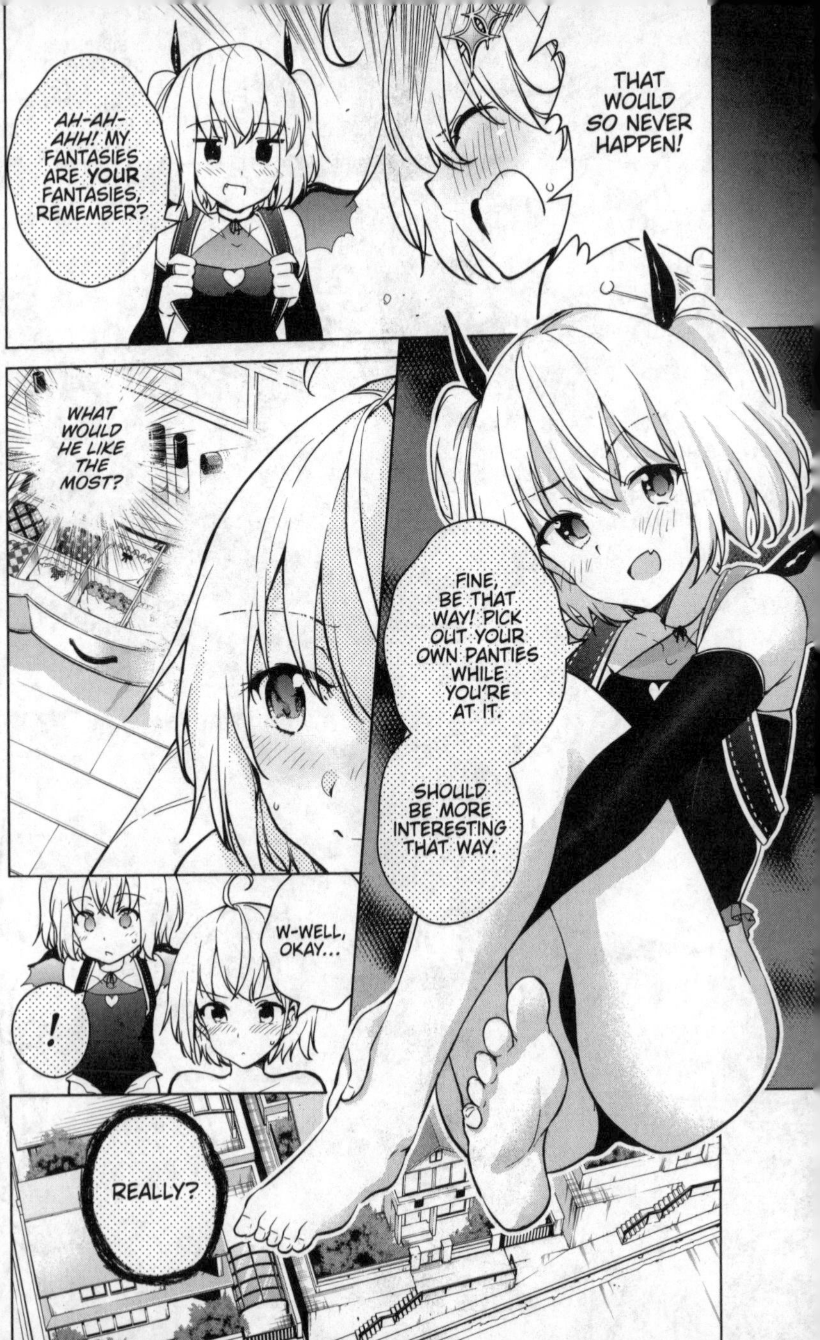
THAT WOULD SO NEVER HAPPEN!
AH-AH-AHH! MY FANTASIES ARE YOUR FANTASIES, REMEMBER?
FINE, BE THAT WAY! PICK OUT YOUR OWN PANTIES WHILE YOU'RE AT IT.
SHOULD BE MORE INTERESTING THAT WAY.
WHAT WOULD HE LIKE THE MOST?
W-WELL, OKAY...
!
REALLY?

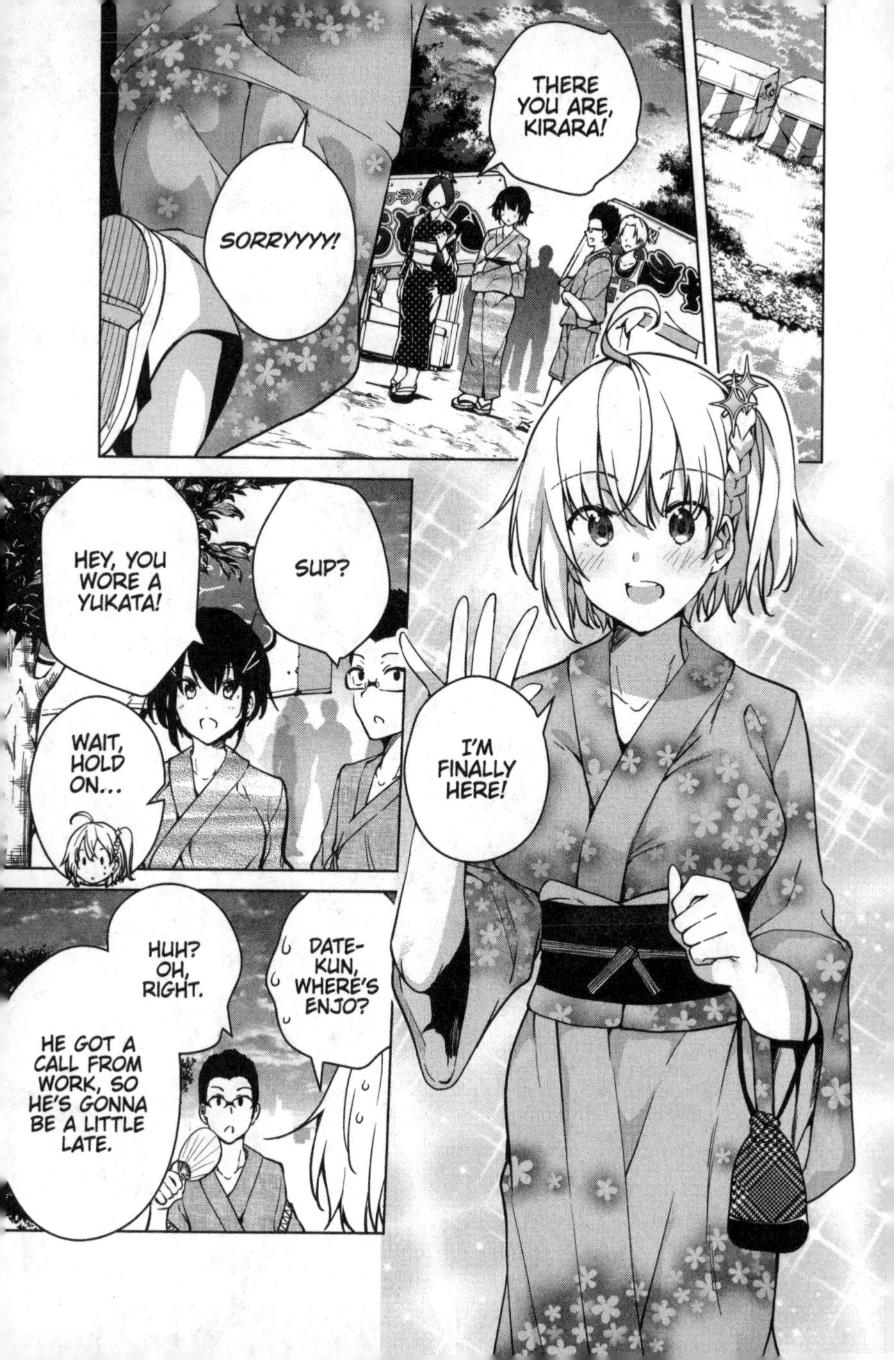
THERE YOU ARE, KIRARA!
SORRYYYY!
I'M FINALLY HERE!
SUP?
HEY, YOU WORE A YUKATA!
WAIT, HOLD ON...
DATE-KUN, WHERE'S ENJO?
HUH? OH, RIGHT.
HE GOT A CALL FROM WORK, SO HE'S GONNA BE A LITTLE LATE.

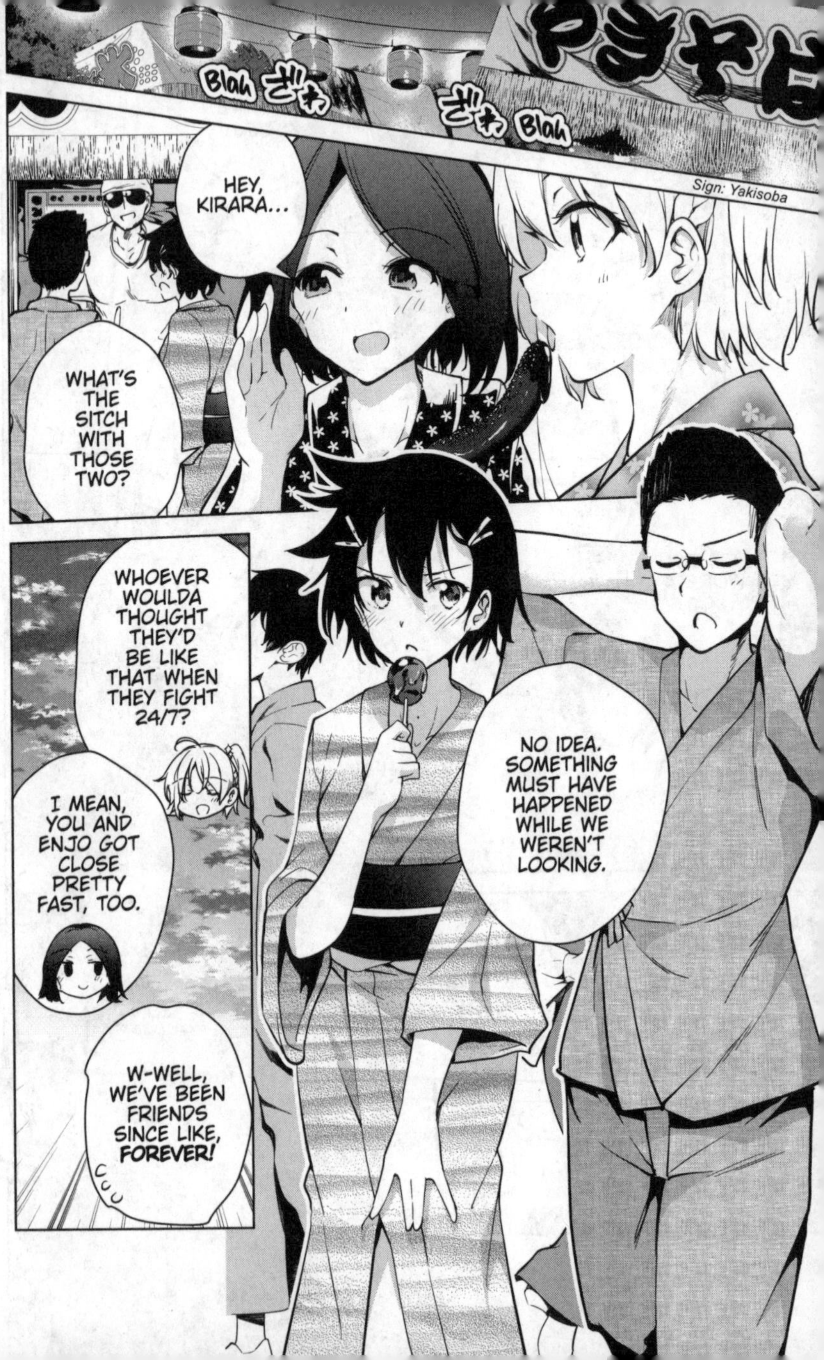
Blah ざわ
ざわ Blah
Sign: Yakisoba
HEY, KIRARA...
WHAT'S THE SITCH WITH THOSE TWO?
NO IDEA. SOMETHING MUST HAVE HAPPENED WHILE WE WEREN'T LOOKING.
WHOEVER WOULDA THOUGHT THEY'D BE LIKE THAT WHEN THEY FIGHT 24/7?
I MEAN, YOU AND ENJO GOT CLOSE PRETTY FAST, TOO.
W-WELL, WE'VE BEEN FRIENDS SINCE LIKE, **FOREVER!**

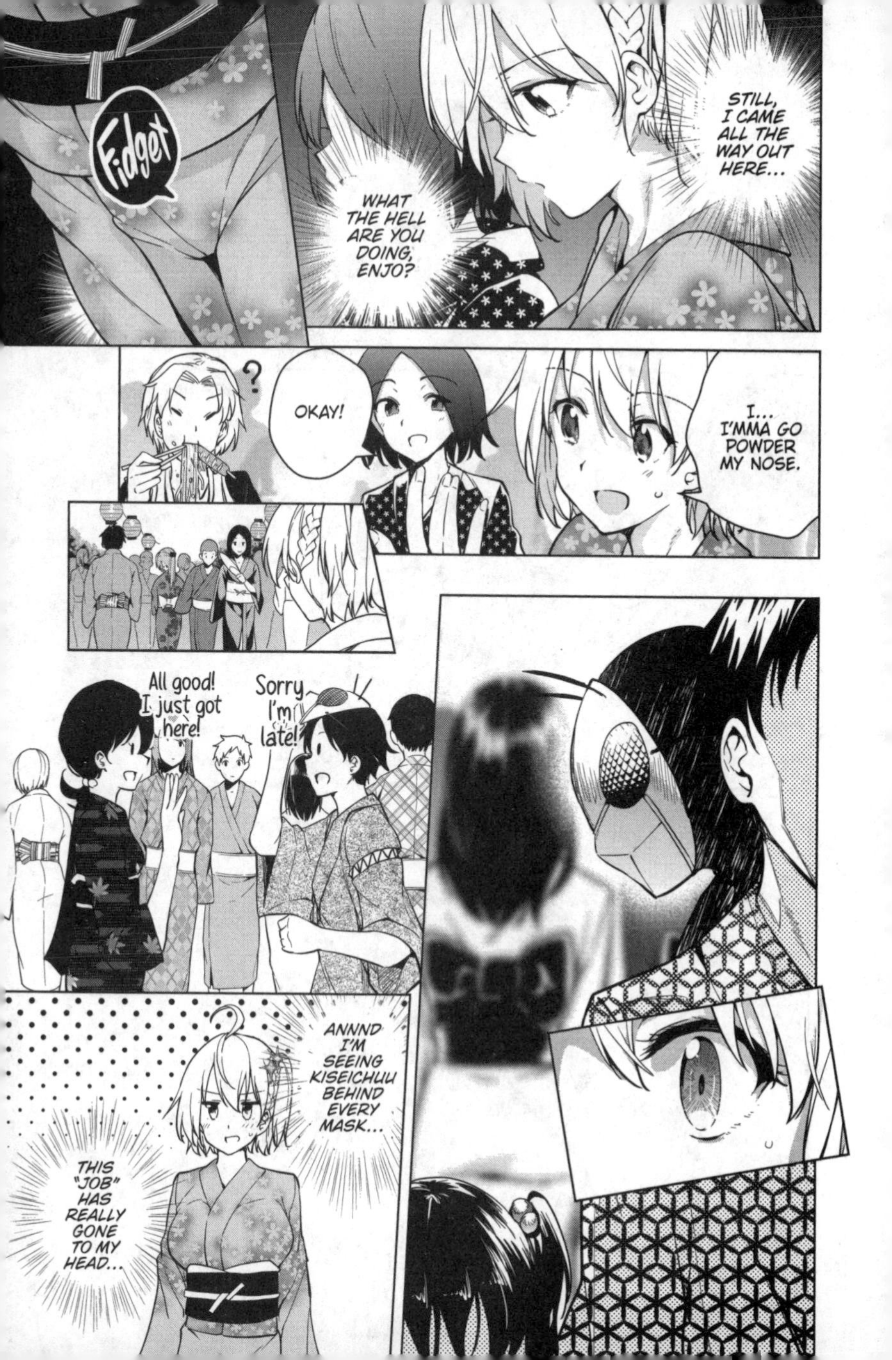
STILL, I CAME ALL THE WAY OUT HERE...
WHAT THE HELL ARE YOU DOING, ENJO?
Fidget
I... I'MMA GO POWDER MY NOSE.
OKAY!
?
Sorry I'm late!
All good! I just got here!
ANNND I'M SEEING KISEICHUU BEHIND EVERY MASK...
THIS "JOB" HAS REALLY GONE TO MY HEAD...

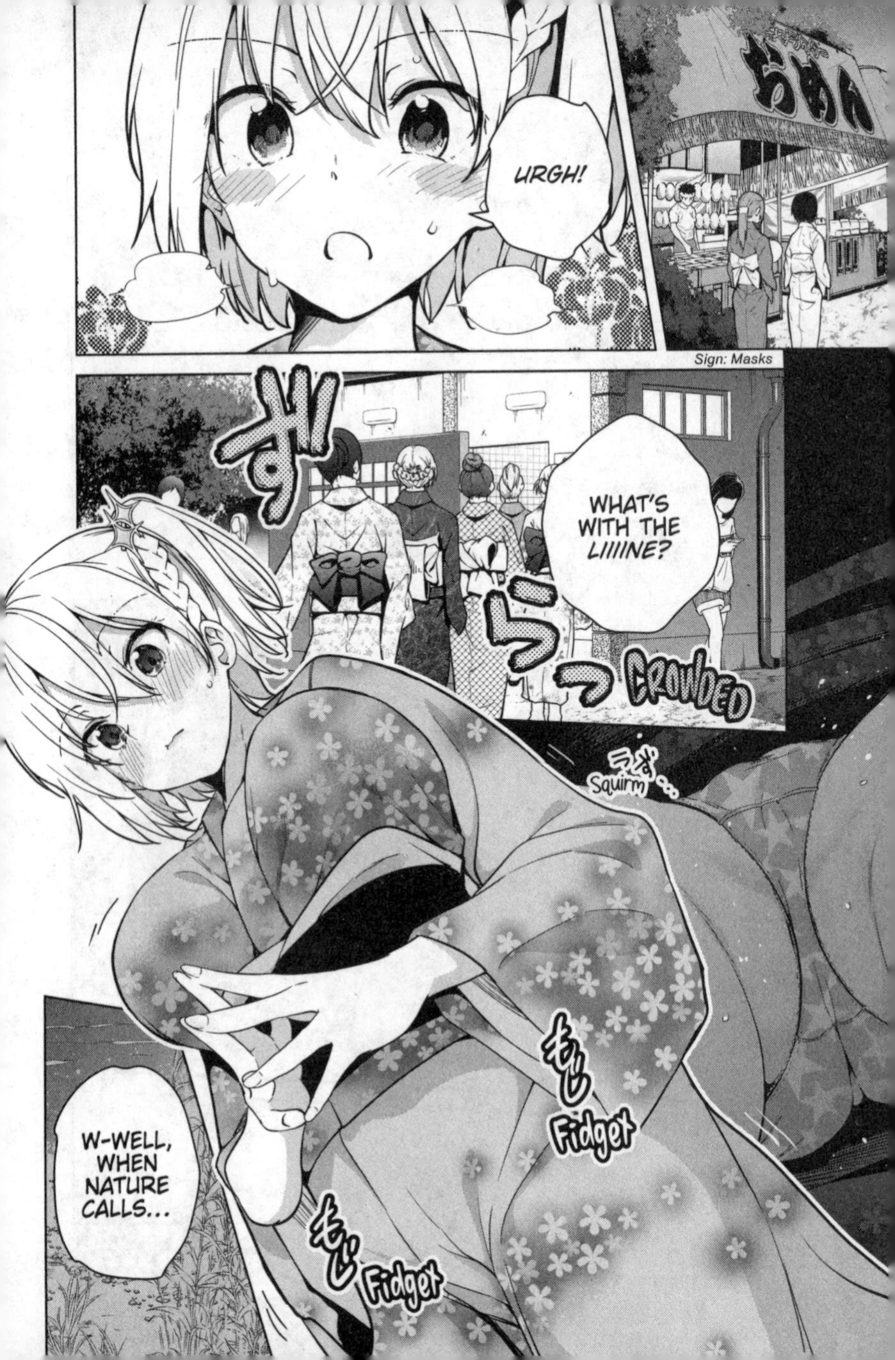
URGH!
Sign: Masks
ずらっ
CROWDED
WHAT'S WITH THE LIIIINE?
そわ…
Squirm…
W-WELL, WHEN NATURE CALLS…
もじ
Fidget
もじ
Fidget

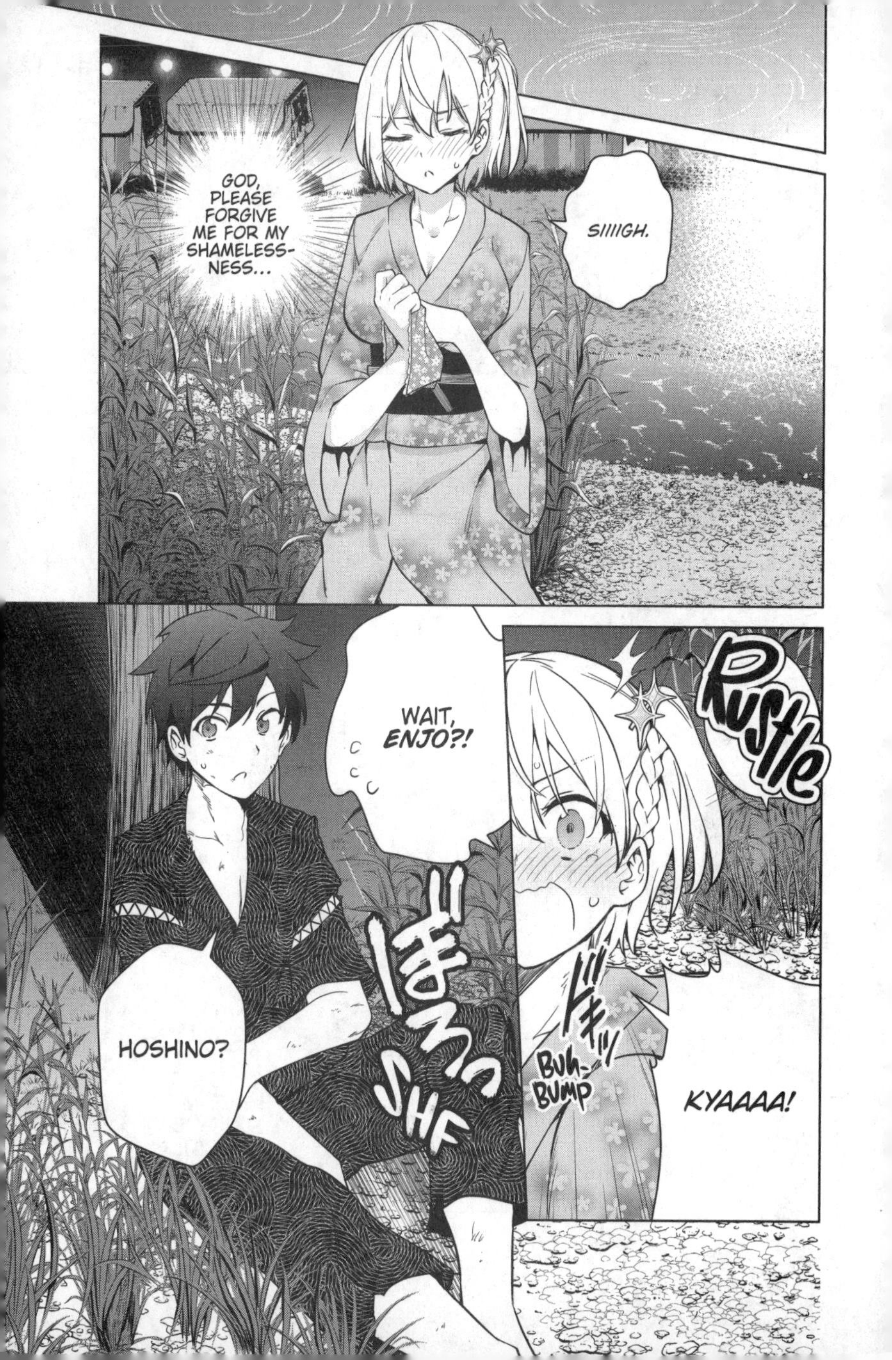
SIIIIGH.
GOD, PLEASE FORGIVE ME FOR MY SHAMELESS-NESS...
Rustle
ドキッ
BUH-BUMP
KYAAAA!
WAIT, ENJO?!
ぽろっ
SHF
HOSHINO?

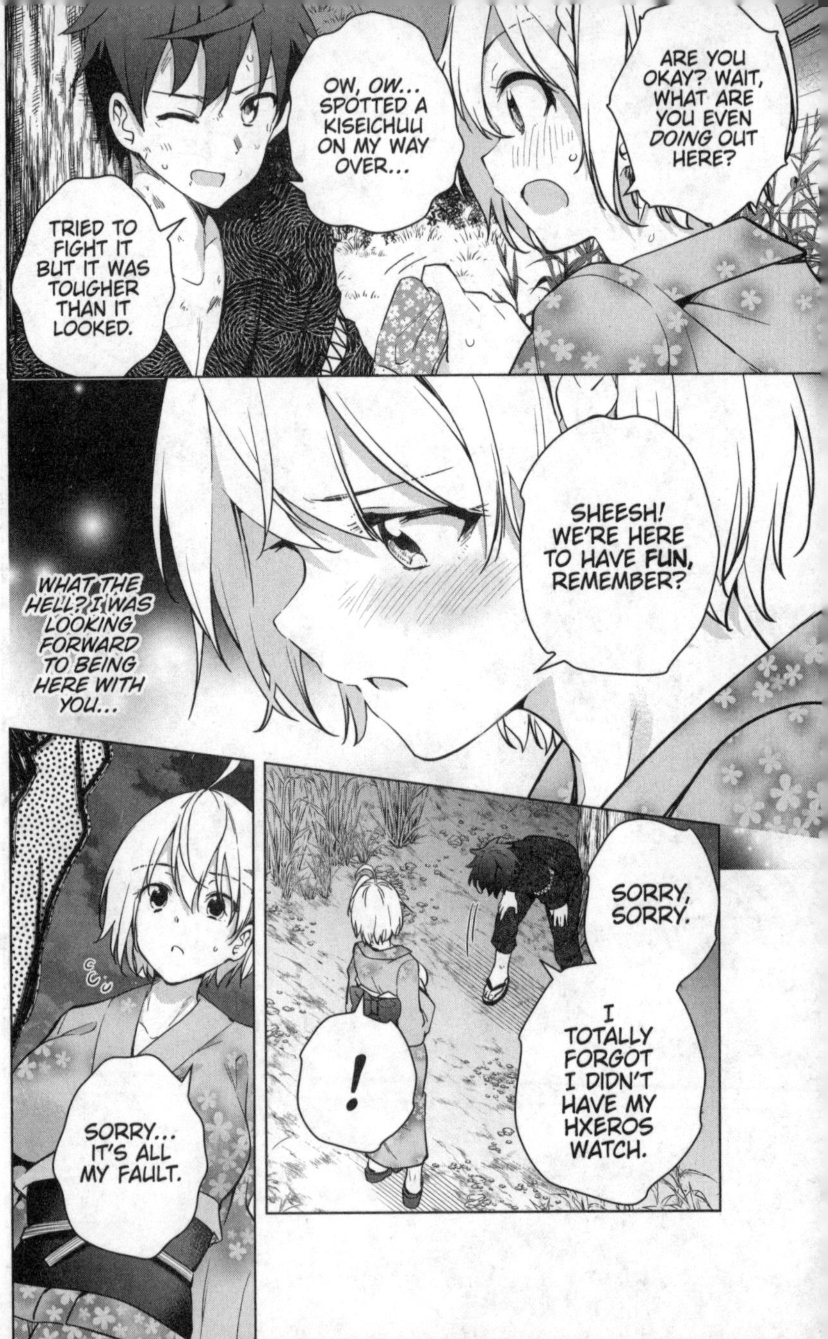
ARE YOU OKAY? WAIT, WHAT ARE YOU EVEN *DOING* OUT HERE?
OW, OW... SPOTTED A KISEICHUU ON MY WAY OVER...
TRIED TO FIGHT IT BUT IT WAS TOUGHER THAN IT LOOKED.
SHEESH! WE'RE HERE TO HAVE **FUN**, REMEMBER?
WHAT THE HELL? I WAS LOOKING FORWARD TO BEING HERE WITH YOU...
SORRY, SORRY.
I TOTALLY FORGOT I DIDN'T HAVE MY HXEROS WATCH.
!
SORRY... IT'S ALL MY FAULT.

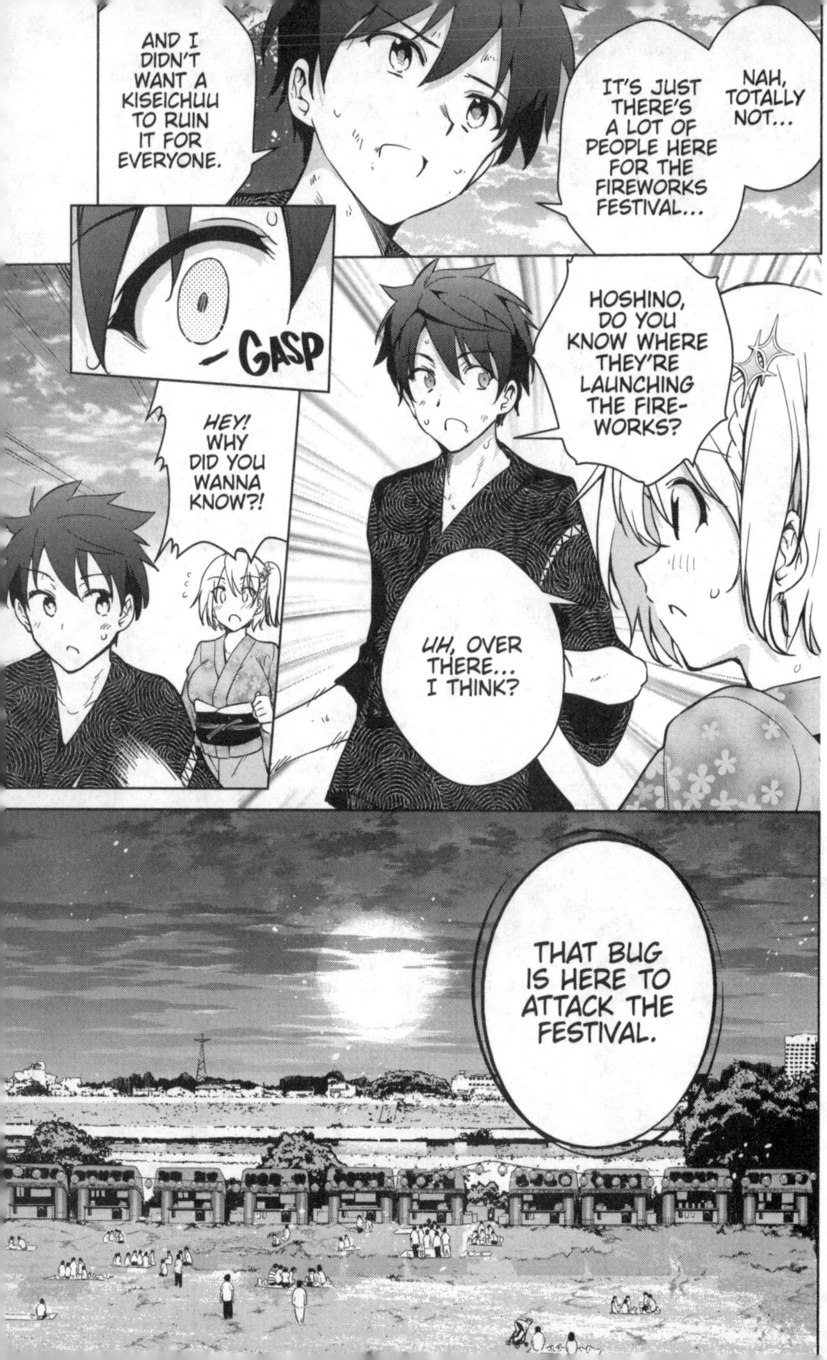
NAH, TOTALLY NOT...
IT'S JUST THERE'S A LOT OF PEOPLE HERE FOR THE FIREWORKS FESTIVAL...
AND I DIDN'T WANT A KISEICHUU TO RUIN IT FOR EVERYONE.
GASP
HOSHINO, DO YOU KNOW WHERE THEY'RE LAUNCHING THE FIRE-WORKS?
UH, OVER THERE... I THINK?
HEY! WHY DID YOU WANNA KNOW?!
THAT BUG IS HERE TO ATTACK THE FESTIVAL.

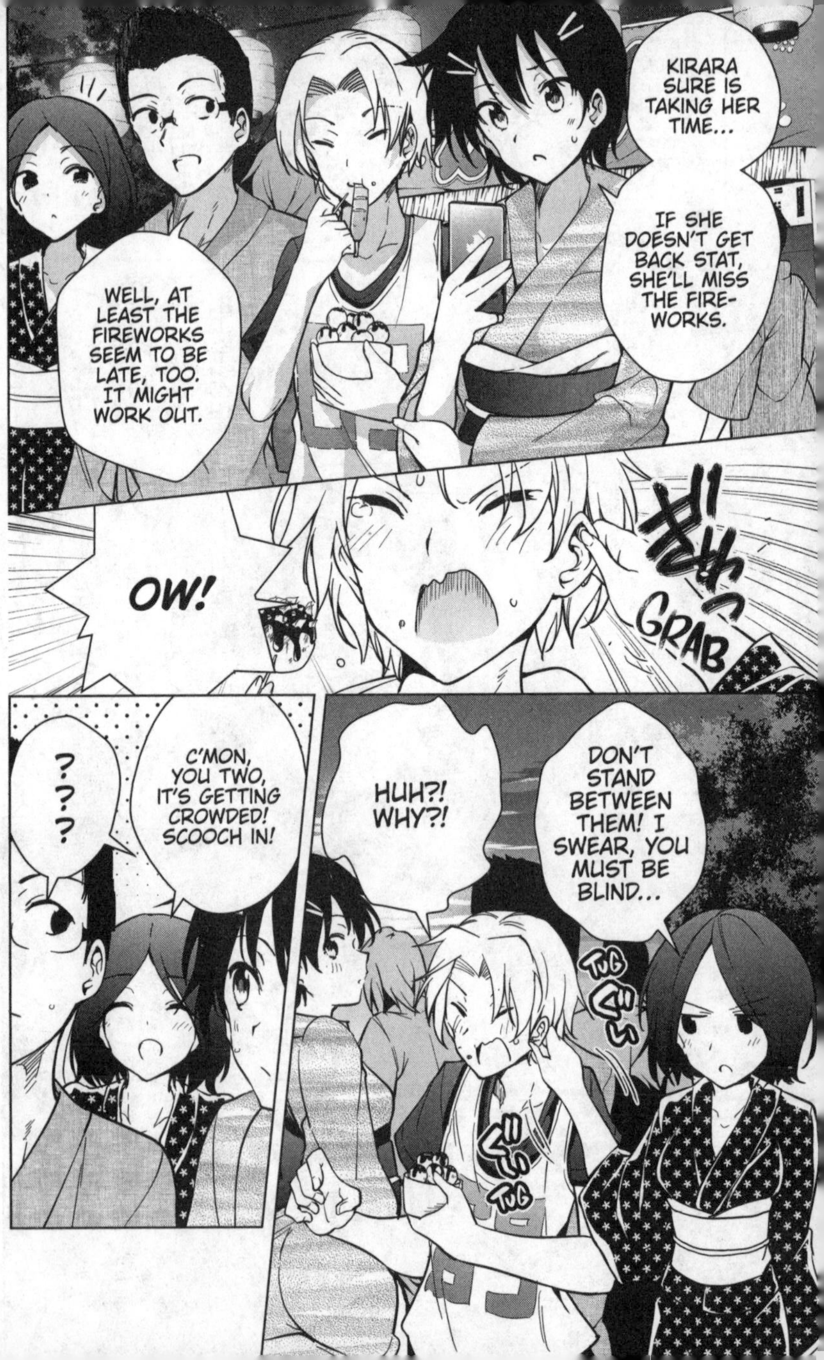
KIRARA SURE IS TAKING HER TIME...
IF SHE DOESN'T GET BACK STAT, SHE'LL MISS THE FIRE-WORKS.
WELL, AT LEAST THE FIREWORKS SEEM TO BE LATE, TOO. IT MIGHT WORK OUT.
GRAB
OW!
DON'T STAND BETWEEN THEM! I SWEAR, YOU MUST BE BLIND...
TUG
HUH?! WHY?!
TUG
C'MON, YOU TWO, IT'S GETTING CROWDED! SCOOCH IN!
???

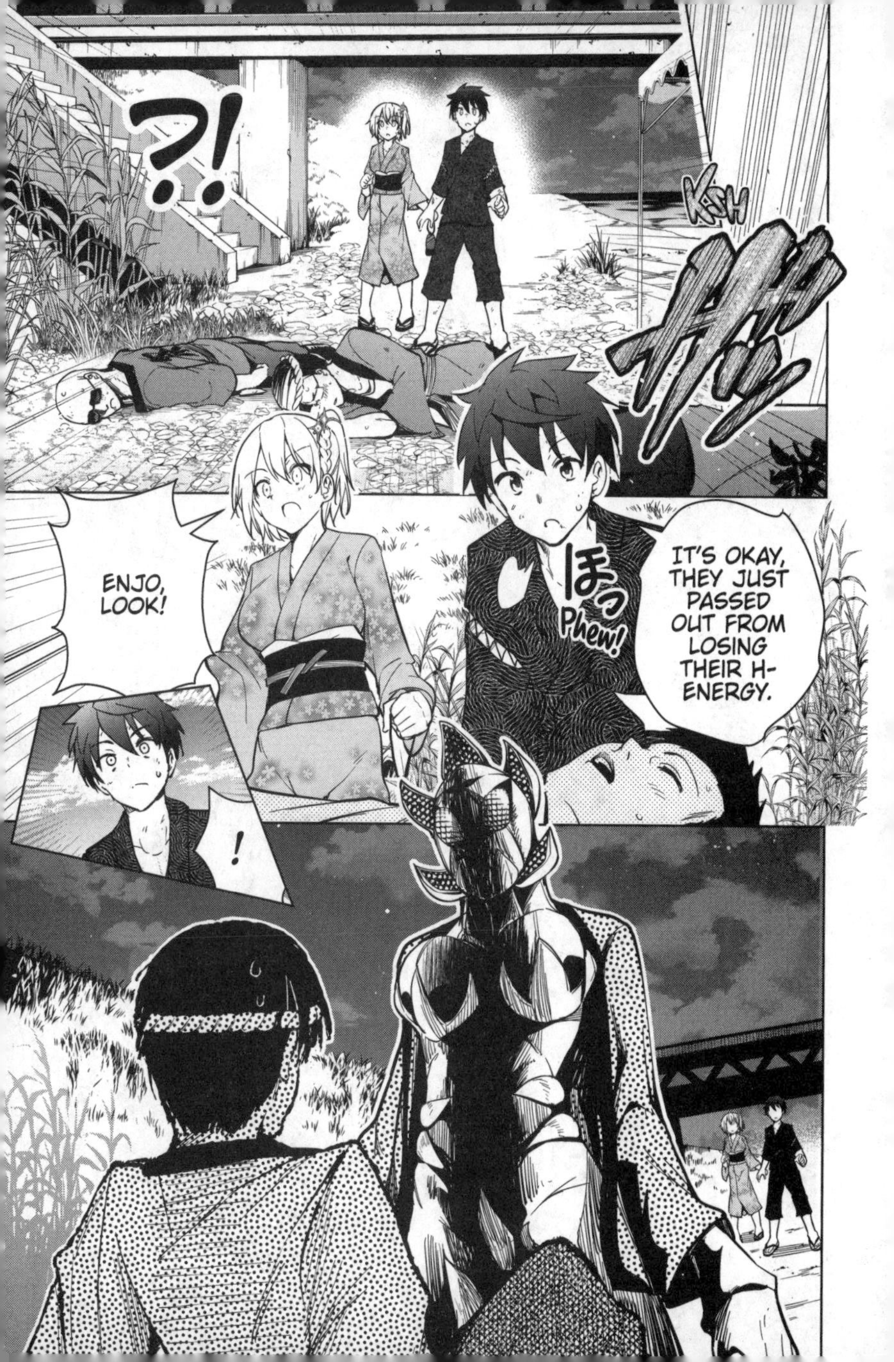
?!
KSSH
IT'S OKAY, THEY JUST PASSED OUT FROM LOSING THEIR H-ENERGY.
ほっ Phew!
ENJO, LOOK!
!

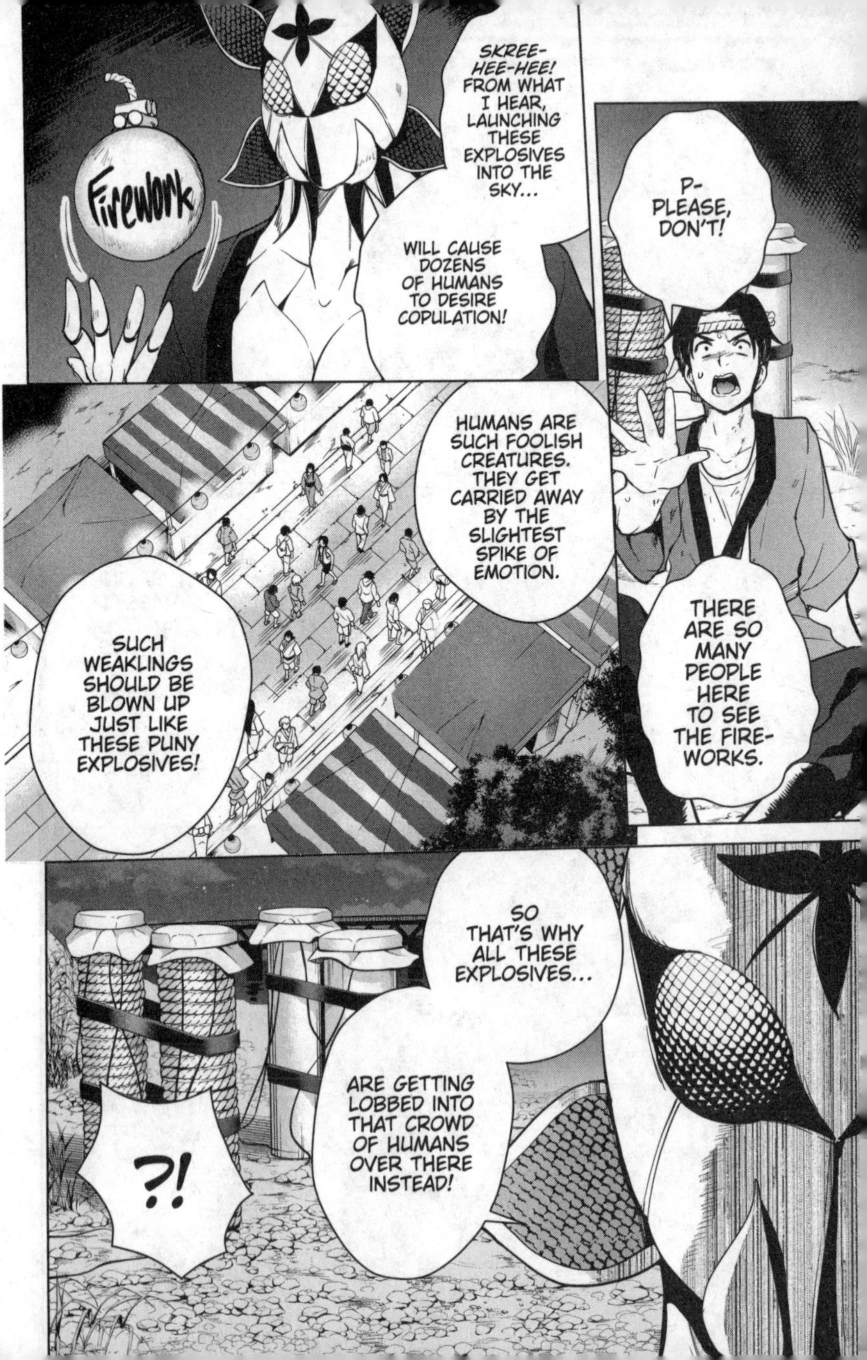
P-
PLEASE, DON'T!
THERE ARE SO MANY PEOPLE HERE TO SEE THE FIRE-WORKS.
SKREE-HEE-HEE! FROM WHAT I HEAR, LAUNCHING THESE EXPLOSIVES INTO THE SKY...
WILL CAUSE DOZENS OF HUMANS TO DESIRE COPULATION!
Firework
HUMANS ARE SUCH FOOLISH CREATURES. THEY GET CARRIED AWAY BY THE SLIGHTEST SPIKE OF EMOTION.
SUCH WEAKLINGS SHOULD BE BLOWN UP JUST LIKE THESE PUNY EXPLOSIVES!
SO THAT'S WHY ALL THESE EXPLOSIVES...
ARE GETTING LOBBED INTO THAT CROWD OF HUMANS OVER THERE INSTEAD!
?!

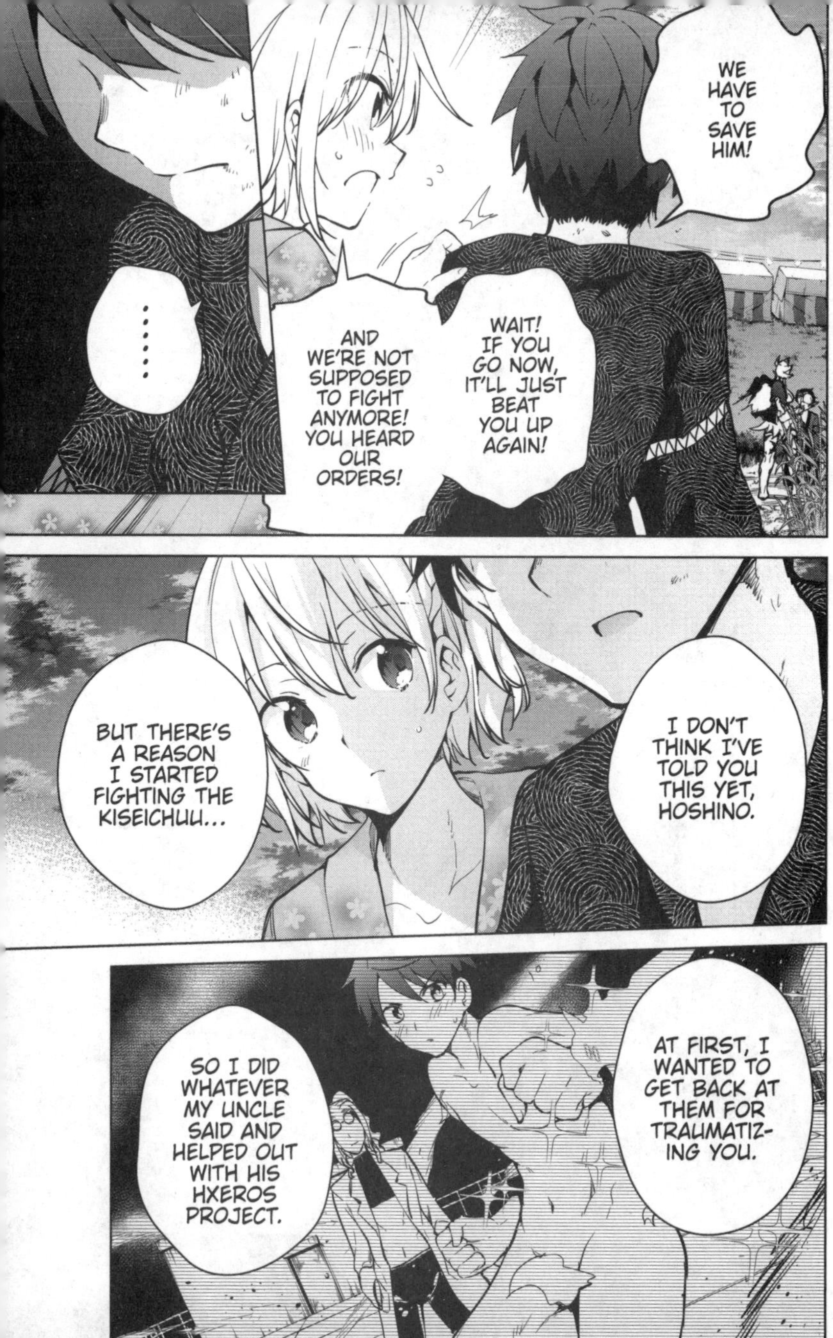
WE HAVE TO SAVE HIM!
WAIT! IF YOU GO NOW, IT'LL JUST BEAT YOU UP AGAIN!
AND WE'RE NOT SUPPOSED TO FIGHT ANYMORE! YOU HEARD OUR ORDERS!
......
I DON'T THINK I'VE TOLD YOU THIS YET, HOSHINO.
BUT THERE'S A REASON I STARTED FIGHTING THE KISEICHUU...
AT FIRST, I WANTED TO GET BACK AT THEM FOR TRAUMATIZ-ING YOU.
SO I DID WHATEVER MY UNCLE SAID AND HELPED OUT WITH HIS HXEROS PROJECT.

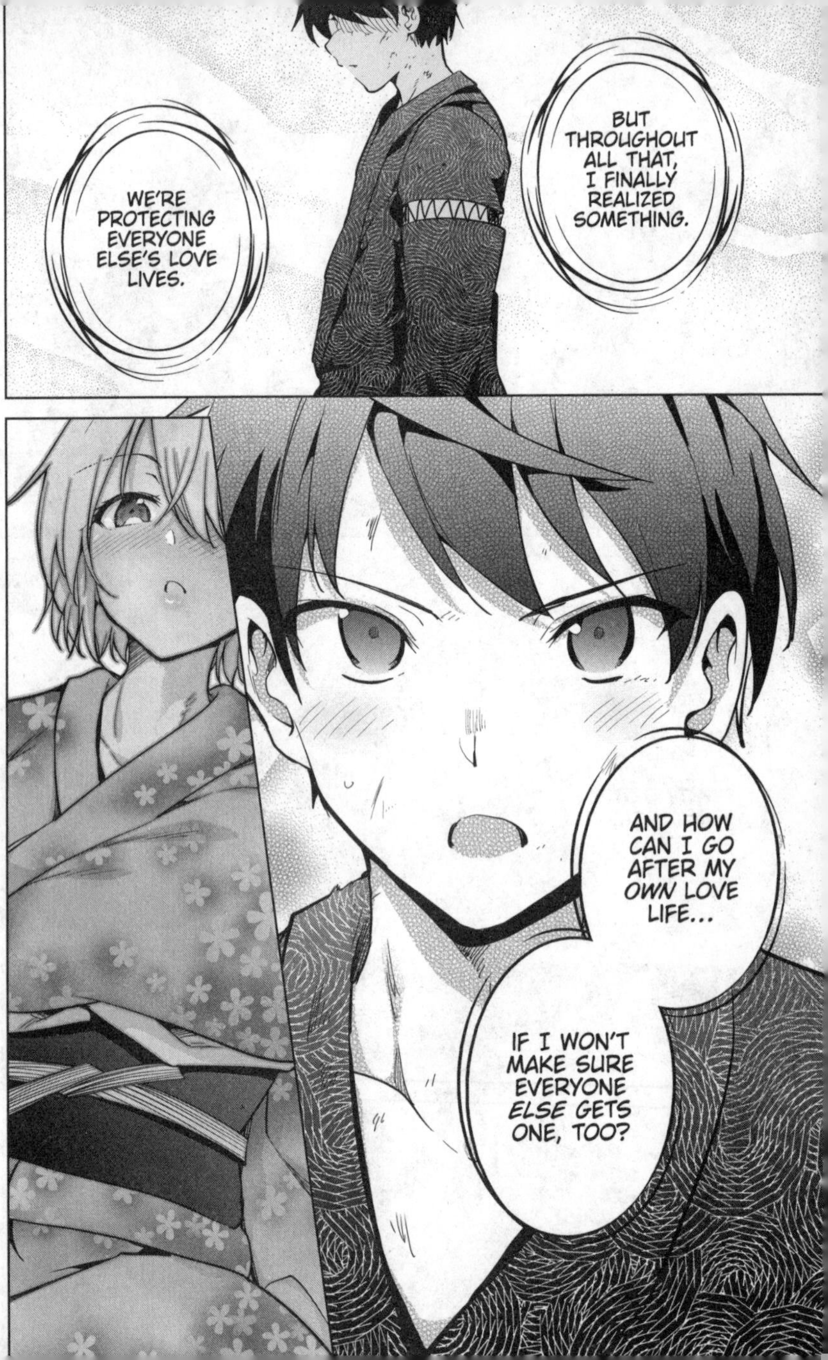
BUT THROUGHOUT ALL THAT, I FINALLY REALIZED SOMETHING.
WE'RE PROTECTING EVERYONE ELSE'S LOVE LIVES.
AND HOW CAN I GO AFTER MY *OWN* LOVE LIFE...
IF I WON'T MAKE SURE EVERYONE *ELSE* GETS ONE, TOO?

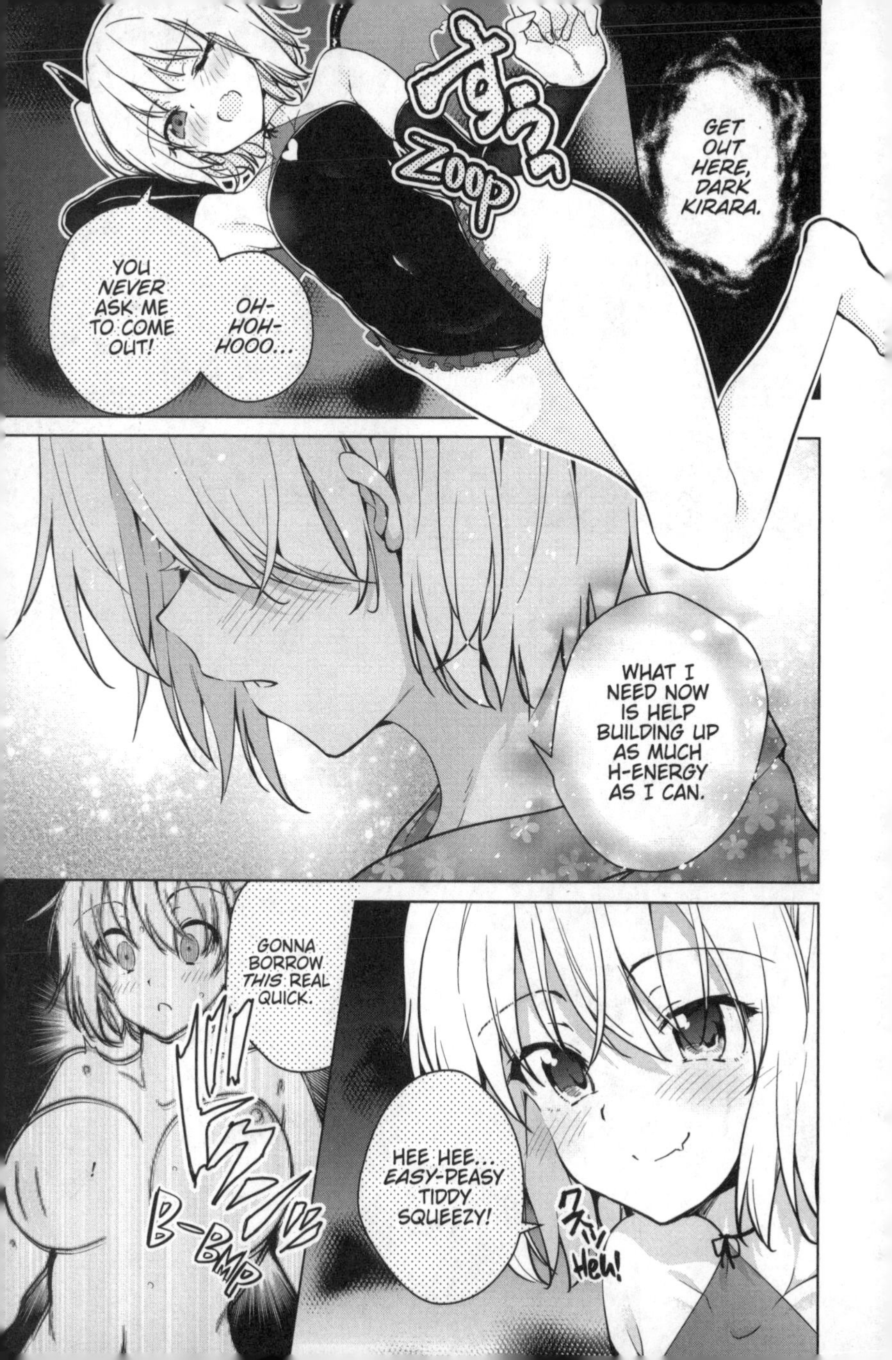
GET OUT HERE, DARK KIRARA.
ZOOP
OH-HOH-HOOO...
YOU NEVER ASK ME TO COME OUT!
WHAT I NEED NOW IS HELP BUILDING UP AS MUCH H-ENERGY AS I CAN.
HEE HEE... EASY-PEASY TIDDY SQUEEZY!
HEH!
GONNA BORROW THIS REAL QUICK.
B-BMP

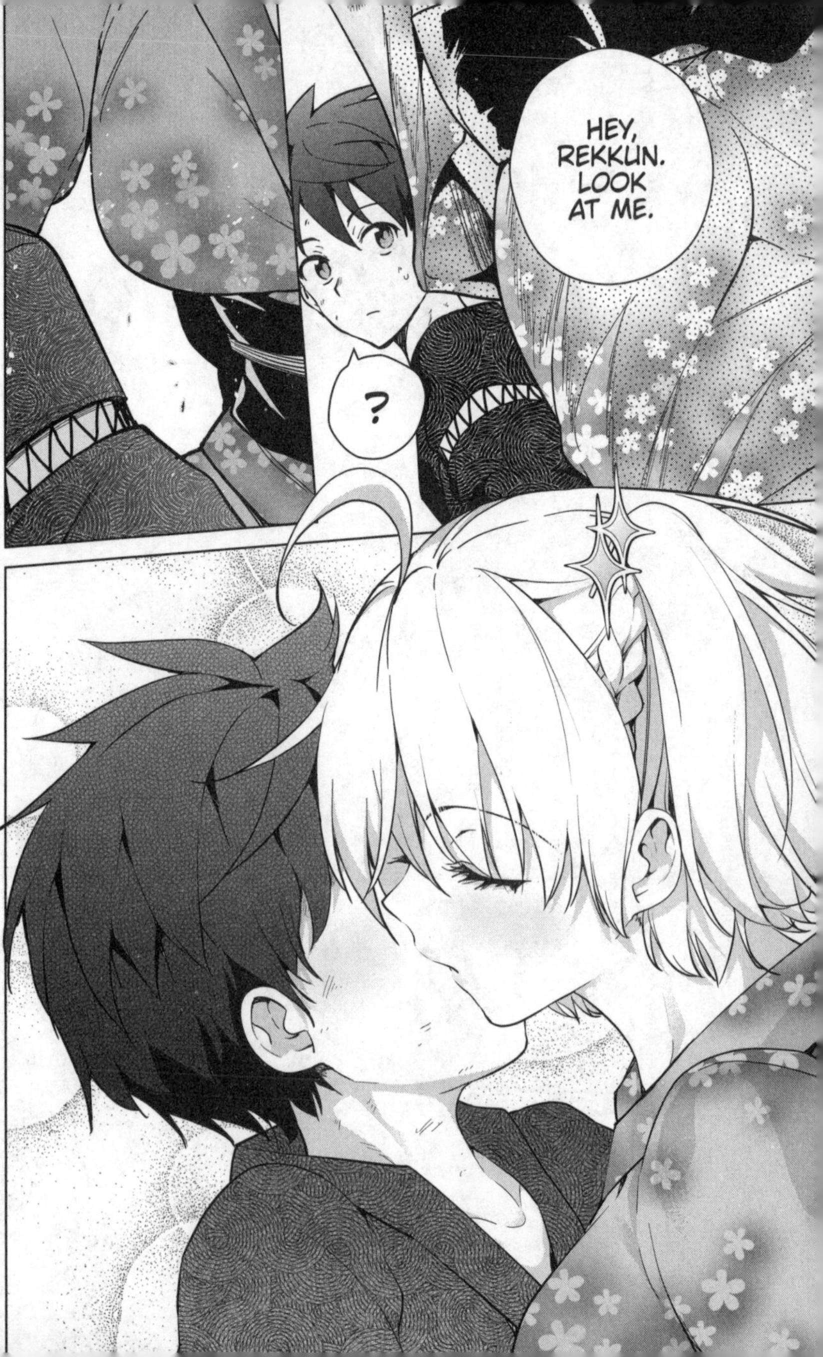
HEY, REKKUN. LOOK AT ME.
?

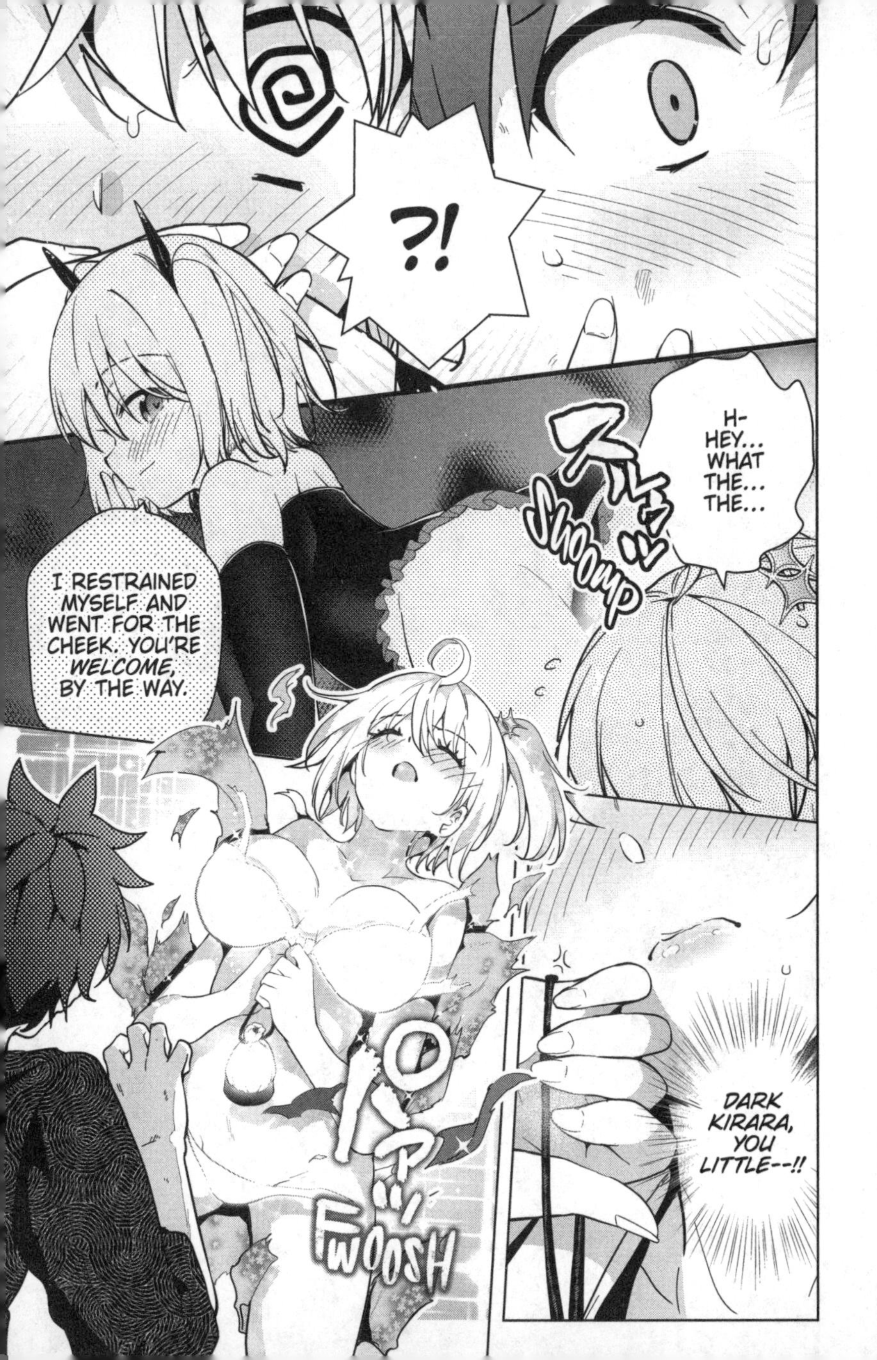
?!
H-HEY... WHAT THE... THE...
Shoomp
I RESTRAINED MYSELF AND WENT FOR THE CHEEK. YOU'RE *WELCOME*, BY THE WAY.
DARK KIRARA, YOU LITTLE--!!
FWOOSH

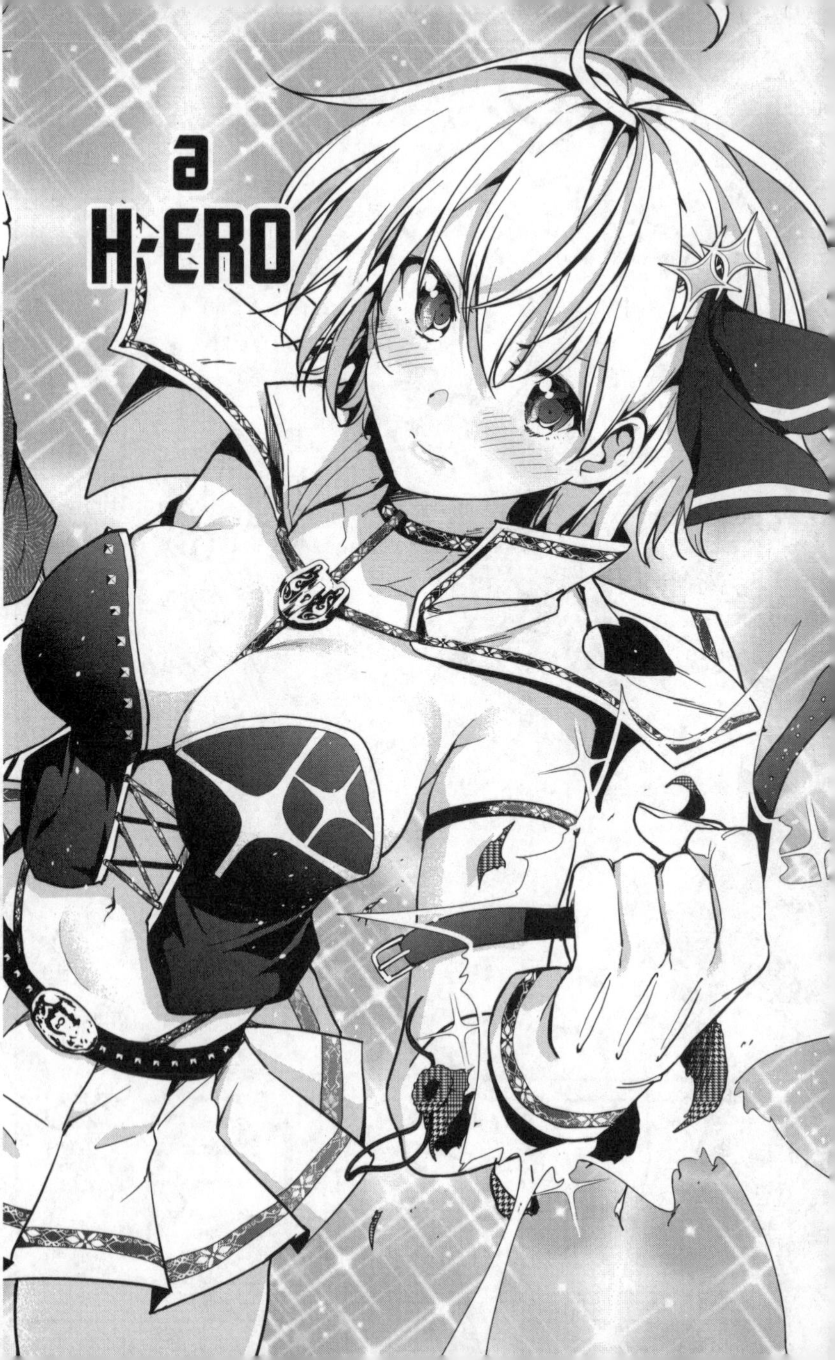
a
H-ERO

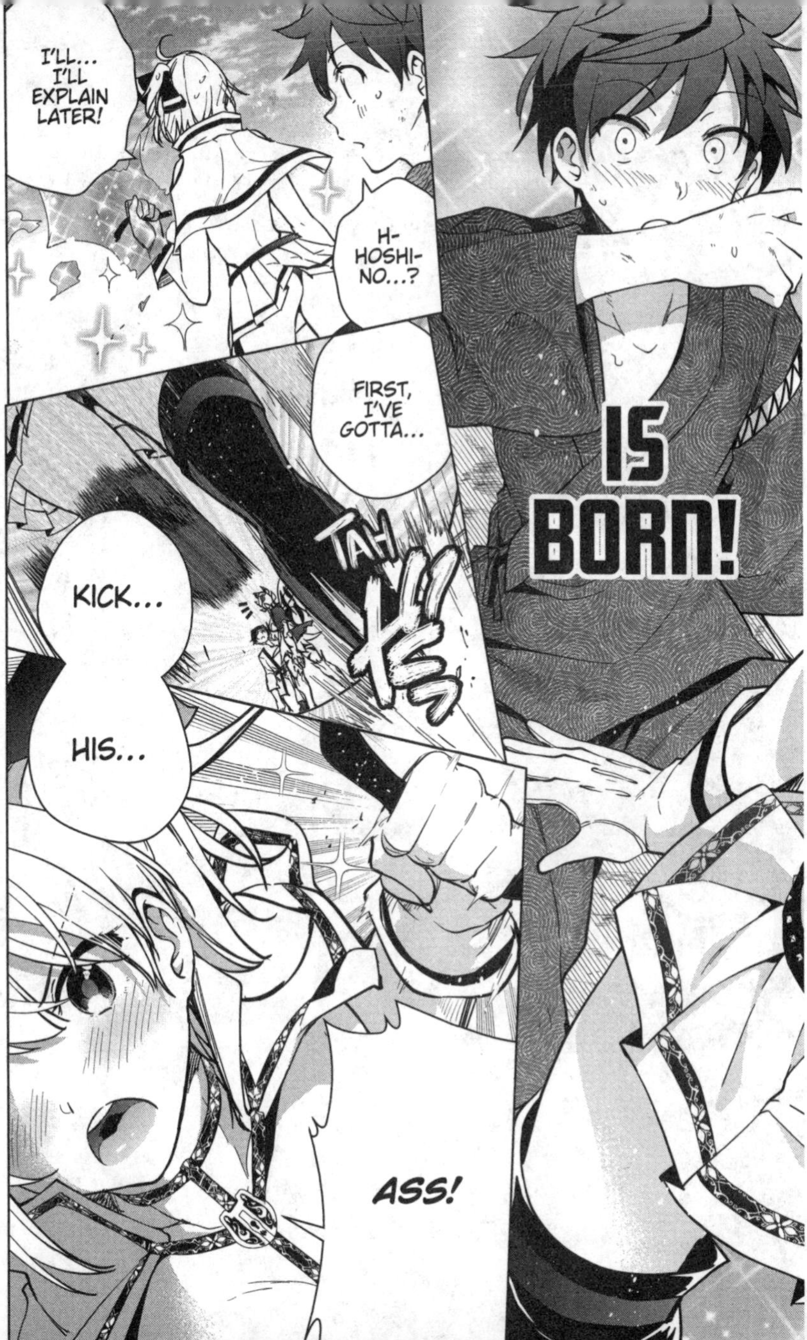

IS BORN!
H-HOSHINO...?
I'LL... I'LL EXPLAIN LATER!
FIRST, I'VE GOTTA...
TAH
KICK...
HIS...
ASS!

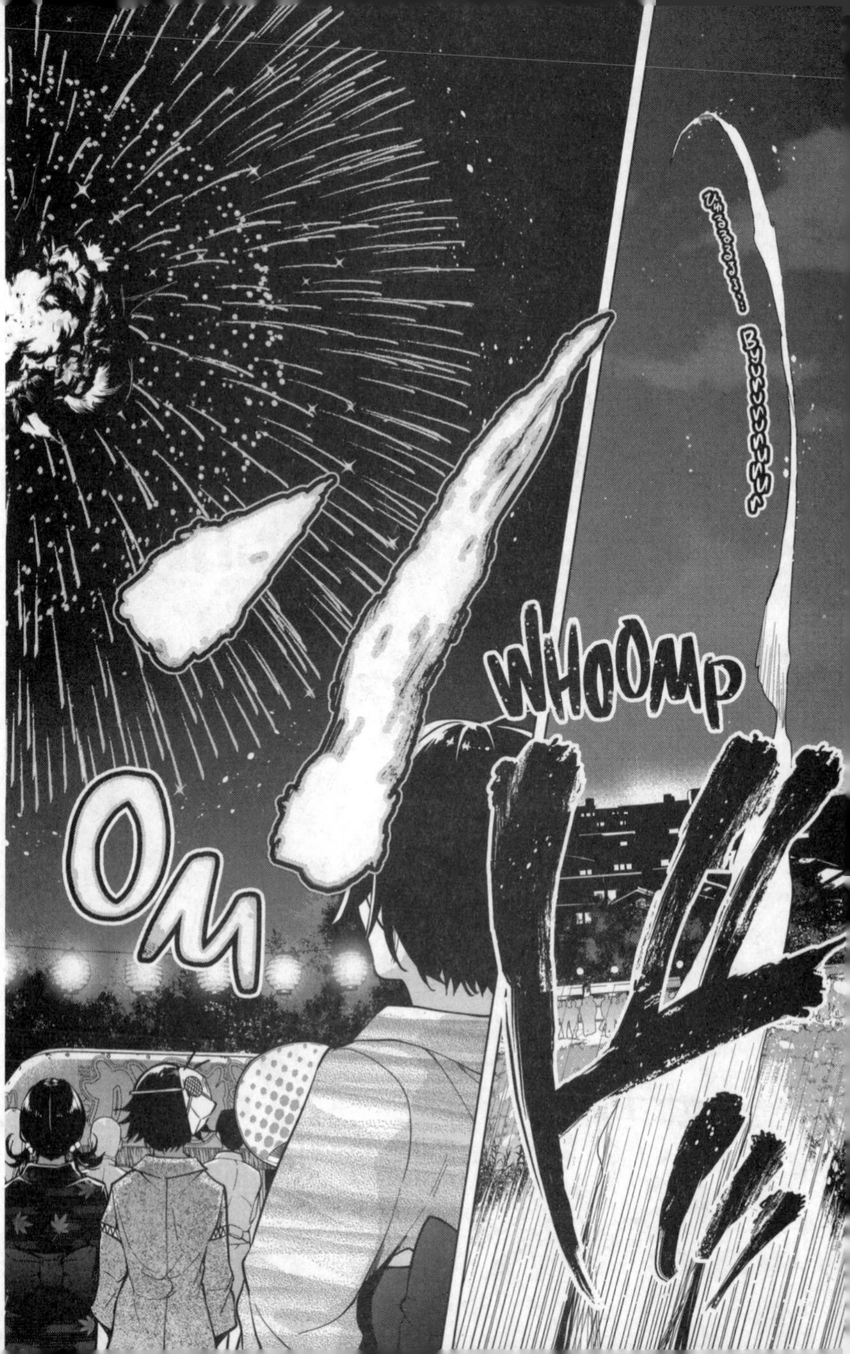
WHOOMP
OM

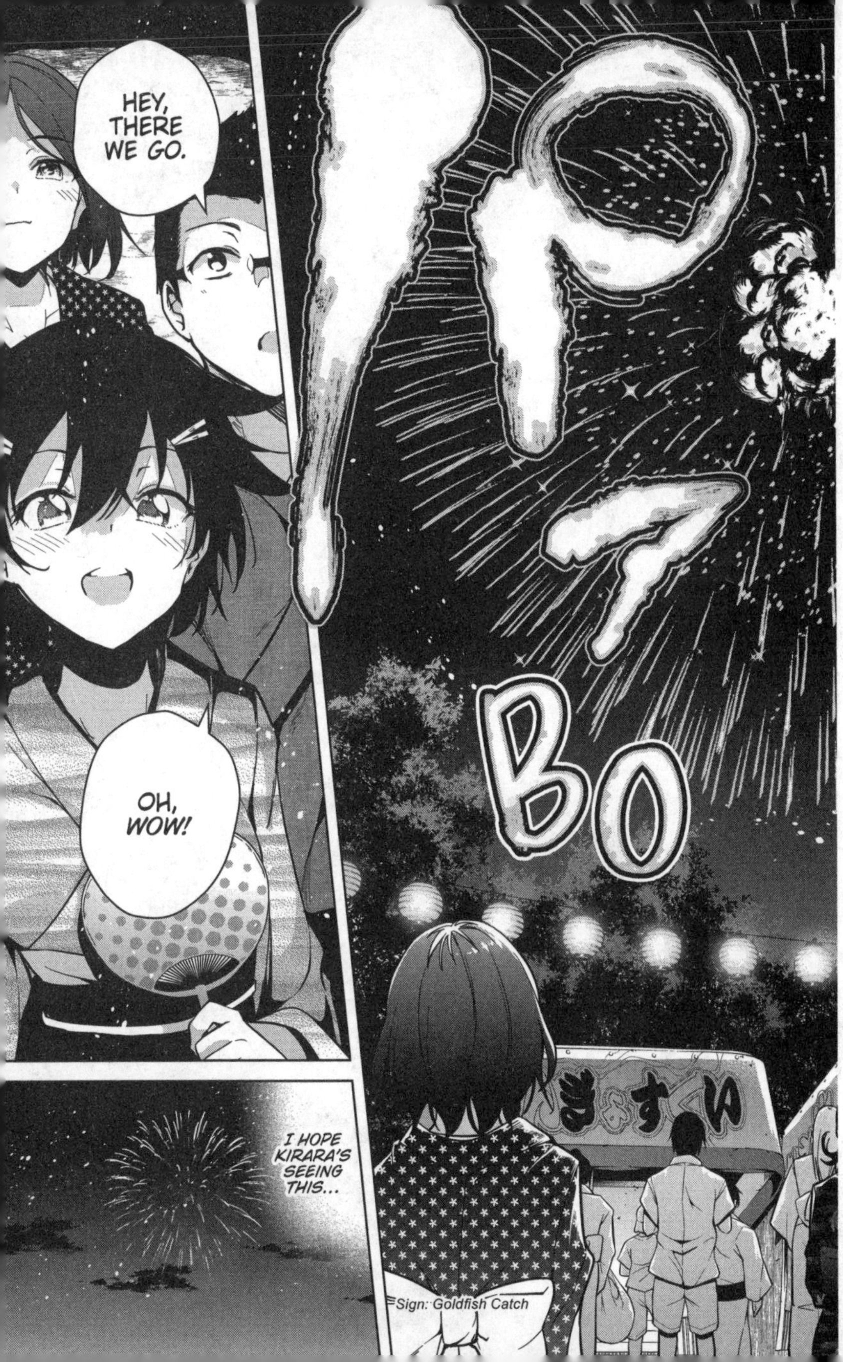

BO
Sign: Goldfish Catch
HEY, THERE WE GO.
OH, WOW!
I HOPE KIRARA'S SEEING THIS...

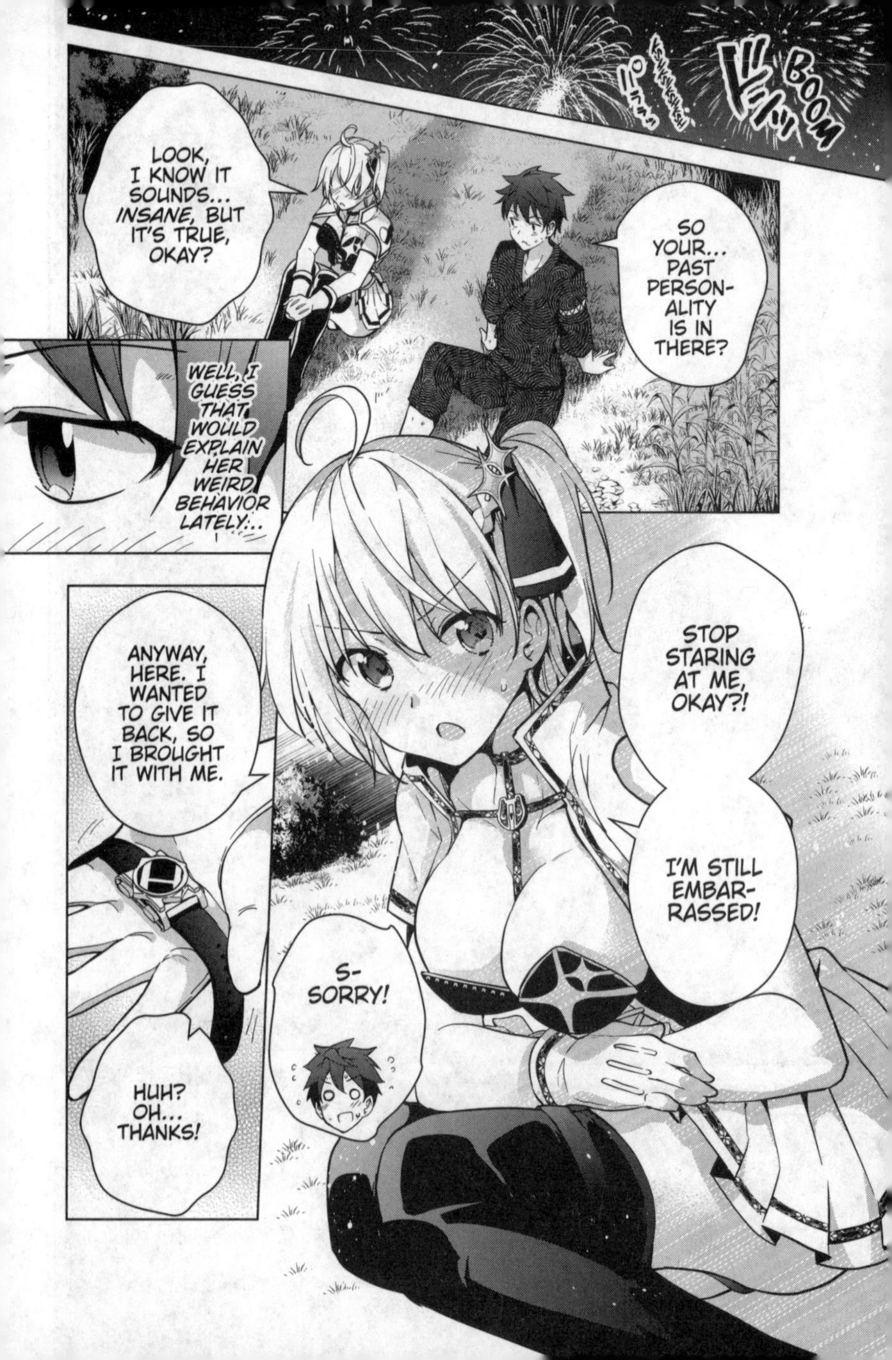
BOOM
KSHKSHKSHKSH
SO YOUR... PAST PERSONALITY IS IN THERE?
LOOK, I KNOW IT SOUNDS... *INSANE*, BUT IT'S TRUE, OKAY?
STOP STARING AT ME, OKAY?!
I'M STILL EMBARRASSED!
S-SORRY!
WELL, I GUESS THAT WOULD EXPLAIN HER WEIRD BEHAVIOR LATELY...
ANYWAY, HERE. I WANTED TO GIVE IT BACK, SO I BROUGHT IT WITH ME.
HUH? OH... THANKS!

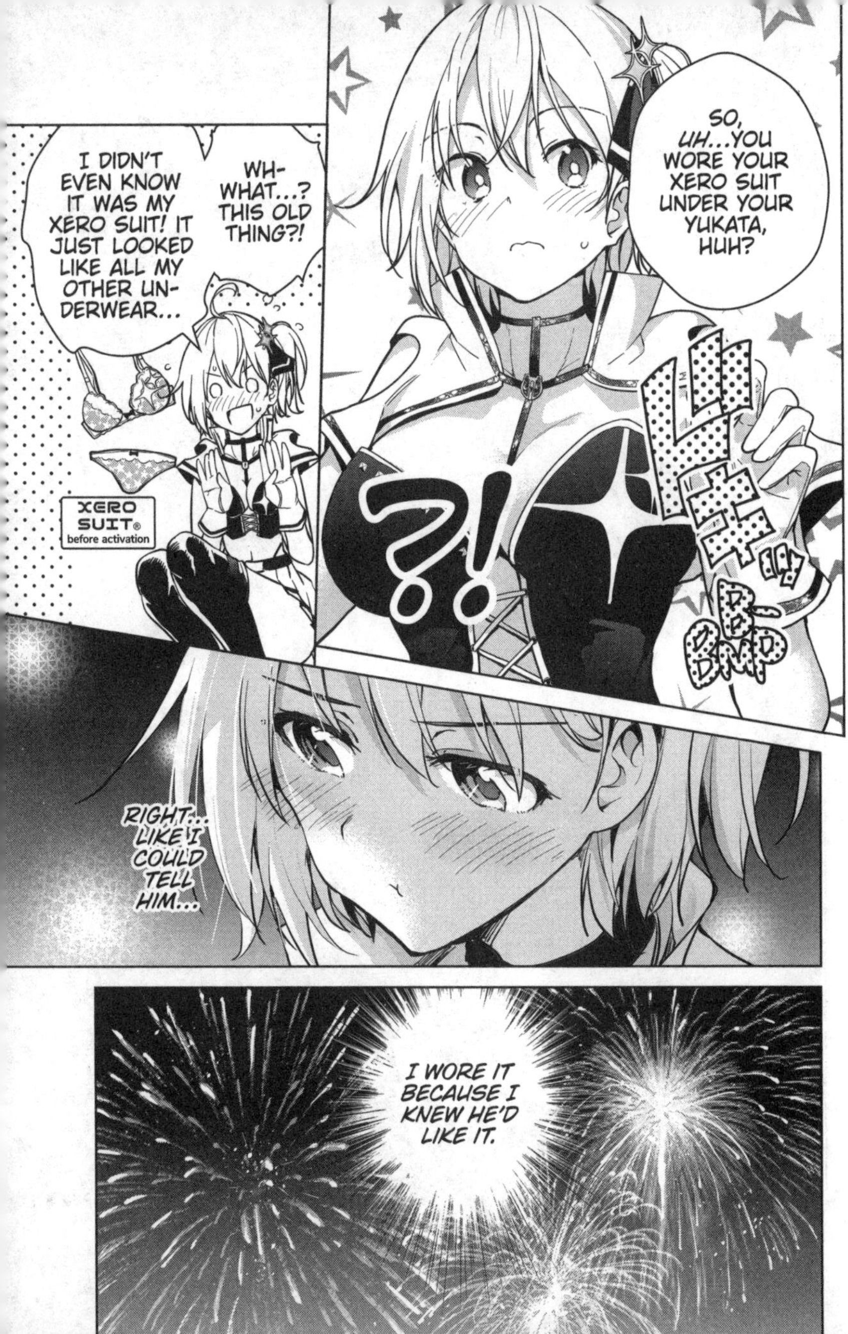
SO, UH...YOU WORE YOUR XERO SUIT UNDER YOUR YUKATA, HUH?
?!
WH-WHAT...? THIS OLD THING?!
I DIDN'T EVEN KNOW IT WAS MY XERO SUIT! IT JUST LOOKED LIKE ALL MY OTHER UNDERWEAR...
XERO SUIT® before activation
RIGHT... LIKE I COULD TELL HIM...
I WORE IT BECAUSE I KNEW HE'D LIKE IT.

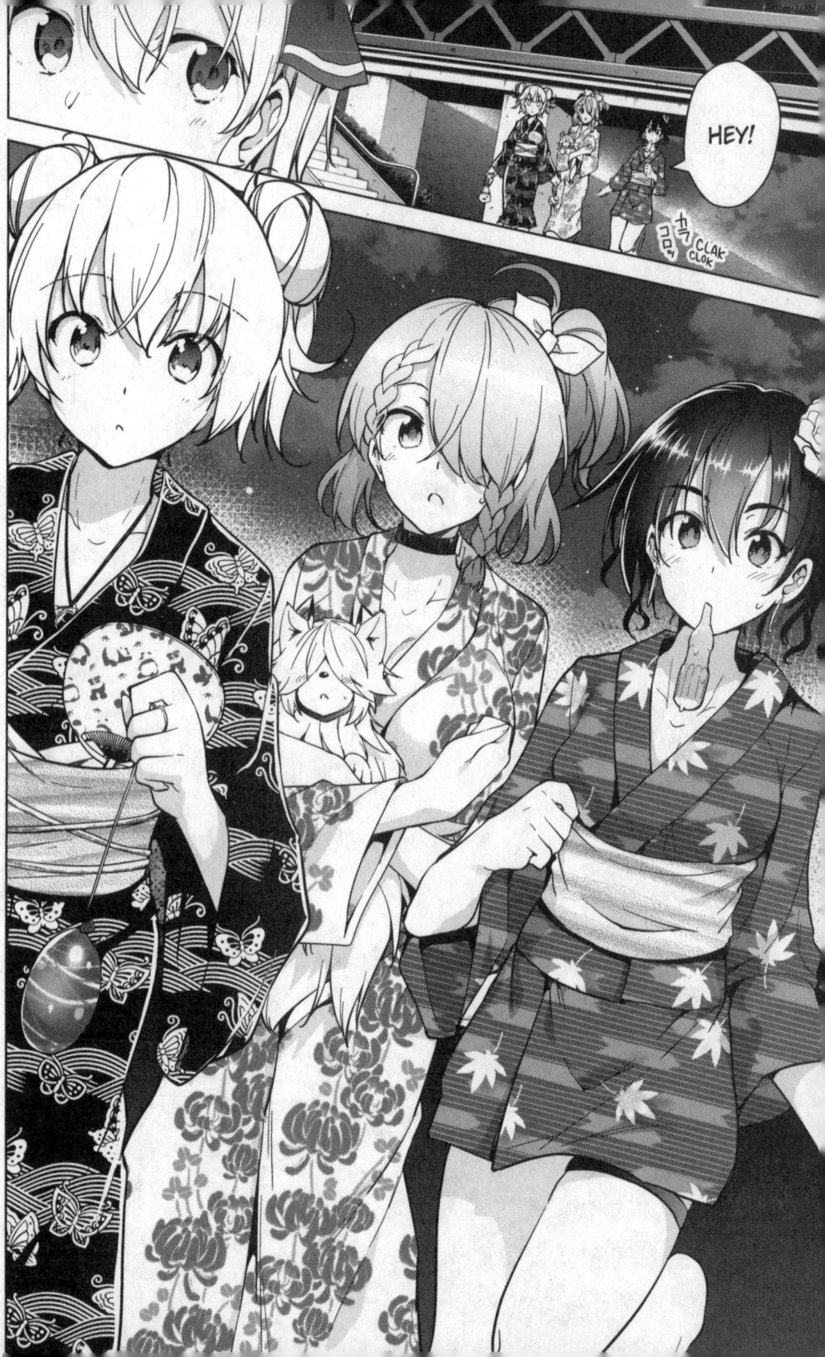
HEY!
カラ コロッ
CLAK CLOK

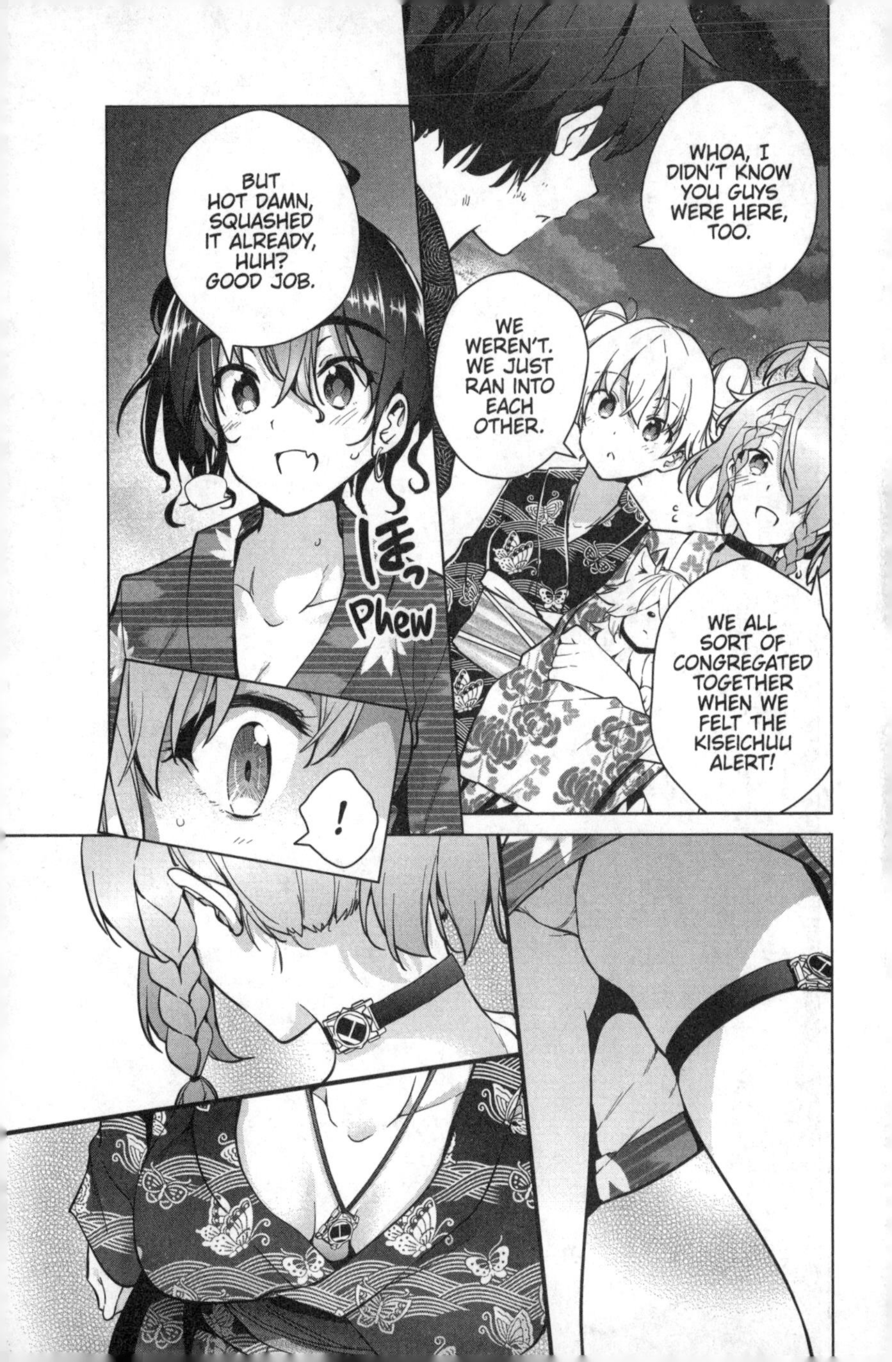
WHOA, I DIDN'T KNOW YOU GUYS WERE HERE, TOO.
WE WEREN'T. WE JUST RAN INTO EACH OTHER.
WE ALL SORT OF CONGREGATED TOGETHER WHEN WE FELT THE KISEICHUU ALERT!
BUT HOT DAMN, SQUASHED IT ALREADY, HUH? GOOD JOB.
ほっ
Phew
!

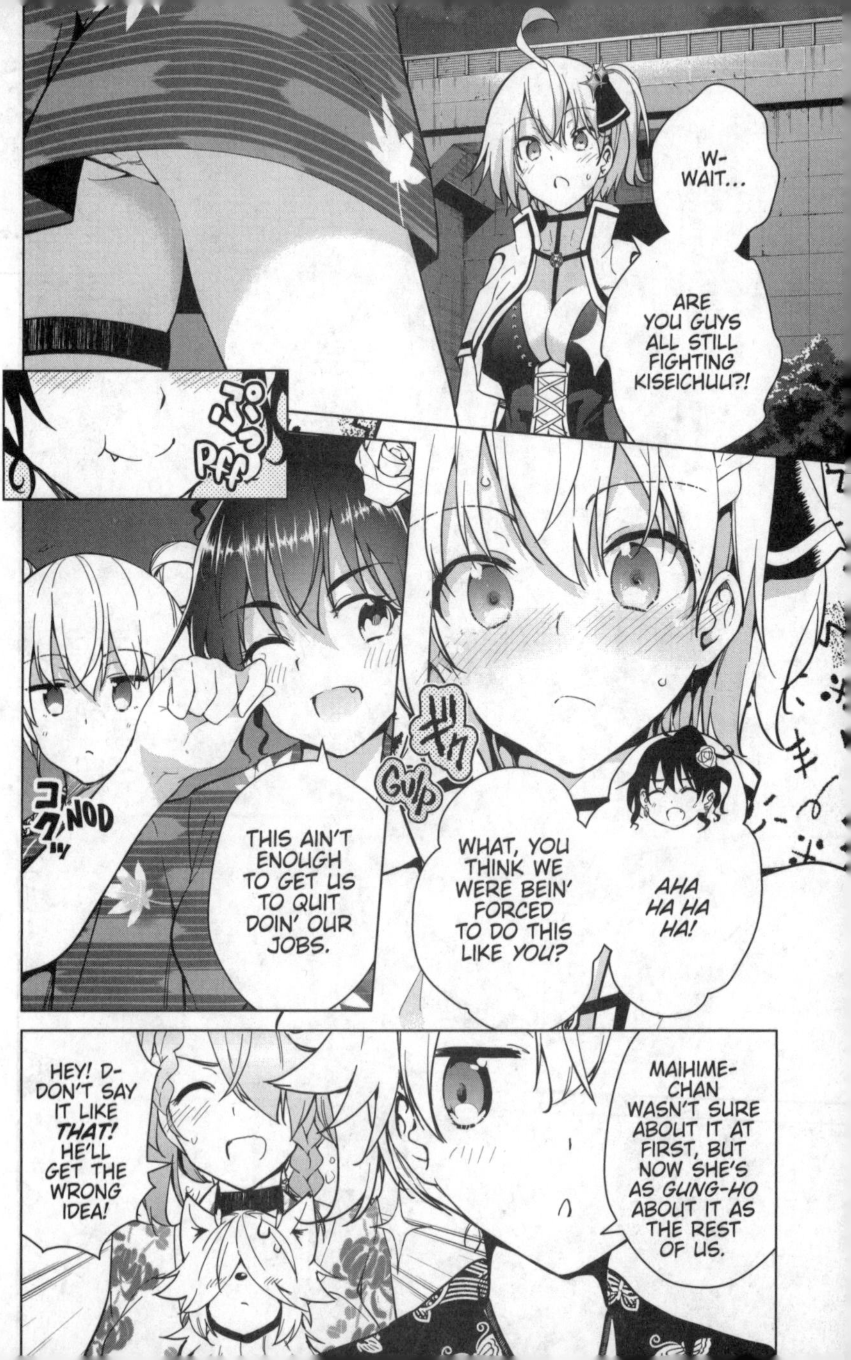
W- WAIT...
ARE YOU GUYS ALL STILL FIGHTING KISEICHUU?!
ぷっ PFF
AHA HA HA HA!
ギク GULP
WHAT, YOU THINK WE WERE BEIN' FORCED TO DO THIS LIKE *YOU?*
THIS AIN'T ENOUGH TO GET US TO QUIT DOIN' OUR JOBS.
コクッ NOD
MAIHIME-CHAN WASN'T SURE ABOUT IT AT FIRST, BUT NOW SHE'S AS *GUNG-HO* ABOUT IT AS THE REST OF US.
HEY! D-DON'T SAY IT LIKE ***THAT!*** HE'LL GET THE WRONG IDEA!

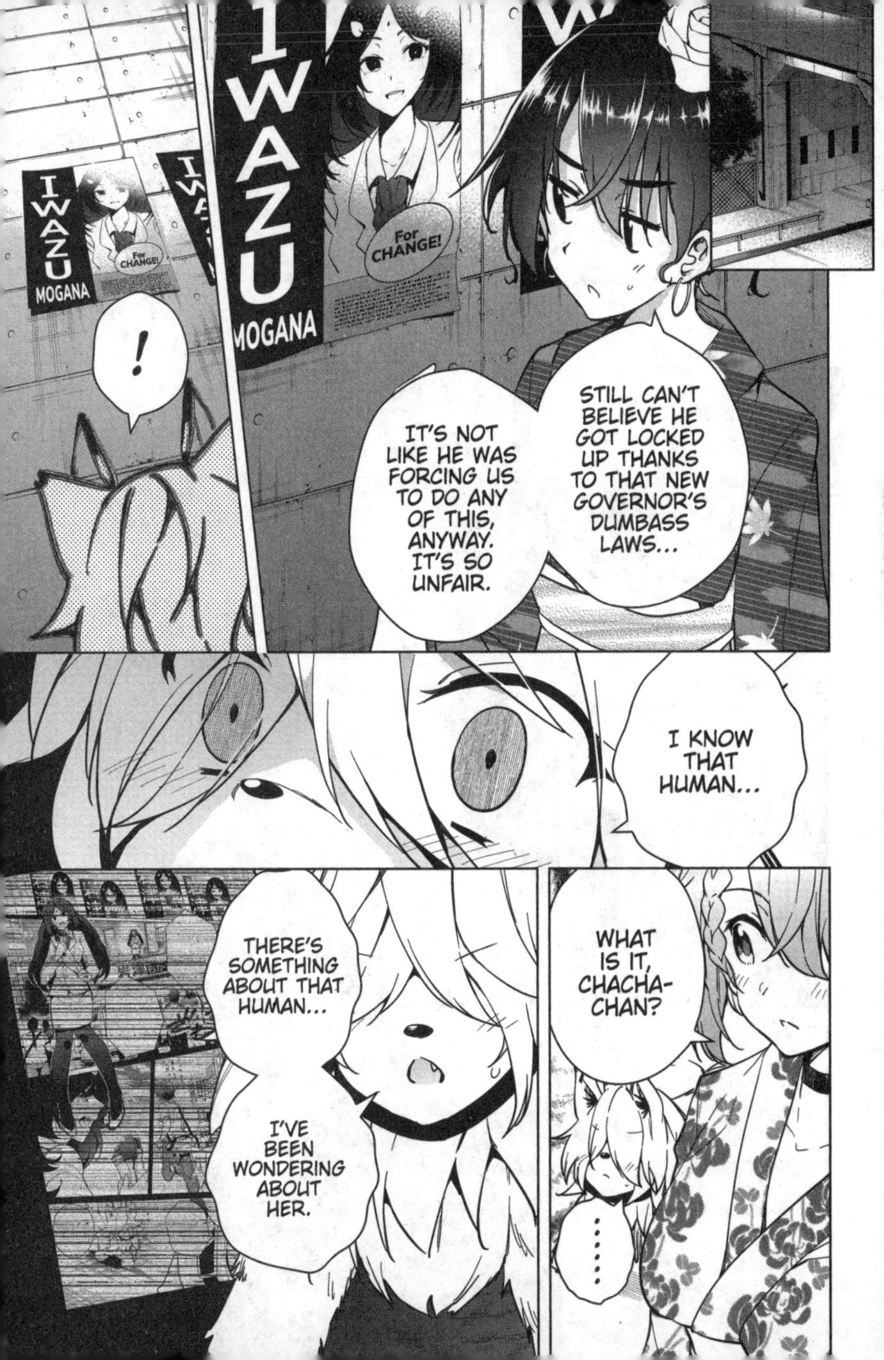

IWAZU MOGANA
For CHANGE!
IWAZU MOGANA
For CHANGE!
STILL CAN'T BELIEVE HE GOT LOCKED UP THANKS TO THAT NEW GOVERNOR'S DUMBASS LAWS...
IT'S NOT LIKE HE WAS FORCING US TO DO ANY OF THIS, ANYWAY. IT'S SO UNFAIR.
!
I KNOW THAT HUMAN...
WHAT IS IT, CHACHA-CHAN?
......
THERE'S SOMETHING ABOUT THAT HUMAN...
I'VE BEEN WONDERING ABOUT HER.

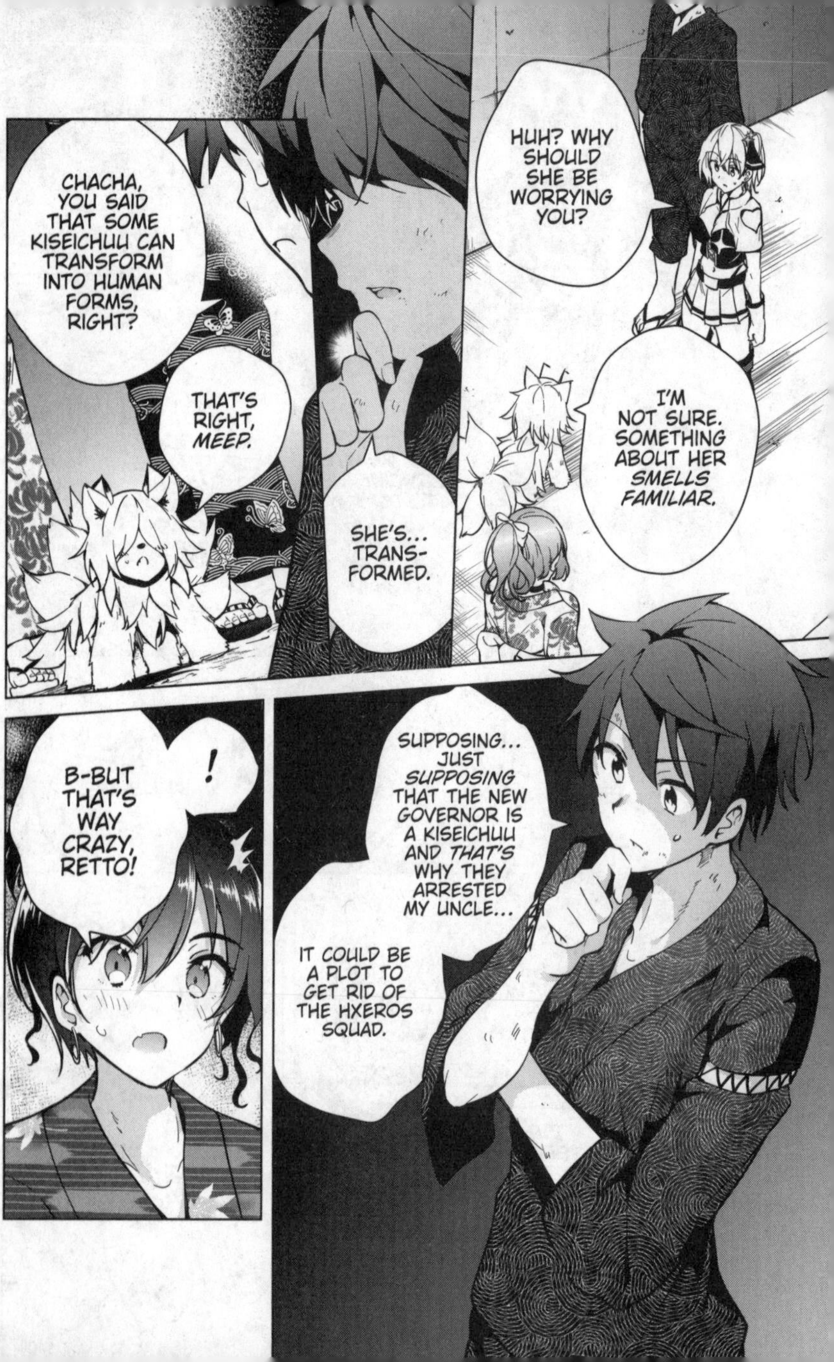
HUH? WHY SHOULD SHE BE WORRYING YOU?
I'M NOT SURE. SOMETHING ABOUT HER *SMELLS FAMILIAR.*
CHACHA, YOU SAID THAT SOME KISEICHUU CAN TRANSFORM INTO HUMAN FORMS, RIGHT?
THAT'S RIGHT, *MEEP.*
SHE'S... TRANS-FORMED.
SUPPOSING... JUST *SUPPOSING* THAT THE NEW GOVERNOR IS A KISEICHUU AND *THAT'S* WHY THEY ARRESTED MY UNCLE...
IT COULD BE A PLOT TO GET RID OF THE HXEROS SQUAD.
!
B-BUT THAT'S WAY CRAZY, RETTO!

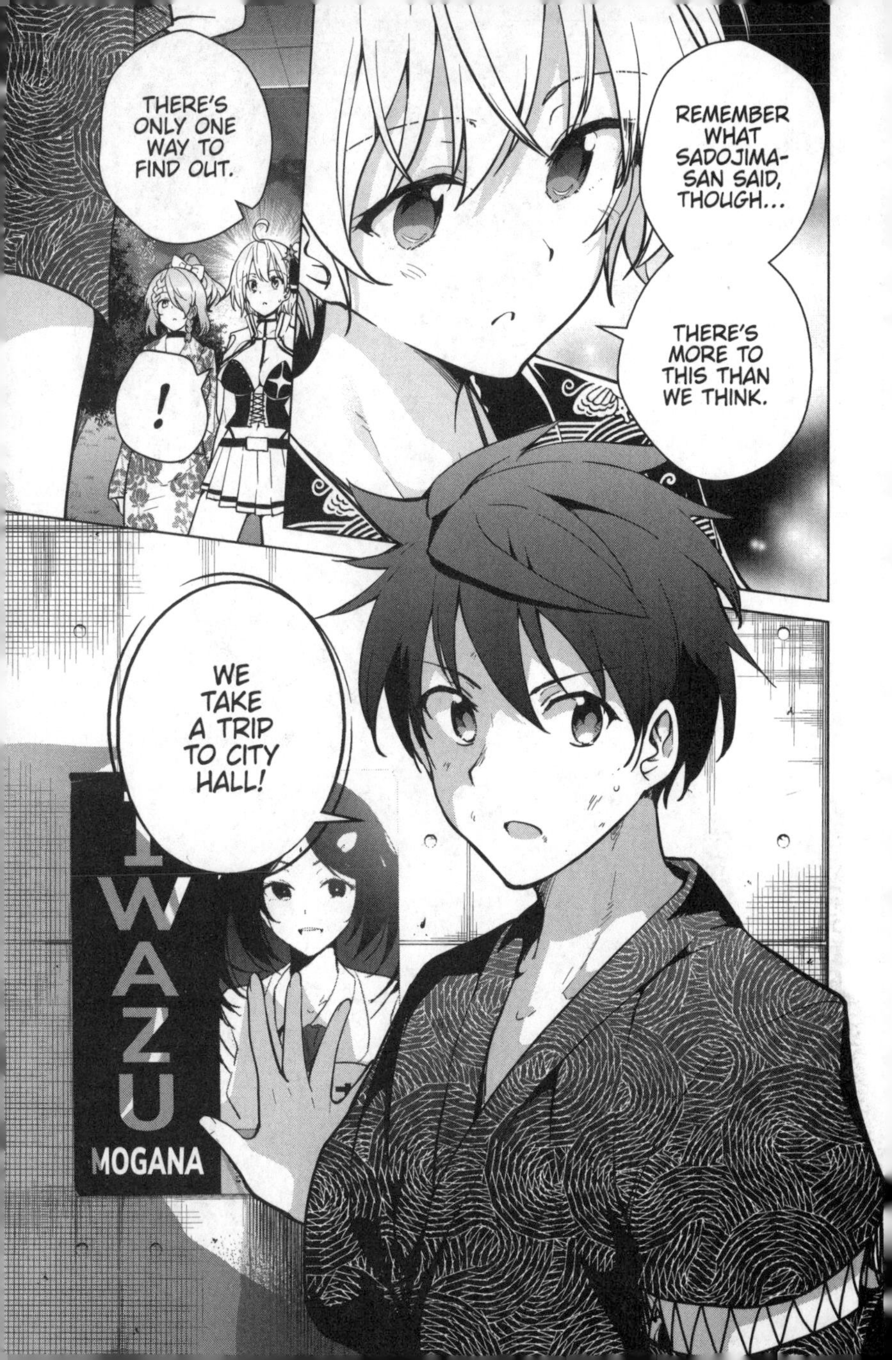
REMEMBER WHAT SADOJIMA-SAN SAID, THOUGH...
THERE'S MORE TO THIS THAN WE THINK.
THERE'S ONLY ONE WAY TO FIND OUT.
!
WE TAKE A TRIP TO CITY HALL!
IWAZU
MOGANA

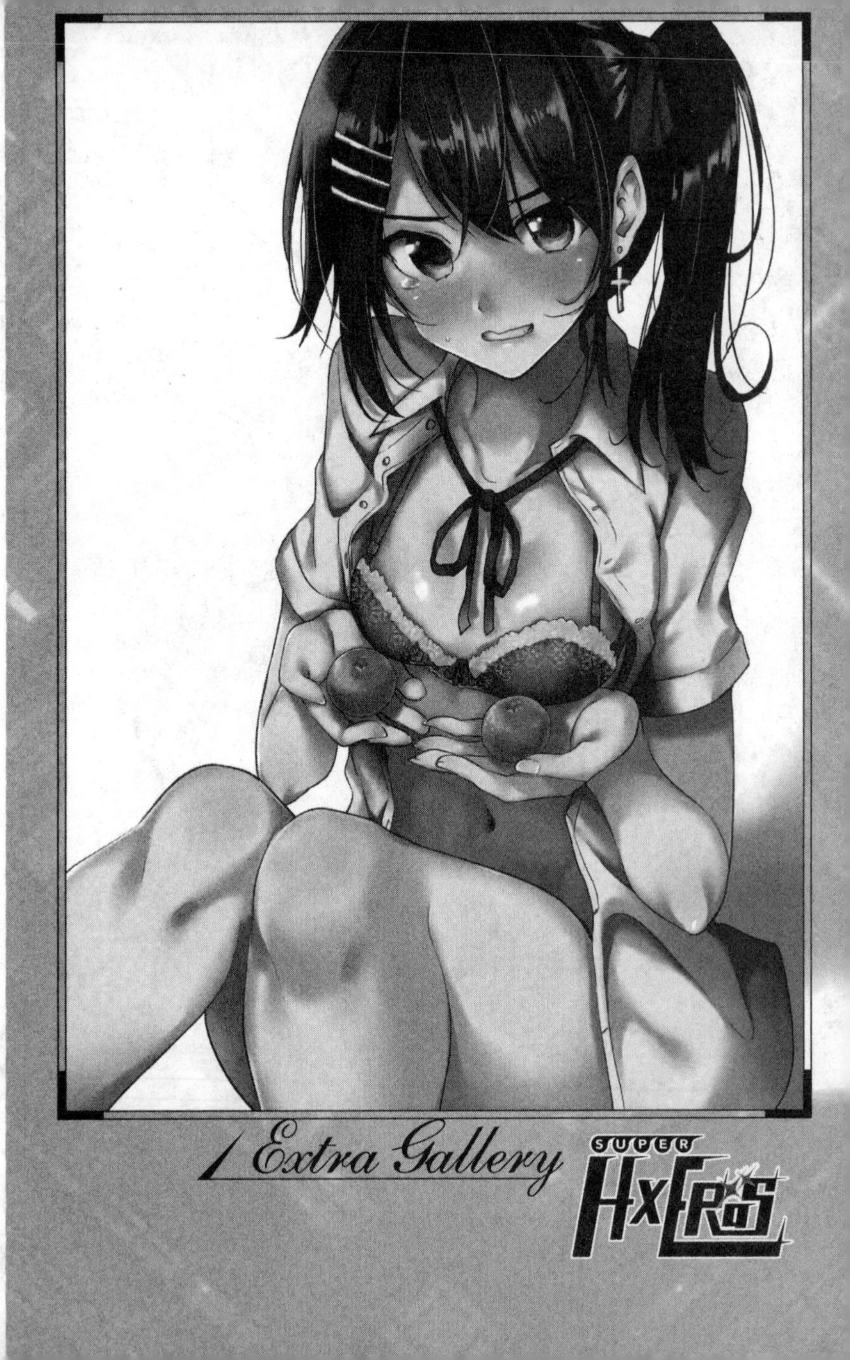

Extra Gallery

SUPER HxEROS

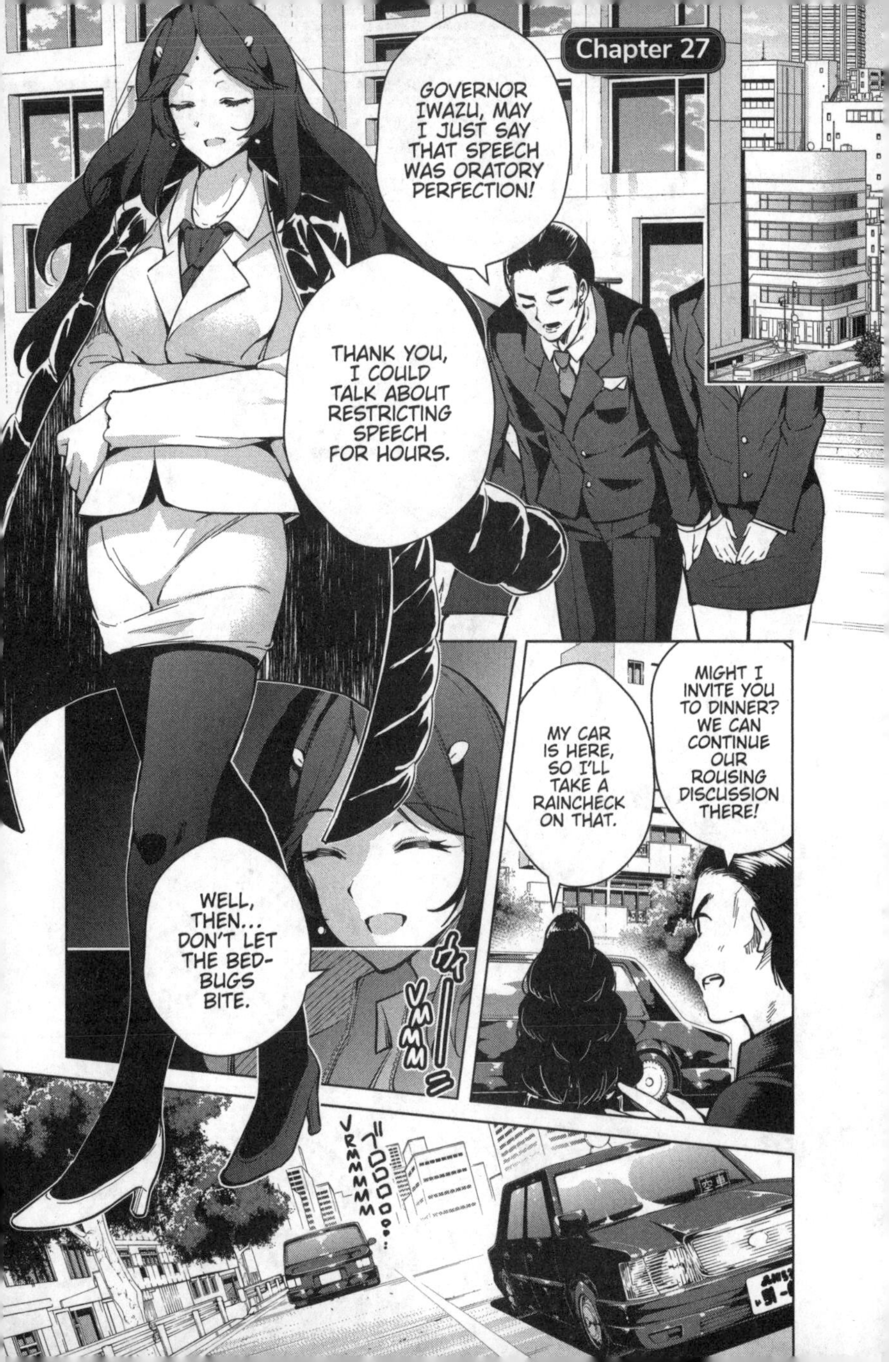
Chapter 27
GOVERNOR IWAZU, MAY I JUST SAY THAT SPEECH WAS ORATORY PERFECTION!
THANK YOU, I COULD TALK ABOUT RESTRICTING SPEECH FOR HOURS.
MIGHT I INVITE YOU TO DINNER? WE CAN CONTINUE OUR ROUSING DISCUSSION THERE!
MY CAR IS HERE, SO I'LL TAKE A RAINCHECK ON THAT.
WELL, THEN... DON'T LET THE BED-BUGS BITE.
VMMMM
VRMMMMM

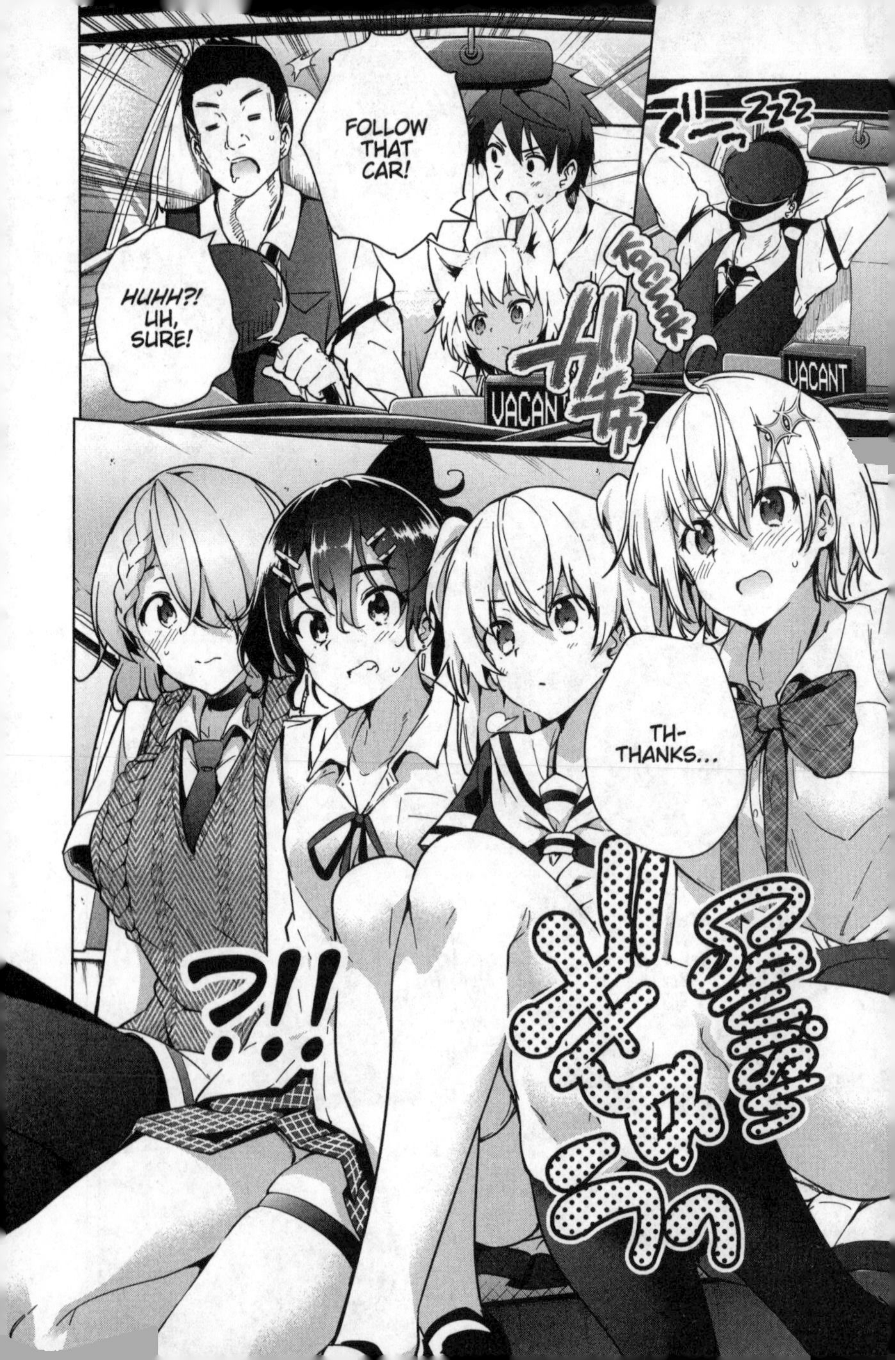
Zzzz
FOLLOW THAT CAR!
HUHH?! UH, SURE!
Kachak
TH-THANKS...
Swish
?!!

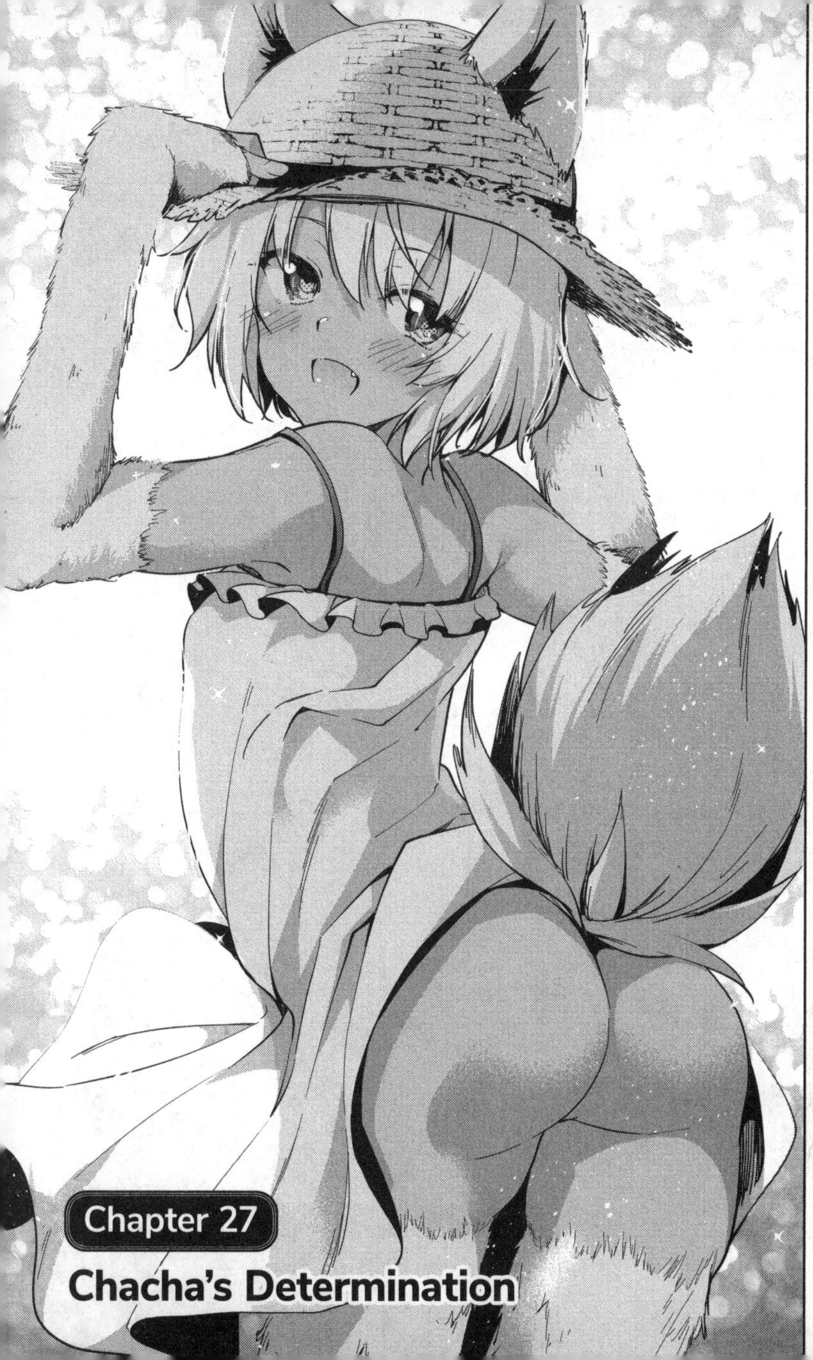

Chapter 27

Chacha's Determination

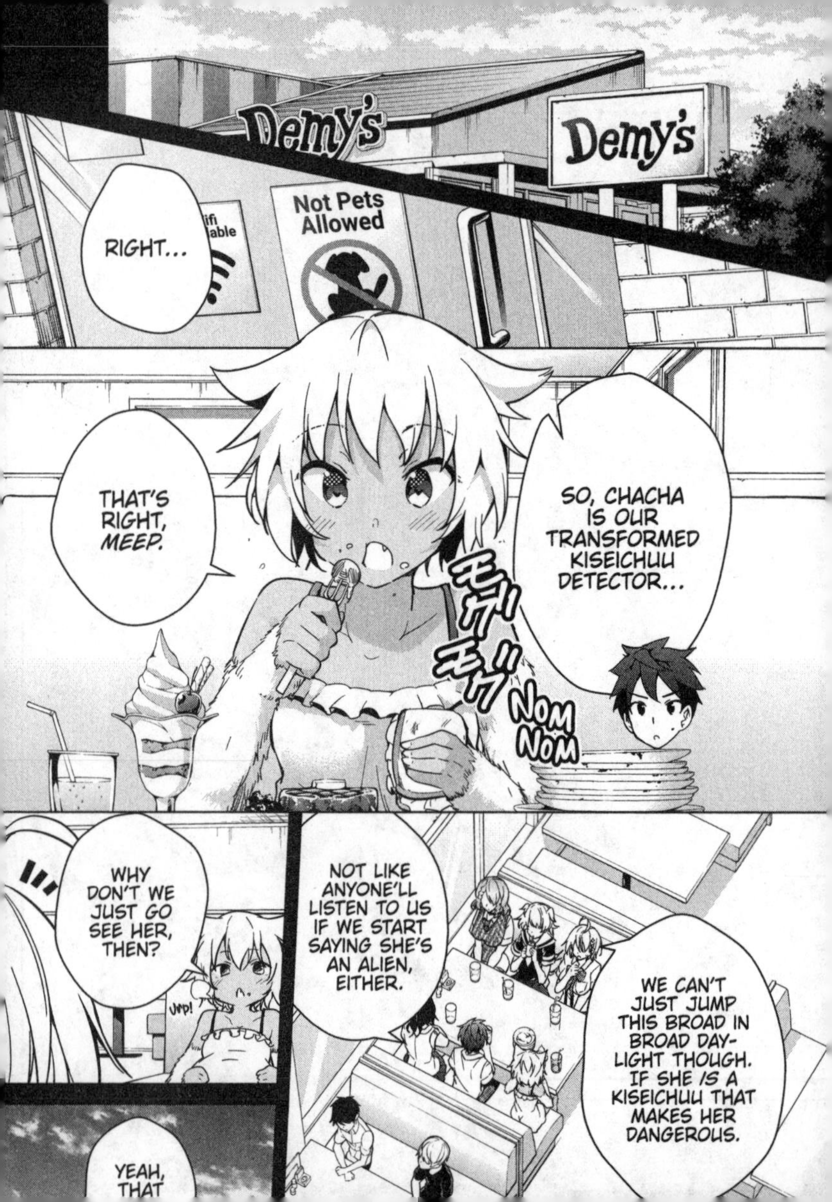
Demy's
Demy's
Not Pets Allowed
RIGHT…
SO, CHACHA IS OUR TRANSFORMED KISEICHUU DETECTOR…
THAT'S RIGHT, *MEEP.*
モグモグ
NOM NOM
WE CAN'T JUST JUMP THIS BROAD IN BROAD DAY-LIGHT THOUGH. IF SHE *IS* A KISEICHUU THAT MAKES HER DANGEROUS.
NOT LIKE ANYONE'LL LISTEN TO US IF WE START SAYING SHE'S AN ALIEN, EITHER.
WHY DON'T WE JUST GO SEE HER, THEN?
UMP!
YEAH, THAT

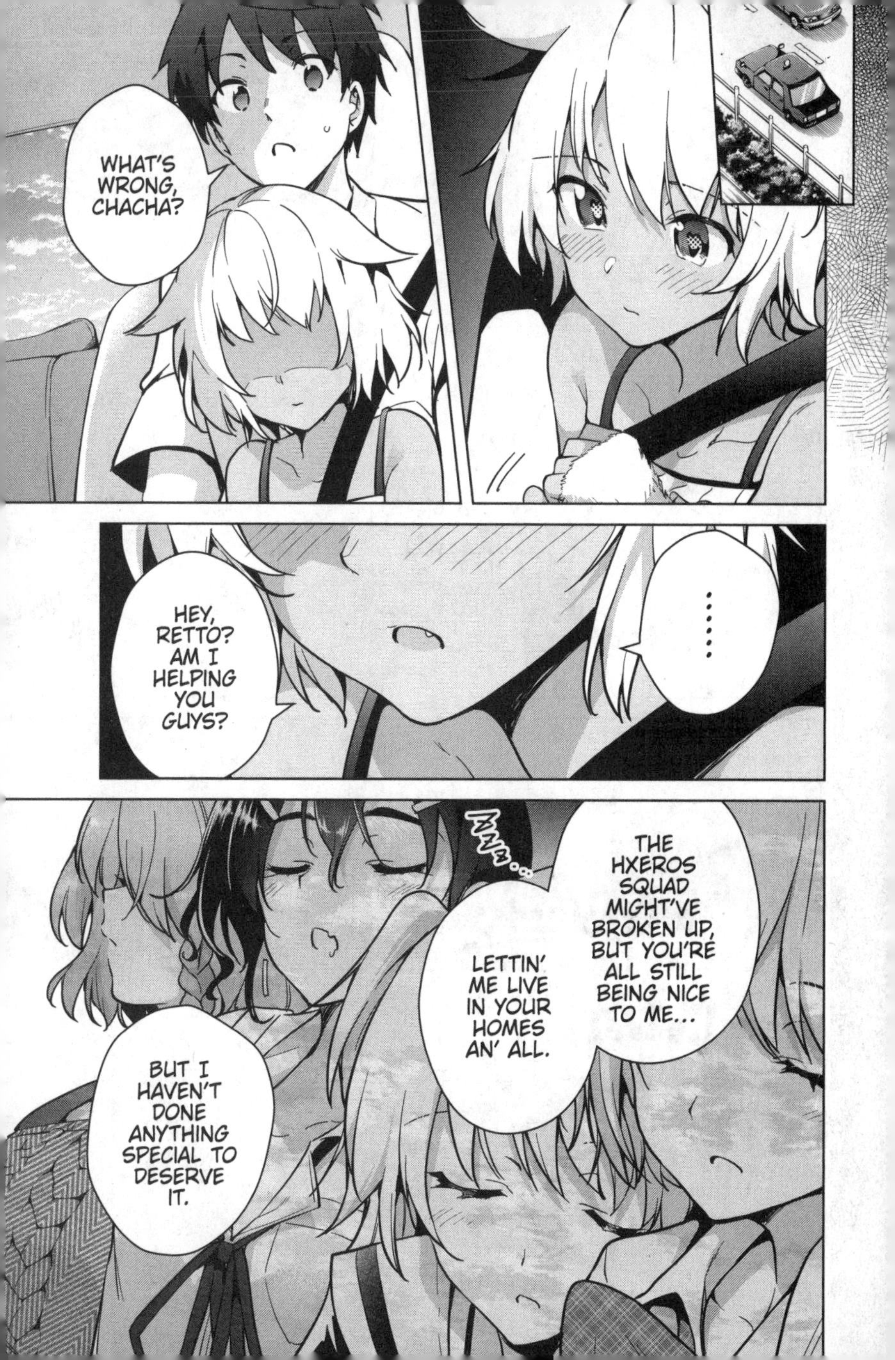
WHAT'S WRONG, CHACHA?
......
HEY, RETTO? AM I HELPING YOU GUYS?
THE HXEROS SQUAD MIGHT'VE BROKEN UP, BUT YOU'RE ALL STILL BEING NICE TO ME...
LETTIN' ME LIVE IN YOUR HOMES AN' ALL.
BUT I HAVEN'T DONE ANYTHING SPECIAL TO DESERVE IT.

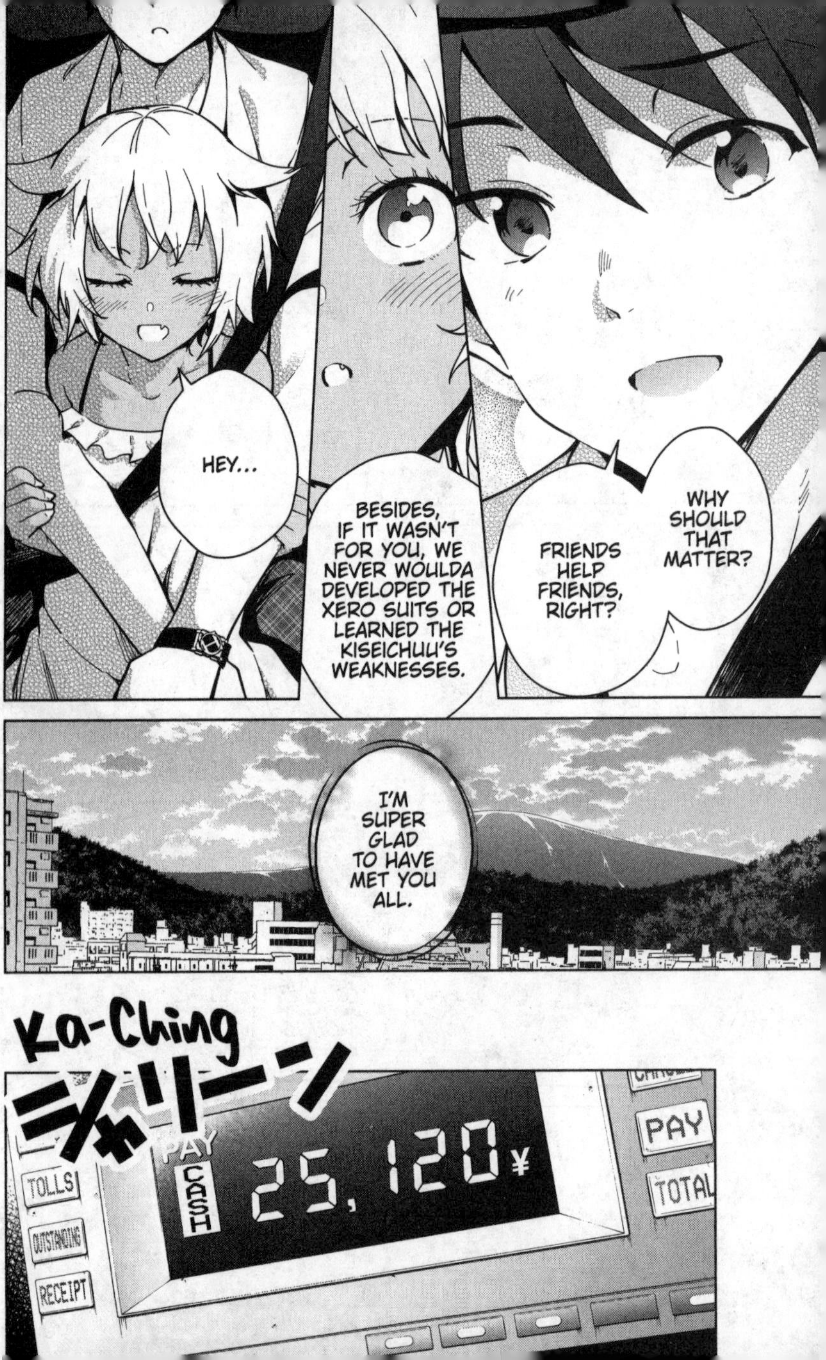
WHY SHOULD THAT MATTER?
FRIENDS HELP FRIENDS, RIGHT?
BESIDES, IF IT WASN'T FOR YOU, WE NEVER WOULDA DEVELOPED THE XERO SUITS OR LEARNED THE KISEICHUU'S WEAKNESSES.
HEY...
I'M SUPER GLAD TO HAVE MET YOU ALL.
Ka-Ching
ジャリーン
PAY
TOTAL
PAY
CASH
25,120¥
TOLLS
OUTSTANDING
RECEIPT

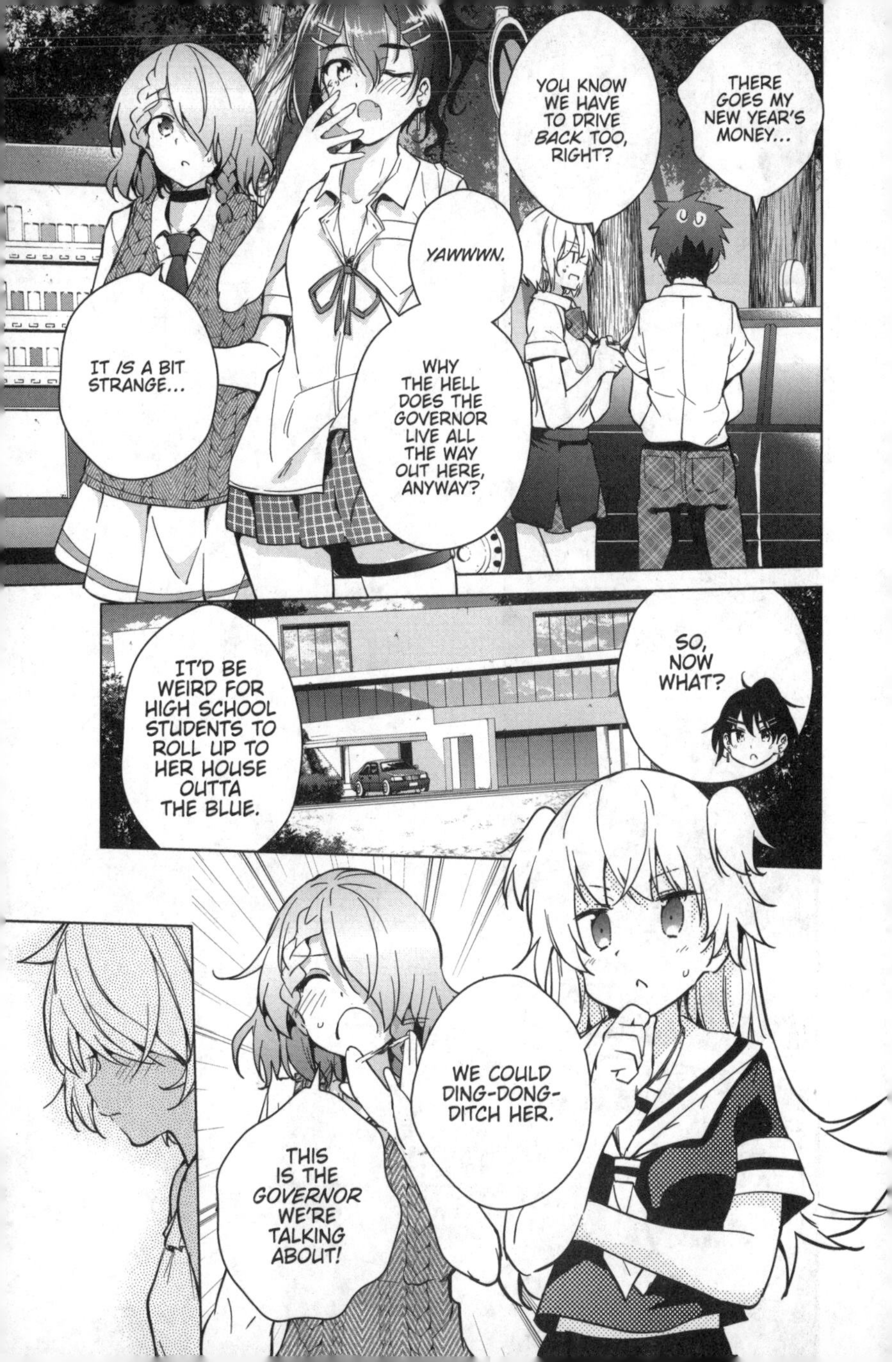
THERE GOES MY NEW YEAR'S MONEY...
YOU KNOW WE HAVE TO DRIVE *BACK* TOO, RIGHT?
YAWWWN.
WHY THE HELL DOES THE GOVERNOR LIVE ALL THE WAY OUT HERE, ANYWAY?
IT *IS* A BIT STRANGE...
SO, NOW WHAT?
IT'D BE WEIRD FOR HIGH SCHOOL STUDENTS TO ROLL UP TO HER HOUSE OUTTA THE BLUE.
WE COULD DING-DONG-DITCH HER.
THIS IS THE *GOVERNOR* WE'RE TALKING ABOUT!

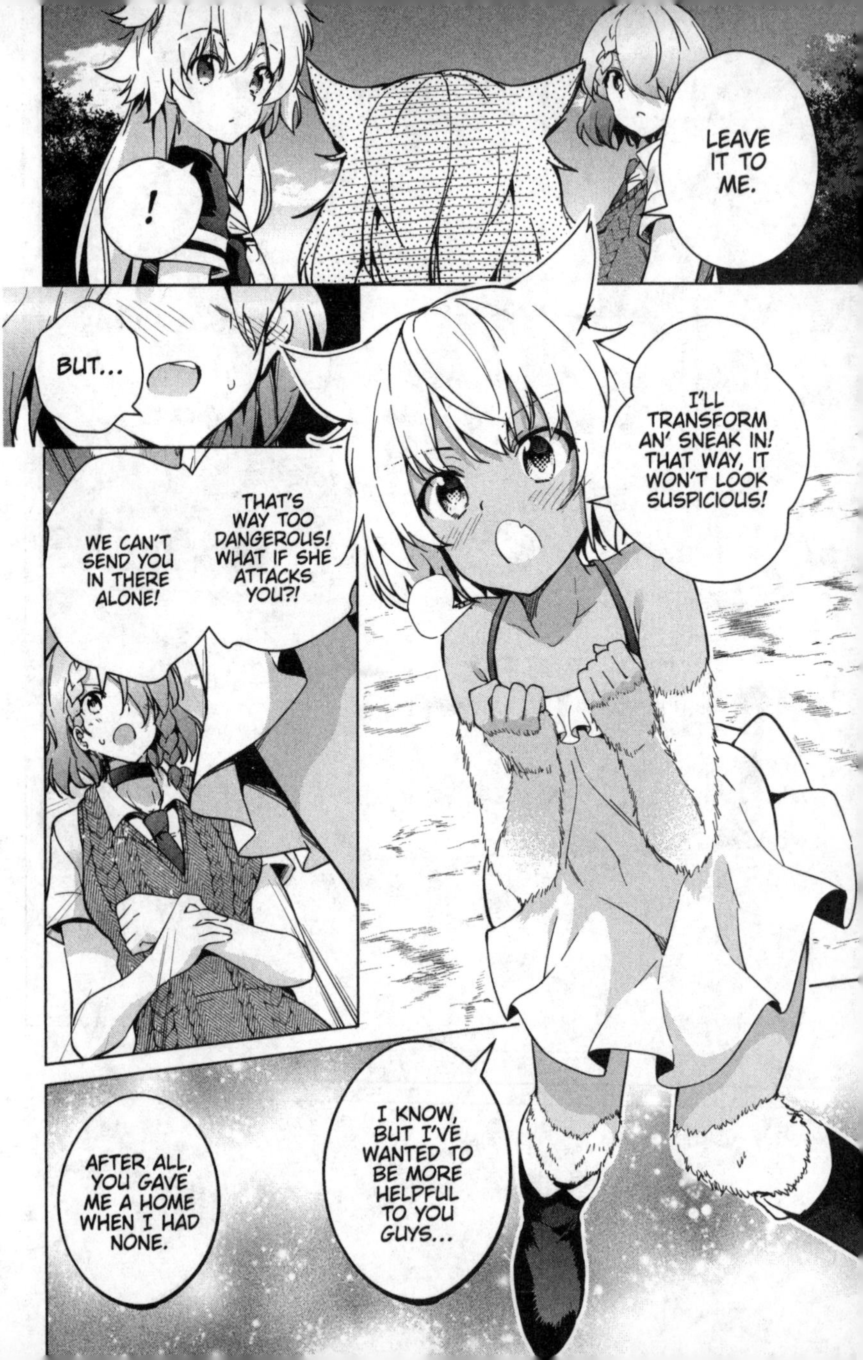
LEAVE IT TO ME.
!
I'LL TRANSFORM AN' SNEAK IN! THAT WAY, IT WON'T LOOK SUSPICIOUS!
BUT...
THAT'S WAY TOO DANGEROUS! WHAT IF SHE ATTACKS YOU?!
WE CAN'T SEND YOU IN THERE ALONE!
I KNOW, BUT I'VE WANTED TO BE MORE HELPFUL TO YOU GUYS...
AFTER ALL, YOU GAVE ME A HOME WHEN I HAD NONE.

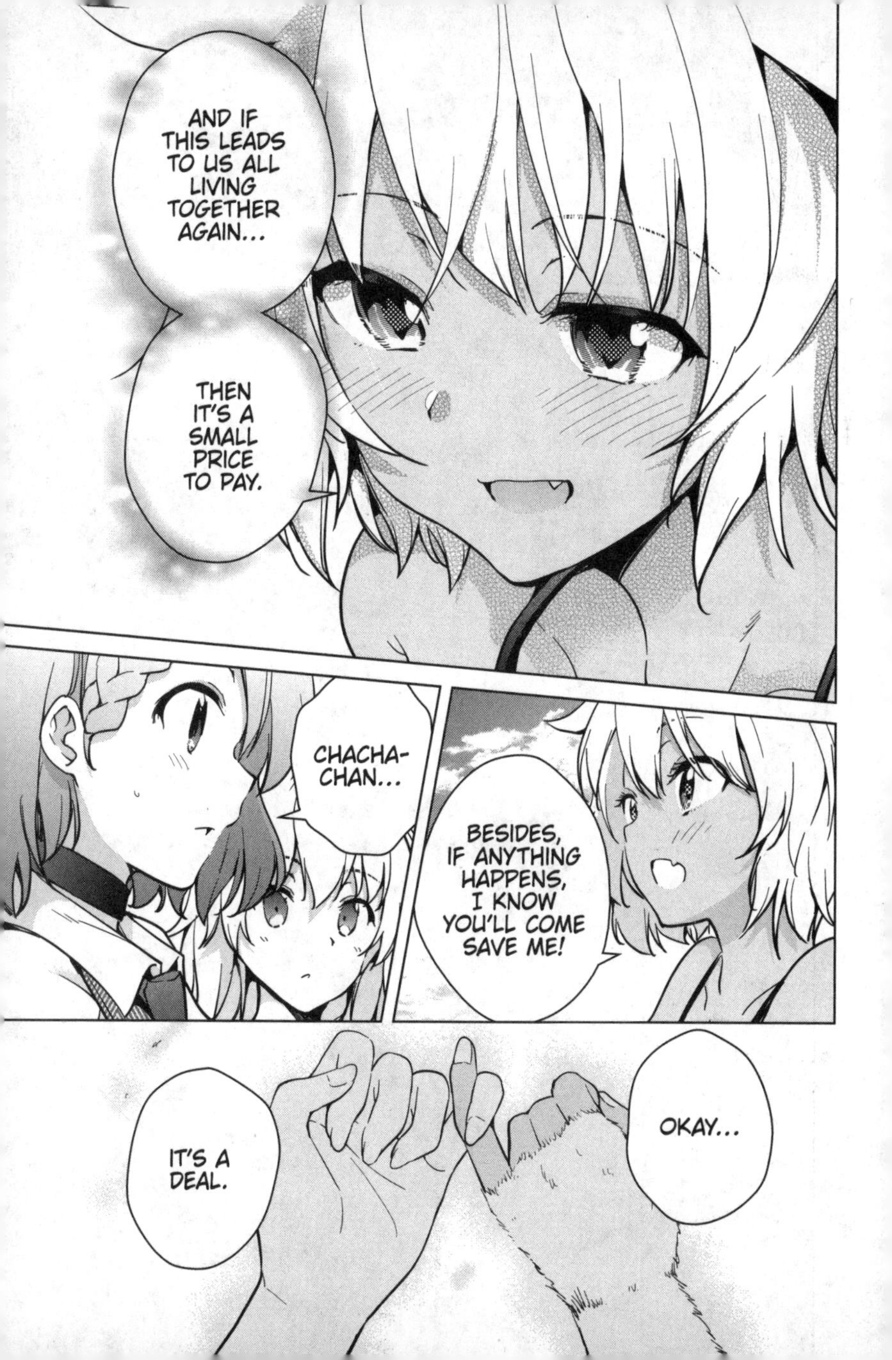
AND IF THIS LEADS TO US ALL LIVING TOGETHER AGAIN...
THEN IT'S A SMALL PRICE TO PAY.
BESIDES, IF ANYTHING HAPPENS, I KNOW YOU'LL COME SAVE ME!
CHACHA-CHAN...
OKAY...
IT'S A DEAL.

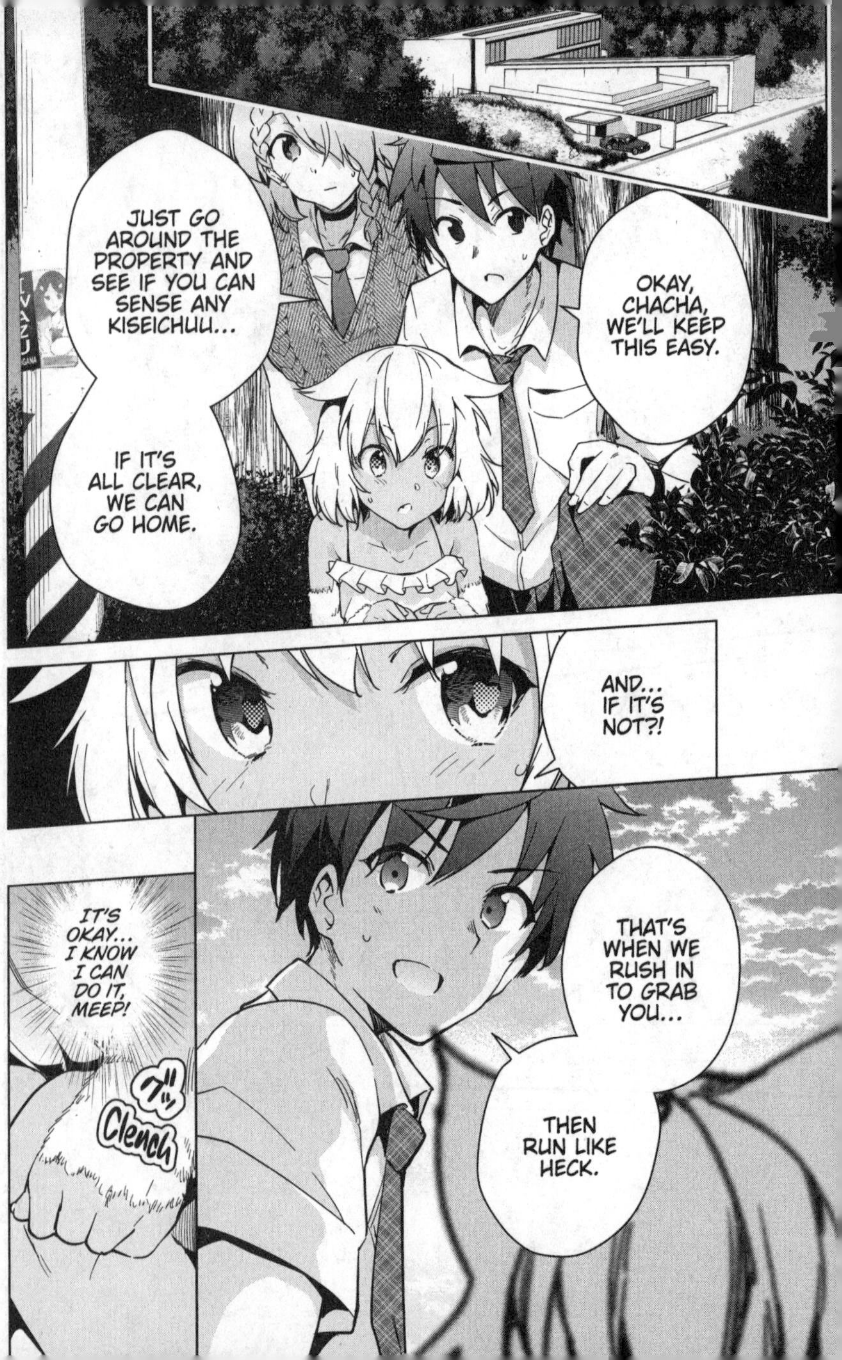
OKAY, CHACHA, WE'LL KEEP THIS EASY.
JUST GO AROUND THE PROPERTY AND SEE IF YOU CAN SENSE ANY KISEICHUU...
IF IT'S ALL CLEAR, WE CAN GO HOME.
AND... IF IT'S NOT?!
THAT'S WHEN WE RUSH IN TO GRAB YOU...
THEN RUN LIKE HECK.
IT'S OKAY... I KNOW I CAN DO IT, MEEP!
Clench

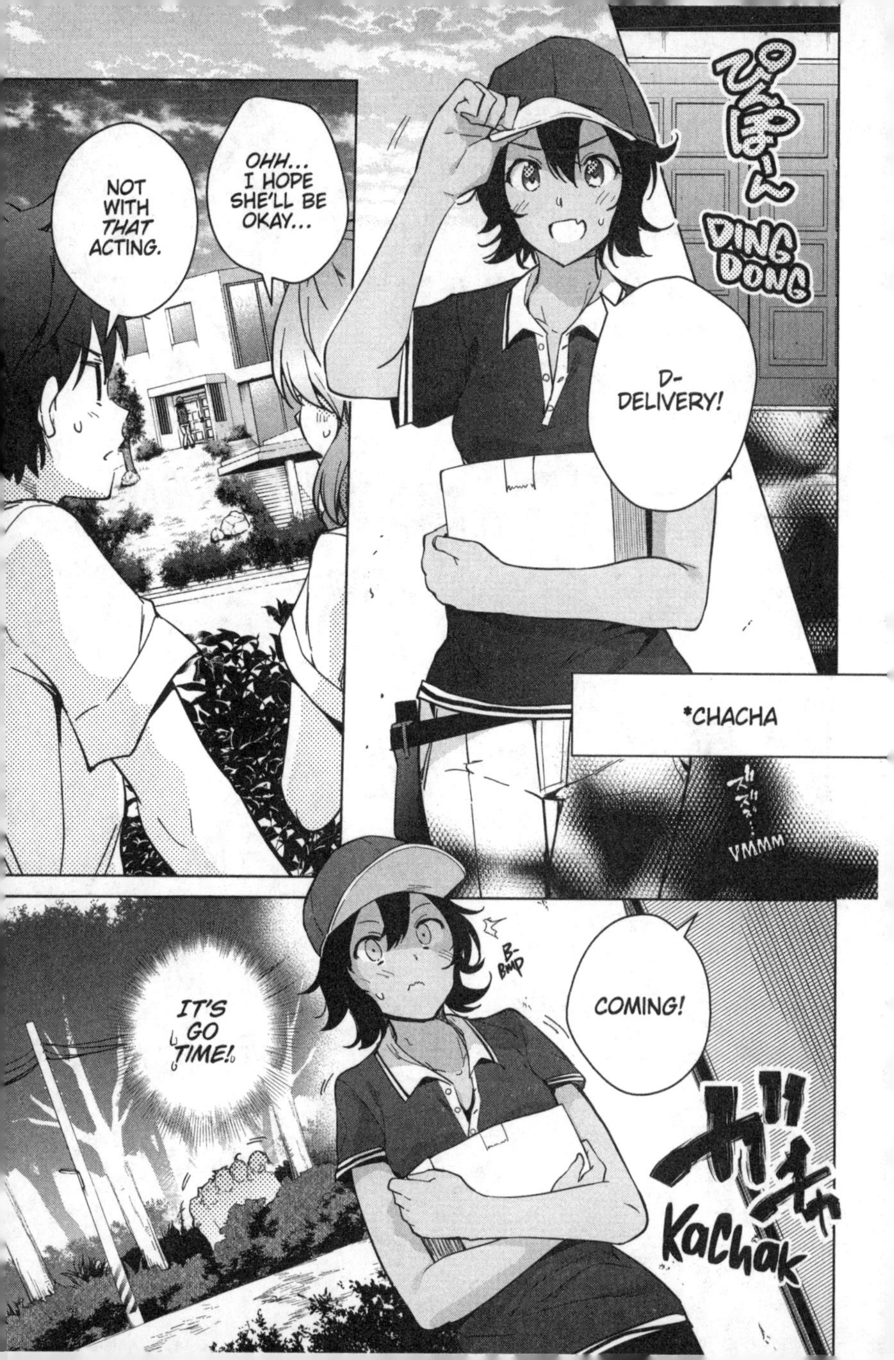
ぴんぽ〜ん
DING DONG
D-DELIVERY!
*CHACHA
VMMM
OHH... I HOPE SHE'LL BE OKAY...
NOT WITH *THAT* ACTING.
ガチャ
KaChak
COMING!
B-BMP
IT'S GO TIME!

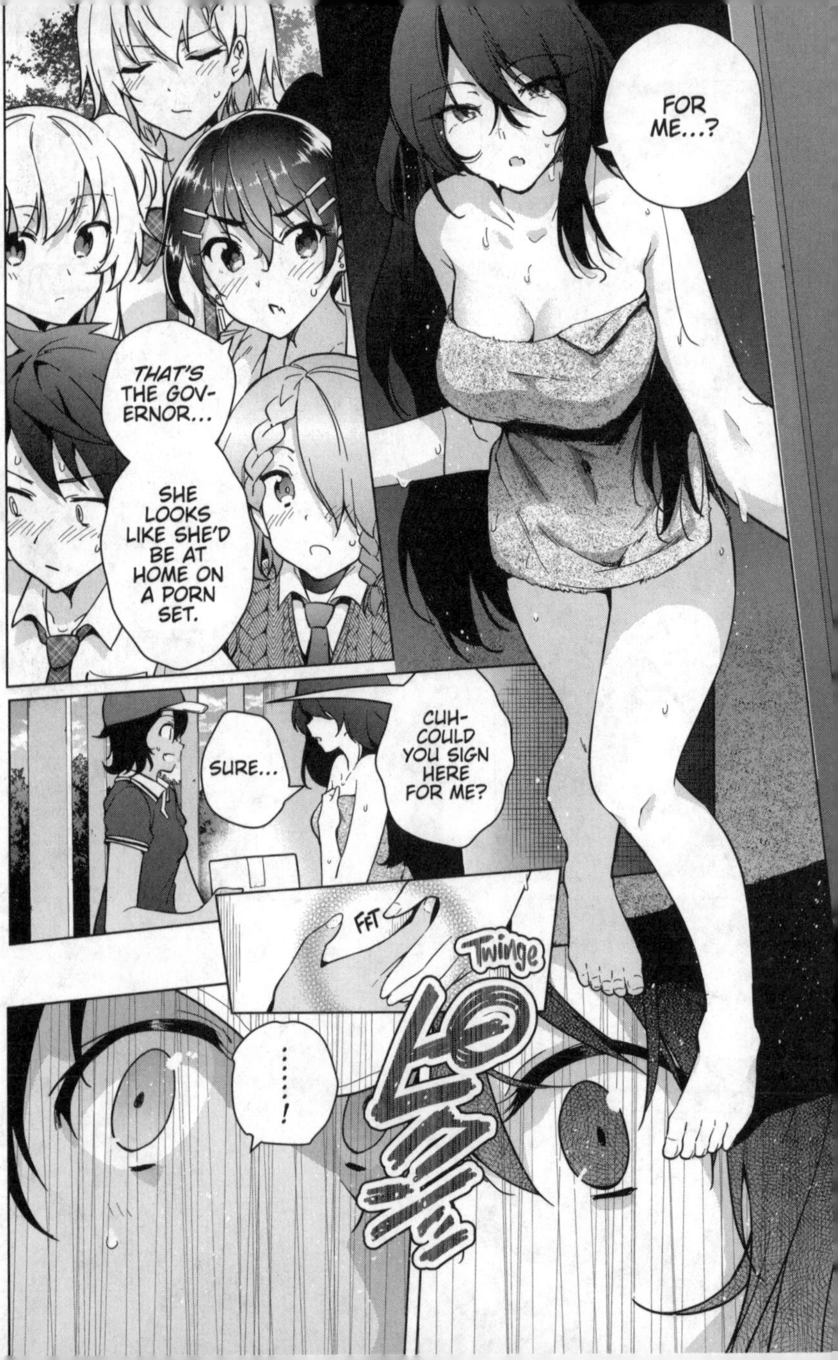
FOR ME...?
THAT'S THE GOV-ERNOR...
SHE LOOKS LIKE SHE'D BE AT HOME ON A PORN SET.
CUH-COULD YOU SIGN HERE FOR ME?
SURE...
FFT
Twinge
......!

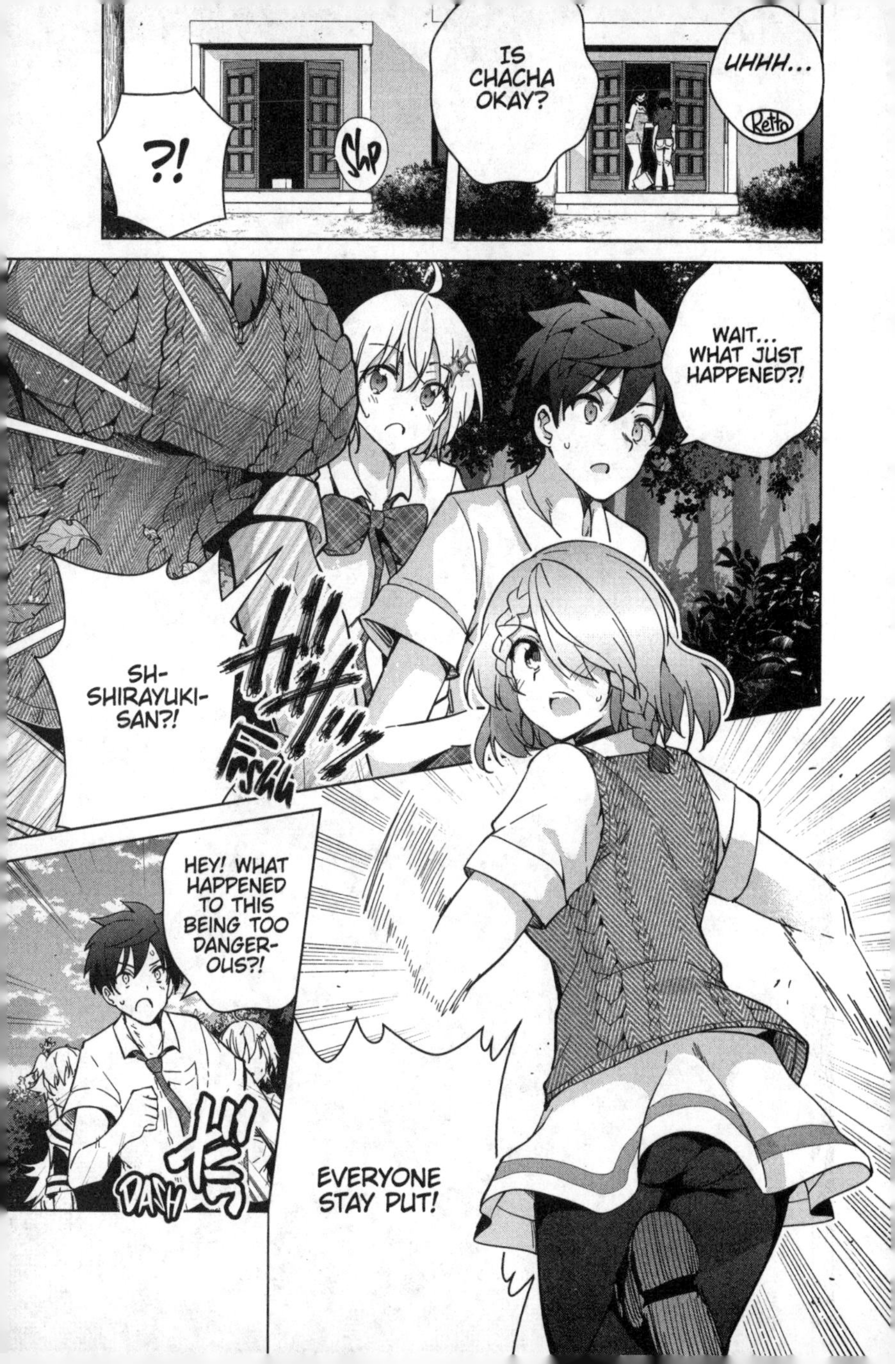
UHHH...
Retto
IS CHACHA OKAY?
Shp
?!
WAIT... WHAT JUST HAPPENED?!
SH-SHIRAYUKI-SAN?!
Frshu
EVERYONE STAY PUT!
HEY! WHAT HAPPENED TO THIS BEING TOO DANGEROUS?!
DASH

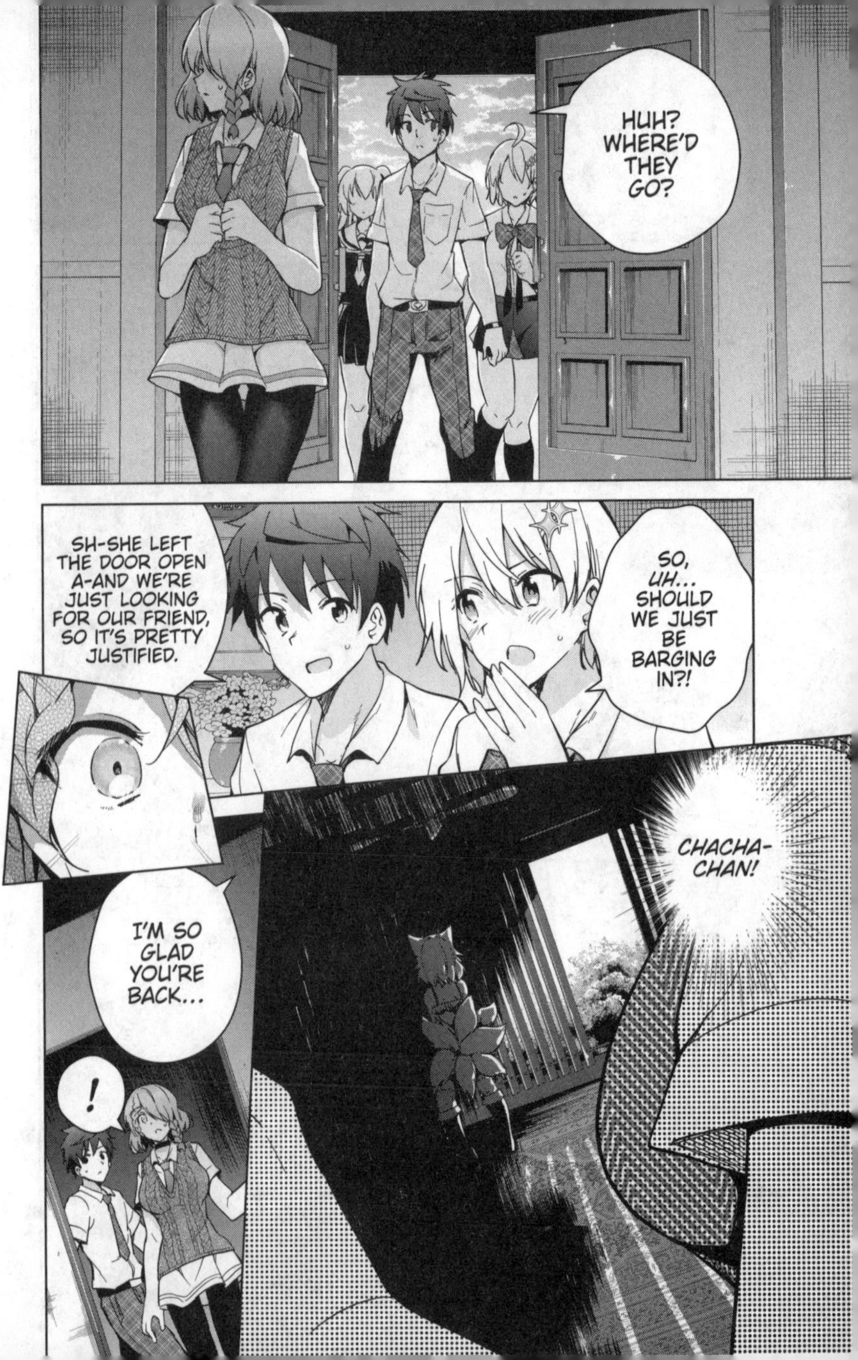
HUH? WHERE'D THEY GO?
SO, UH... SHOULD WE JUST BE BARGING IN?!
SH-SHE LEFT THE DOOR OPEN A-AND WE'RE JUST LOOKING FOR OUR FRIEND, SO IT'S PRETTY JUSTIFIED.
CHACHA-CHAN!
I'M SO GLAD YOU'RE BACK...
!

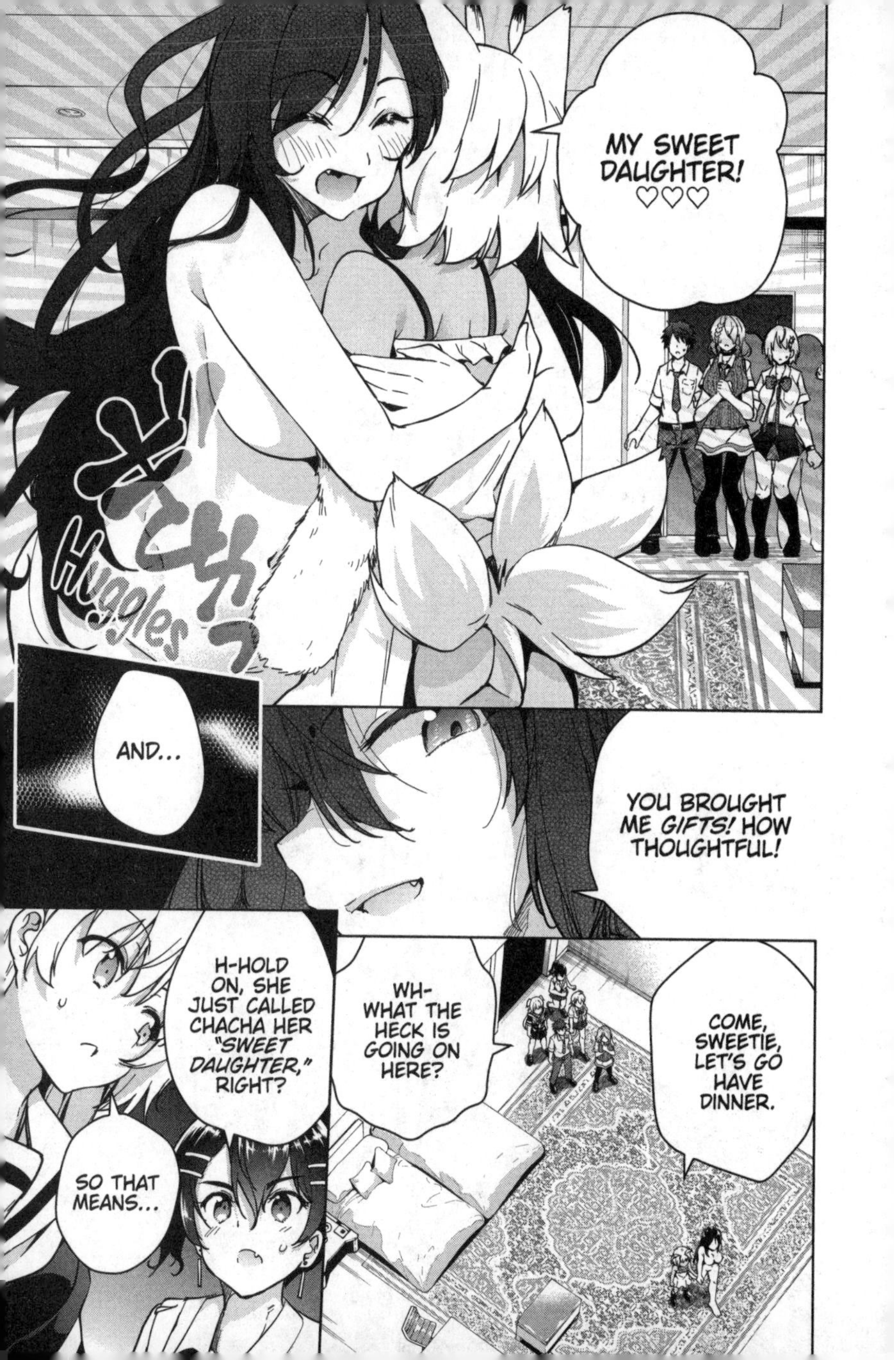
MY SWEET DAUGHTER! ♡♡♡
Huggles
AND...
YOU BROUGHT ME *GIFTS!* HOW THOUGHTFUL!
COME, SWEETIE, LET'S GO HAVE DINNER.
WH-WHAT THE HECK IS GOING ON HERE?
H-HOLD ON, SHE JUST CALLED CHACHA HER "*SWEET DAUGHTER,*" RIGHT?
SO THAT MEANS...

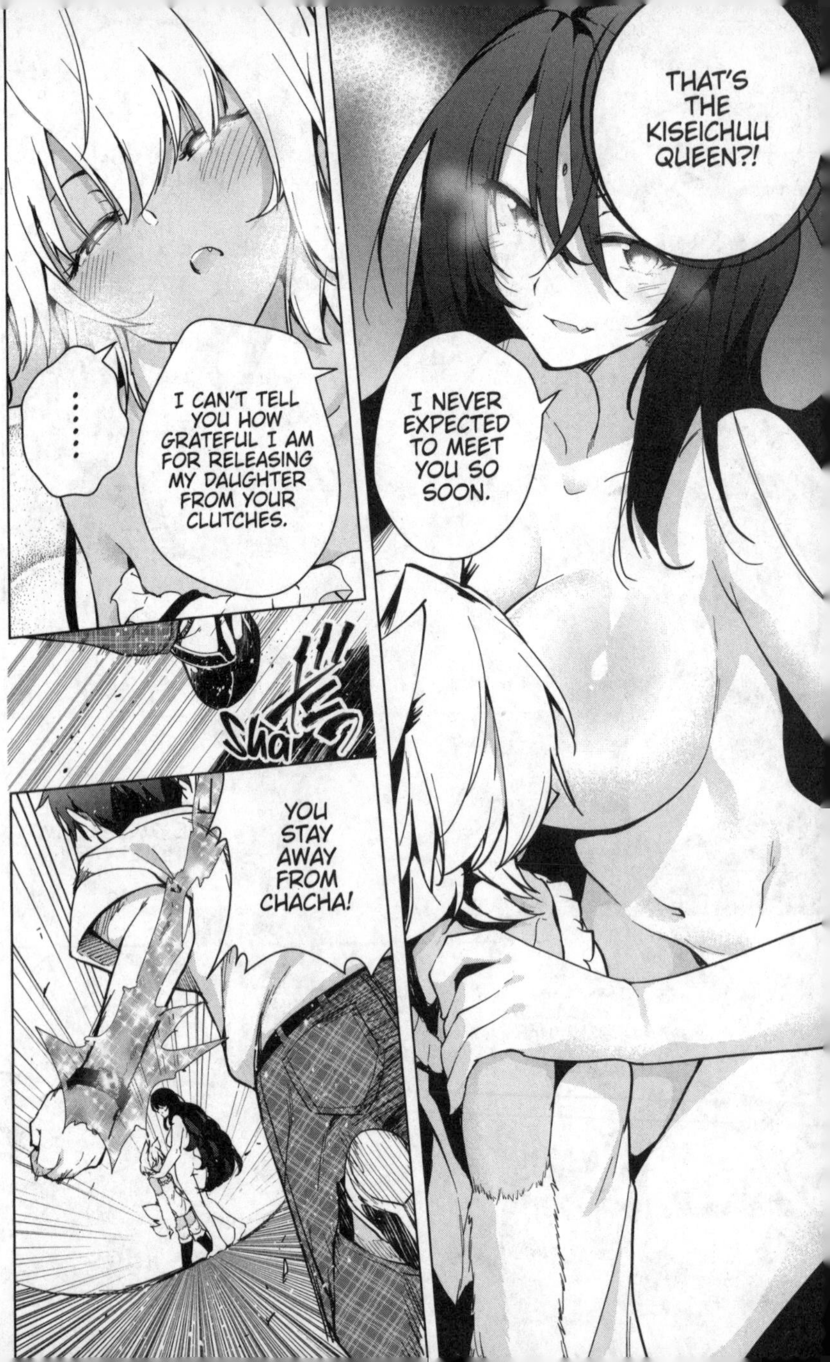
THAT'S THE KISEICHUU QUEEN?!
I NEVER EXPECTED TO MEET YOU SO SOON.
I CAN'T TELL YOU HOW GRATEFUL I AM FOR RELEASING MY DAUGHTER FROM YOUR CLUTCHES.
......
YOU STAY AWAY FROM CHACHA!

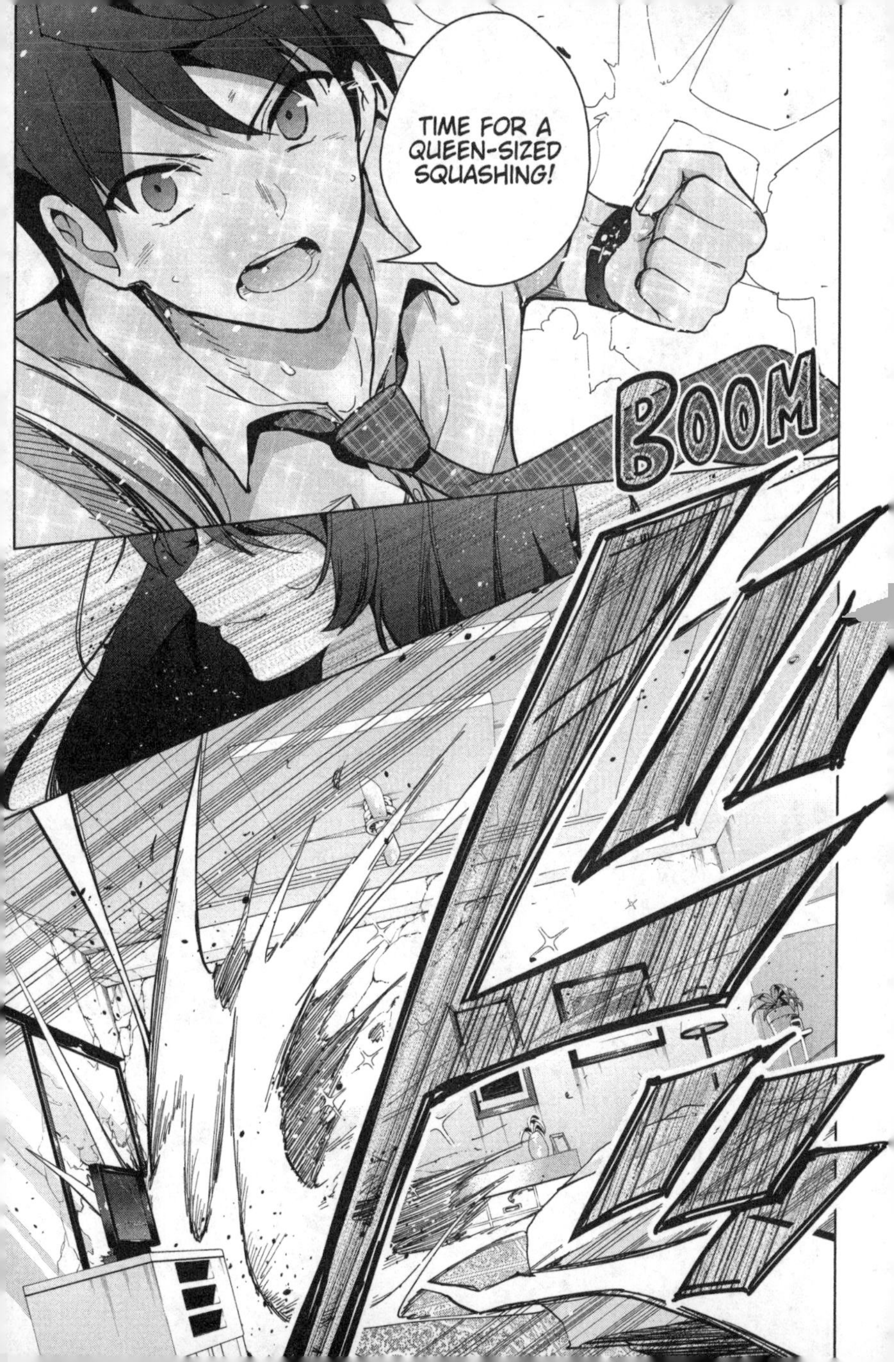
TIME FOR A QUEEN-SIZED SQUASHING!
BOOM

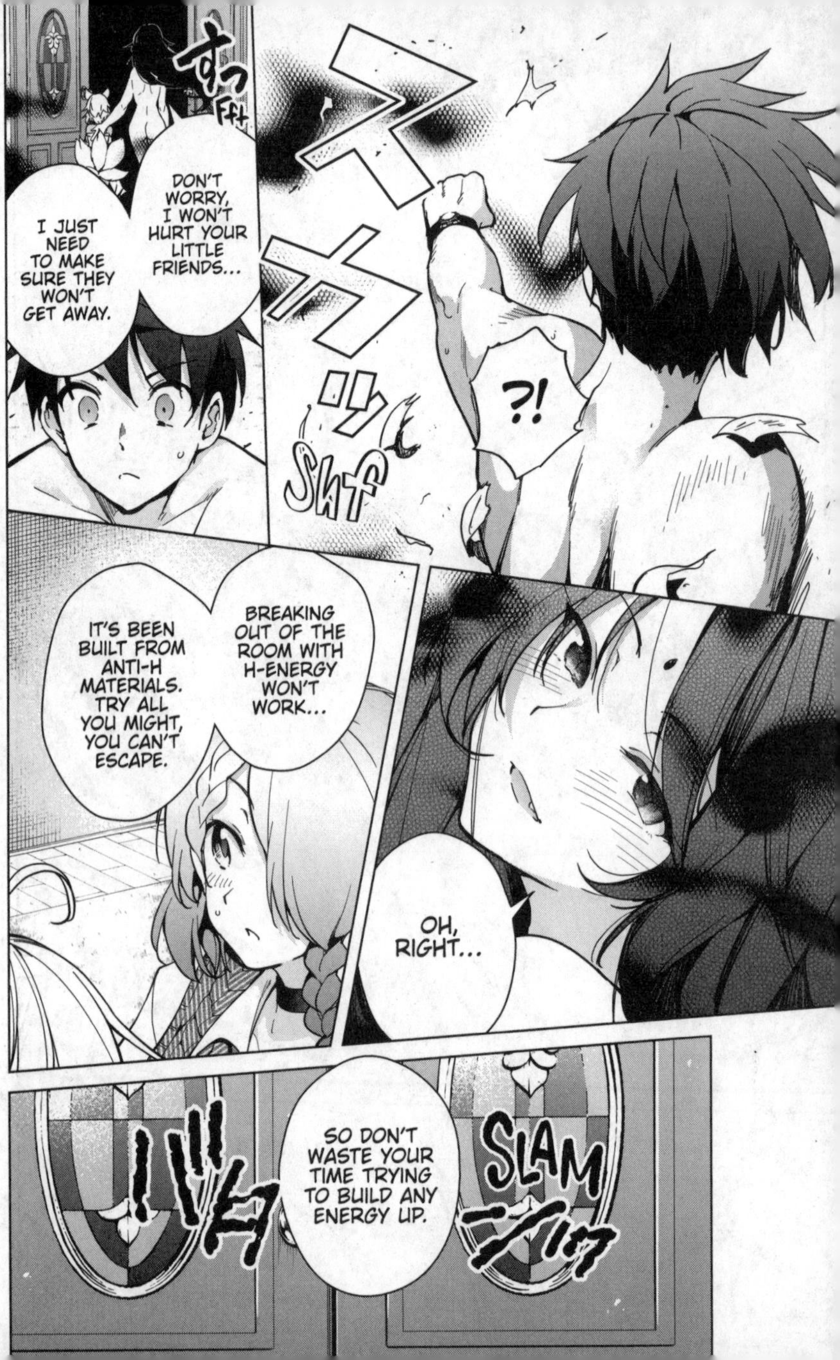
?!
Shf
すっ
Fft
DON'T WORRY, I WON'T HURT YOUR LITTLE FRIENDS...
I JUST NEED TO MAKE SURE THEY WON'T GET AWAY.
OH, RIGHT...
BREAKING OUT OF THE ROOM WITH H-ENERGY WON'T WORK...
IT'S BEEN BUILT FROM ANTI-H MATERIALS. TRY ALL YOU MIGHT, YOU CAN'T ESCAPE.
SLAM
SO DON'T WASTE YOUR TIME TRYING TO BUILD ANY ENERGY UP.

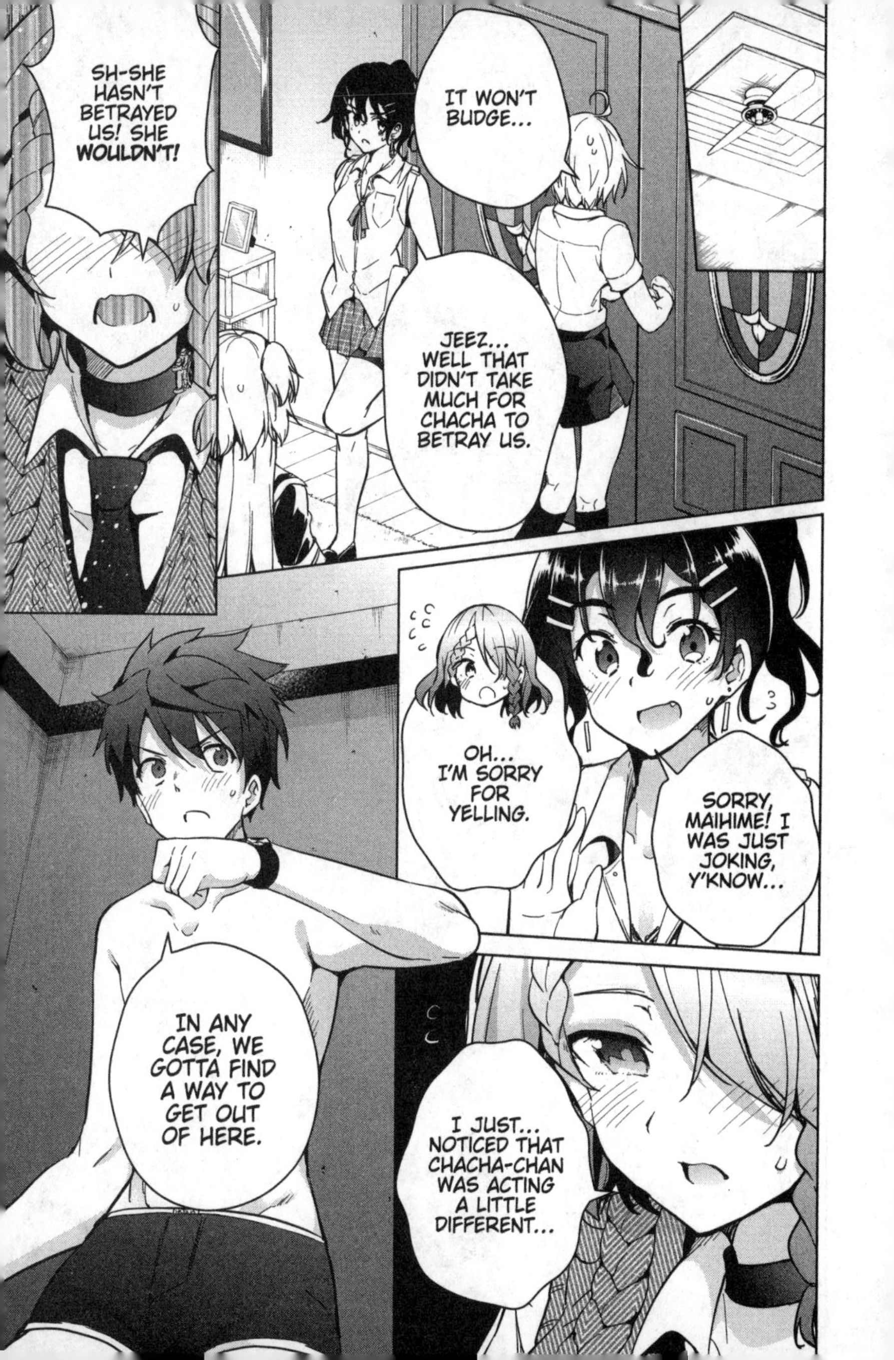
IT WON'T BUDGE...
JEEZ... WELL THAT DIDN'T TAKE MUCH FOR CHACHA TO BETRAY US.
SH-SHE HASN'T BETRAYED US! SHE WOULDN'T!
SORRY, MAIHIME! I WAS JUST JOKING, Y'KNOW...
OH... I'M SORRY FOR YELLING.
I JUST... NOTICED THAT CHACHA-CHAN WAS ACTING A LITTLE DIFFERENT...
IN ANY CASE, WE GOTTA FIND A WAY TO GET OUT OF HERE.

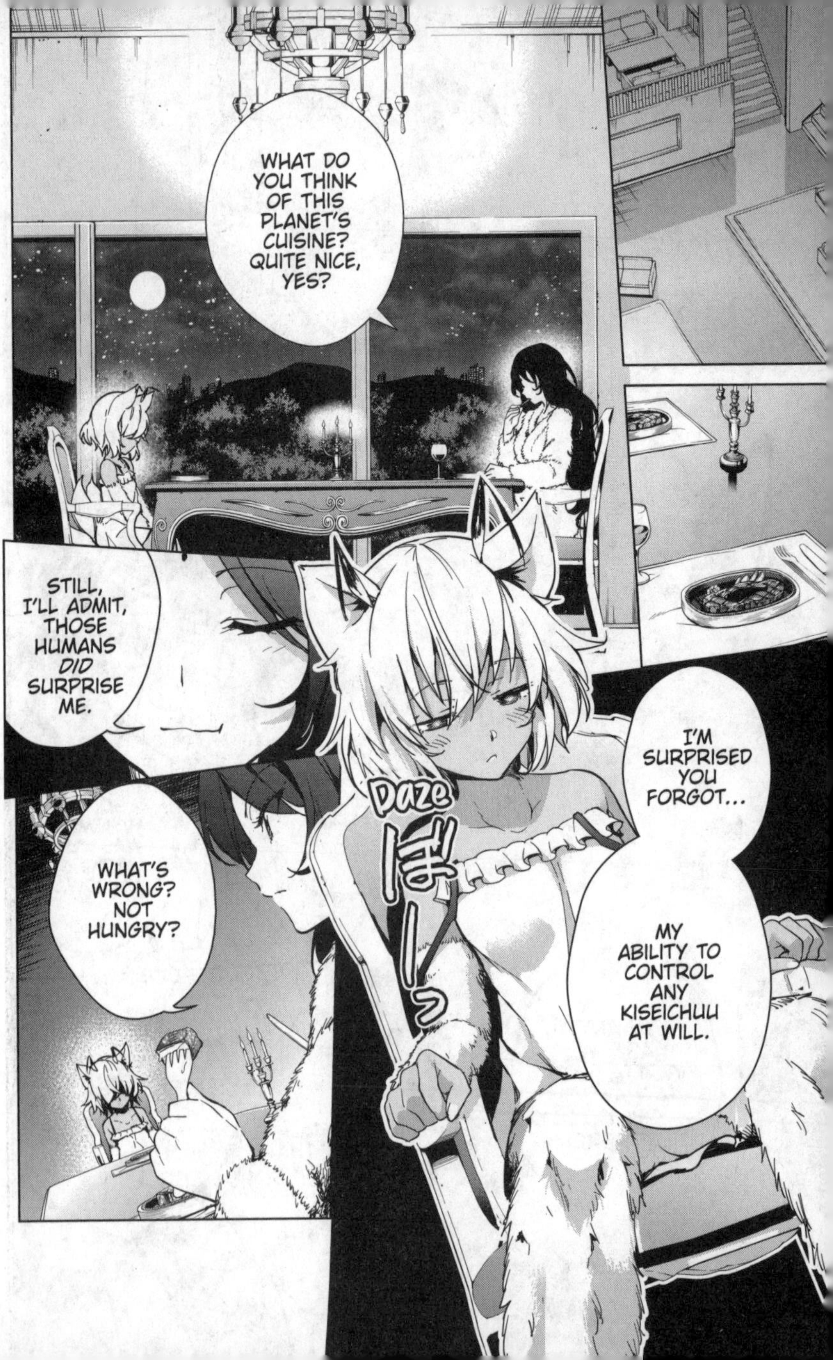
WHAT DO YOU THINK OF THIS PLANET'S CUISINE? QUITE NICE, YES?
DAZE
I'M SURPRISED YOU FORGOT...
MY ABILITY TO CONTROL ANY KISEICHUU AT WILL.
STILL, I'LL ADMIT, THOSE HUMANS *DID* SURPRISE ME.
WHAT'S WRONG? NOT HUNGRY?

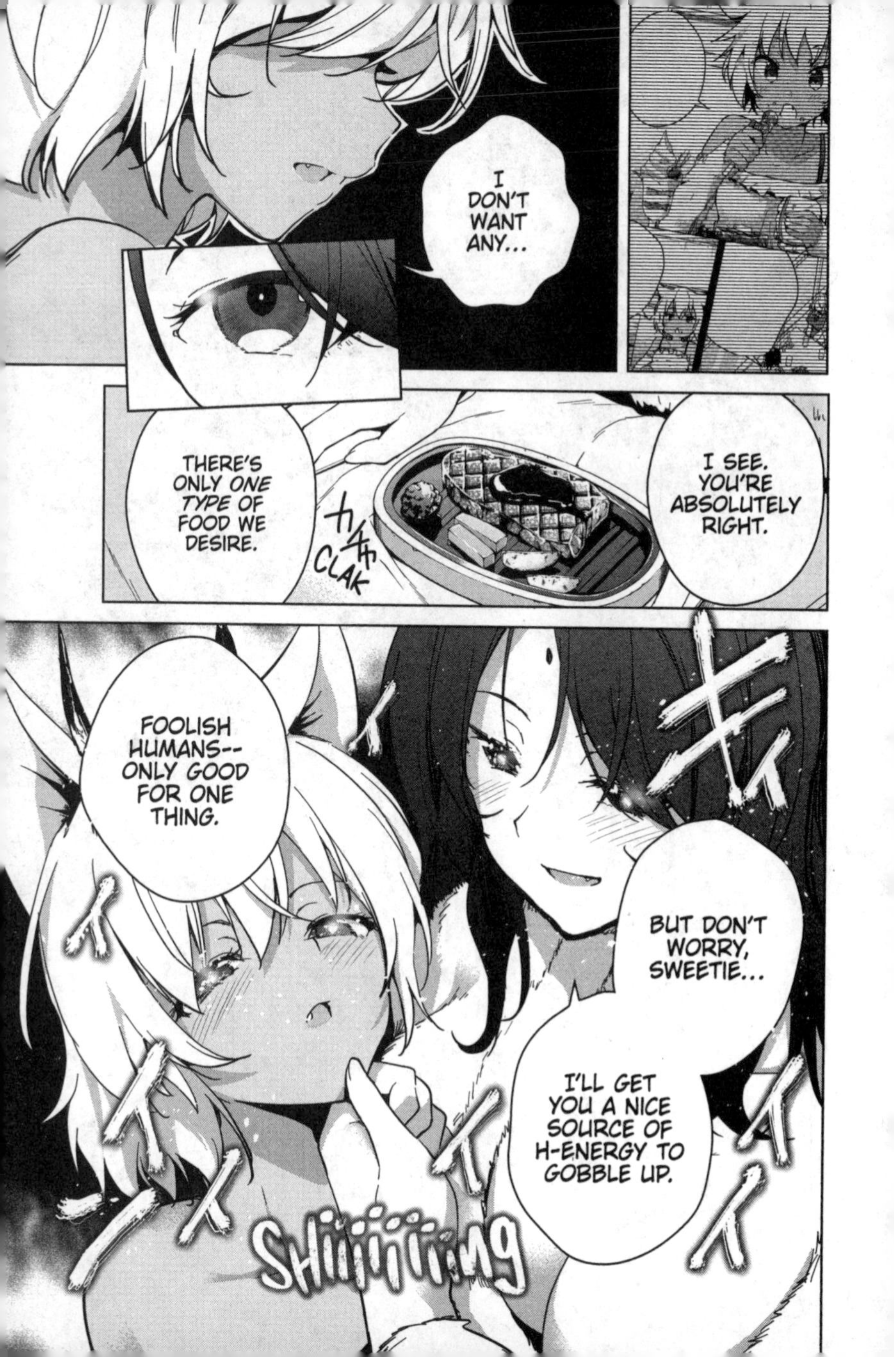

I DON'T WANT ANY...
I SEE. YOU'RE ABSOLUTELY RIGHT.
CLAK
THERE'S ONLY *ONE TYPE* OF FOOD WE DESIRE.
FOOLISH HUMANS-- ONLY GOOD FOR ONE THING.
BUT DON'T WORRY, SWEETIE...
I'LL GET YOU A NICE SOURCE OF H-ENERGY TO GOBBLE UP.
SHIIIIIIING

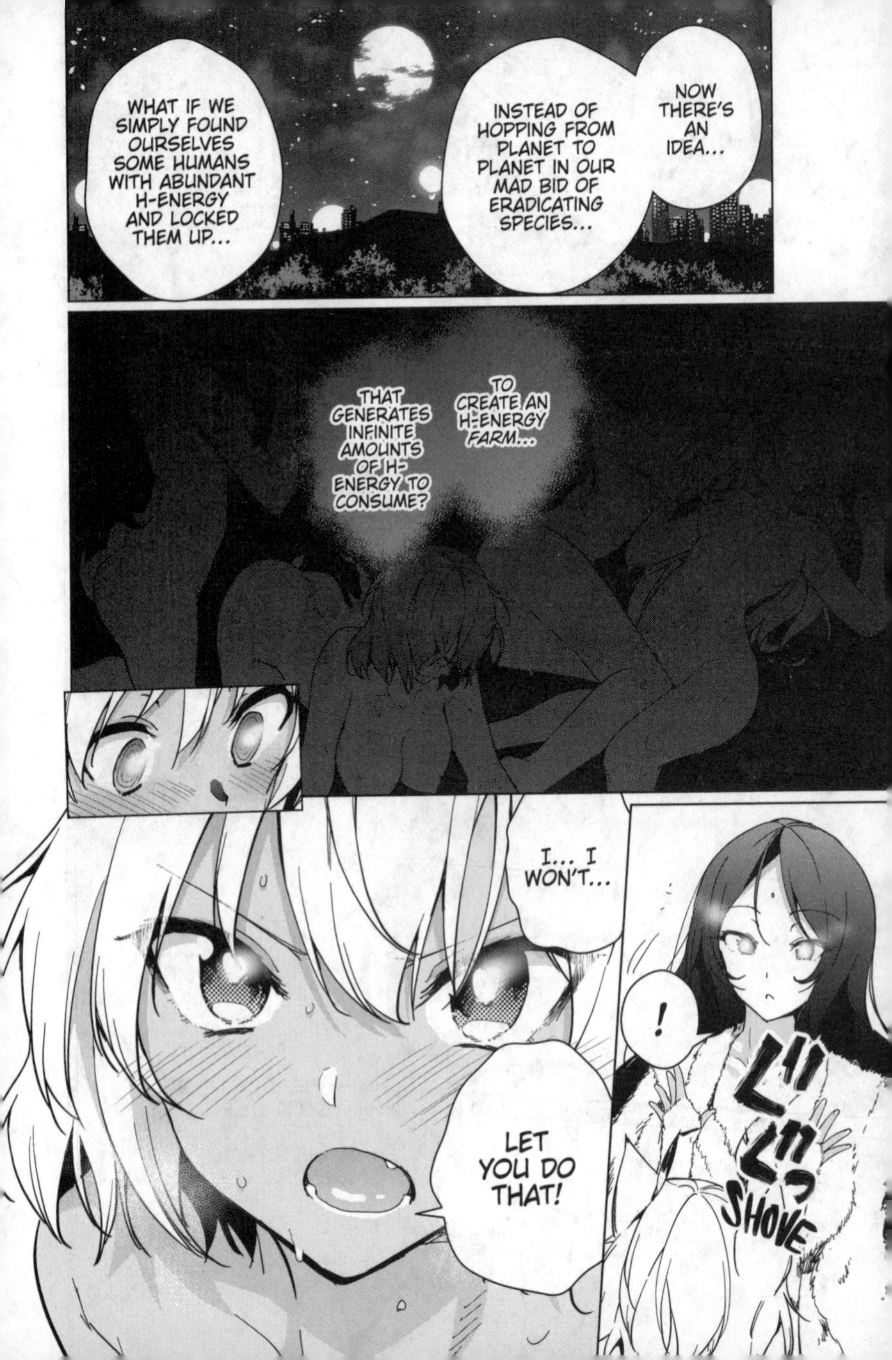
NOW THERE'S AN IDEA...
INSTEAD OF HOPPING FROM PLANET TO PLANET IN OUR MAD BID OF ERADICATING SPECIES...
WHAT IF WE SIMPLY FOUND OURSELVES SOME HUMANS WITH ABUNDANT H-ENERGY AND LOCKED THEM UP...
TO CREATE AN H-ENERGY FARM...
THAT GENERATES INFINITE AMOUNTS OF H-ENERGY TO CONSUME?
I... I WON'T...
!
LET YOU DO THAT!
SHOVE

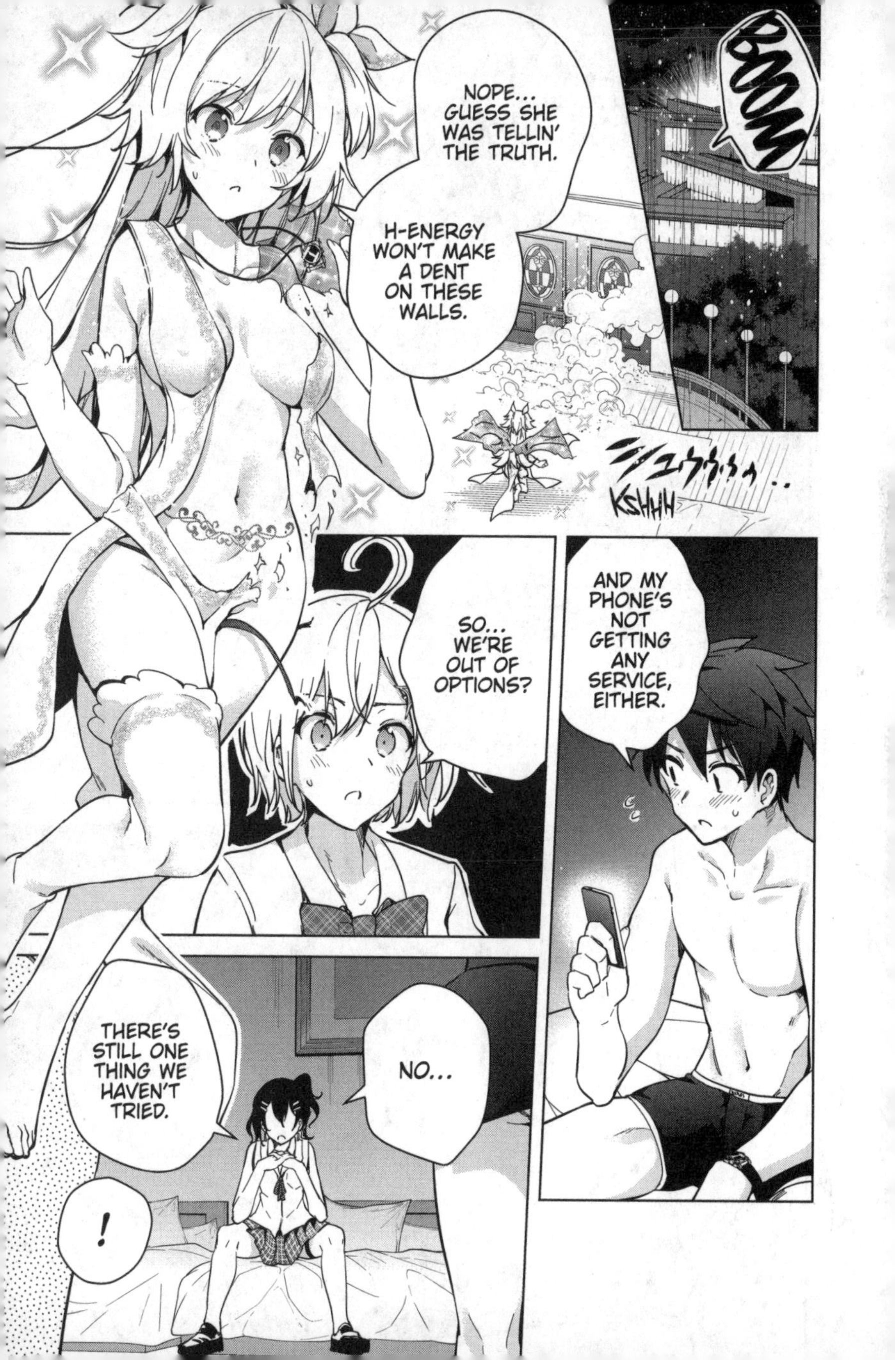
BOOM
KSHHH
NOPE... GUESS SHE WAS TELLIN' THE TRUTH.
H-ENERGY WON'T MAKE A DENT ON THESE WALLS.
AND MY PHONE'S NOT GETTING ANY SERVICE, EITHER.
SO... WE'RE OUT OF OPTIONS?
NO...
THERE'S STILL ONE THING WE HAVEN'T TRIED.
!

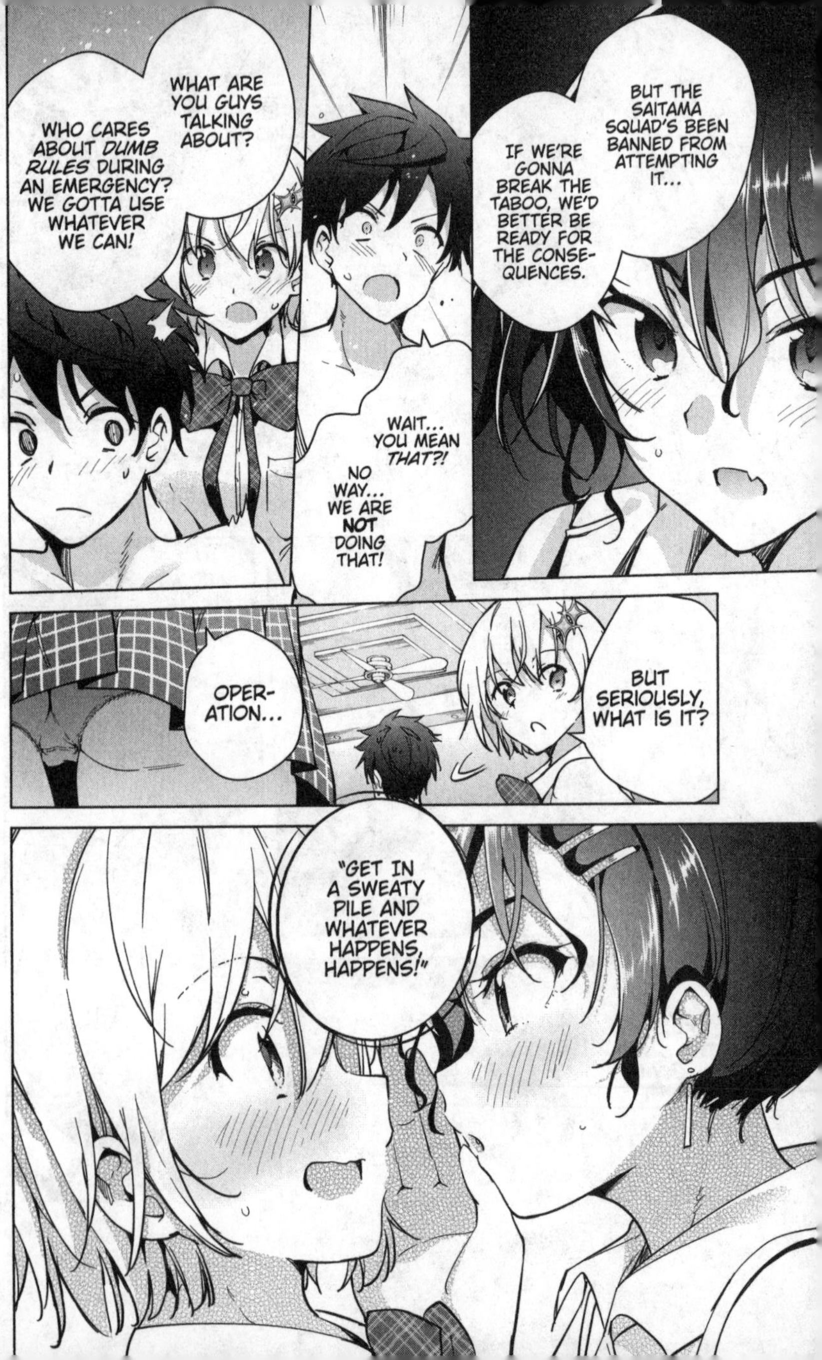
BUT THE SAITAMA SQUAD'S BEEN BANNED FROM ATTEMPTING IT...
IF WE'RE GONNA BREAK THE TABOO, WE'D BETTER BE READY FOR THE CONSE-QUENCES.
WAIT... YOU MEAN *THAT*?!
NO WAY... WE ARE **NOT** DOING THAT!
WHAT ARE YOU GUYS TALKING ABOUT?
WHO CARES ABOUT *DUMB RULES* DURING AN EMERGENCY? WE GOTTA USE WHATEVER WE CAN!
BUT SERIOUSLY, WHAT IS IT?
OPER-ATION...
"GET IN A SWEATY PILE AND WHATEVER HAPPENS, HAPPENS!"

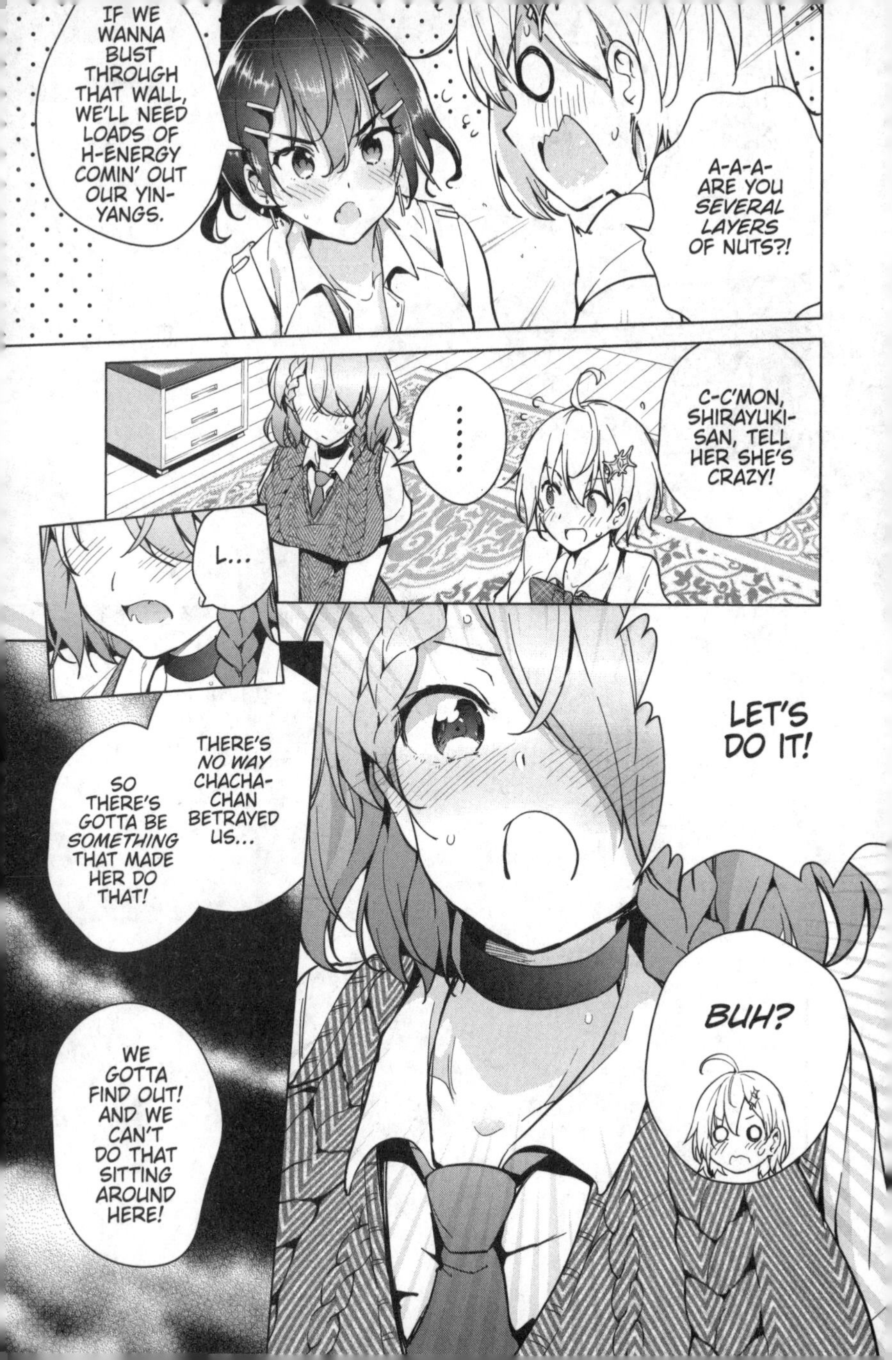
A-A-A-ARE YOU SEVERAL LAYERS OF NUTS?!
IF WE WANNA BUST THROUGH THAT WALL, WE'LL NEED LOADS OF H-ENERGY COMIN' OUT OUR YIN-YANGS.
C-C'MON, SHIRAYUKI-SAN, TELL HER SHE'S CRAZY!
......
L...
LET'S DO IT!
BUH?
THERE'S NO WAY CHACHA-CHAN BETRAYED US...
SO THERE'S GOTTA BE SOMETHING THAT MADE HER DO THAT!
WE GOTTA FIND OUT! AND WE CAN'T DO THAT SITTING AROUND HERE!

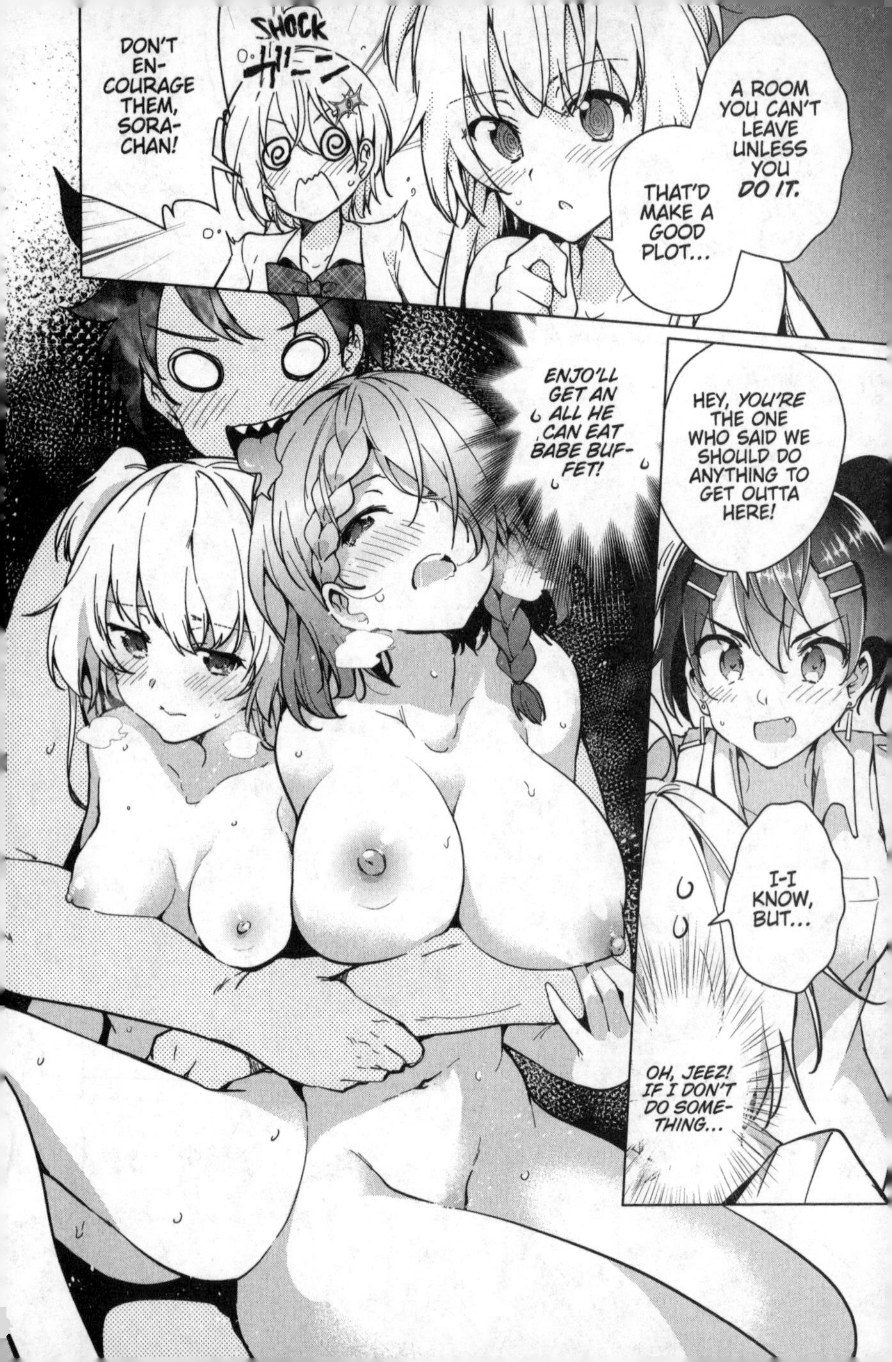
A ROOM YOU CAN'T LEAVE UNLESS YOU *DO IT.*
THAT'D MAKE A GOOD PLOT...
SHOCK
DON'T EN-COURAGE THEM, SORA-CHAN!
HEY, *YOU'RE* THE ONE WHO SAID WE SHOULD DO ANYTHING TO GET OUTTA HERE!
I-I KNOW, BUT...
OH, JEEZ! IF I DON'T DO SOME-THING...
ENJO'LL GET AN ALL HE CAN EAT BABE BUF-FET!

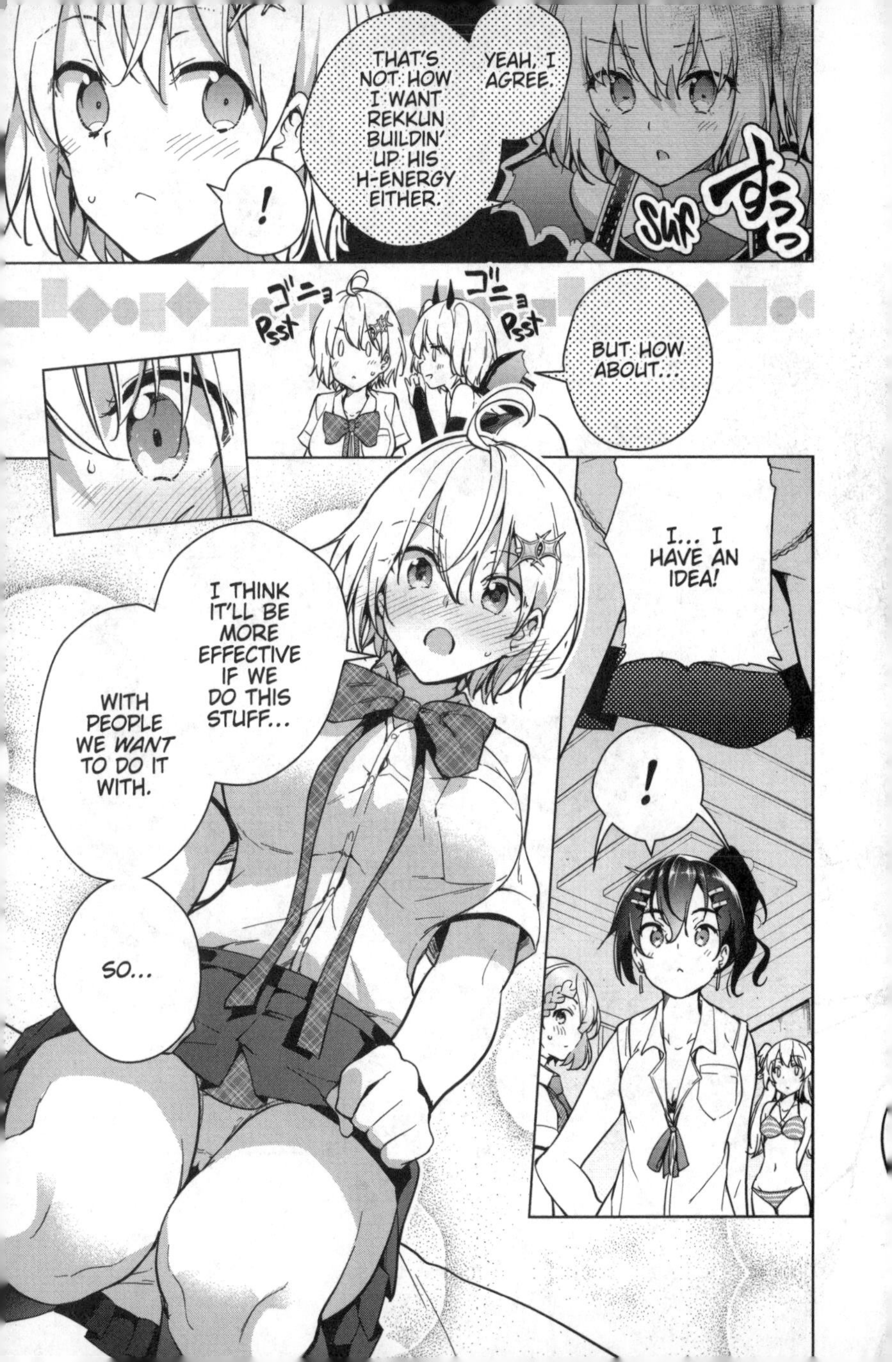
YEAH, I AGREE.
THAT'S NOT HOW I WANT REKKUN BUILDIN' UP HIS H-ENERGY EITHER.
すっ
Suf
!
ゴニョ
Psst
ゴニョ
Psst
BUT HOW ABOUT...
I... I HAVE AN IDEA!
!
I THINK IT'LL BE MORE EFFECTIVE IF WE DO THIS STUFF...
WITH PEOPLE WE *WANT* TO DO IT WITH.
SO...

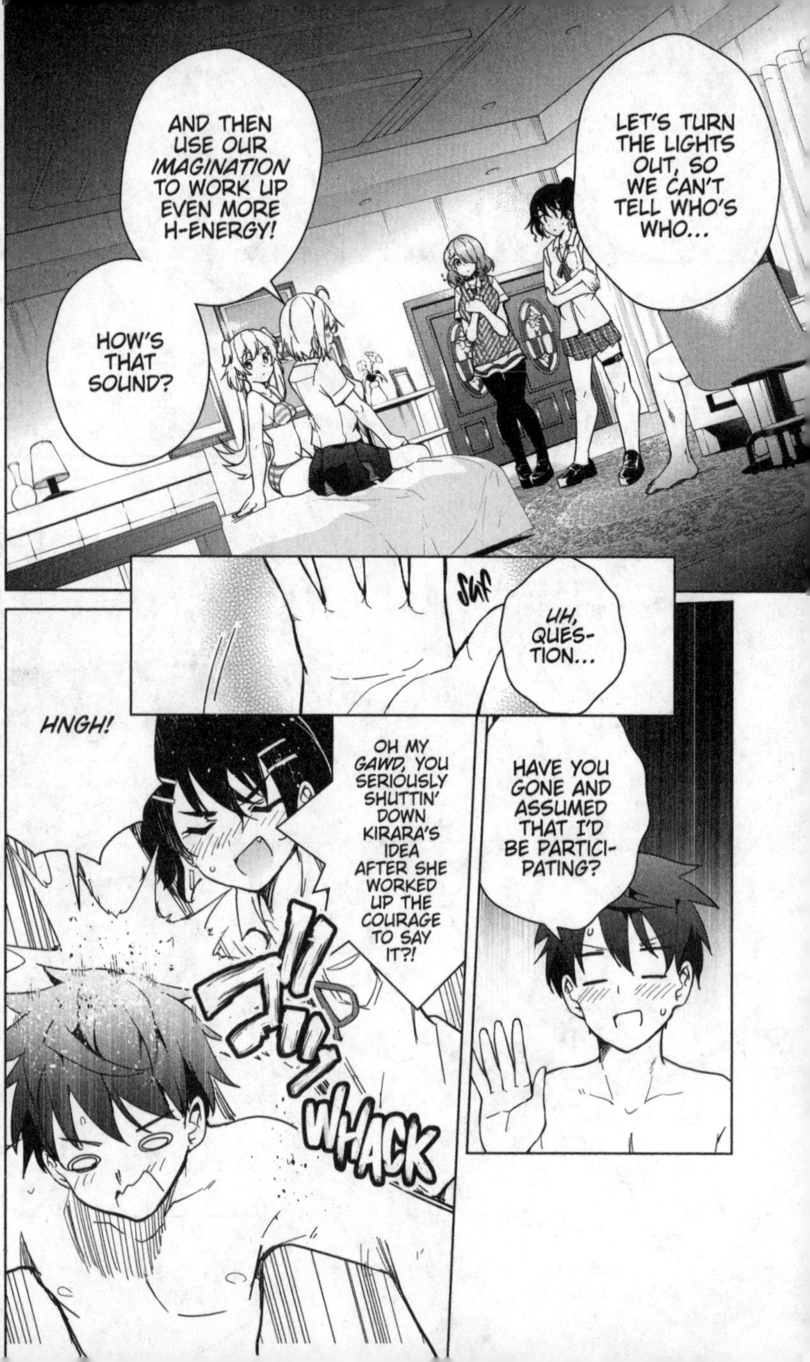
LET'S TURN THE LIGHTS OUT, SO WE CAN'T TELL WHO'S WHO...
AND THEN USE OUR IMAGINATION TO WORK UP EVEN MORE H-ENERGY!
HOW'S THAT SOUND?
SUF
UH, QUESTION...
HAVE YOU GONE AND ASSUMED THAT I'D BE PARTICIPATING?
OH MY GAWD, YOU SERIOUSLY SHUTTIN' DOWN KIRARA'S IDEA AFTER SHE WORKED UP THE COURAGE TO SAY IT?!
HNGH!
WHACK

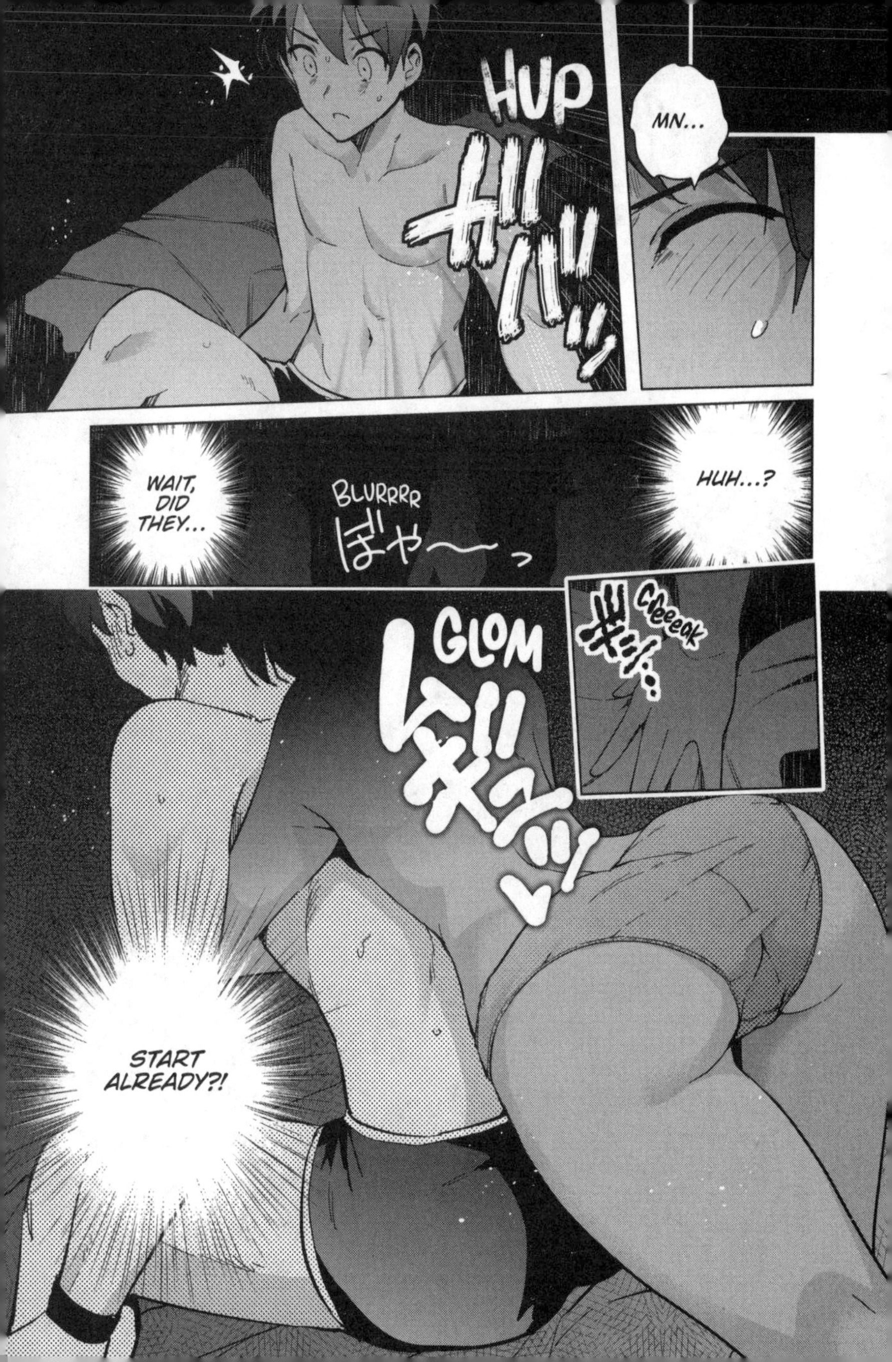
MN...
HUP
HUH...?
BLURRRR
ぼや〜〜っ
WAIT, DID THEY...
Creeeak
GLOM
START ALREADY?!

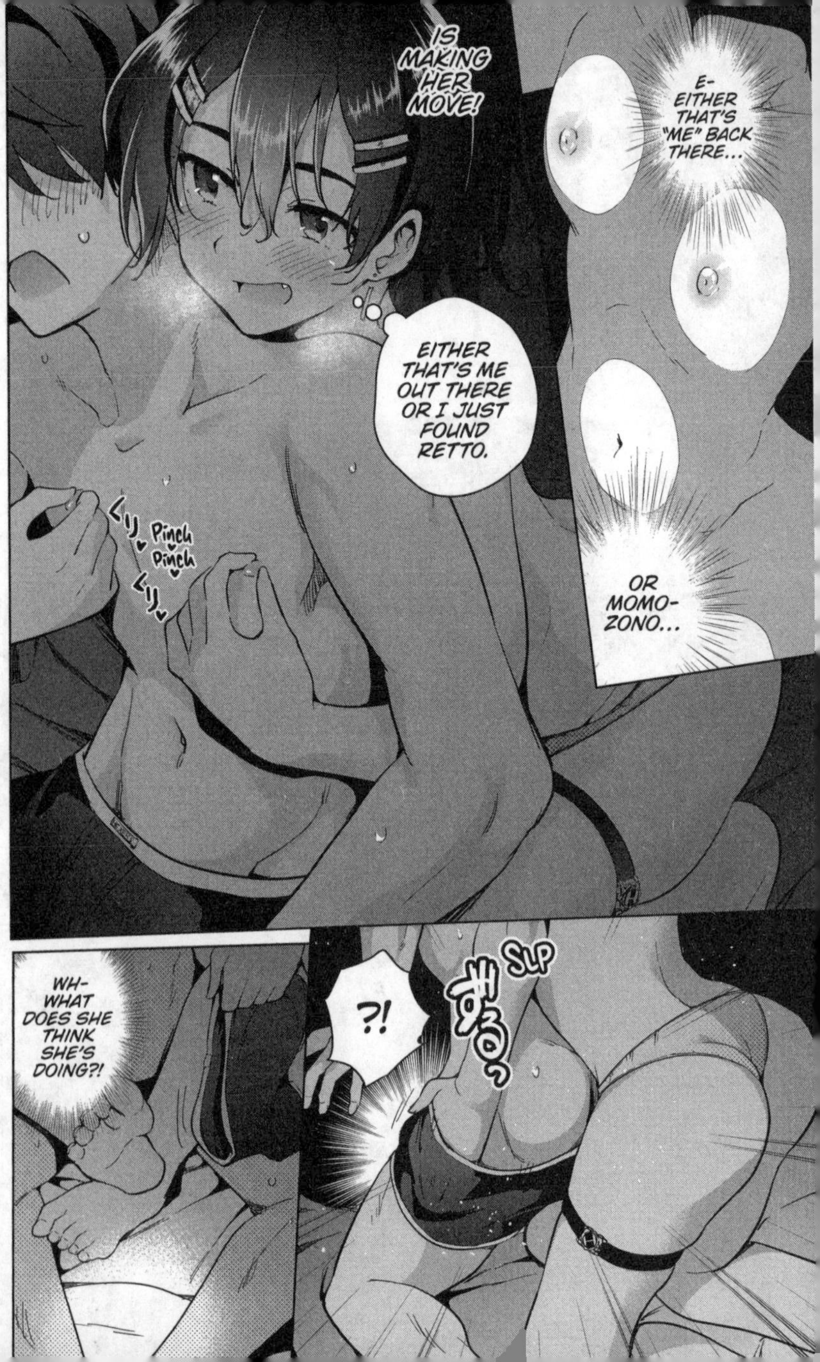
E-EITHER THAT'S "ME" BACK THERE...
OR MOMOZONO...
IS MAKING HER MOVE!
EITHER THAT'S ME OUT THERE OR I JUST FOUND RETTO.
Pinch Pinch
SLP
するっ
?!
WH-WHAT DOES SHE THINK SHE'S DOING?!

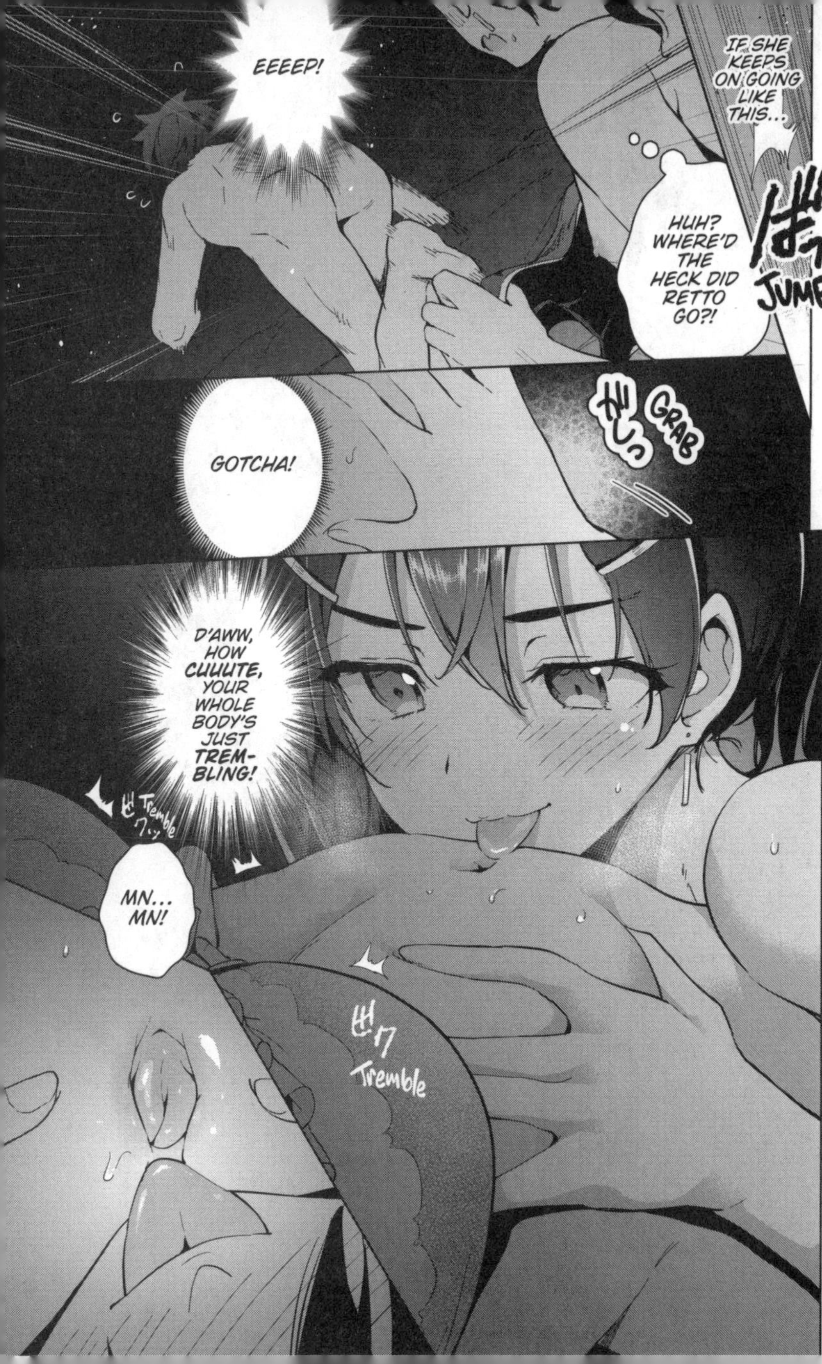
IF SHE KEEPS ON GOING LIKE THIS…
ぱっ JUMP
HUH? WHERE'D THE HECK DID RETTO GO?!
EEEEP!
がしっ GRAB
GOTCHA!
D'AWW, HOW CUUUTE, YOUR WHOLE BODY'S JUST TREMBLING!
Tremble
MN… MN!
Tremble

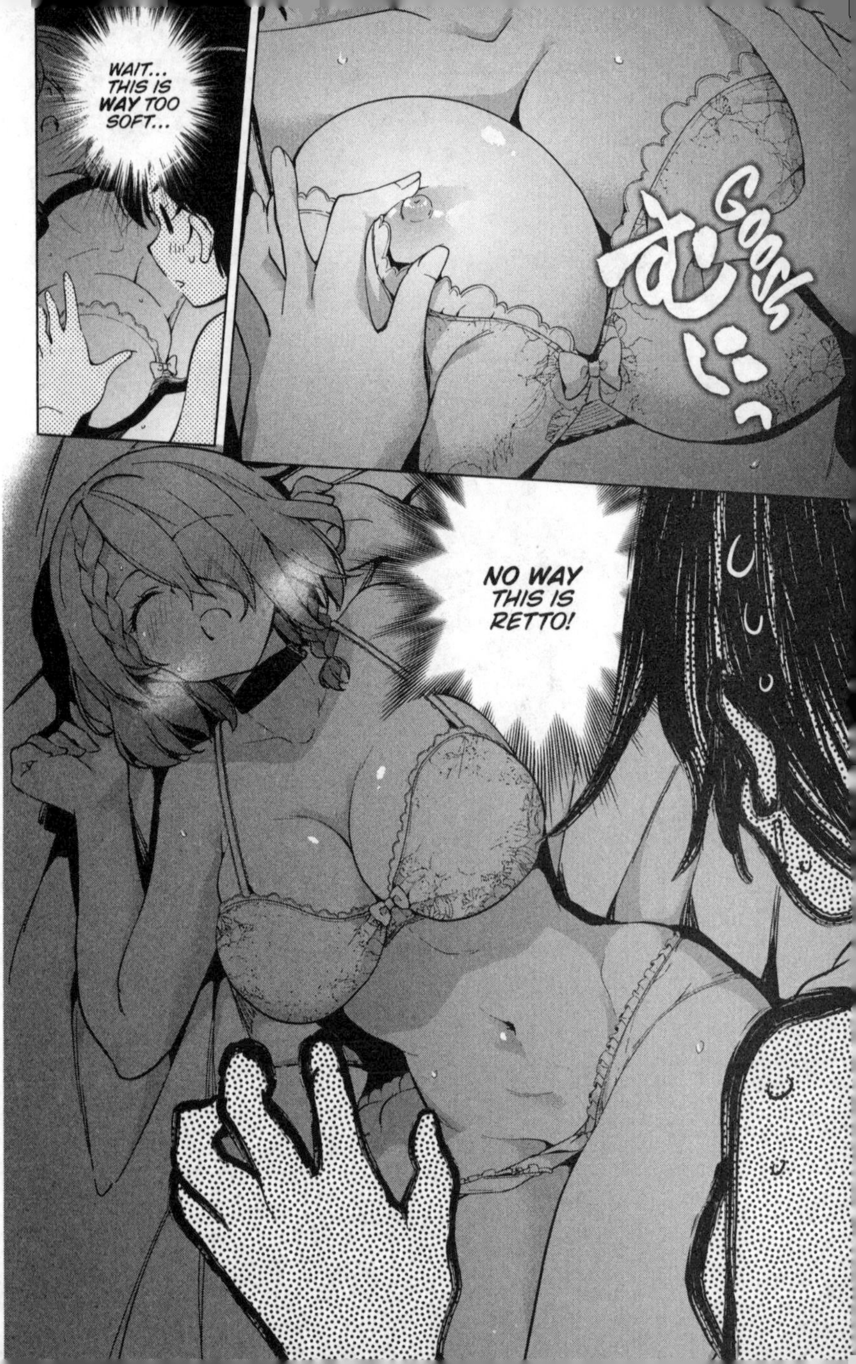
Goosh
むにっ
WAIT... THIS IS WAY TOO SOFT...
NO WAY THIS IS RETTO!

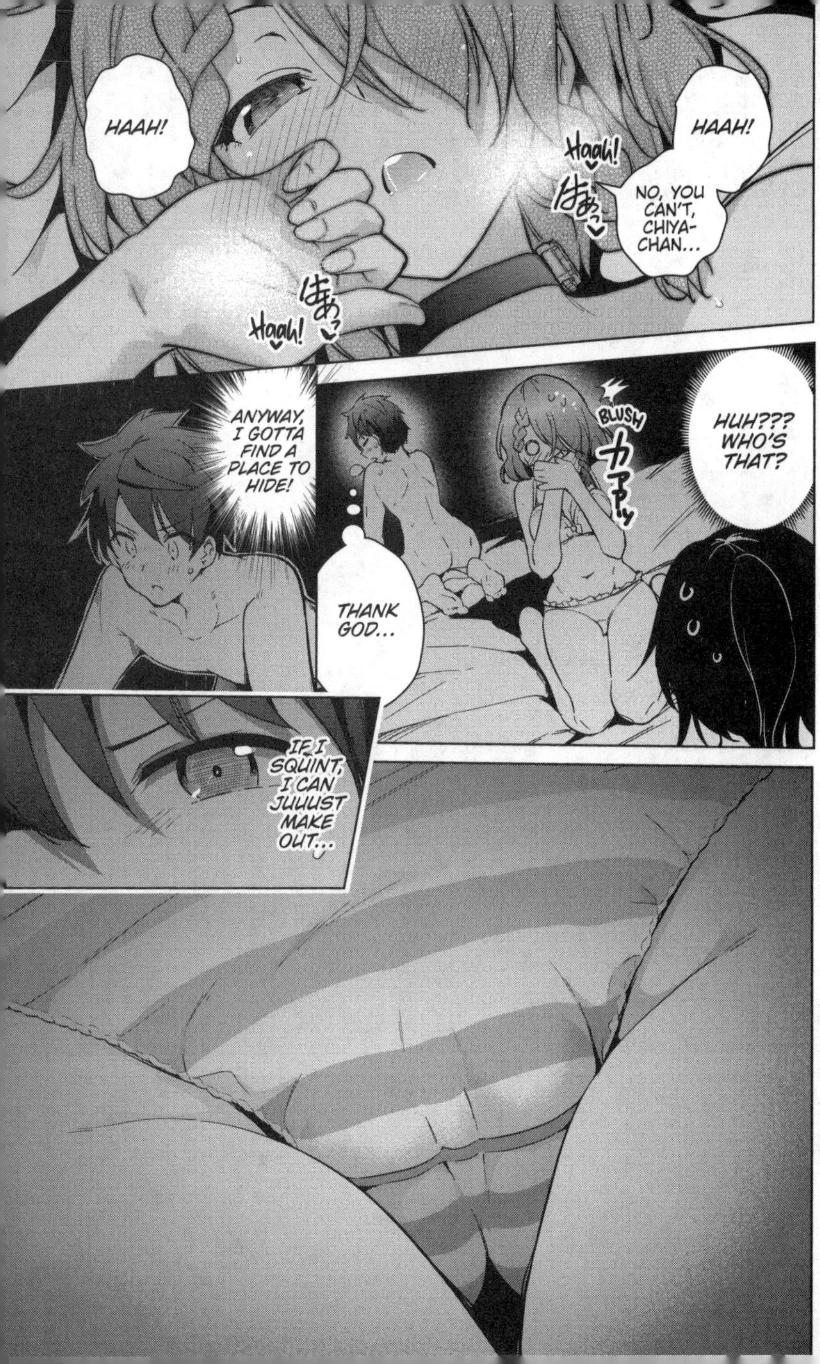
HAAH!
Haah!
はぁっ
NO, YOU CAN'T, CHIYA-CHAN...
HAAH!
はぁっ
Haah!
HUH??? WHO'S THAT?
BLUSH
THANK GOD...
ANYWAY, I GOTTA FIND A PLACE TO HIDE!
IF I SQUINT, I CAN JUUUST MAKE OUT...

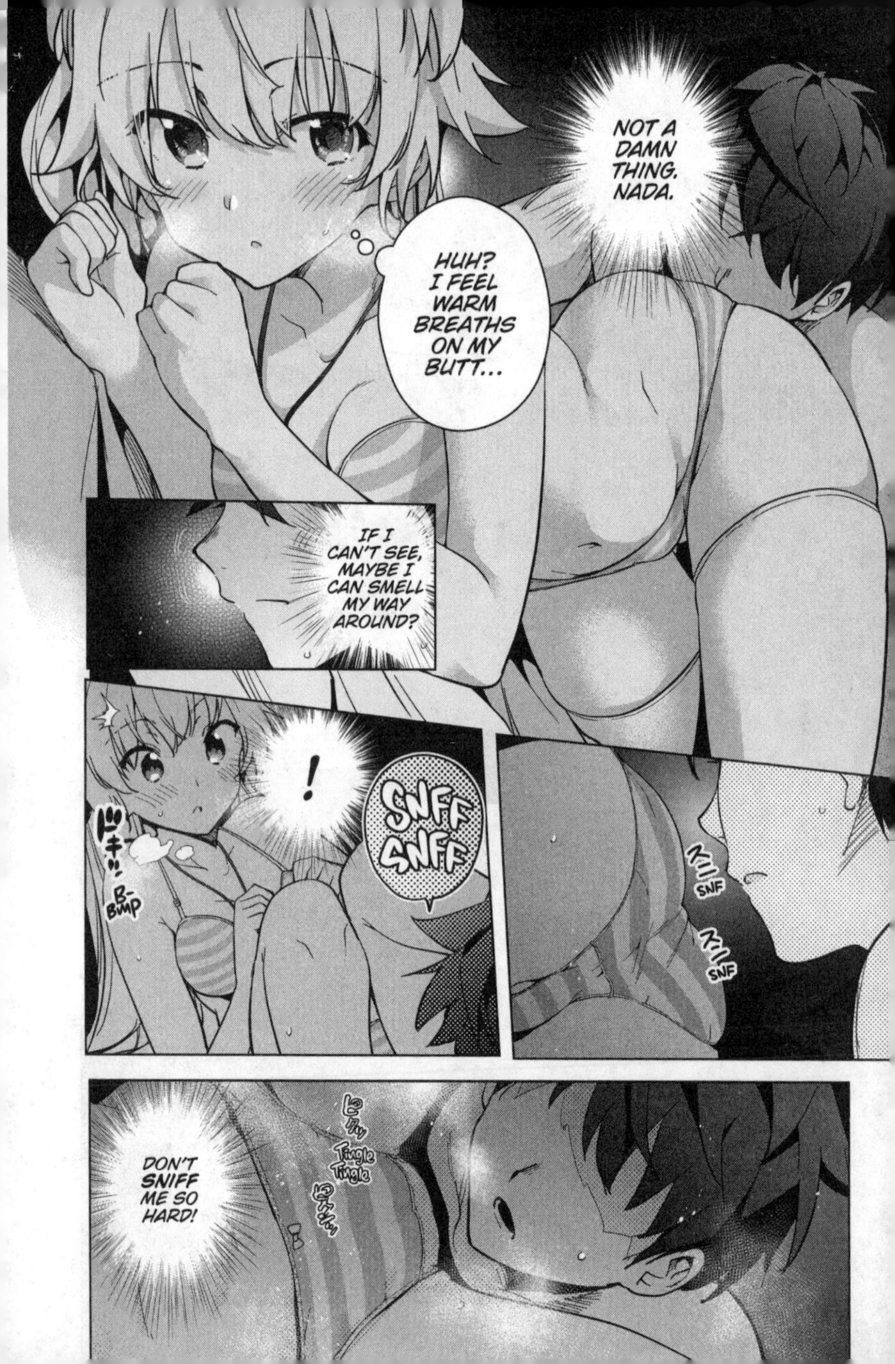
NOT A DAMN THING. NADA.
HUH? I FEEL WARM BREATHS ON MY BUTT...
IF I CAN'T SEE, MAYBE I CAN SMELL MY WAY AROUND?
SNF
SNF
!
SNFF SNFF
ドキッ
B-BUMP
Tingle Tingle
DON'T SNIFF ME SO HARD!

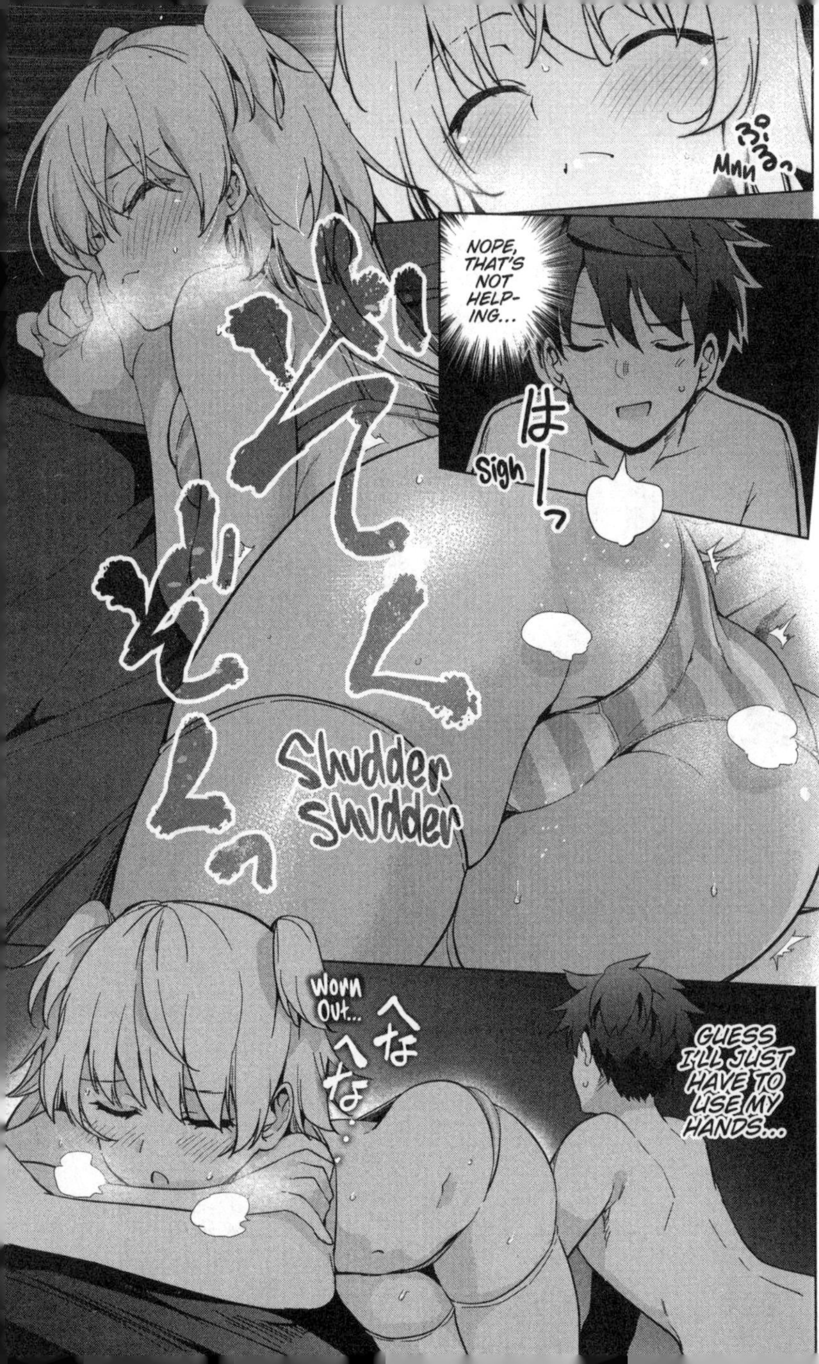
ぷるるっ
Mnn
NOPE, THAT'S NOT HELPING...
はーっ
Sigh
びくんびくんっ
Shudder shudder
GUESS I'LL JUST HAVE TO USE MY HANDS...
Worn out...
へなへなっ

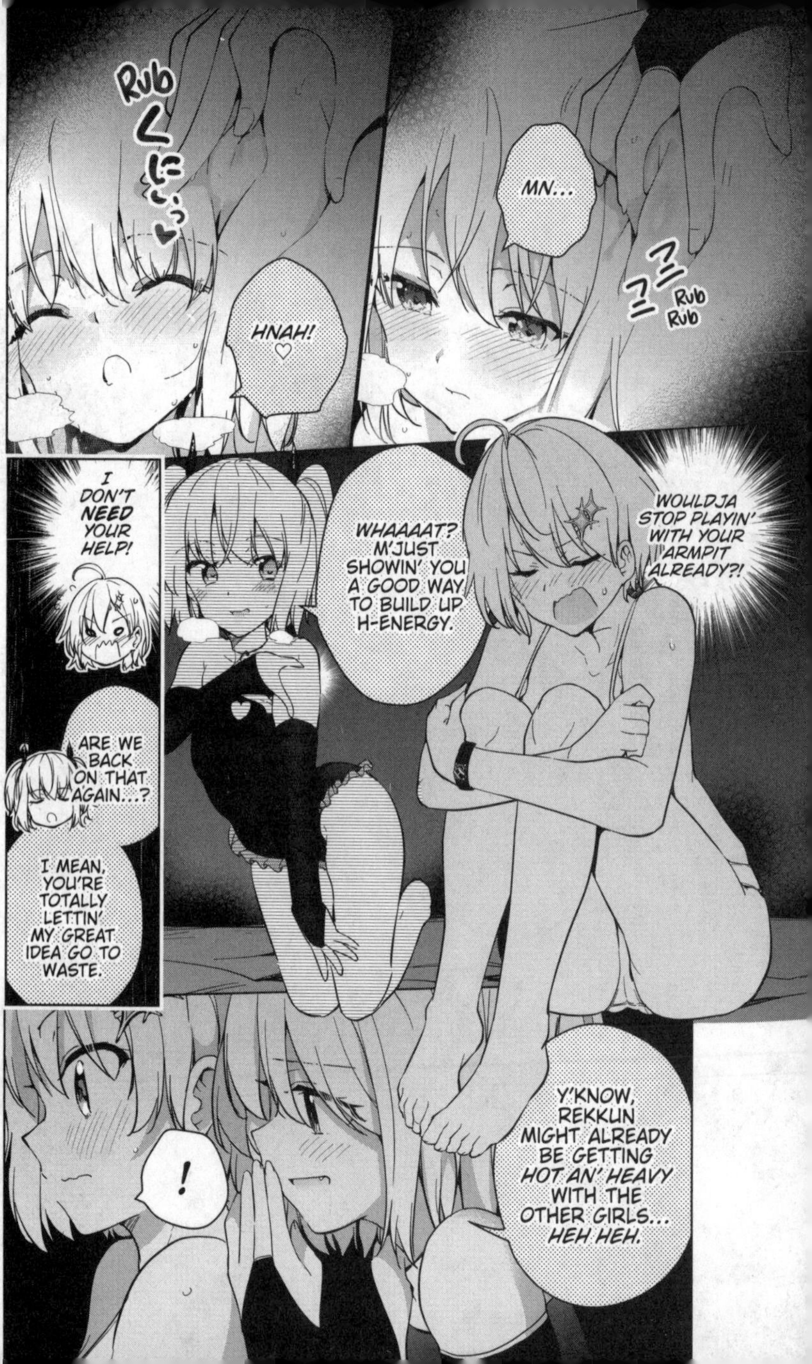
MN...
Rub Rub
Rub
くにっ♥
HNAH! ♡
WOULDJA STOP PLAYIN' WITH YOUR ARMPIT ALREADY?!
WHAAAAT? M'JUST SHOWIN' YOU A GOOD WAY TO BUILD UP H-ENERGY.
I DON'T NEED YOUR HELP!
ARE WE BACK ON THAT AGAIN...?
I MEAN, YOU'RE TOTALLY LETTIN' MY GREAT IDEA GO TO WASTE.
Y'KNOW, REKKUN MIGHT ALREADY BE GETTING HOT AN' HEAVY WITH THE OTHER GIRLS... HEH HEH.
!

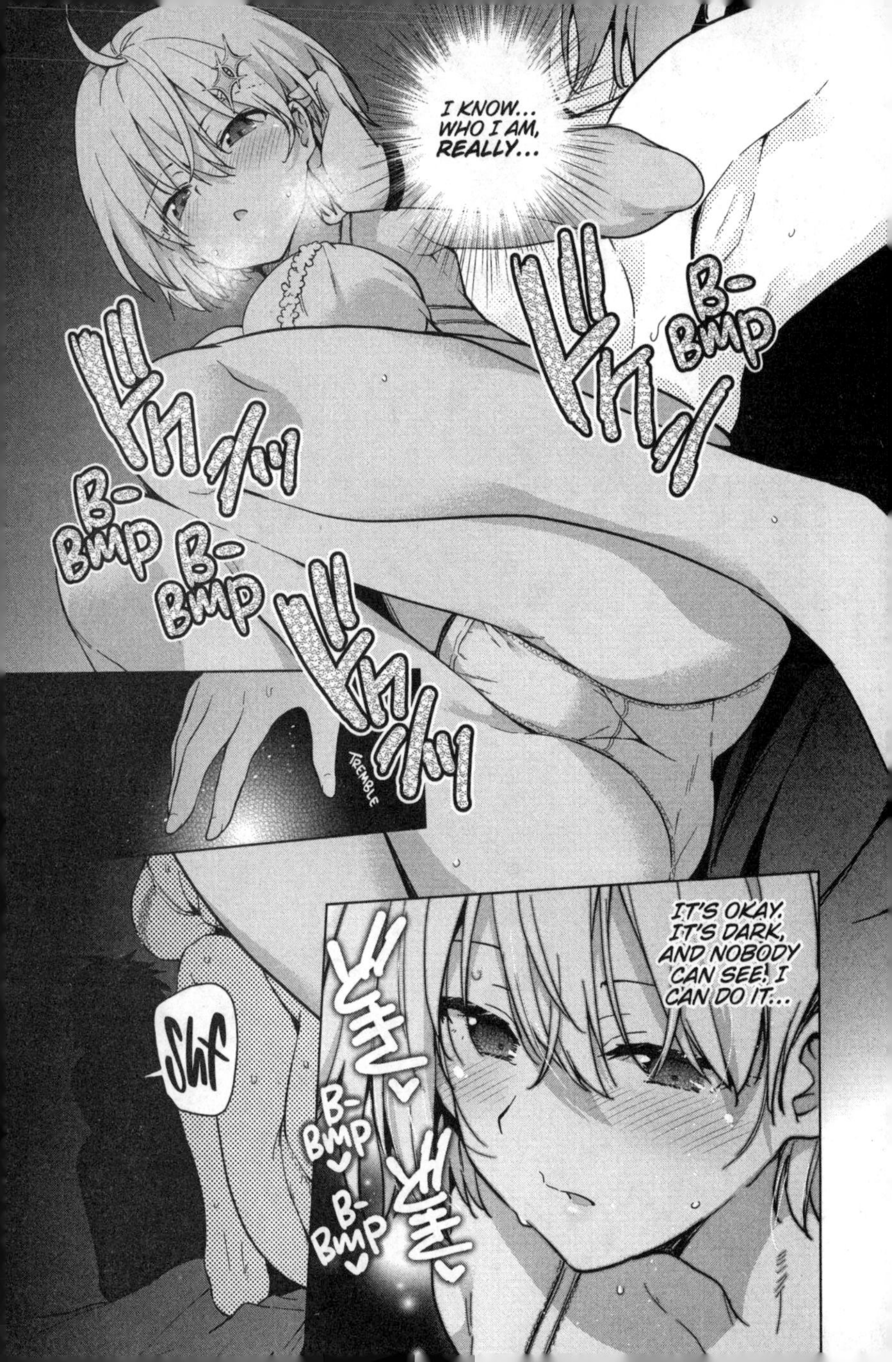

I KNOW... WHO I AM, REALLY...
B-BMP
B-BMP B-BMP
TREMBLE
IT'S OKAY. IT'S DARK, AND NOBODY CAN SEE! I CAN DO IT...
どき
B-BMP
B-BMP
どき
SHF

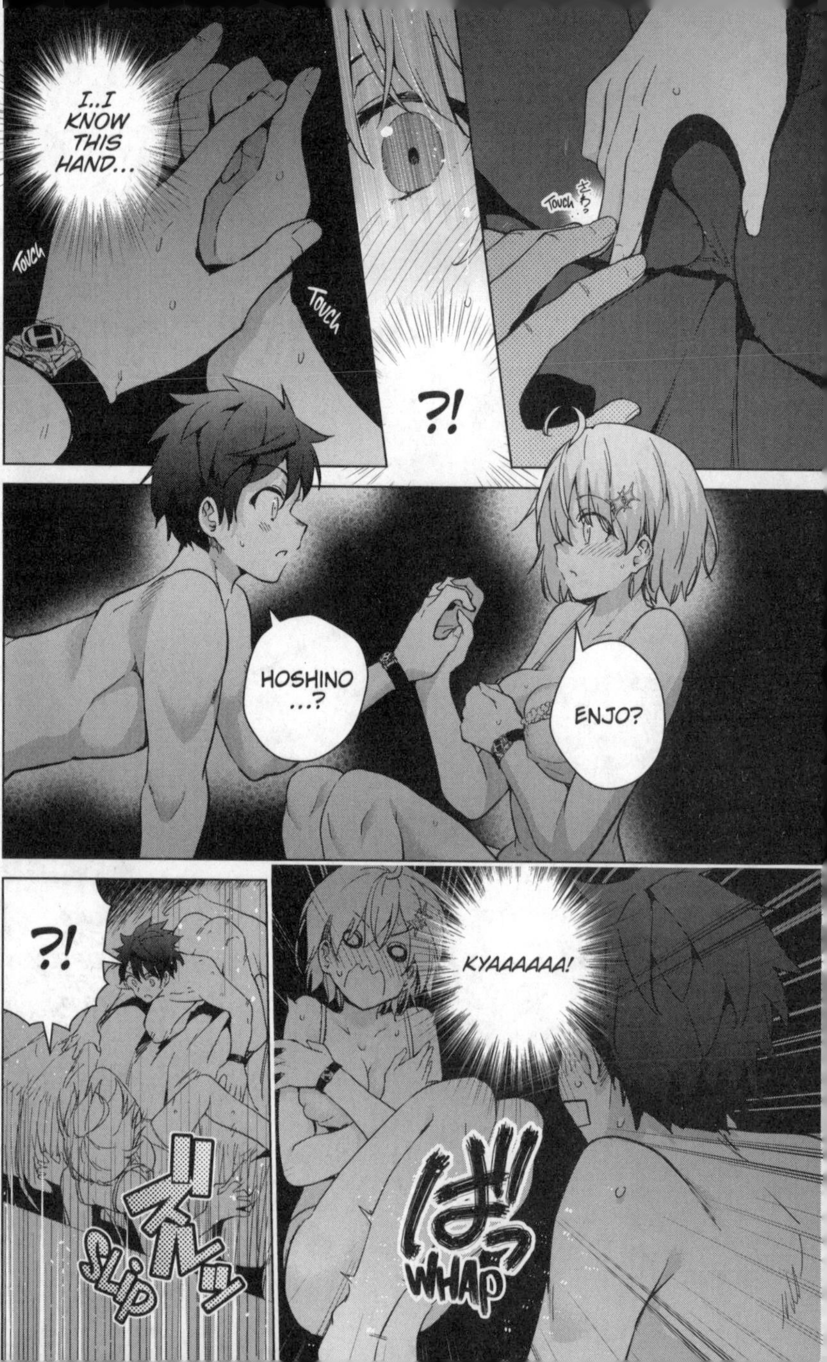
TOUCH
さわっ
?!
I..I KNOW THIS HAND...
TOUCH
TOUCH
ENJO?
HOSHINO ...?
KYAAAAAA!
ぱっ
WHAP
?!
ズルッ
SLIP

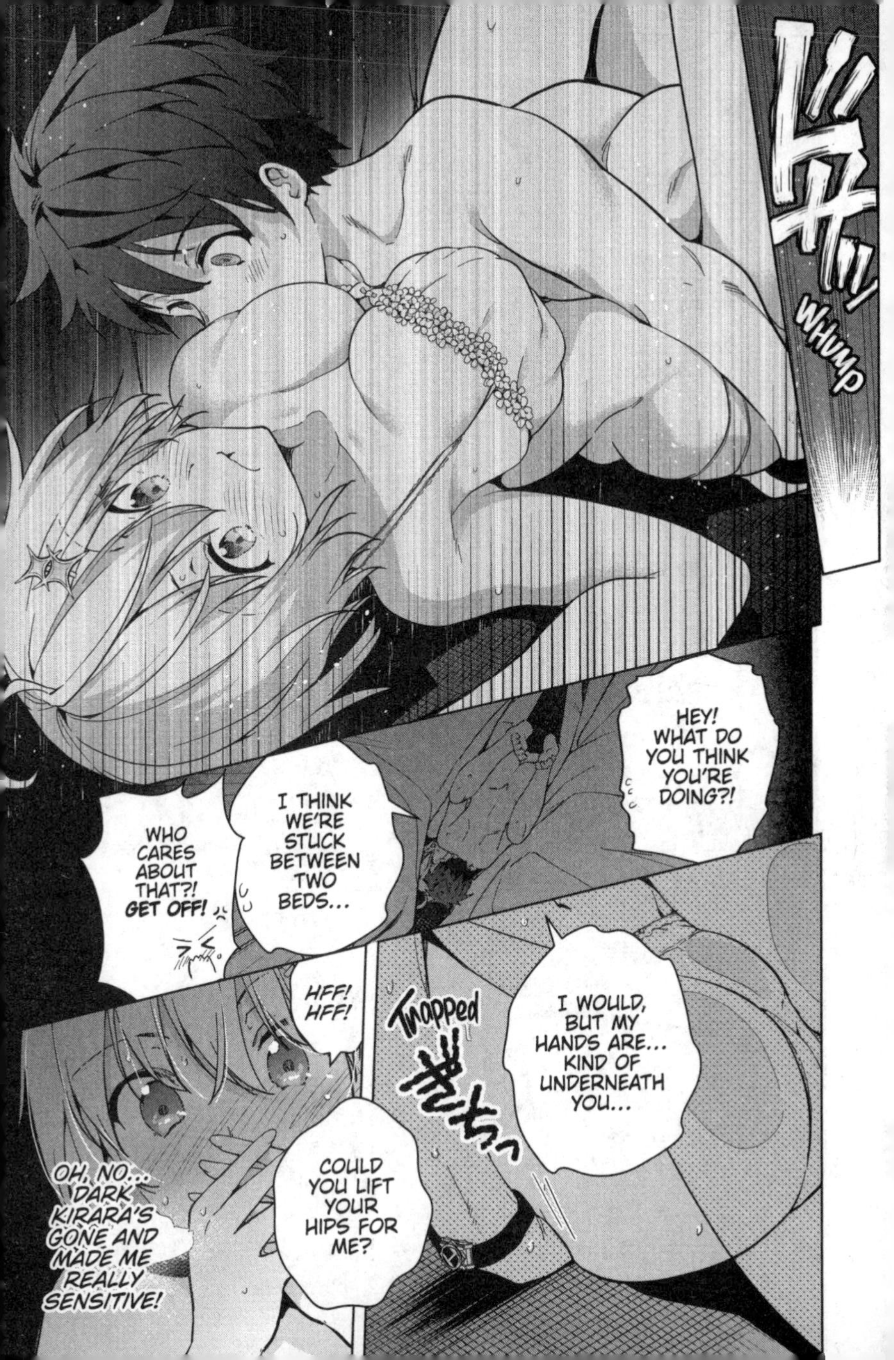
WHUMP
HEY! WHAT DO YOU THINK YOU'RE DOING?!
I THINK WE'RE STUCK BETWEEN TWO BEDS...
WHO CARES ABOUT THAT?! GET OFF!
I WOULD, BUT MY HANDS ARE... KIND OF UNDERNEATH YOU...
Trapped
COULD YOU LIFT YOUR HIPS FOR ME?
HFF! HFF!
OH, NO... DARK KIRARA'S GONE AND MADE ME REALLY SENSITIVE!

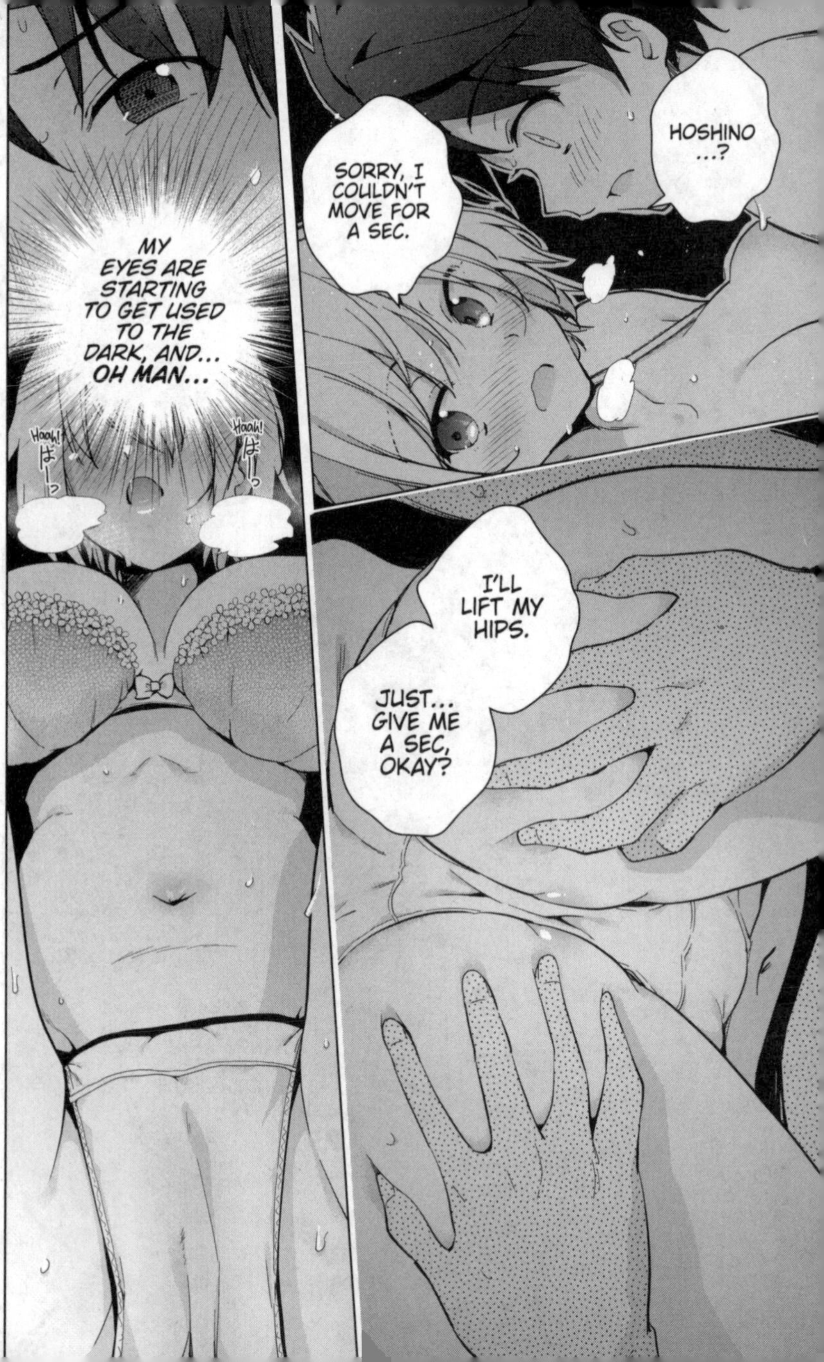
HOSHINO ...?
SORRY, I COULDN'T MOVE FOR A SEC.
I'LL LIFT MY HIPS.
JUST... GIVE ME A SEC, OKAY?
MY EYES ARE STARTING TO GET USED TO THE DARK, AND... OH MAN...
Haah! はーっ
Haah! はーっ

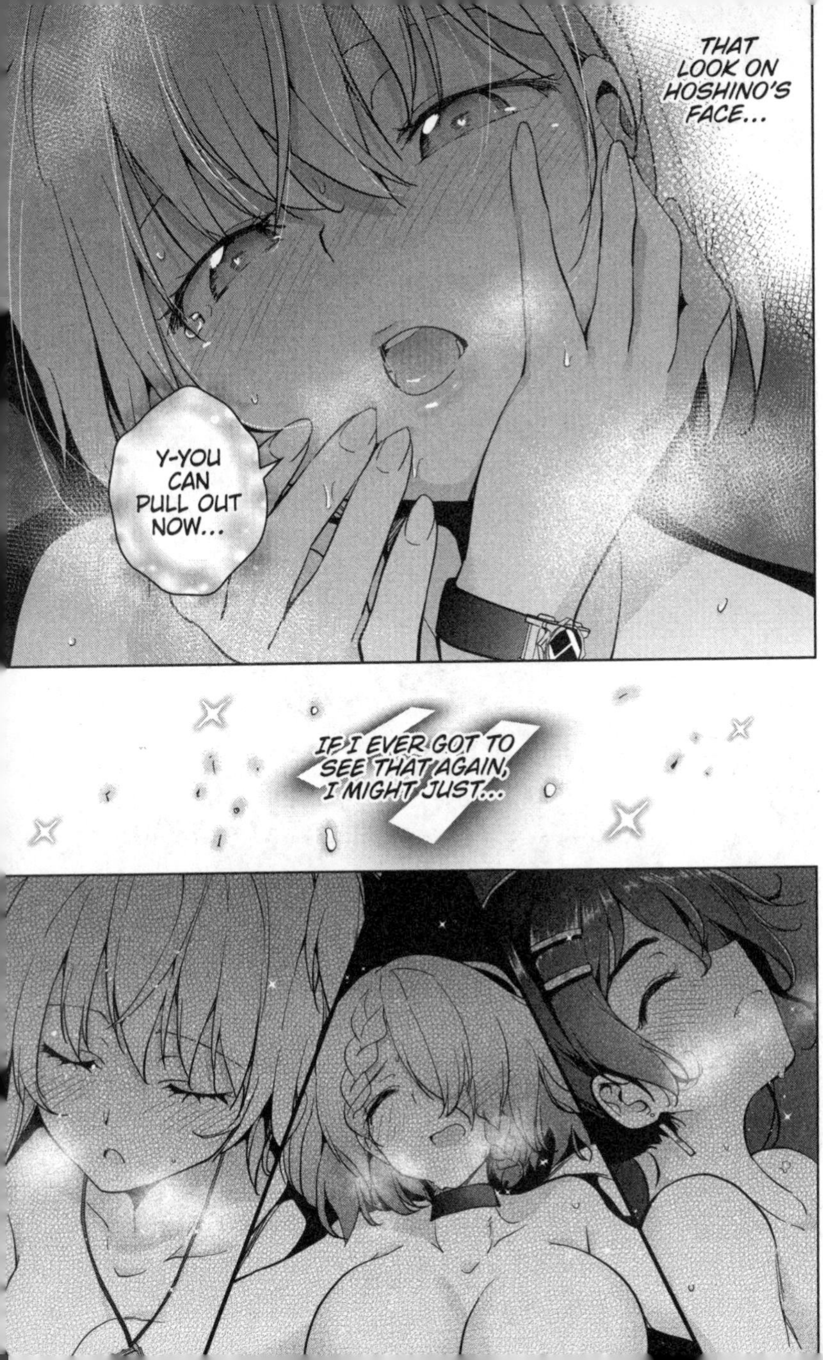
THAT LOOK ON HOSHINO'S FACE...
Y-YOU CAN PULL OUT NOW...
IF I EVER GOT TO SEE THAT AGAIN, I MIGHT JUST...

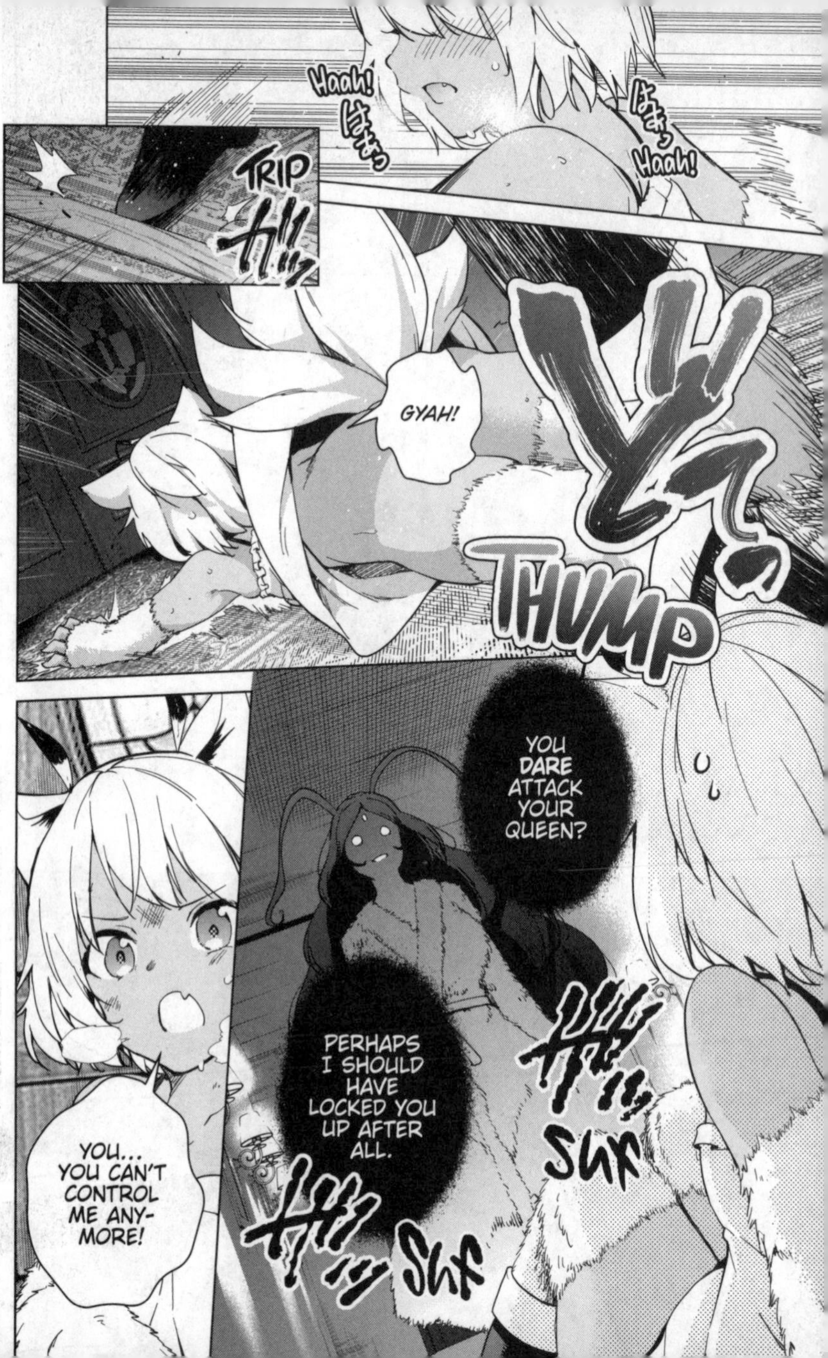
はぁっ Haah!
Haah! はぁっ
TRIP
ガッ
GYAH!
どてっ
THUMP
YOU DARE ATTACK YOUR QUEEN?
PERHAPS I SHOULD HAVE LOCKED YOU UP AFTER ALL.
ザッ Shf
ザッ Shf
YOU... YOU CAN'T CONTROL ME ANY-MORE!

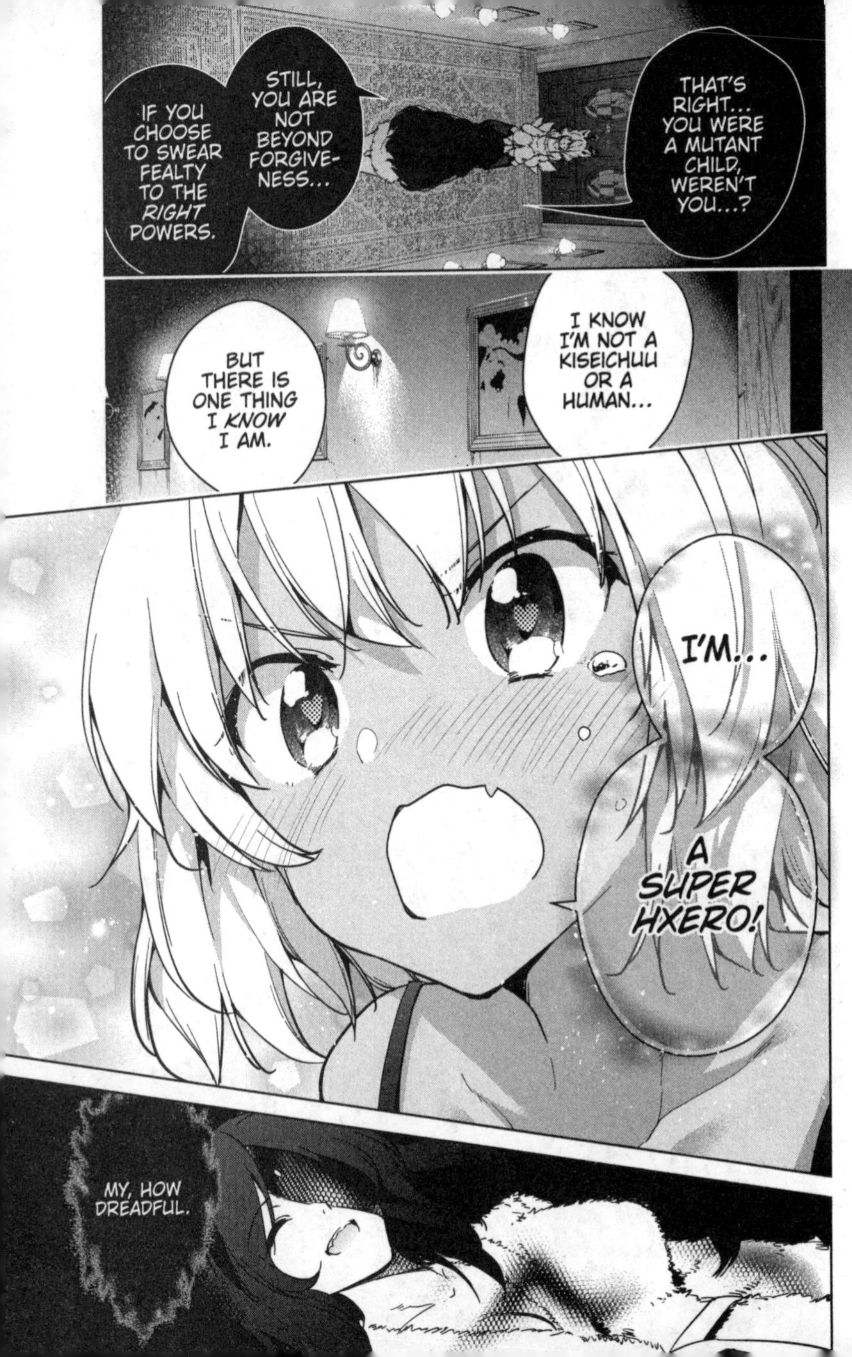
THAT'S RIGHT... YOU WERE A MUTANT CHILD, WEREN'T YOU...?
STILL, YOU ARE NOT BEYOND FORGIVE-NESS...
IF YOU CHOOSE TO SWEAR FEALTY TO THE *RIGHT* POWERS.
I KNOW I'M NOT A KISEICHUU OR A HUMAN...
BUT THERE IS ONE THING I *KNOW* I AM.
I'M...
A SUPER HXERO!
MY, HOW DREADFUL.

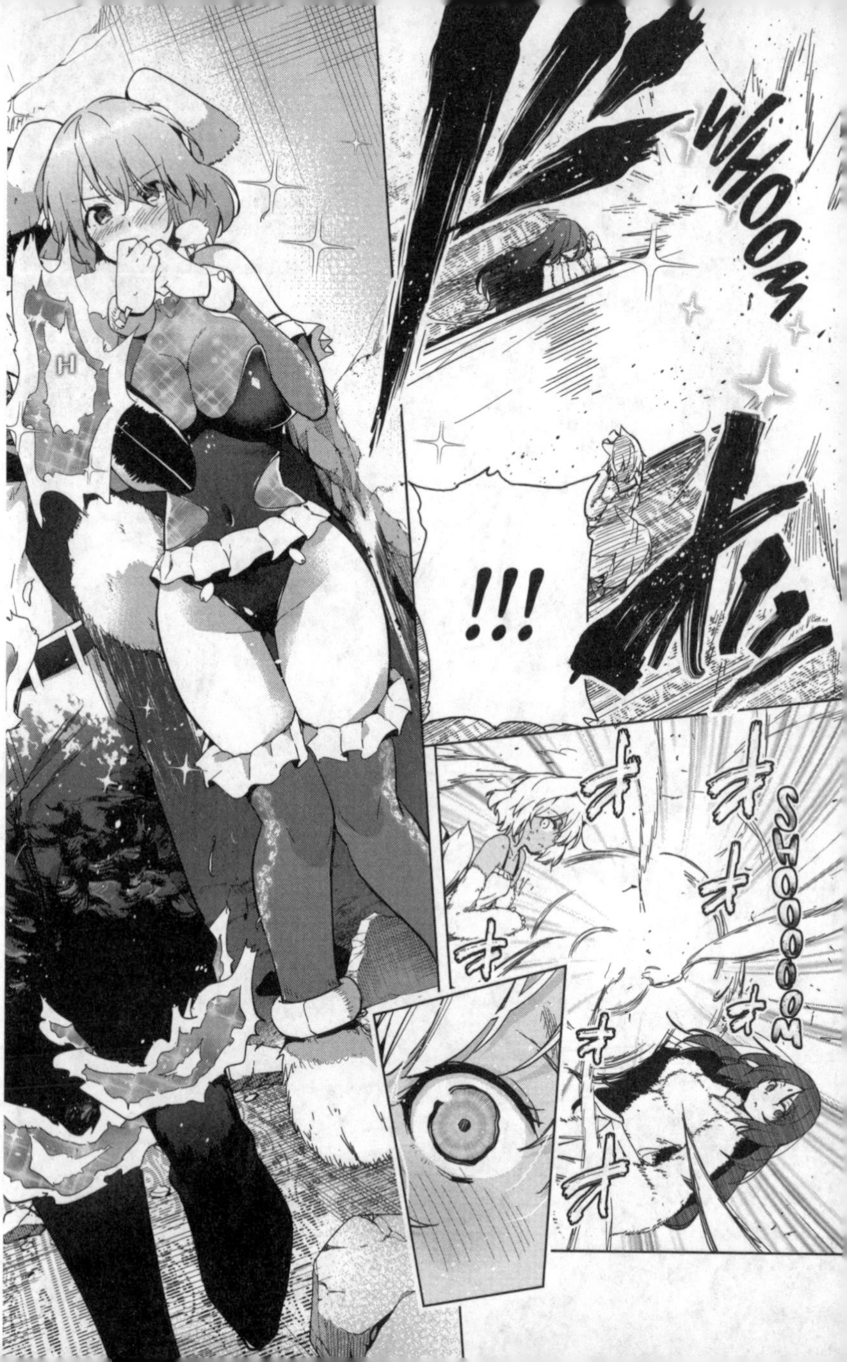
WHOOM
!!!
SHOOOOOOM

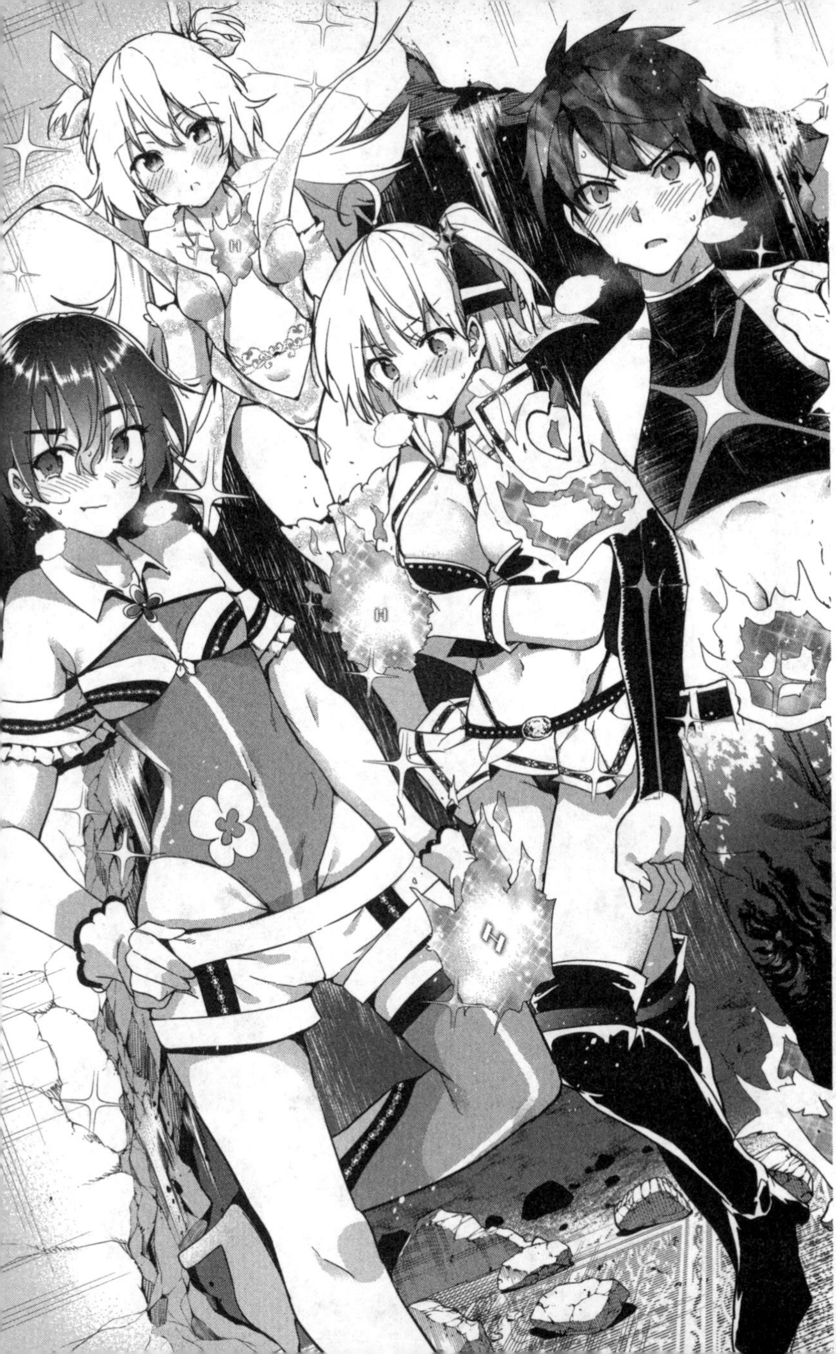

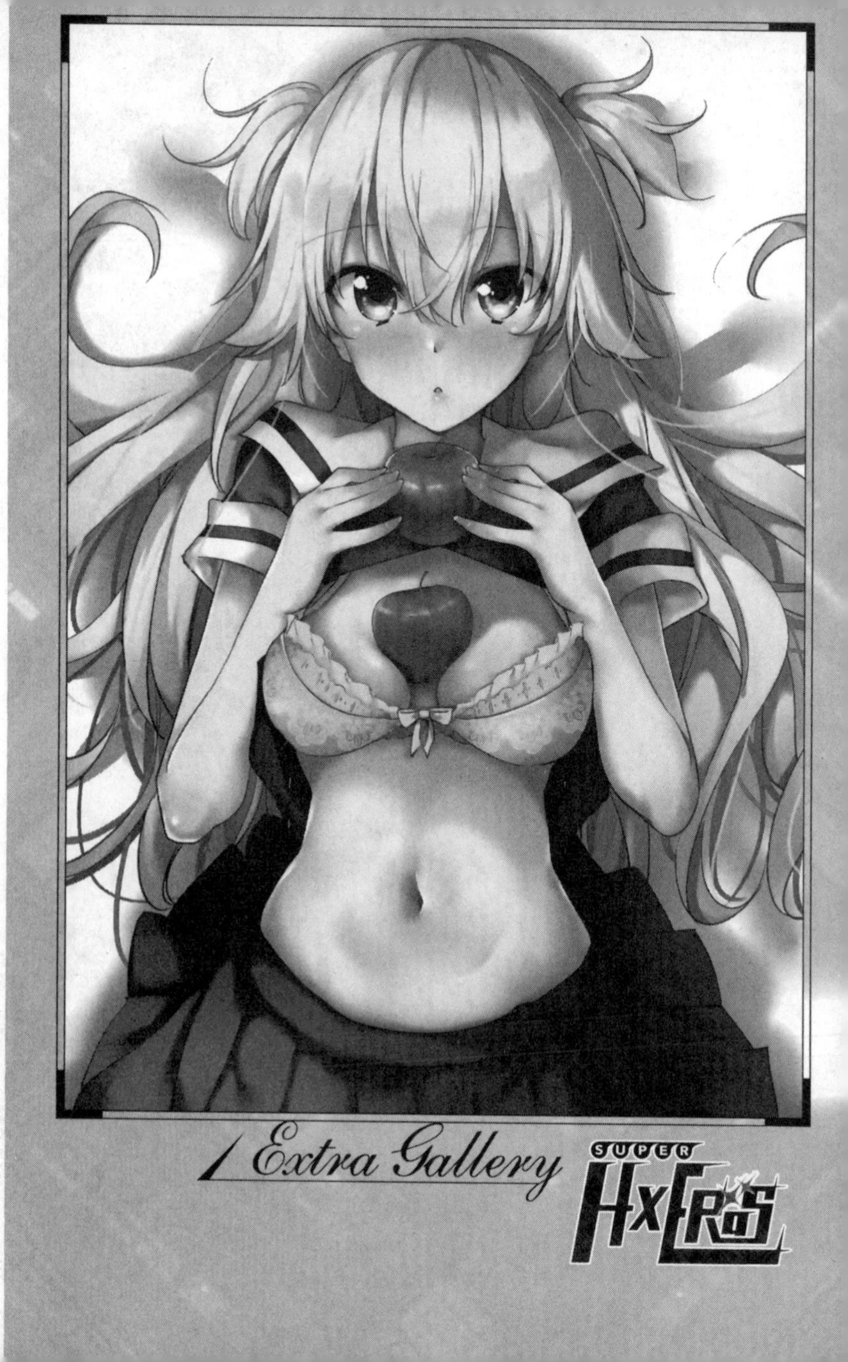

Extra Gallery

SUPER HxEROS

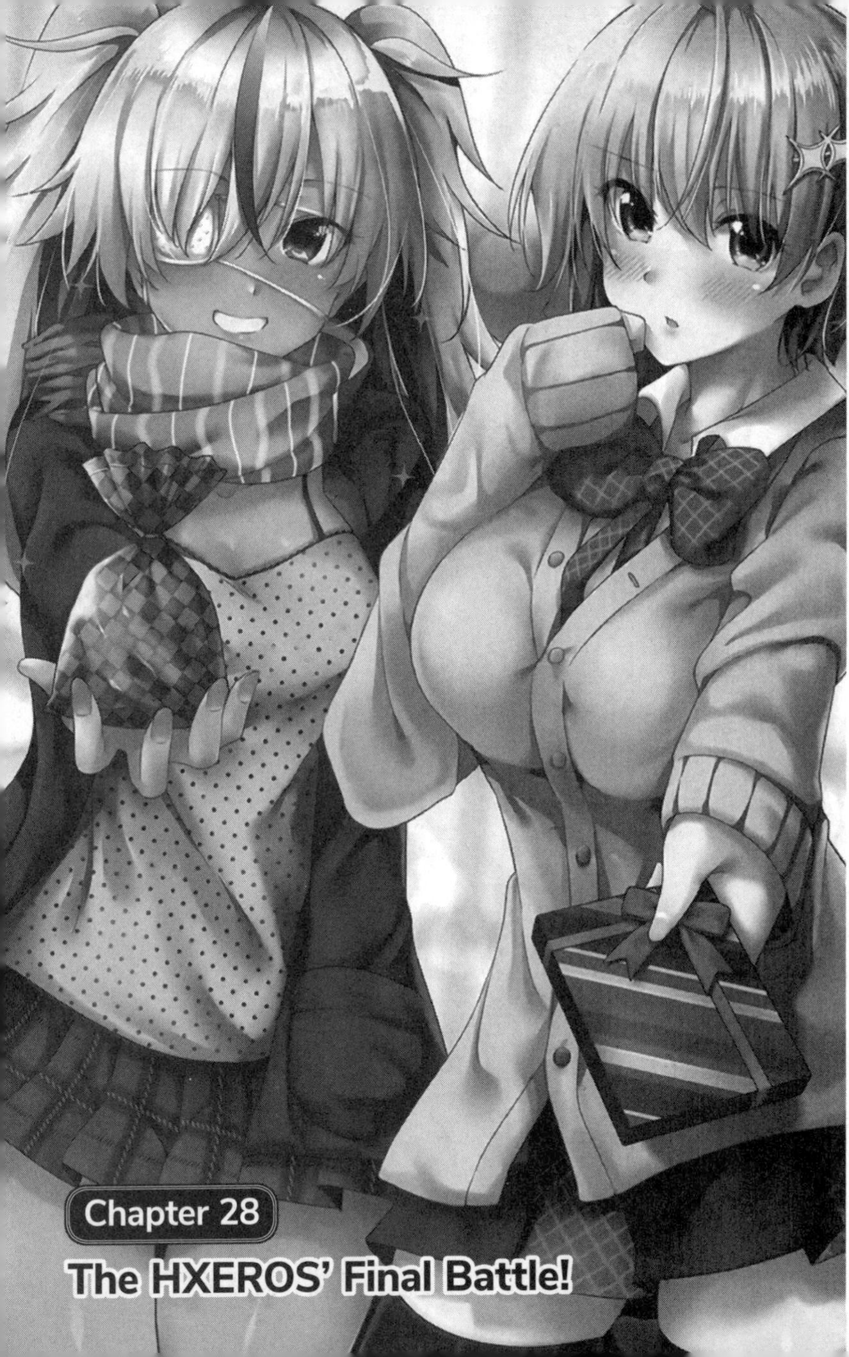
Chapter 28
The HXEROS' Final Battle!

Extra Gallery

SUPER HxEROS

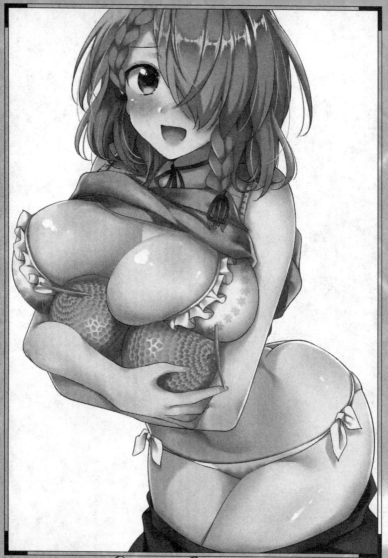

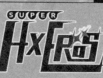

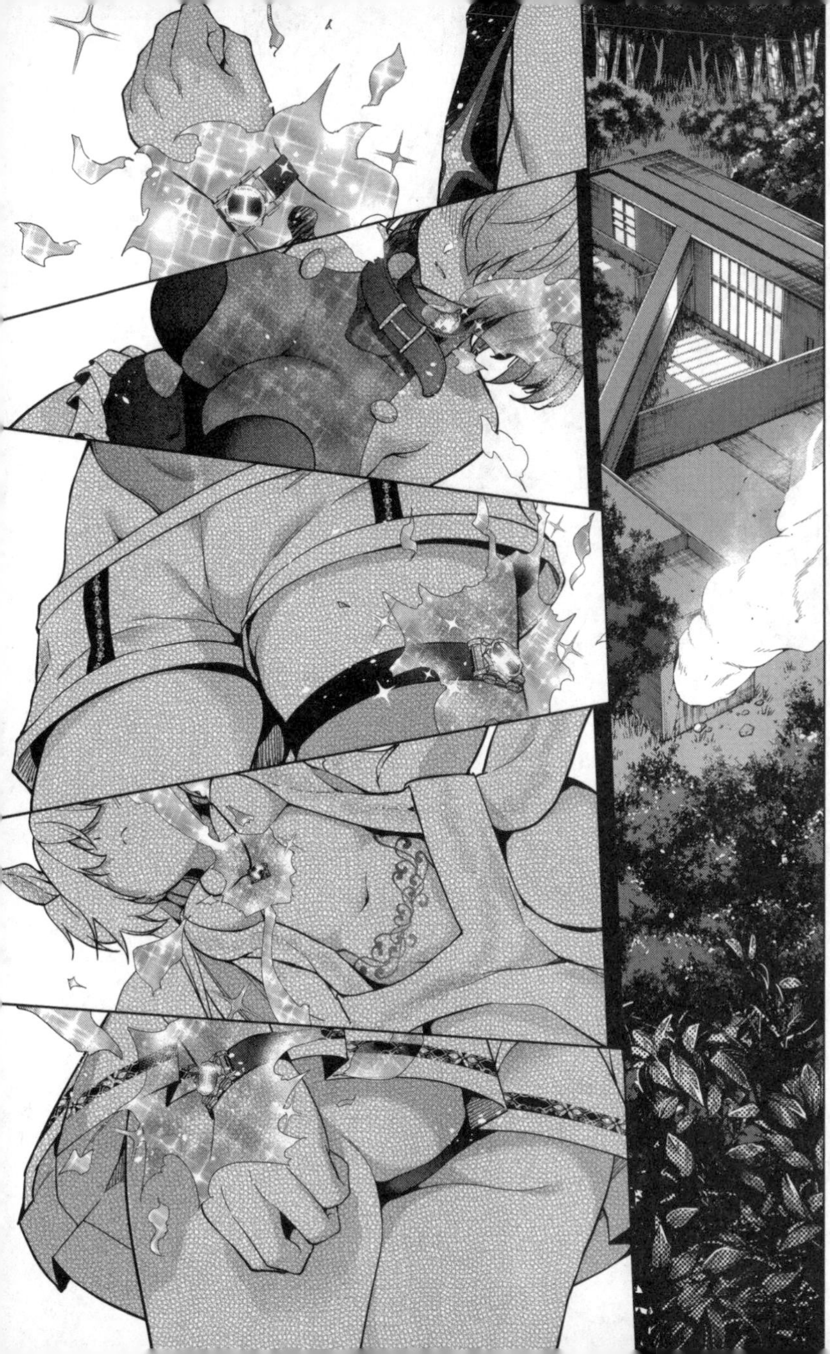

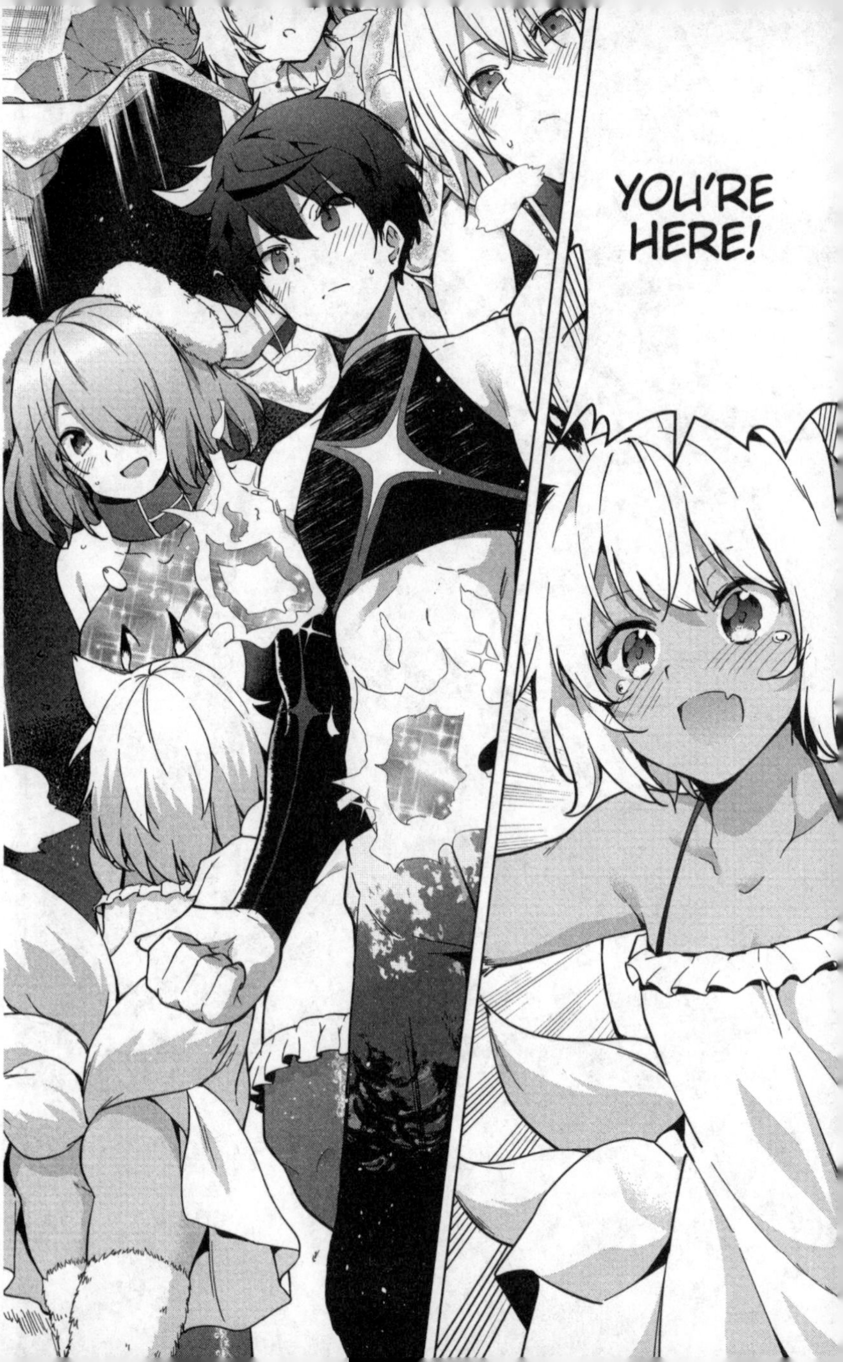
YOU'RE HERE!

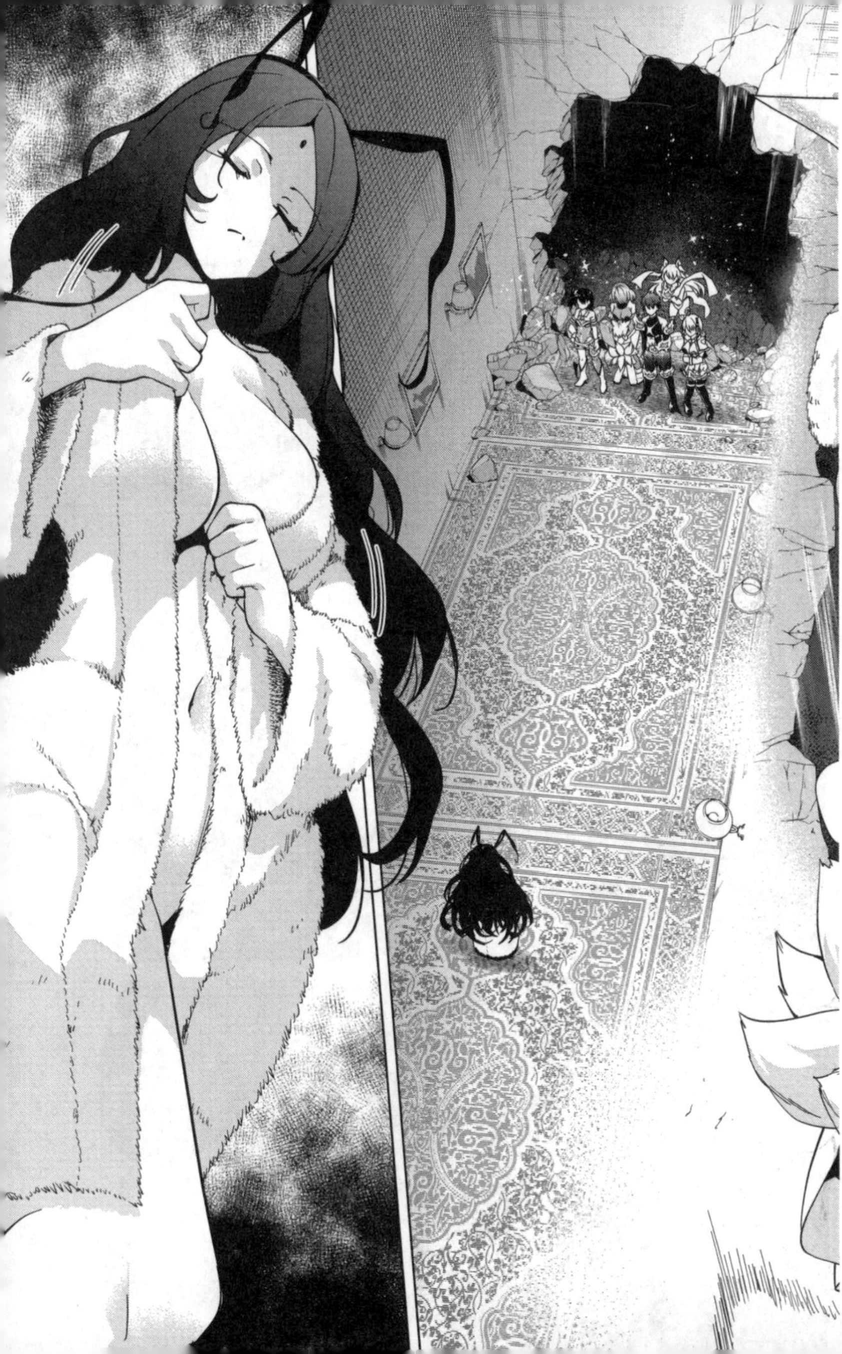

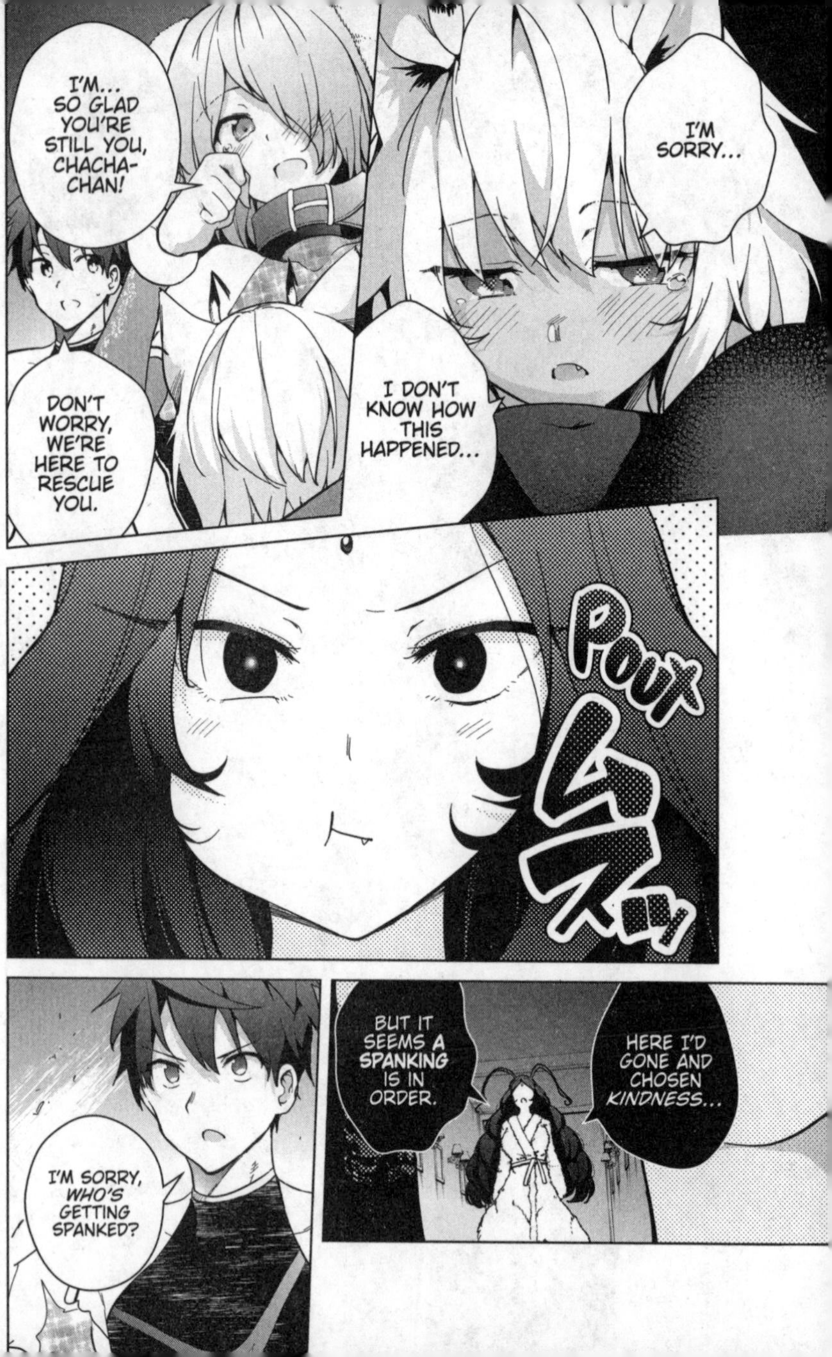
I'M SORRY...
I DON'T KNOW HOW THIS HAPPENED...
I'M... SO GLAD YOU'RE STILL YOU, CHACHA-CHAN!
DON'T WORRY, WE'RE HERE TO RESCUE YOU.
Pout
ムス
HERE I'D GONE AND CHOSEN *KINDNESS*...
BUT IT SEEMS A **SPANKING** IS IN ORDER.
I'M SORRY, *WHO'S* GETTING SPANKED?

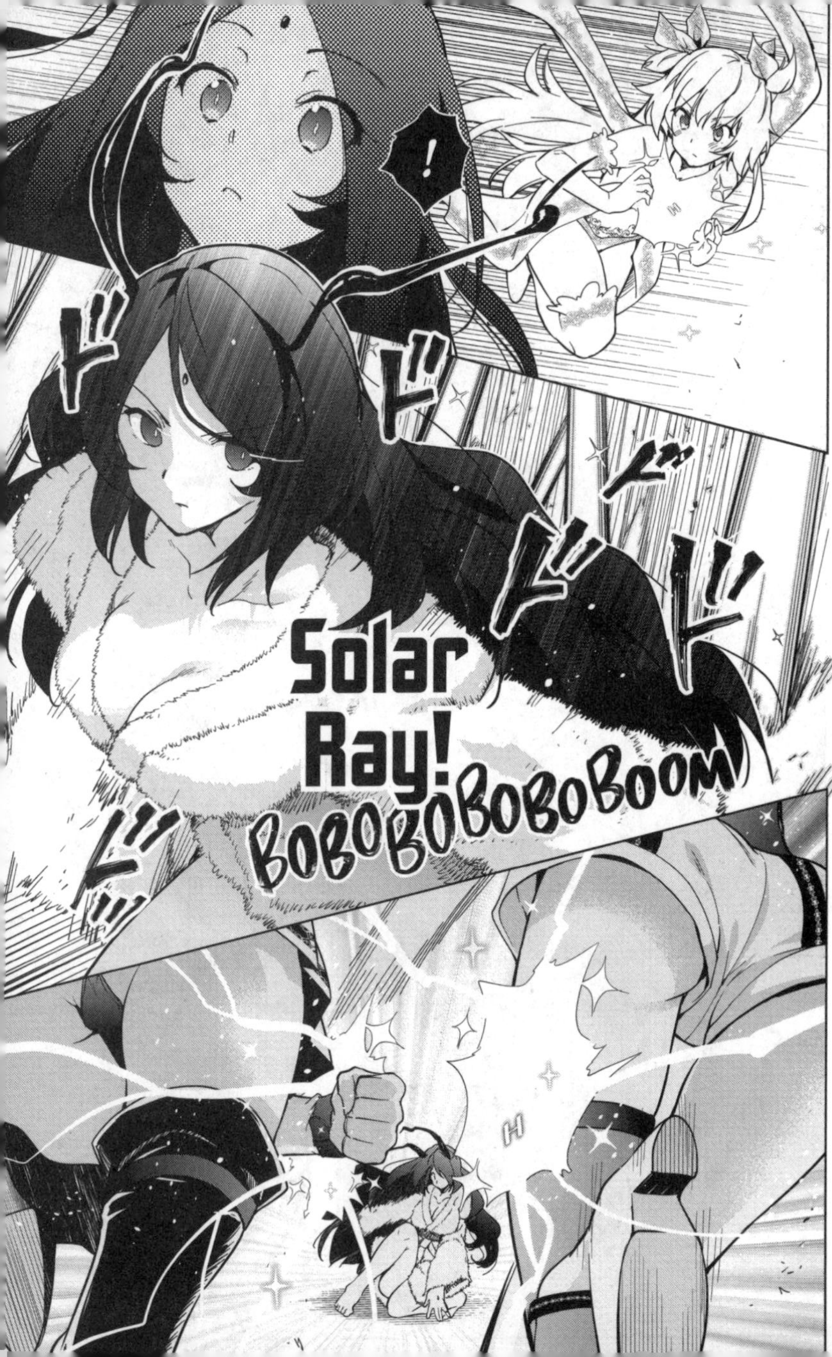

!
ドド
ドド
Solar Ray!
BOBOBOBOBOBoom
ドド

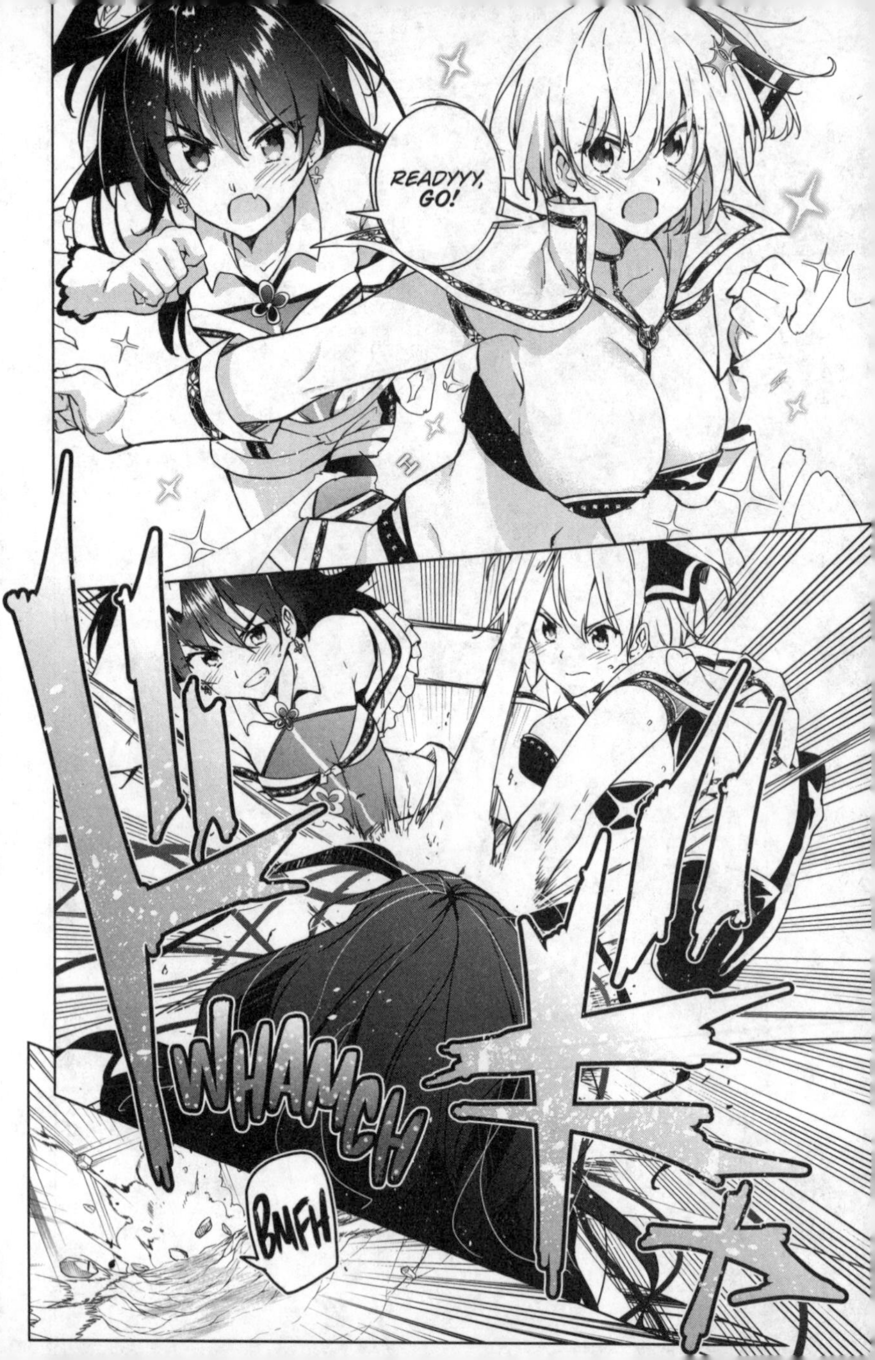
READYYY, GO!
WHAMCH
BMFH

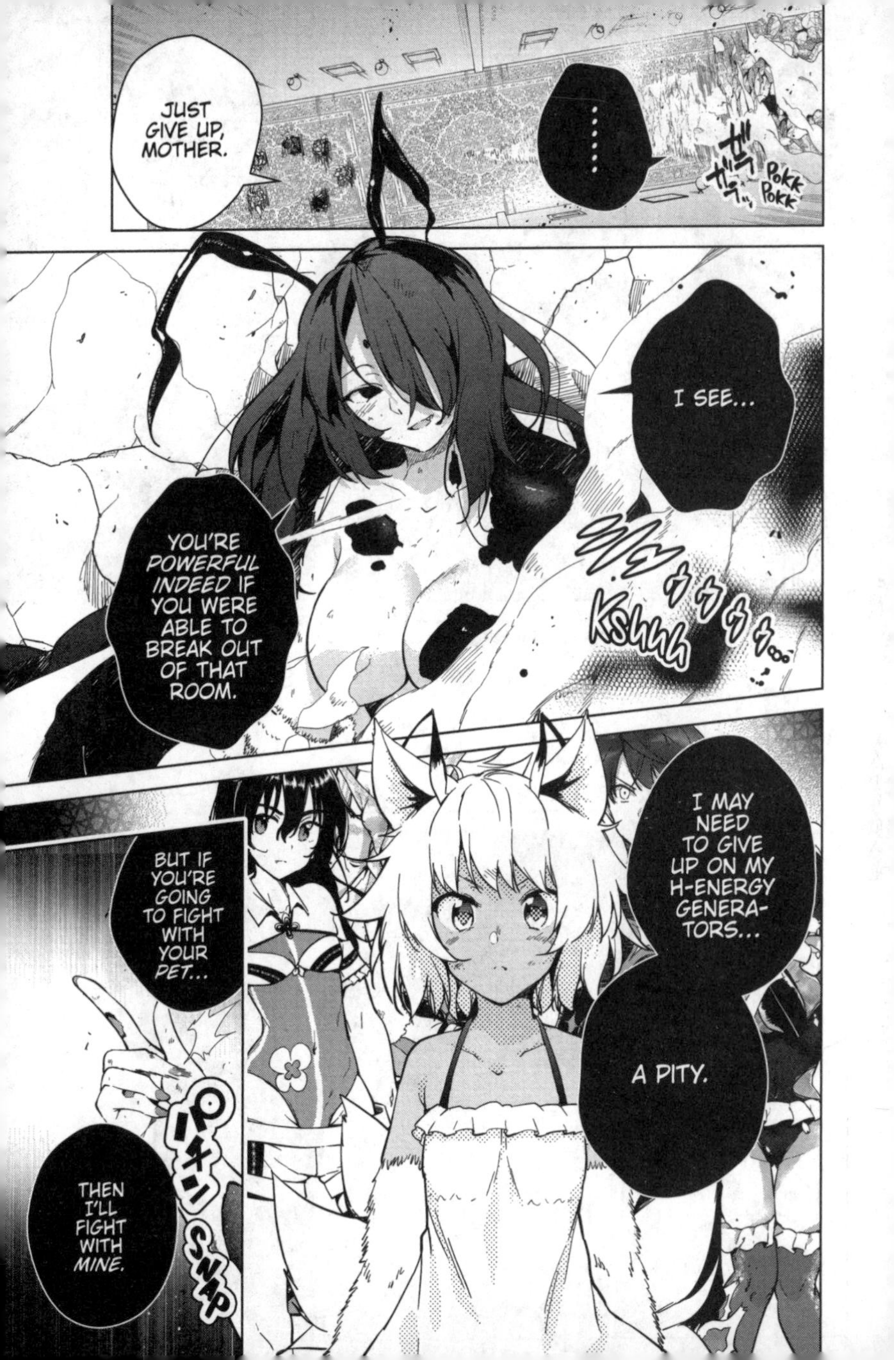
Pokk Pokk
......
JUST GIVE UP, MOTHER.
I SEE...
Kshuh
YOU'RE *POWERFUL INDEED* IF YOU WERE ABLE TO BREAK OUT OF THAT ROOM.
I MAY NEED TO GIVE UP ON MY H-ENERGY GENERATORS...
A PITY.
BUT IF YOU'RE GOING TO FIGHT WITH YOUR *PET*...
SNAP
THEN I'LL FIGHT WITH *MINE*.

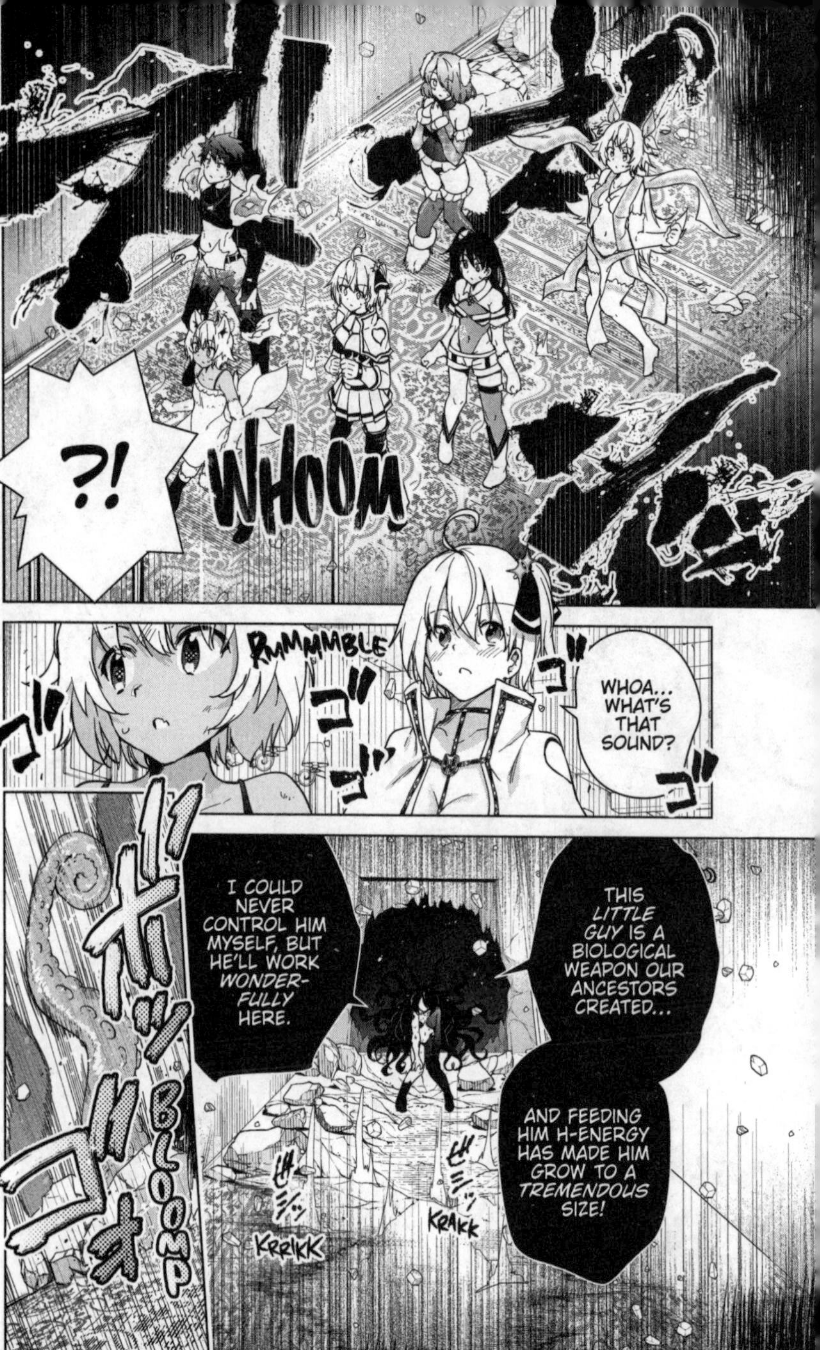
WHOOM
?!
RUMMMBLE
WHOA... WHAT'S THAT SOUND?
THIS LITTLE GUY IS A BIOLOGICAL WEAPON OUR ANCESTORS CREATED...
AND FEEDING HIM H-ENERGY HAS MADE HIM GROW TO A TREMENDOUS SIZE!
I COULD NEVER CONTROL HIM MYSELF, BUT HE'LL WORK WONDERFULLY HERE.
KRAKK
KRRIKK
BLOOMP

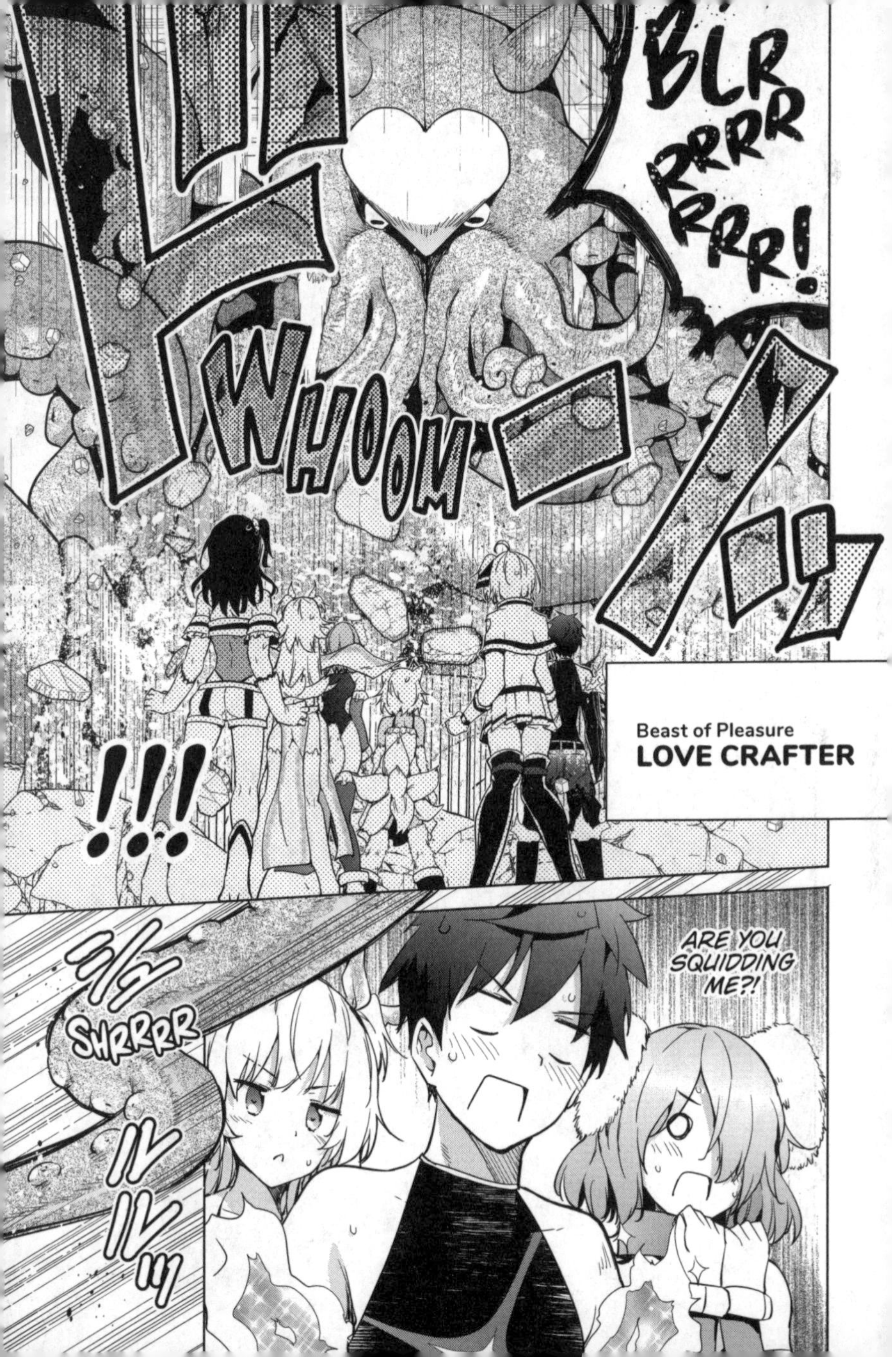
BLRRRRRRRR!
WHOOM—!?
Beast of Pleasure
LOVE CRAFTER
!!!
ARE YOU SQUIDDING ME?!
SHRRRR

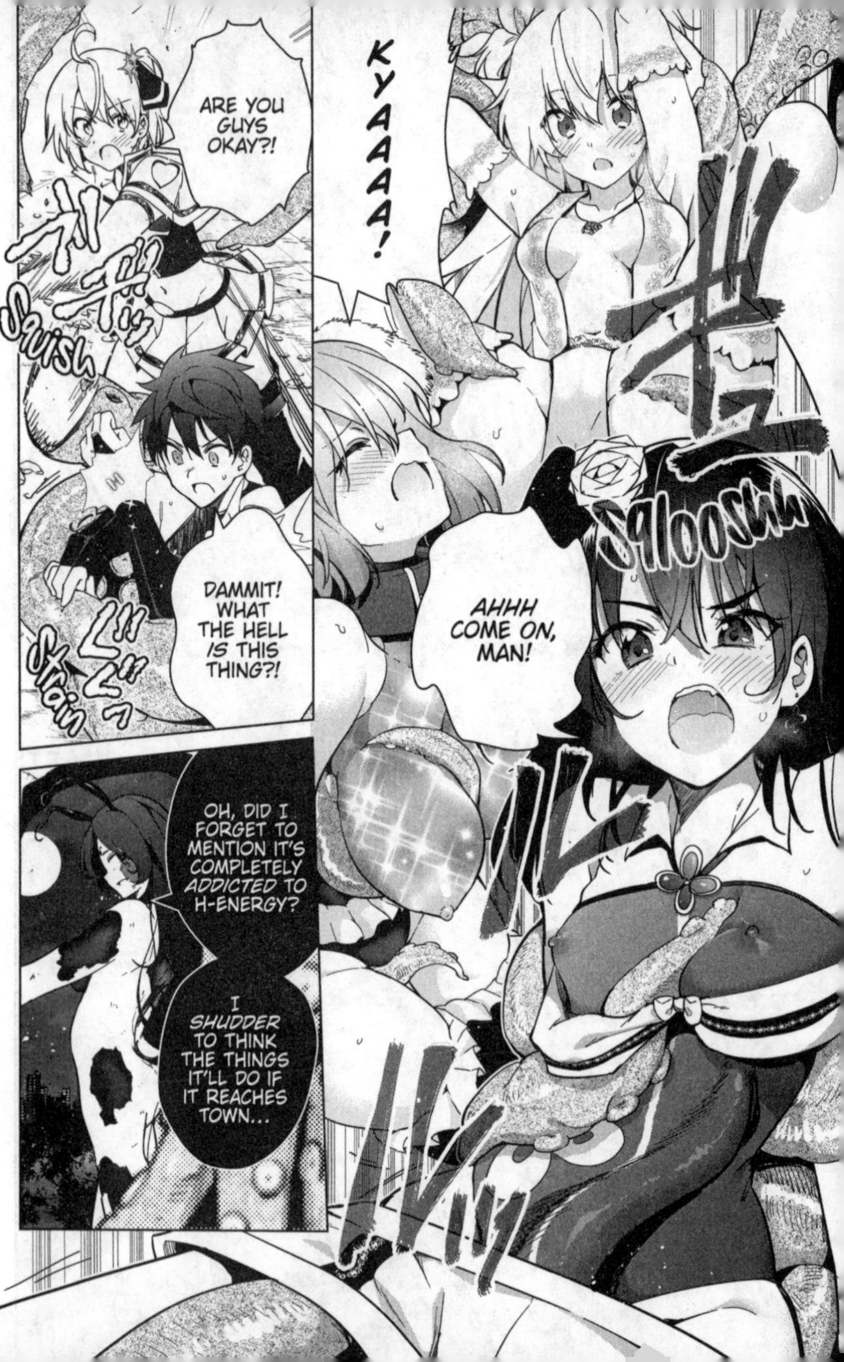
KYAAAAA!
Sploosh
AHHH COME ON, MAN!
ARE YOU GUYS OKAY?!
Squish
DAMMIT! WHAT THE HELL *IS* THIS THING?!
Strain
OH, DID I FORGET TO MENTION IT'S COMPLETELY *ADDICTED* TO H-ENERGY?
I *SHUDDER* TO THINK THE THINGS IT'LL DO IF IT REACHES TOWN...

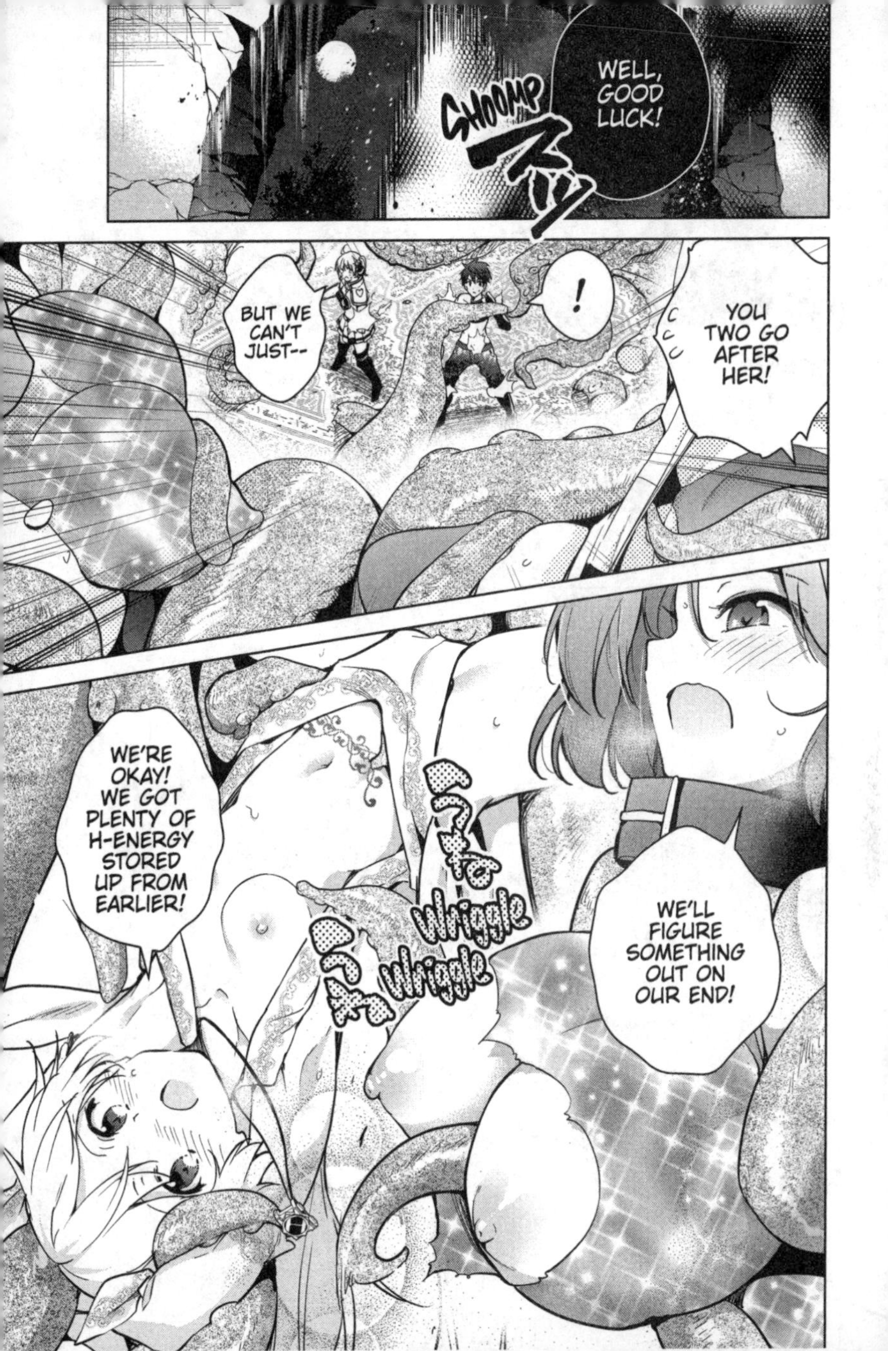
WELL, GOOD LUCK!
SHOOMP
YOU TWO GO AFTER HER!
!
BUT WE CAN'T JUST--
WE'RE OKAY! WE GOT PLENTY OF H-ENERGY STORED UP FROM EARLIER!
wriggle wriggle
WE'LL FIGURE SOMETHING OUT ON OUR END!

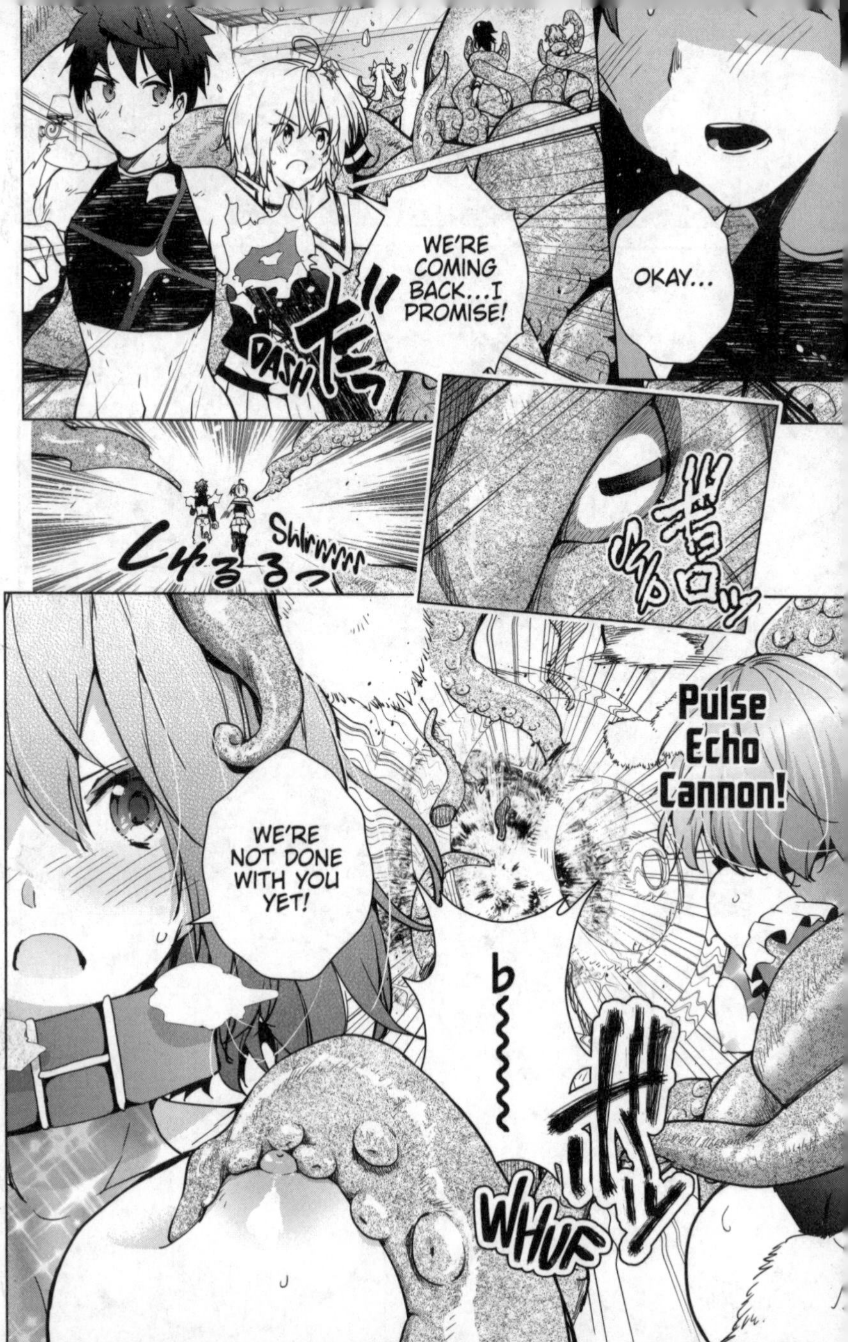
OKAY...
WE'RE COMING BACK...I PROMISE!
DASH
Shlrrrrrr
Pulse Echo Cannon!
WE'RE NOT DONE WITH YOU YET!
WHUF

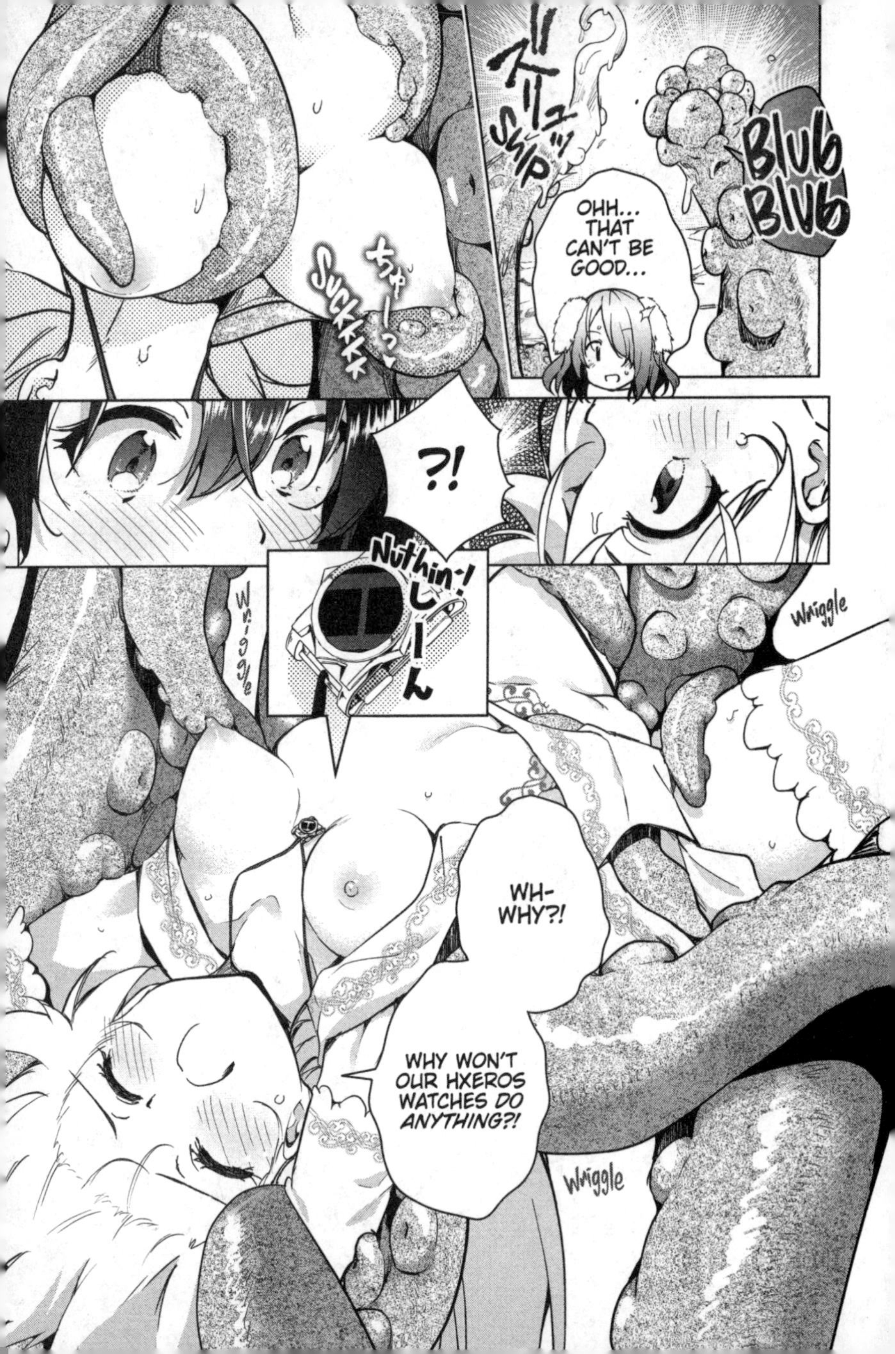
ズリュッ
SWIP
Blub Blub
OHH... THAT CAN'T BE GOOD...
ちゅーっ
SUCKKKK
?!
Nuthin'!
じーん
Wriggle
Wriggle
WH- WHY?!
WHY WON'T OUR HXEROS WATCHES DO ANYTHING?!
Wriggle

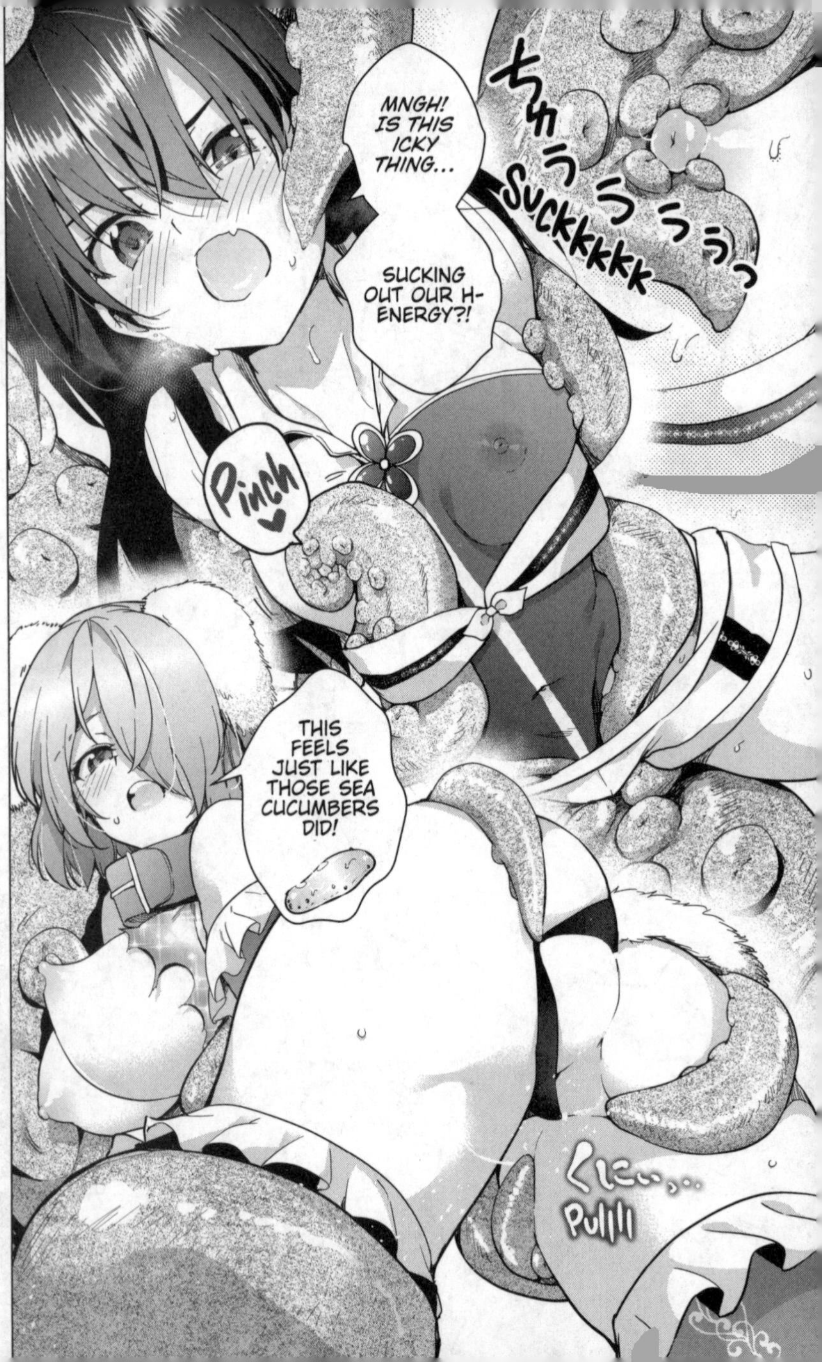
ちゅううううっ
Suckkkkk
MNGH! IS THIS ICKY THING...
SUCKING OUT OUR H-ENERGY?!
Pinch
THIS FEELS JUST LIKE THOSE SEA CUCUMBERS DID!
くにぃ...
Pullll

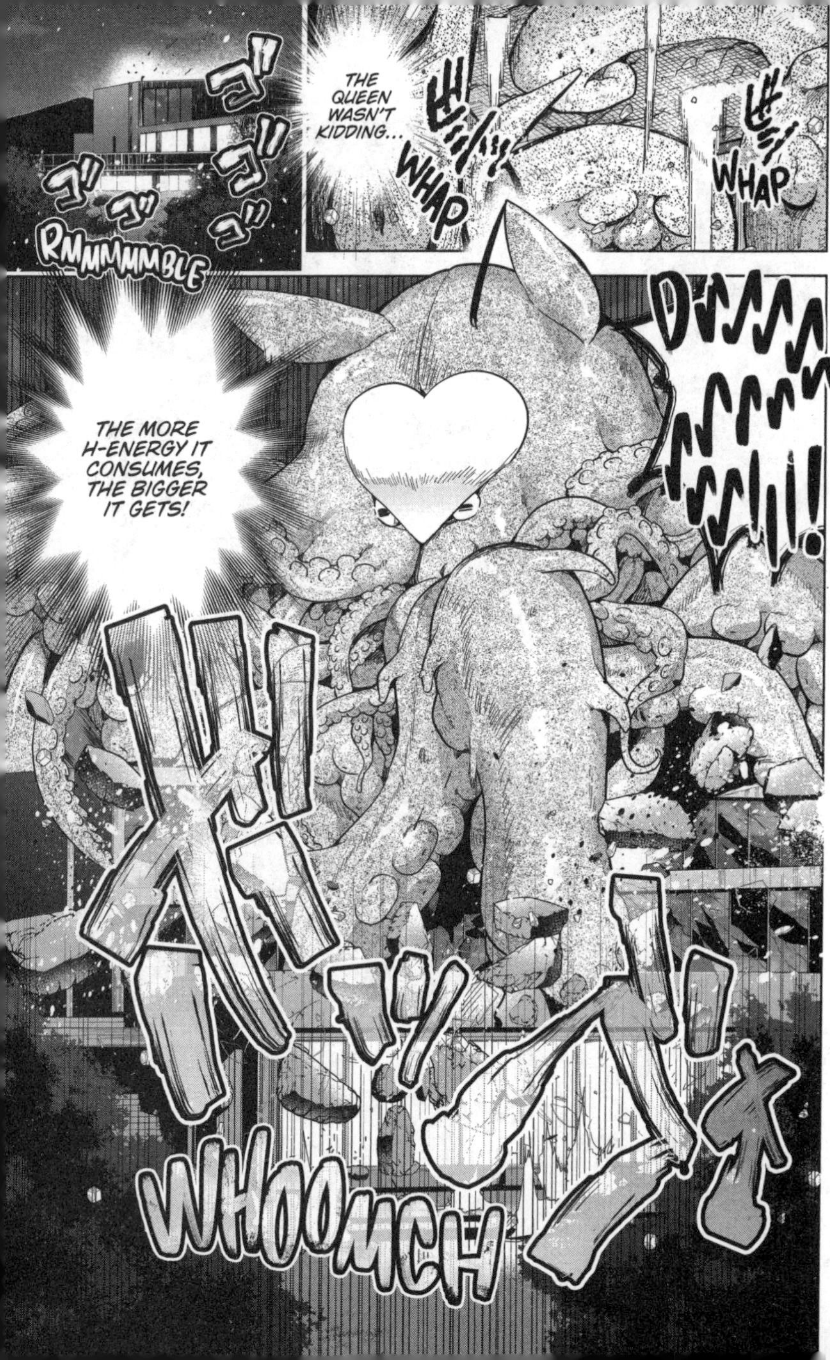
WHAP
THE QUEEN WASN'T KIDDING...
WHAP
RMMMMMBLE
THE MORE H-ENERGY IT CONSUMES, THE BIGGER IT GETS!
WHOOMCH

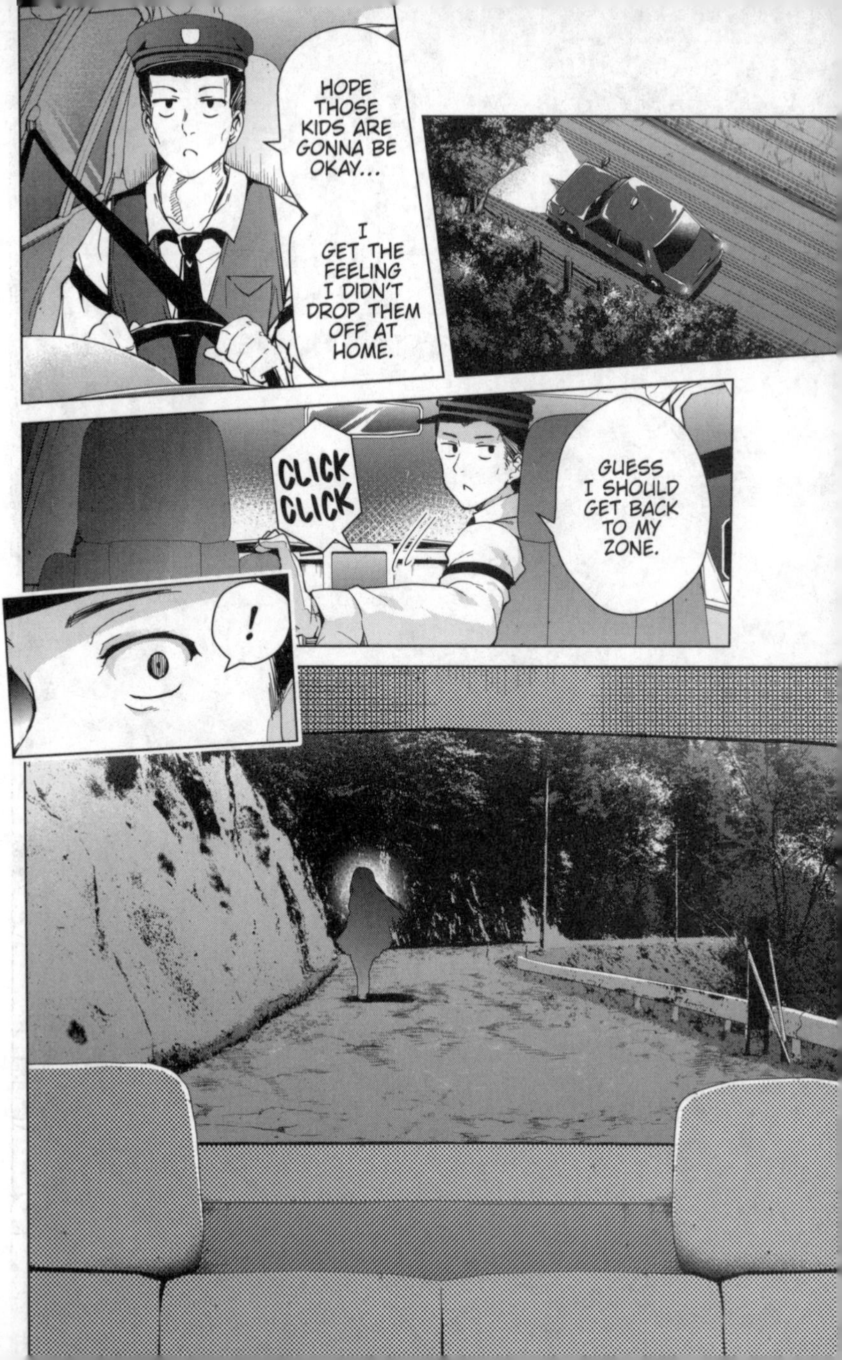
HOPE THOSE KIDS ARE GONNA BE OKAY...
I GET THE FEELING I DIDN'T DROP THEM OFF AT HOME.
GUESS I SHOULD GET BACK TO MY ZONE.
CLICK CLICK
!

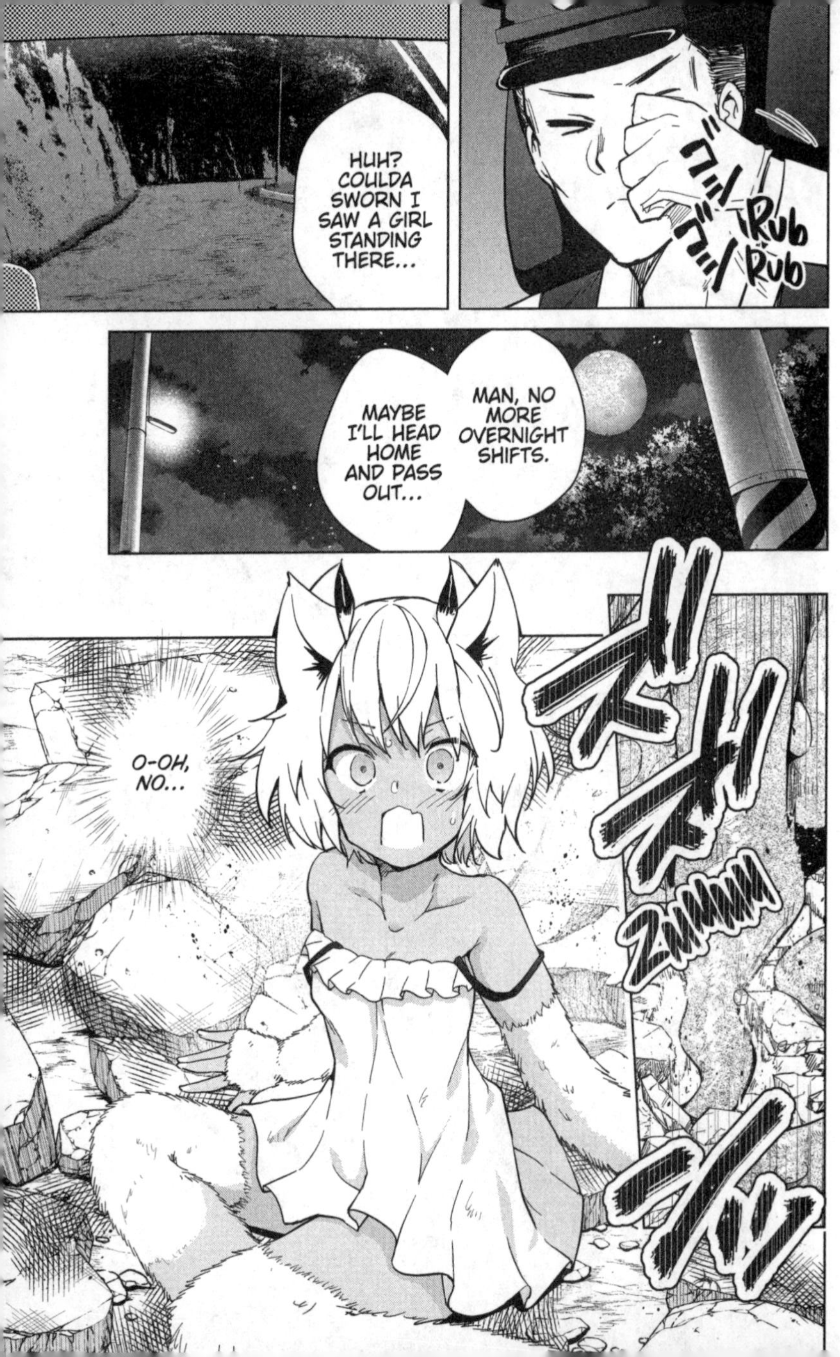
RUB RUB
HUH? COULDA SWORN I SAW A GIRL STANDING THERE...
MAN, NO MORE OVERNIGHT SHIFTS.
MAYBE I'LL HEAD HOME AND PASS OUT...
O-OH, NO...

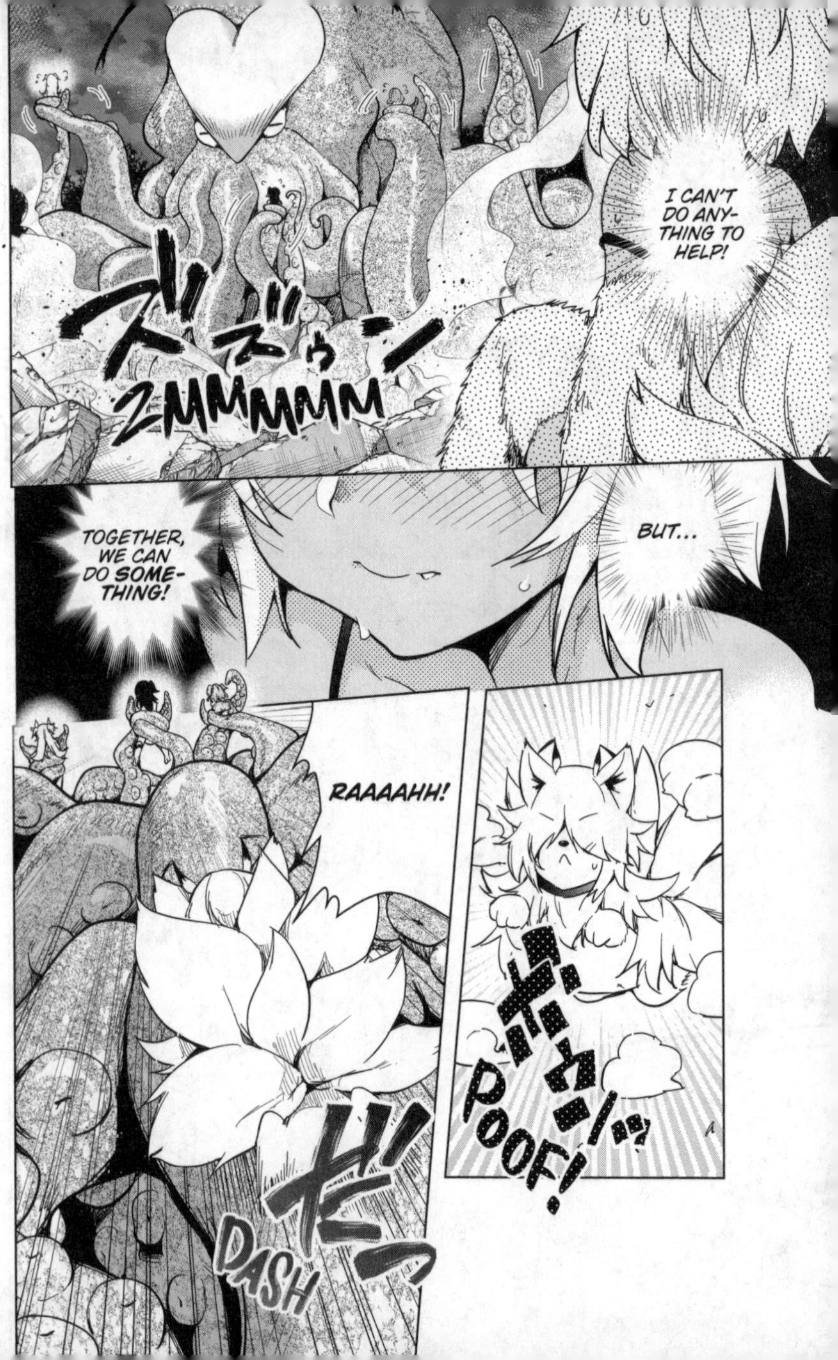

I CAN'T DO ANY-THING TO HELP!
ZMMMMMM
BUT...
TOGETHER, WE CAN DO SOME-THING!
POOF!
RAAAAHH!
DASH

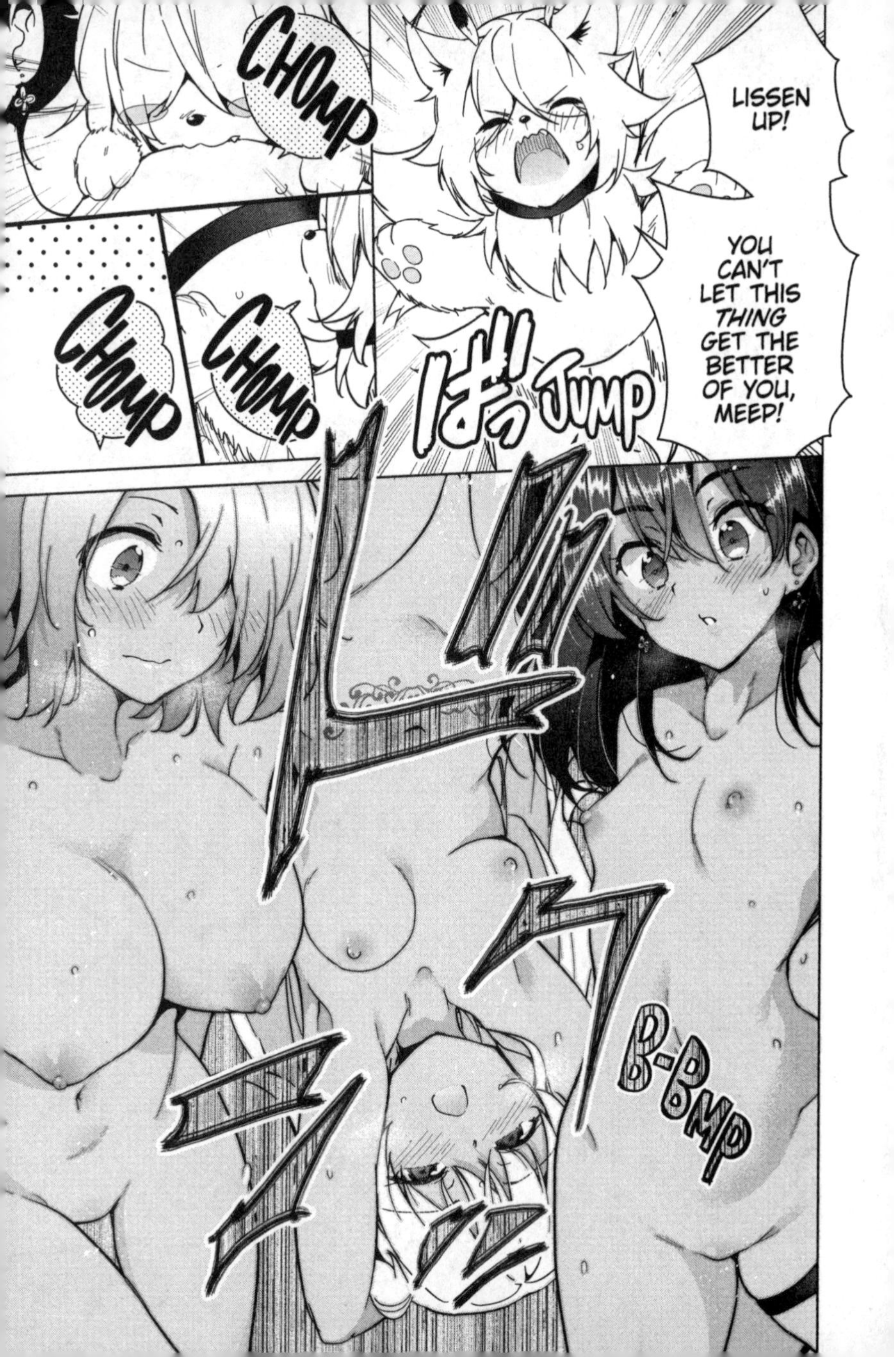
LISSEN UP!
YOU CAN'T LET THIS *THING* GET THE BETTER OF YOU, MEEP!
ぱっ JUMP
CHOMP
CHOMP
CHOMP
B-BMP

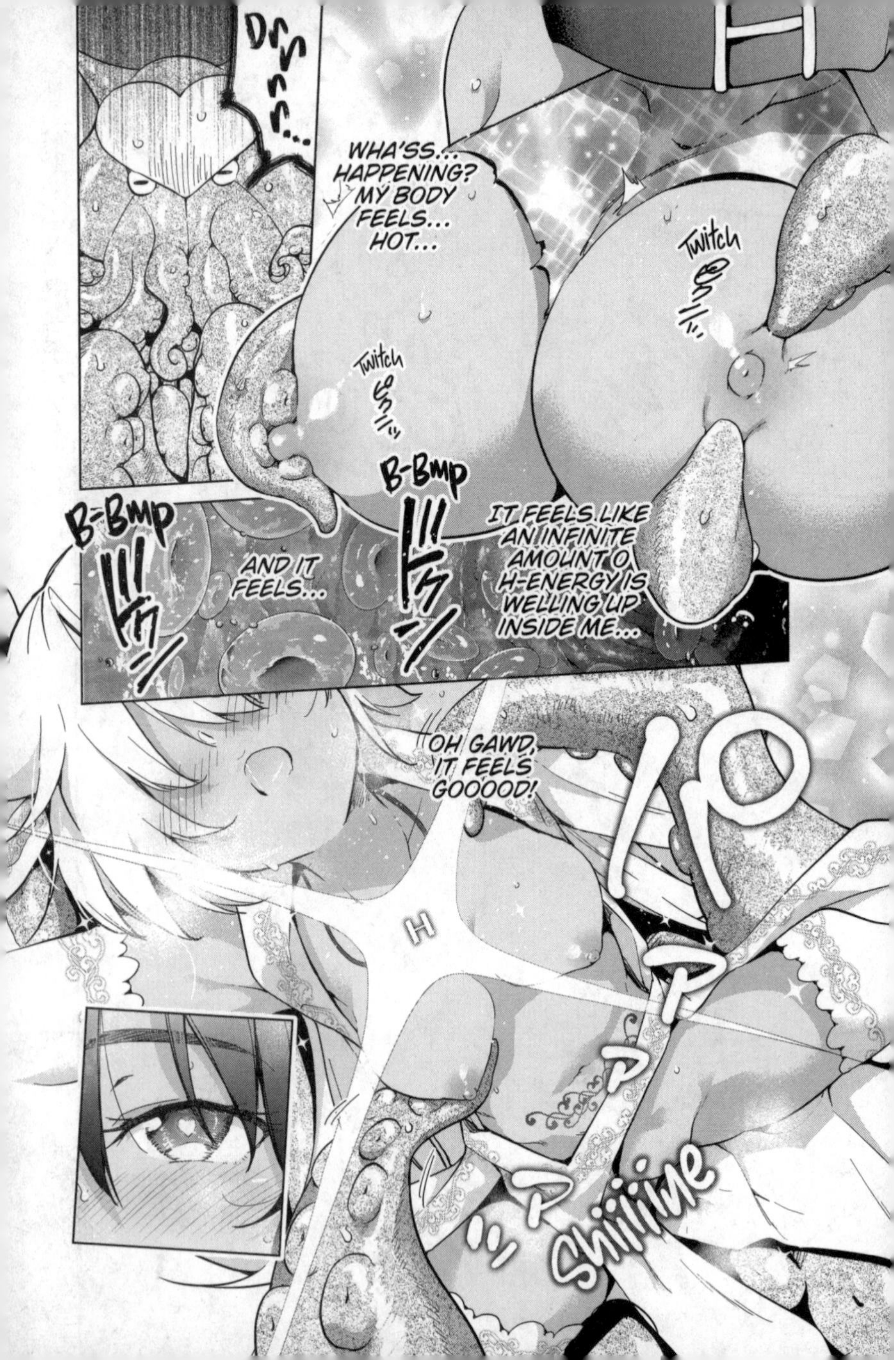

WHA'SS... HAPPENING? MY BODY FEELS... HOT...
Twitch
Twitch
Drrr...
B-Bmp
IT FEELS LIKE AN INFINITE AMOUNT O H-ENERGY IS WELLING UP INSIDE ME...
AND IT FEELS...
B-Bmp
OH GAWD, IT FEELS GOOOOD!
H
Shiiiine

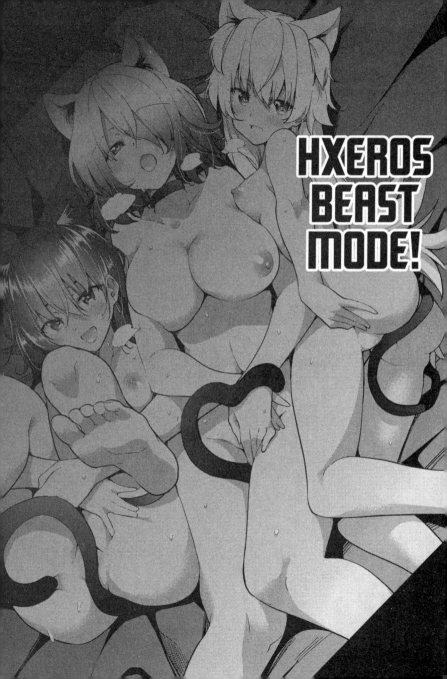

HXEROS BEAST MODE!

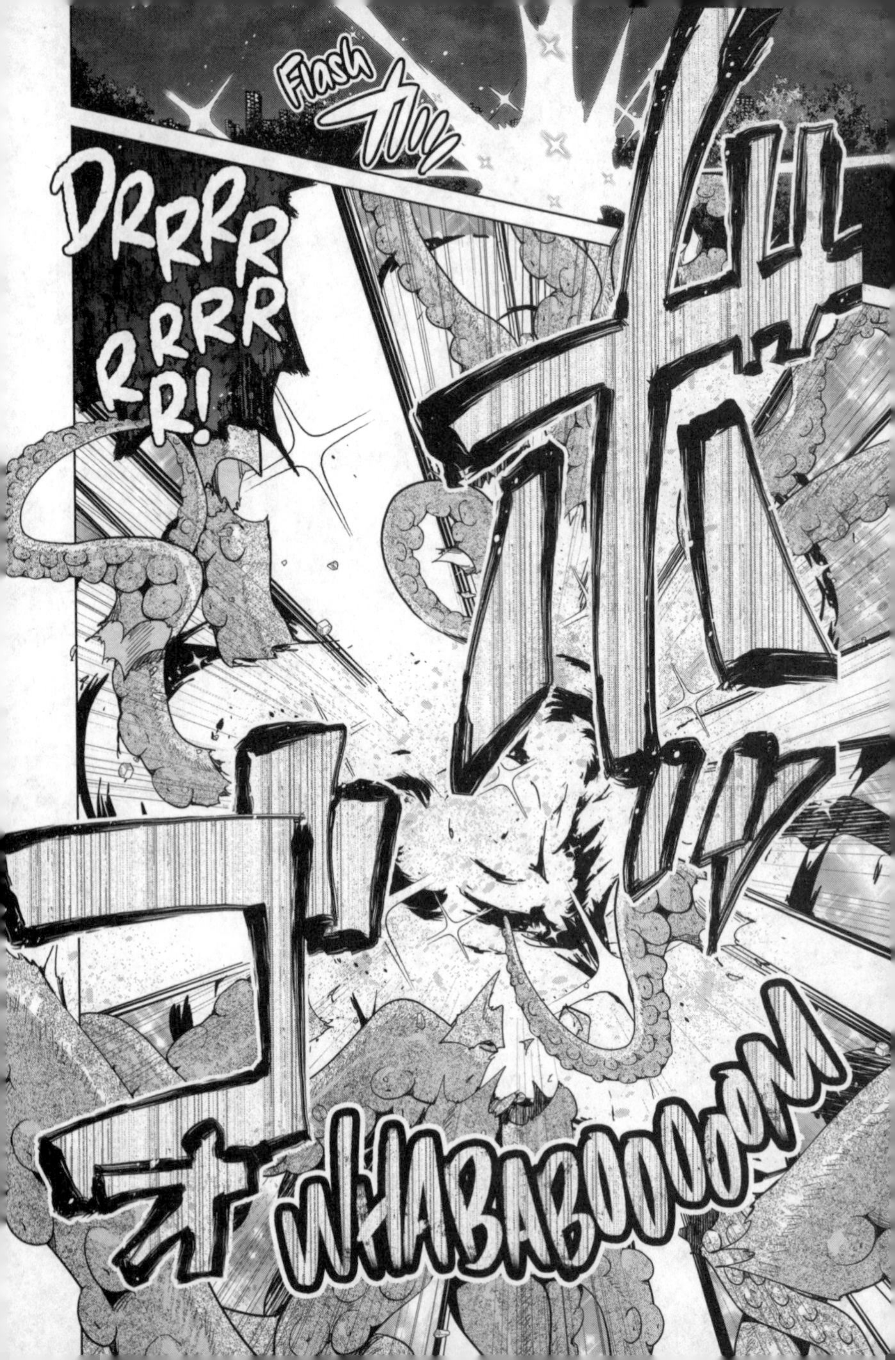
Flash
DRRRR RRRR RRRR R!
WHABABOOOOOM

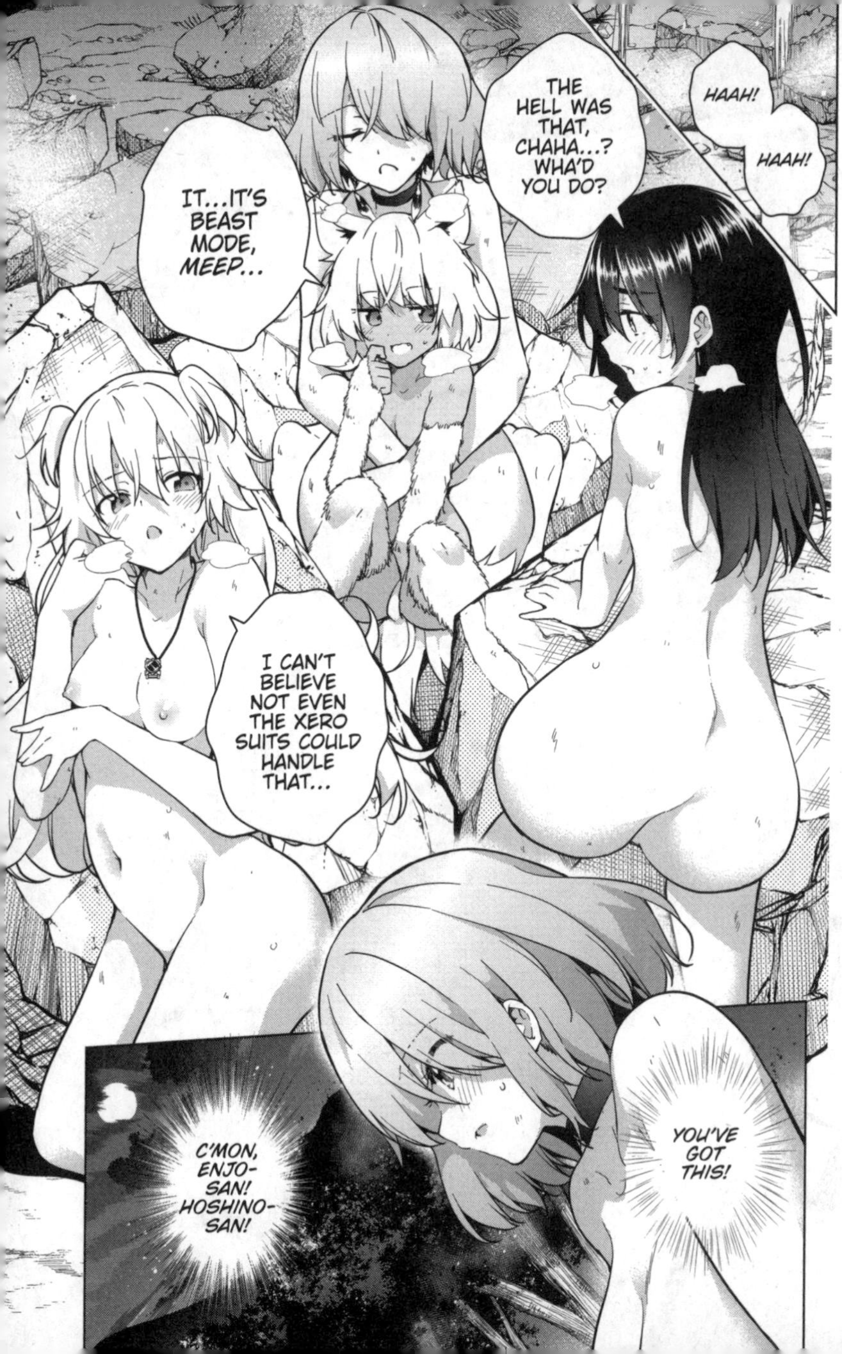
HAAH!
HAAH!
THE HELL WAS THAT, CHAHA...? WHA'D YOU DO?
IT...IT'S BEAST MODE, MEEP...
I CAN'T BELIEVE NOT EVEN THE XERO SUITS COULD HANDLE THAT...
YOU'VE GOT THIS!
C'MON, ENJO-SAN! HOSHINO-SAN!

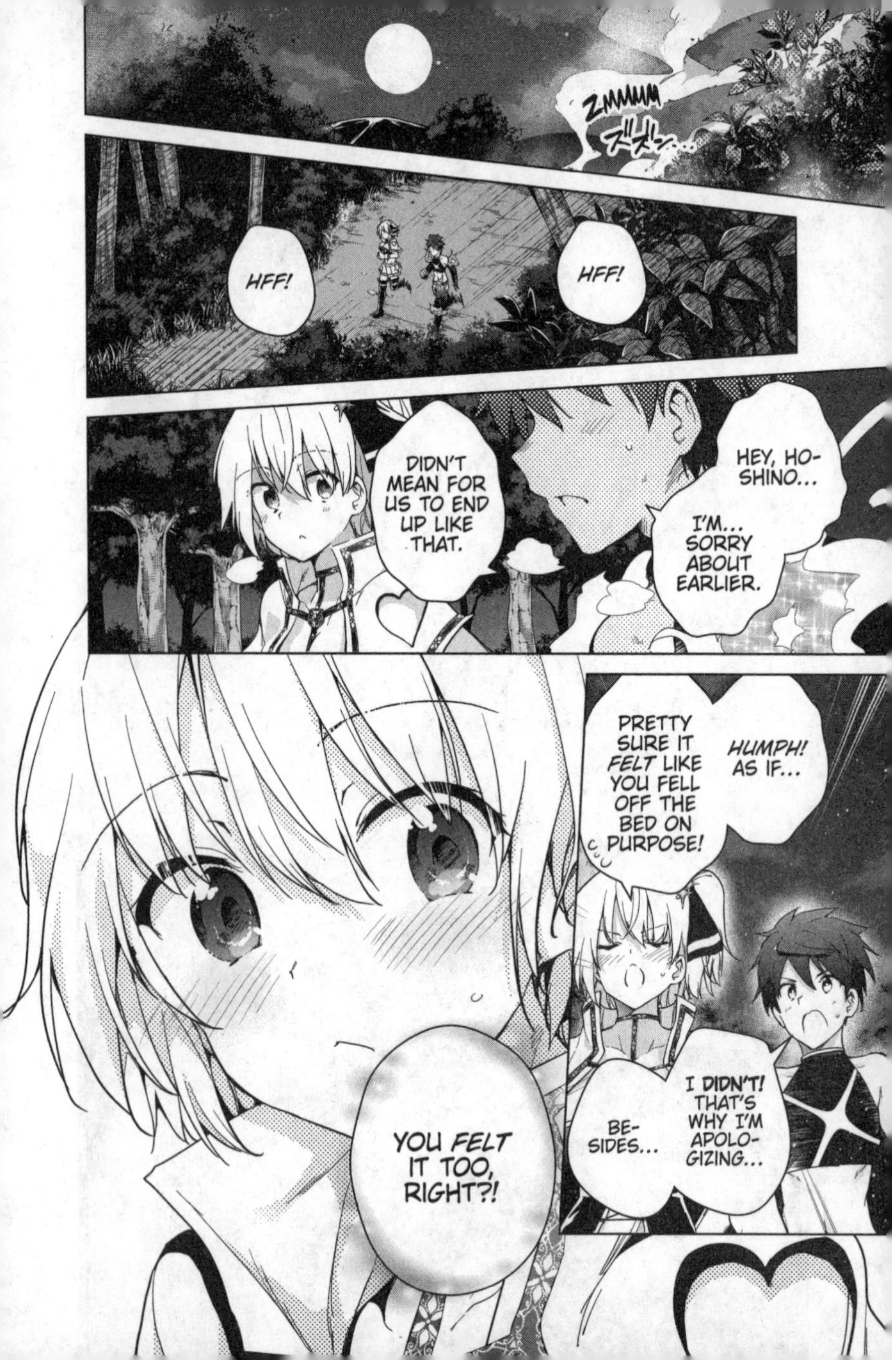
ZMMMM
HFF!
HFF!
HEY, HO-SHINO...
I'M... SORRY ABOUT EARLIER.
DIDN'T MEAN FOR US TO END UP LIKE THAT.
HUMPH! AS IF...
PRETTY SURE IT *FELT* LIKE YOU FELL OFF THE BED ON PURPOSE!
I DIDN'T! THAT'S WHY I'M APOLO-GIZING...
BE-SIDES...
YOU *FELT* IT TOO, RIGHT?!

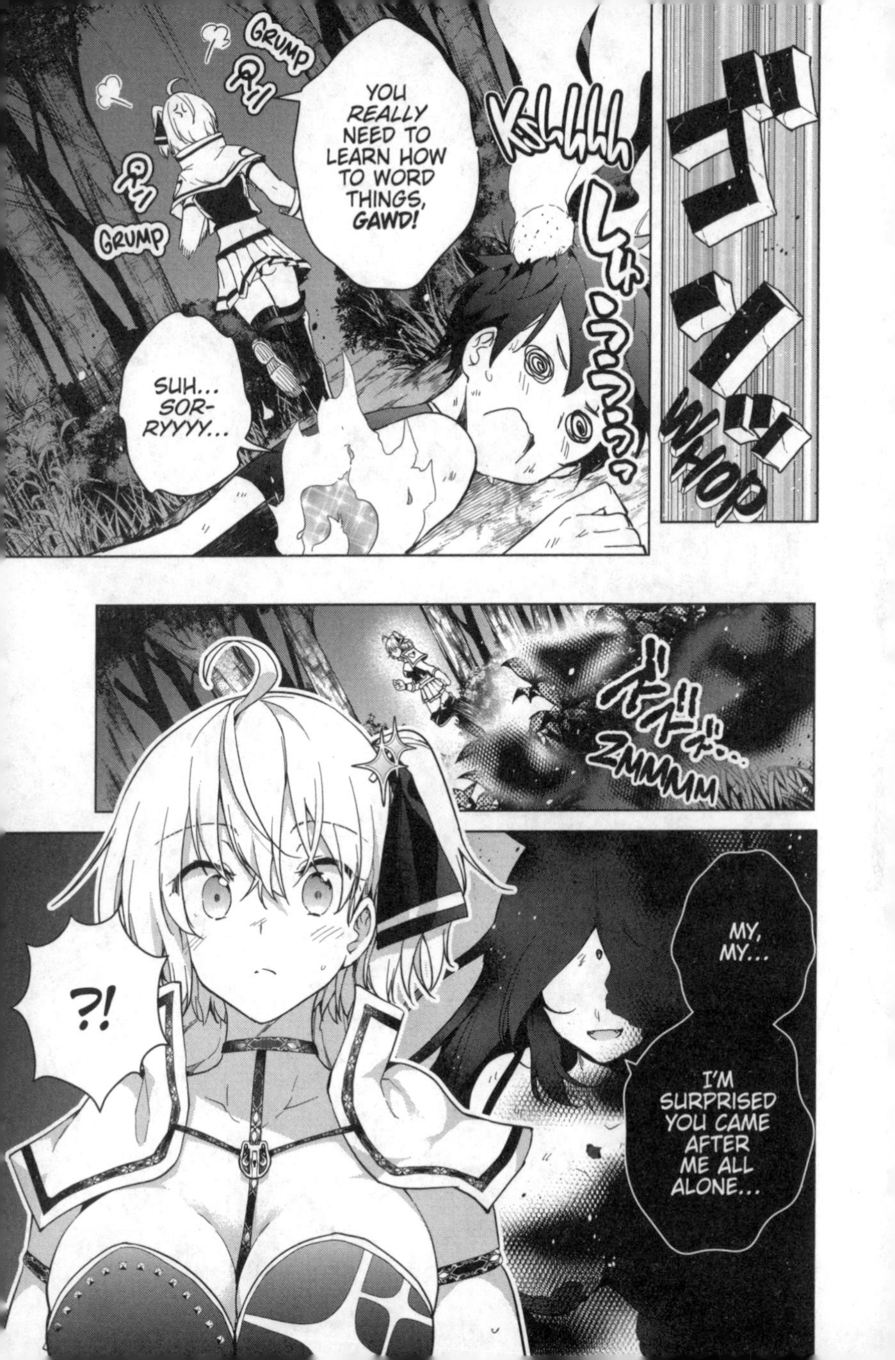
WHOP
Kshhhh
YOU REALLY NEED TO LEARN HOW TO WORD THINGS, GAWD!
GRUMP
GRUMP
SUH... SORRYYYY...
ZMMMM
MY, MY...
I'M SURPRISED YOU CAME AFTER ME ALL ALONE...
?!

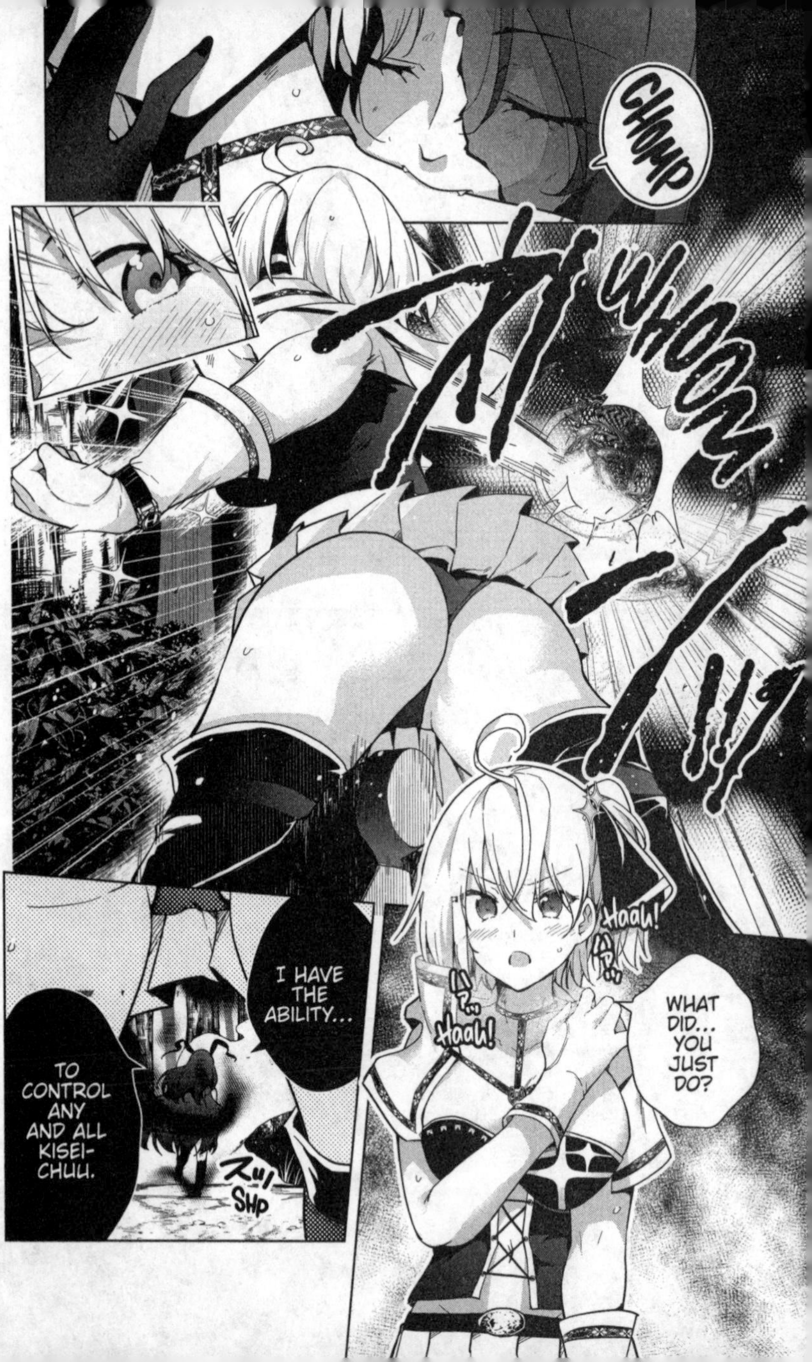

CHOMP
WHOOM!!
Haah!
Haah!
WHAT DID... YOU JUST DO?
I HAVE THE ABILITY...
TO CONTROL ANY AND ALL KISEI-CHUU.
SHP

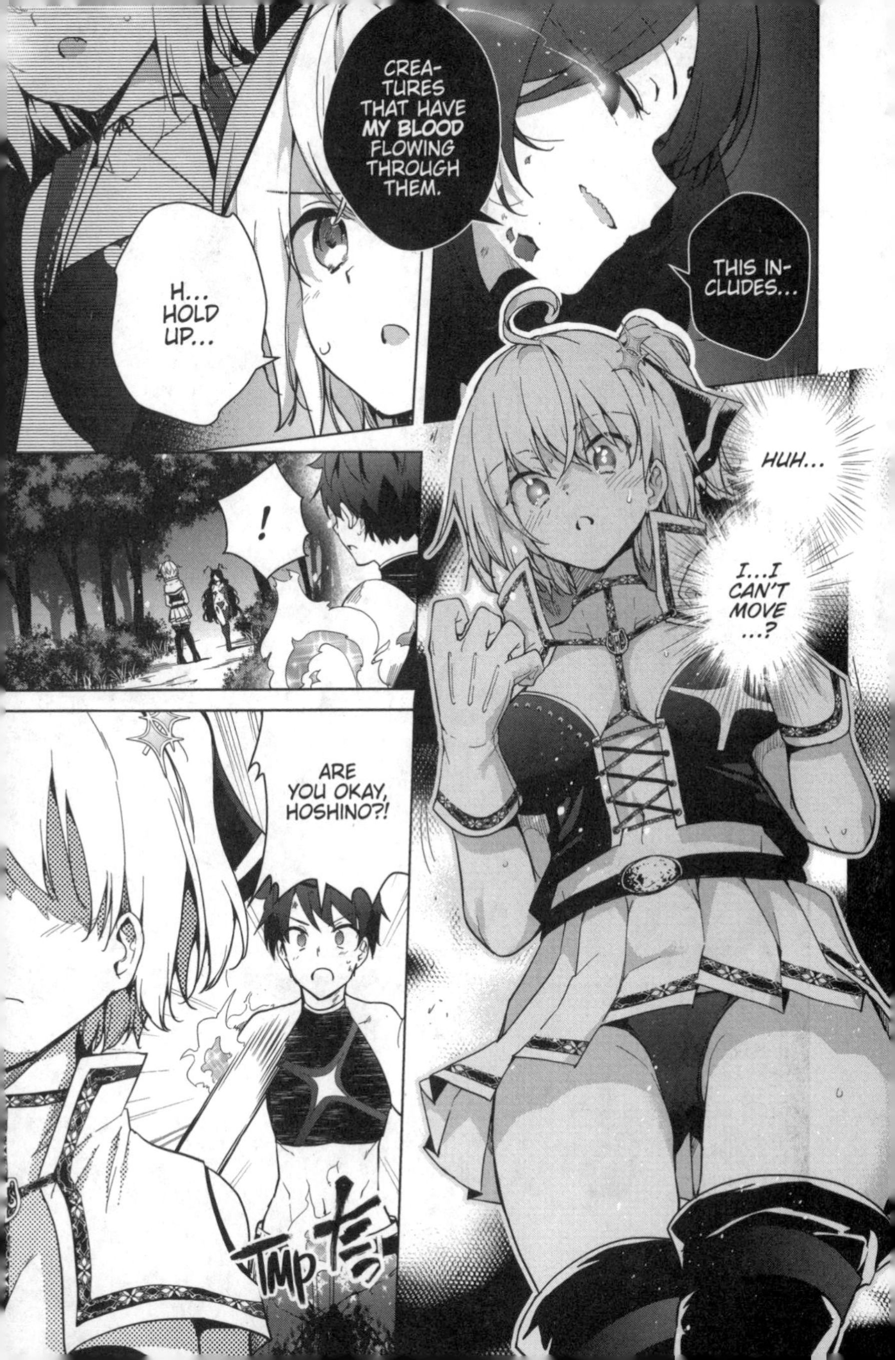
CREA-
TURES
THAT HAVE
MY BLOOD
FLOWING
THROUGH
THEM.
THIS IN-
CLUDES...
H...
HOLD
UP...
HUH...
I...I
CAN'T
MOVE
...?
!
ARE
YOU OKAY,
HOSHINO?!
TMP

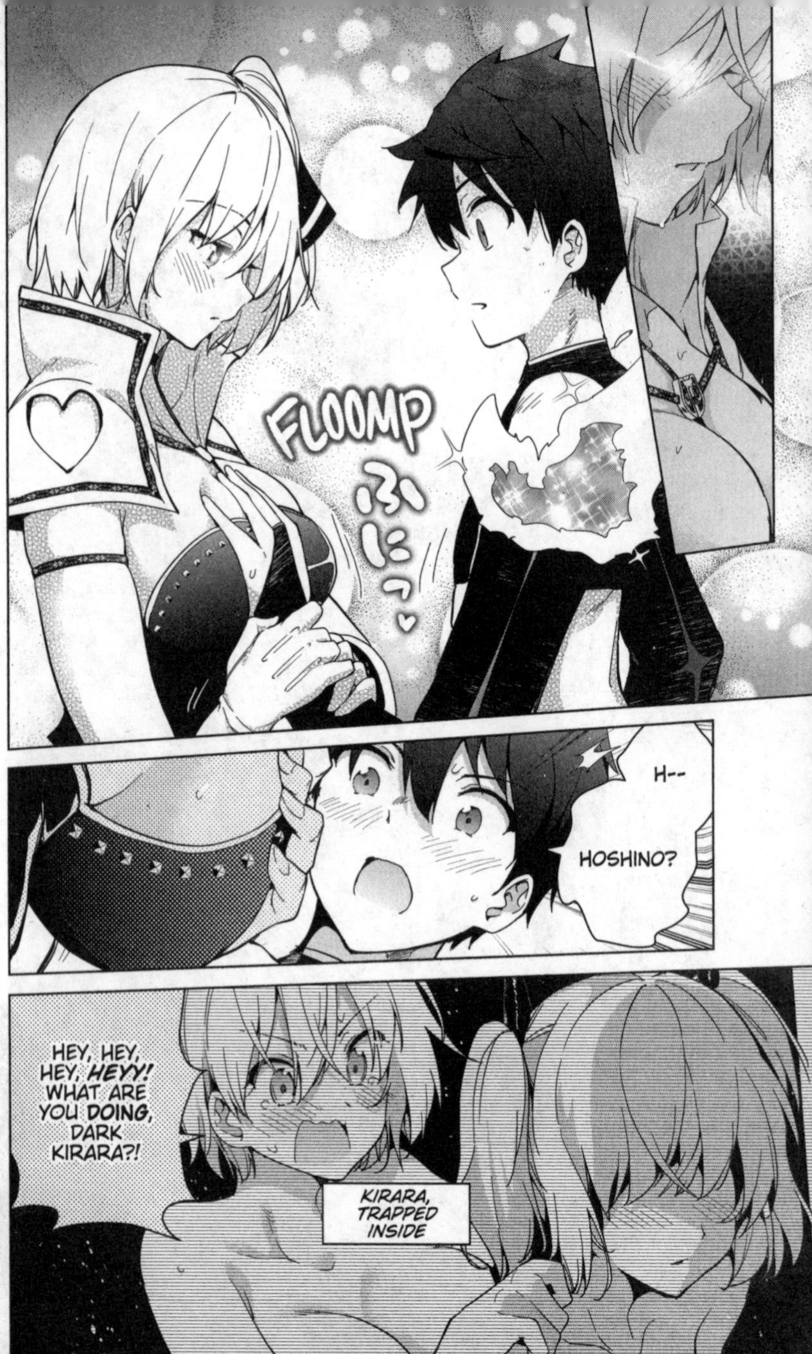
FLOOMP
ふにっ
H--
HOSHINO?
HEY, HEY, HEY, HEYY! WHAT ARE YOU DOING, DARK KIRARA?!
KIRARA, TRAPPED INSIDE

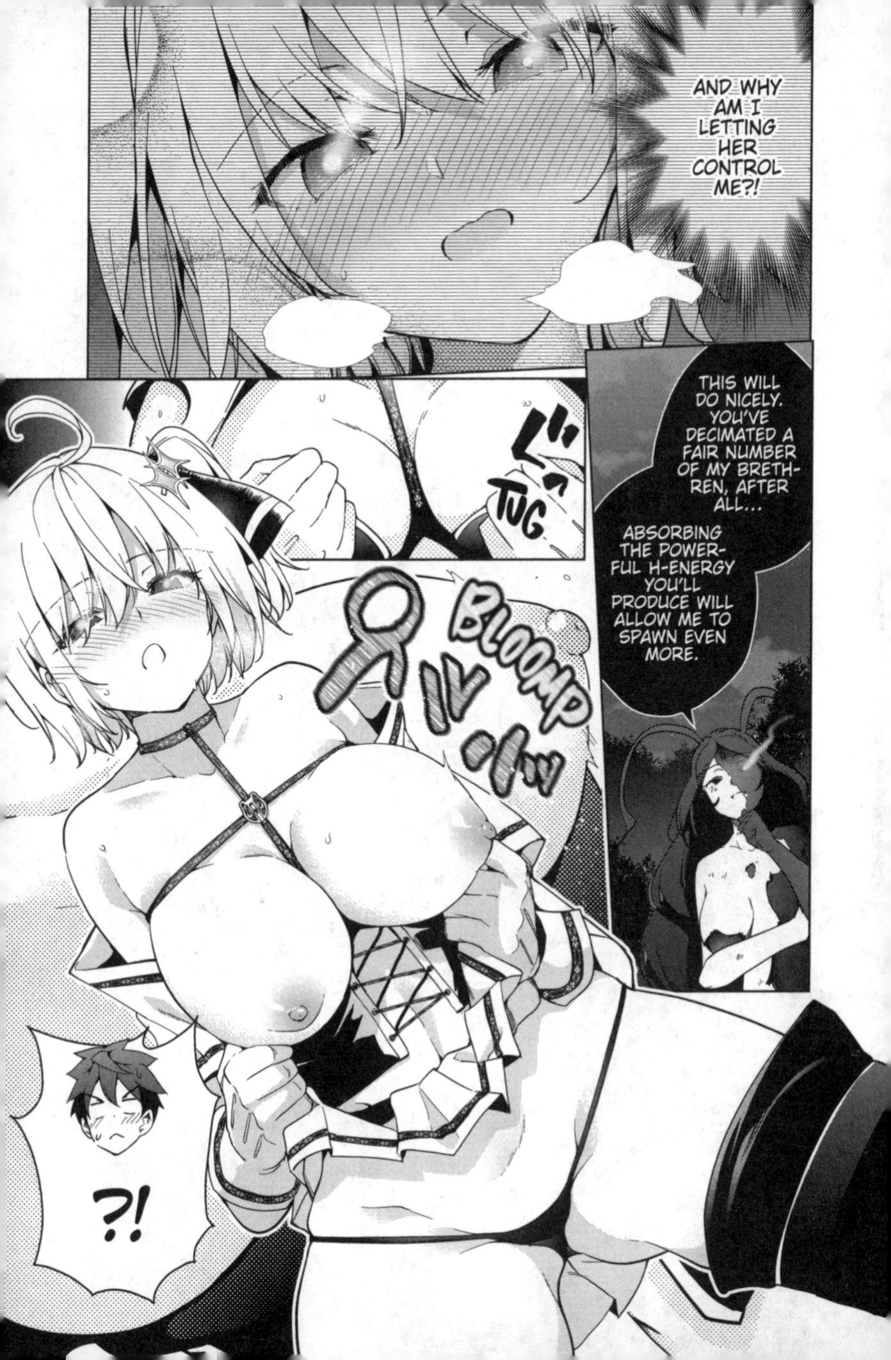
AND WHY AM I LETTING HER CONTROL ME?!
THIS WILL DO NICELY. YOU'VE DECIMATED A FAIR NUMBER OF MY BRETH-REN, AFTER ALL...
ABSORBING THE POWER-FUL H-ENERGY YOU'LL PRODUCE WILL ALLOW ME TO SPAWN EVEN MORE.
TUG
BLOOMP
?!

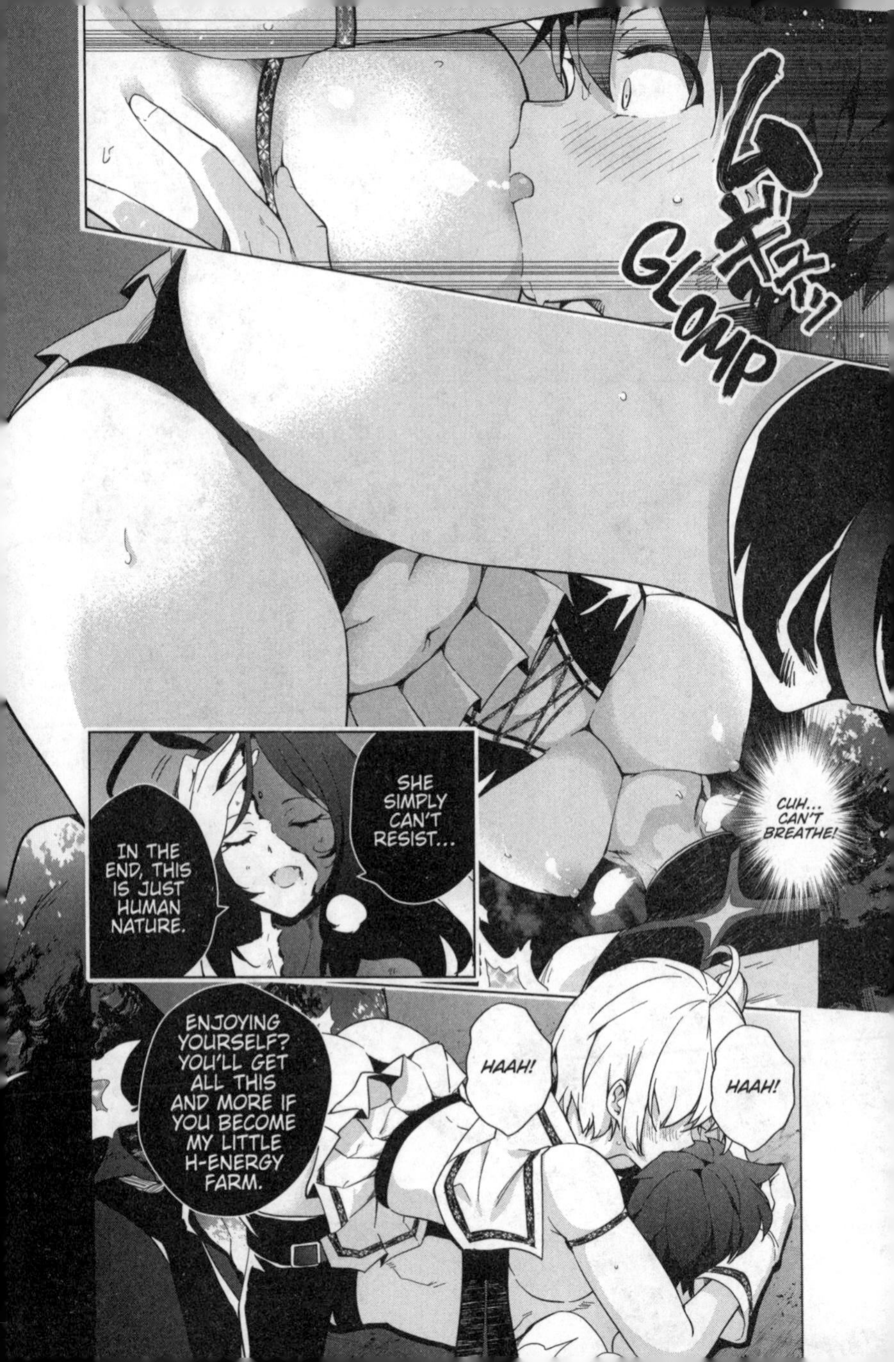
GLOMP
CUH... CAN'T BREATHE!
SHE SIMPLY CAN'T RESIST...
IN THE END, THIS IS JUST HUMAN NATURE.
HAAH!
HAAH!
ENJOYING YOURSELF? YOU'LL GET ALL THIS AND MORE IF YOU BECOME MY LITTLE H-ENERGY FARM.

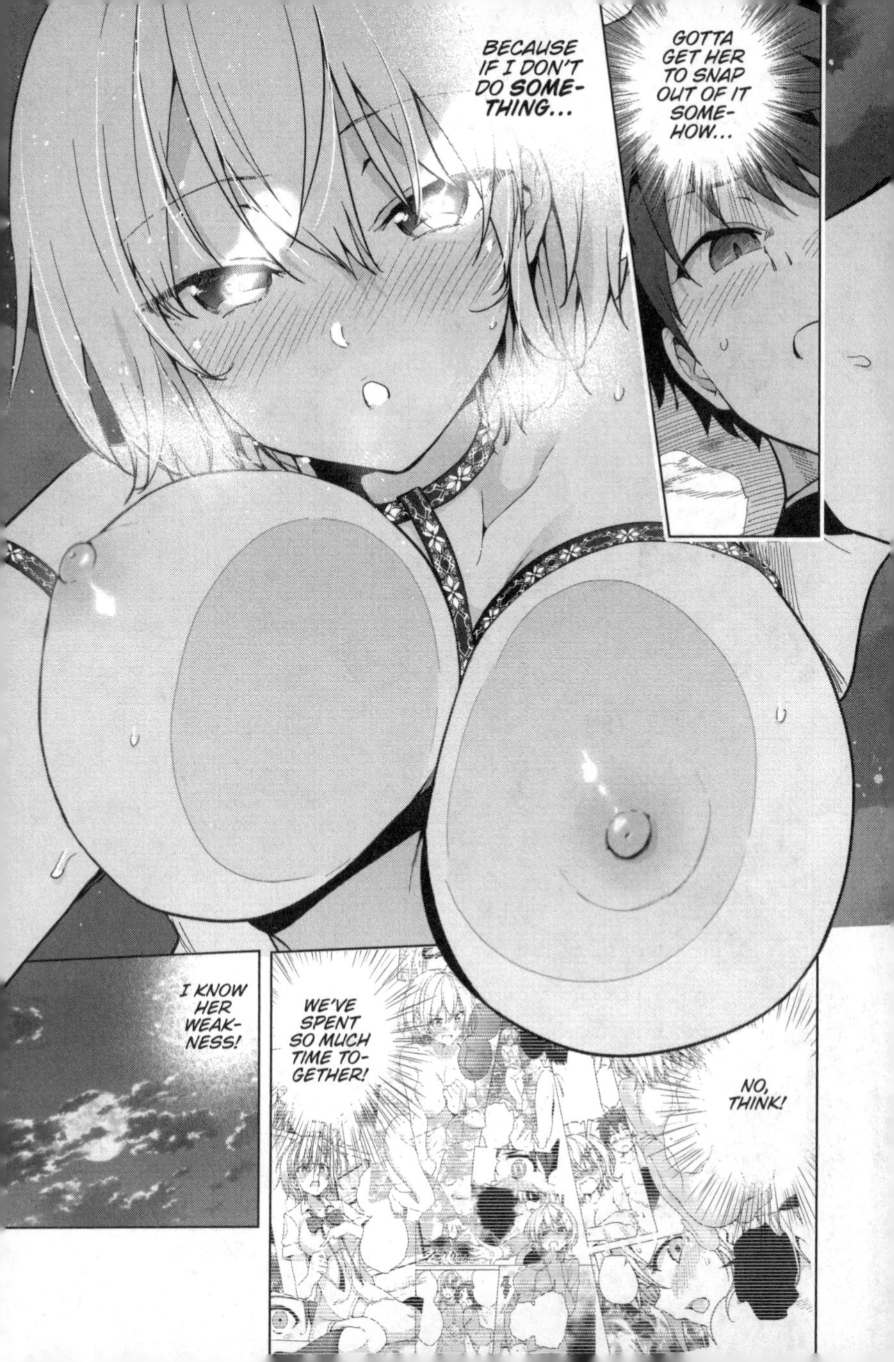
GOTTA GET HER TO SNAP OUT OF IT SOMEHOW...
BECAUSE IF I DON'T DO SOMETHING...
NO, THINK!
WE'VE SPENT SO MUCH TIME TOGETHER!
I KNOW HER WEAKNESS!

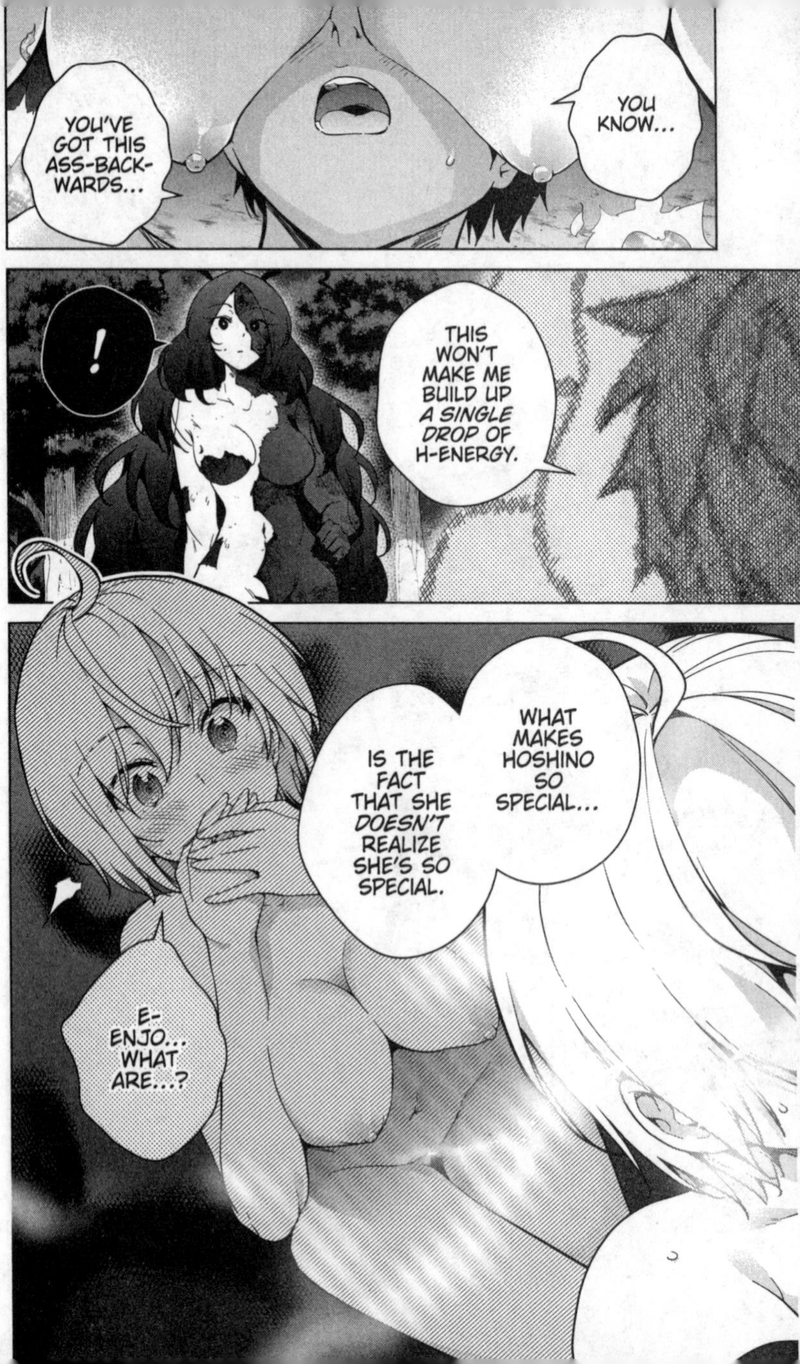
YOU KNOW...
YOU'VE GOT THIS ASS-BACKWARDS...
THIS WON'T MAKE ME BUILD UP *A SINGLE DROP* OF H-ENERGY.
!
WHAT MAKES HOSHINO SO SPECIAL...
IS THE FACT THAT SHE *DOESN'T* REALIZE SHE'S SO SPECIAL.
E-ENJO... WHAT ARE...?

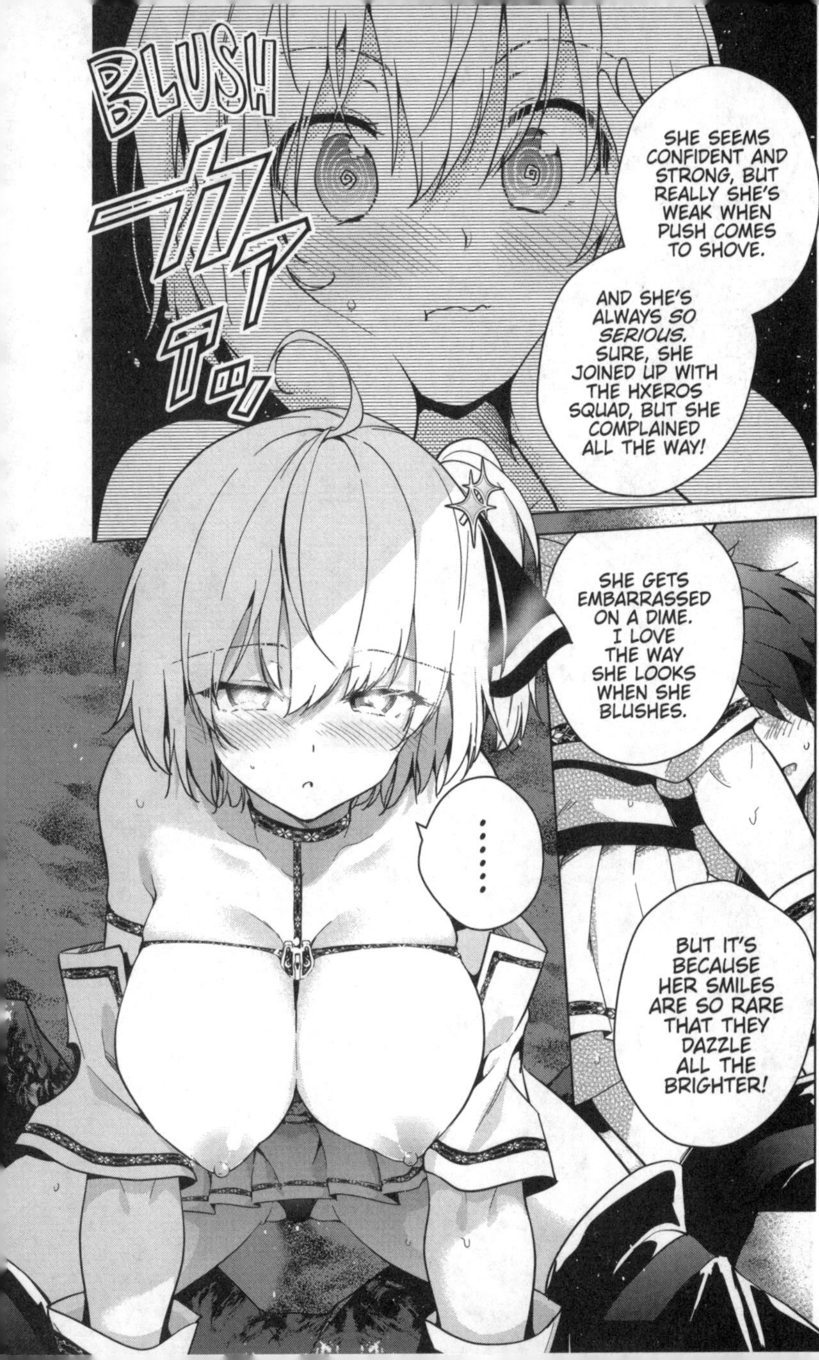
SHE SEEMS CONFIDENT AND STRONG, BUT REALLY SHE'S WEAK WHEN PUSH COMES TO SHOVE.
AND SHE'S ALWAYS SO *SERIOUS.* SURE, SHE JOINED UP WITH THE HXEROS SQUAD, BUT SHE COMPLAINED ALL THE WAY!
BLUSH
SHE GETS EMBARRASSED ON A DIME. I LOVE THE WAY SHE LOOKS WHEN SHE BLUSHES.
BUT IT'S BECAUSE HER SMILES ARE SO RARE THAT THEY DAZZLE ALL THE BRIGHTER!
......

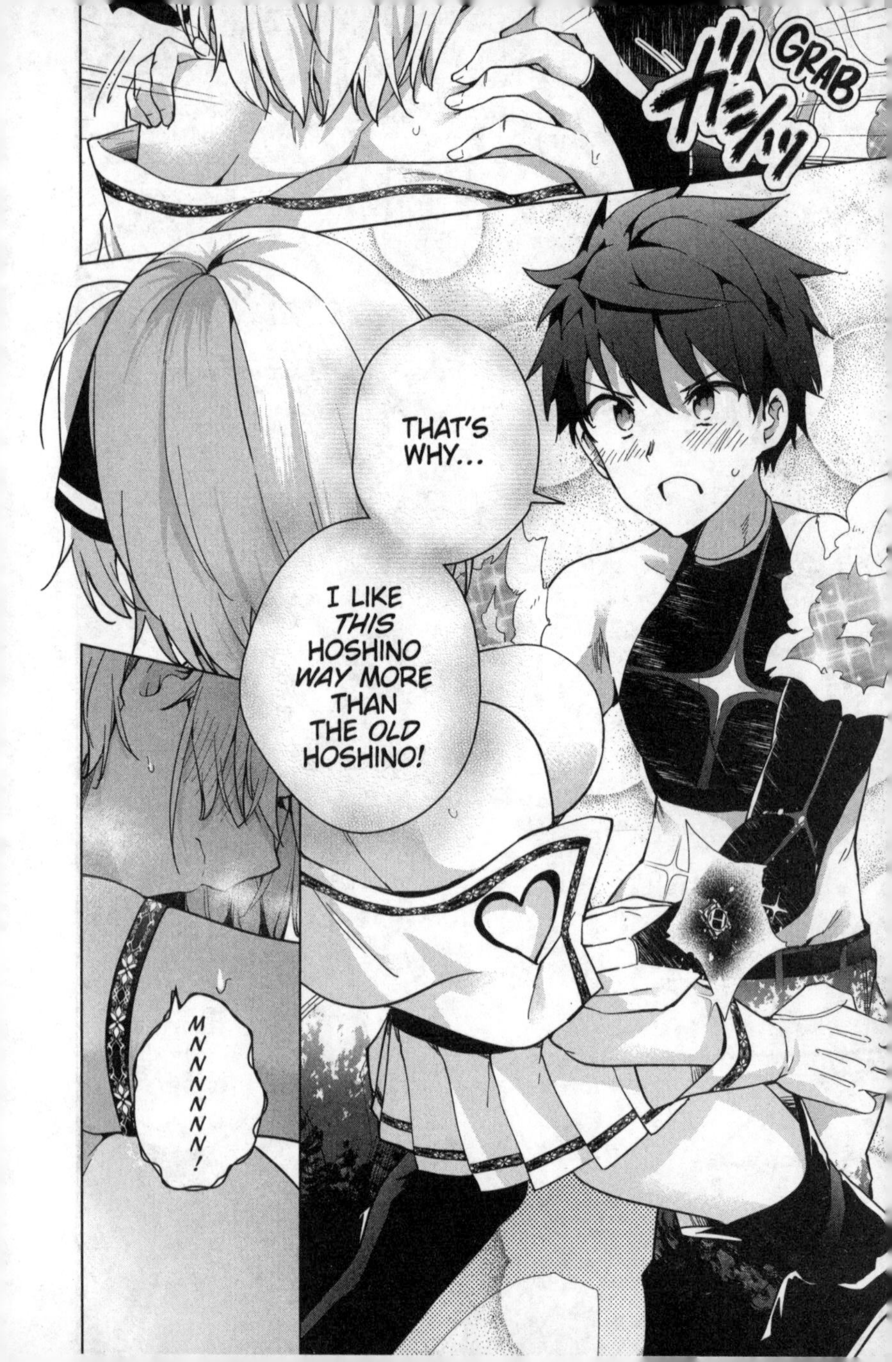
GRAB
ガシッ
THAT'S WHY...
I LIKE *THIS* HOSHINO *WAY* MORE THAN THE *OLD* HOSHINO!
MNNNNNN!

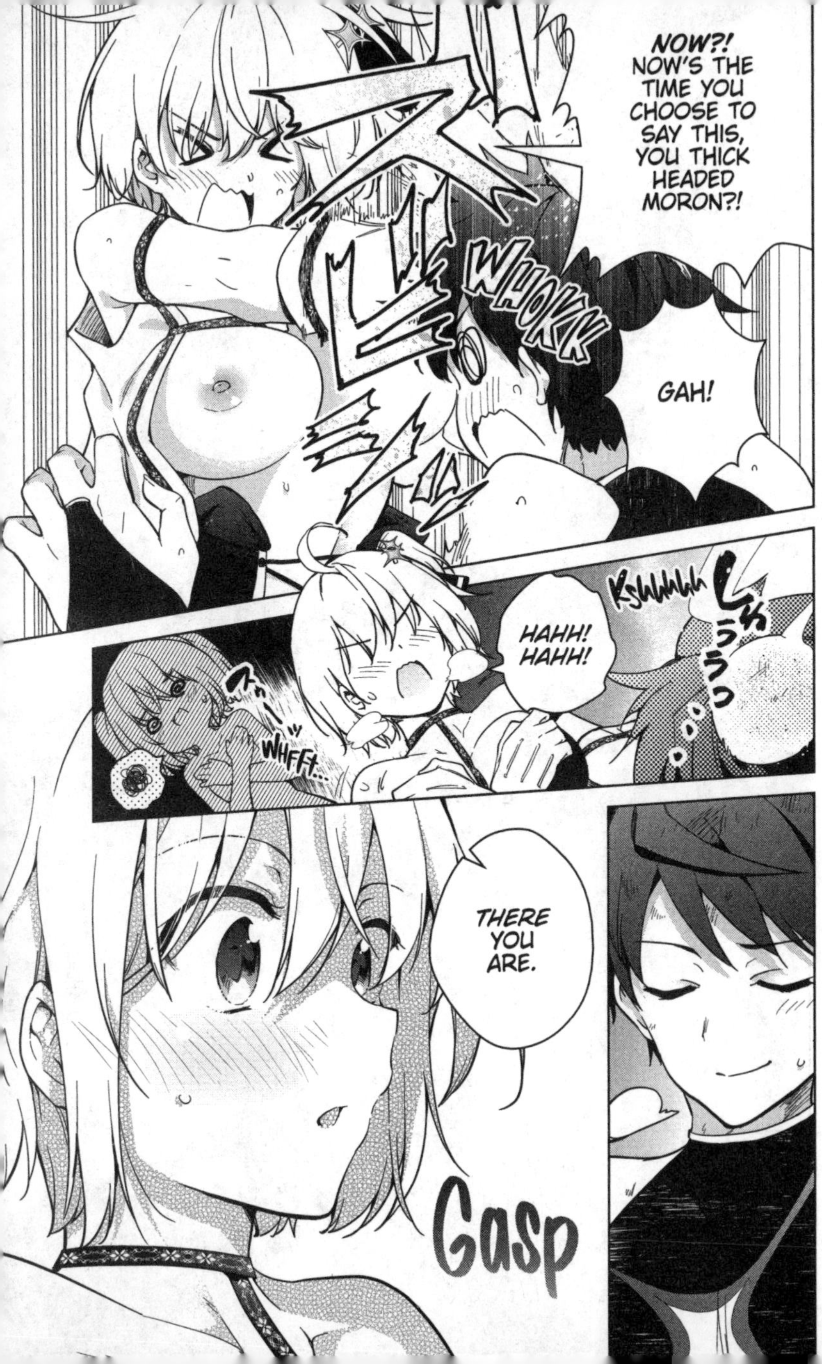
NOW?! NOW'S THE TIME YOU CHOOSE TO SAY THIS, YOU THICK HEADED MORON?!
WHOKK
GAH!
KSHHHHH
HAHH! HAHH!
WHFFT...
THERE YOU ARE.
Gasp

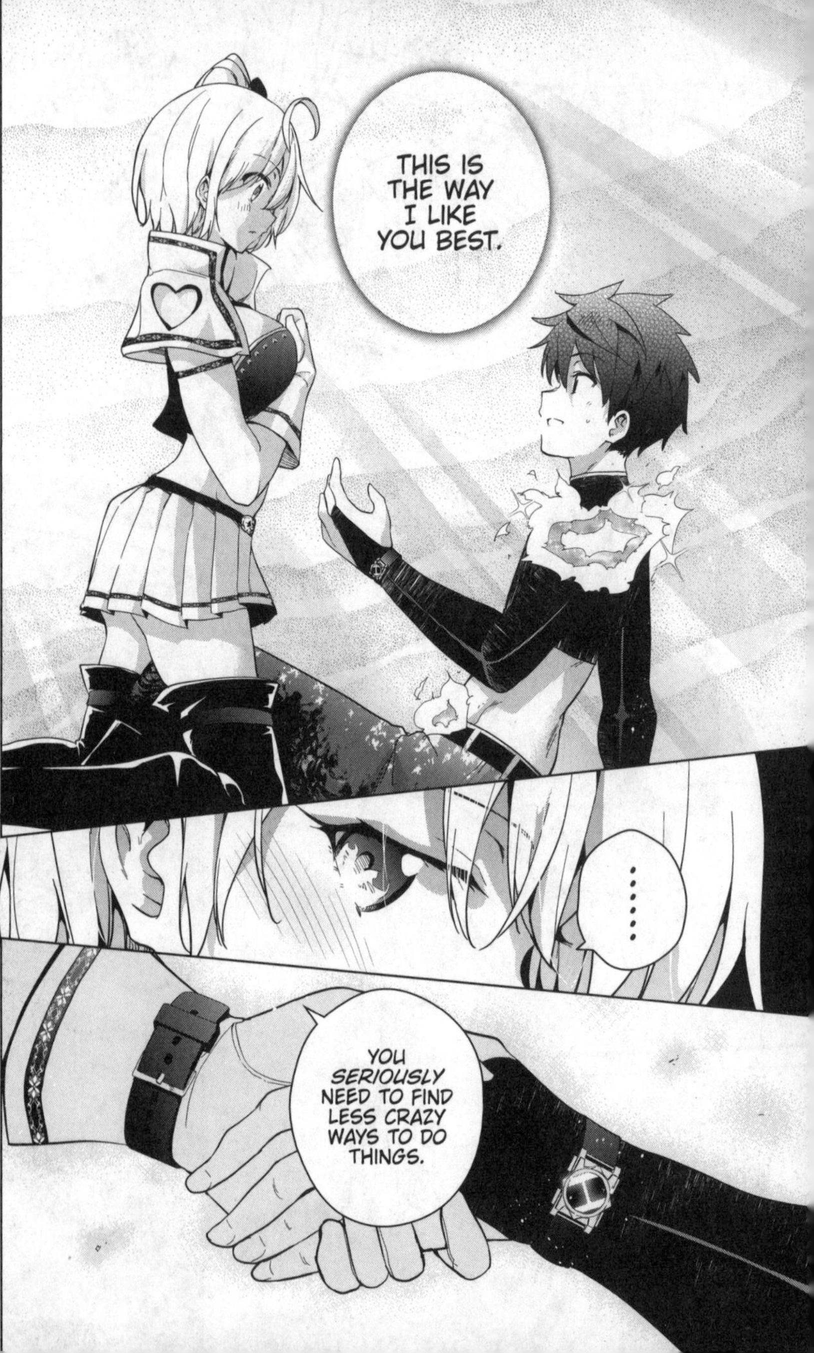
THIS IS THE WAY I LIKE YOU BEST.
......
YOU SERIOUSLY NEED TO FIND LESS CRAZY WAYS TO DO THINGS.

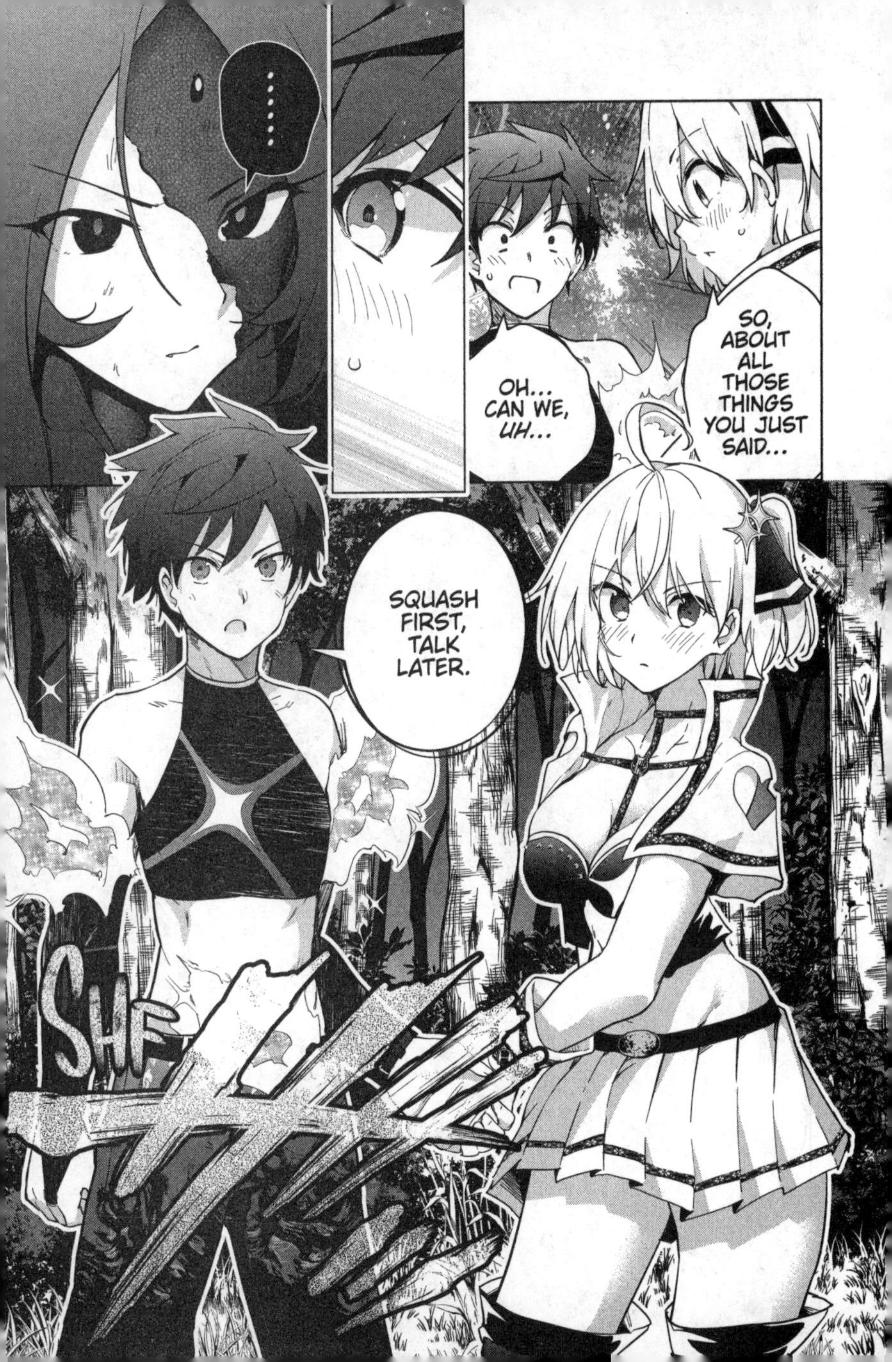
SO, ABOUT ALL THOSE THINGS YOU JUST SAID...
OH... CAN WE, UH...
SQUASH FIRST, TALK LATER.
SHF

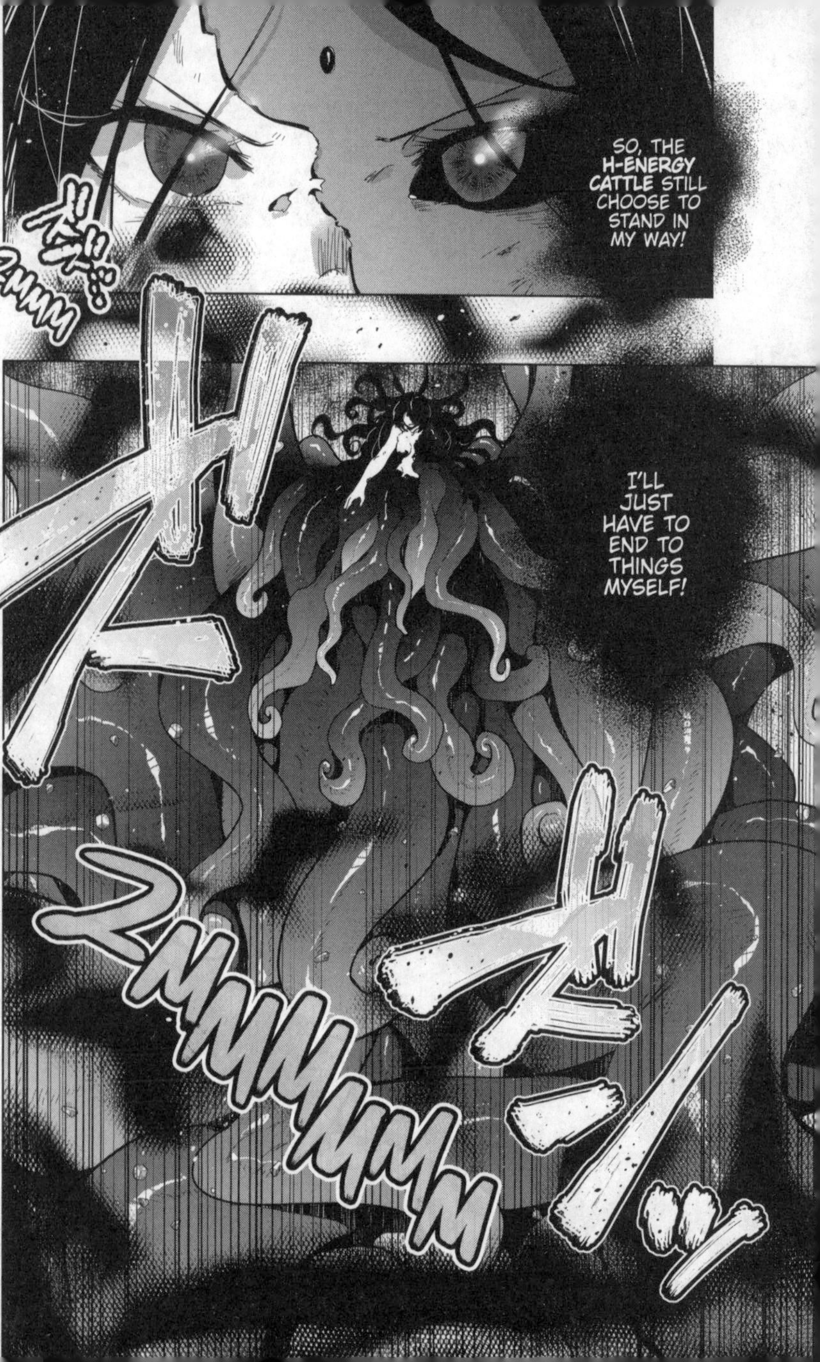
SO, THE **H-ENERGY CATTLE** STILL CHOOSE TO STAND IN MY WAY!
ZMMM
I'LL JUST HAVE TO END TO THINGS MYSELF!
ZMMMMMMMMM

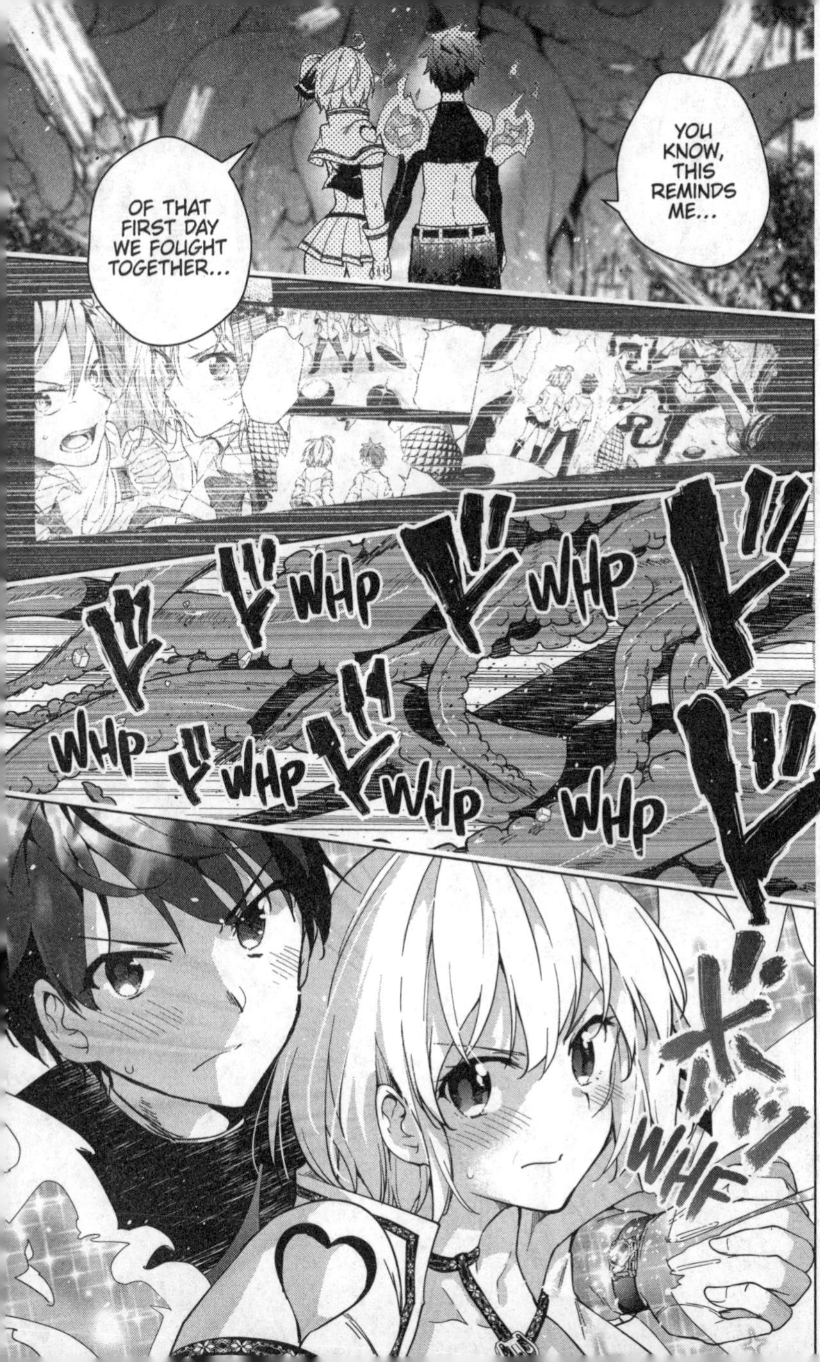

YOU KNOW, THIS REMINDS ME...
OF THAT FIRST DAY WE FOUGHT TOGETHER...
WHP
WHP
WHP
WHP
WHP
WHP
WHF

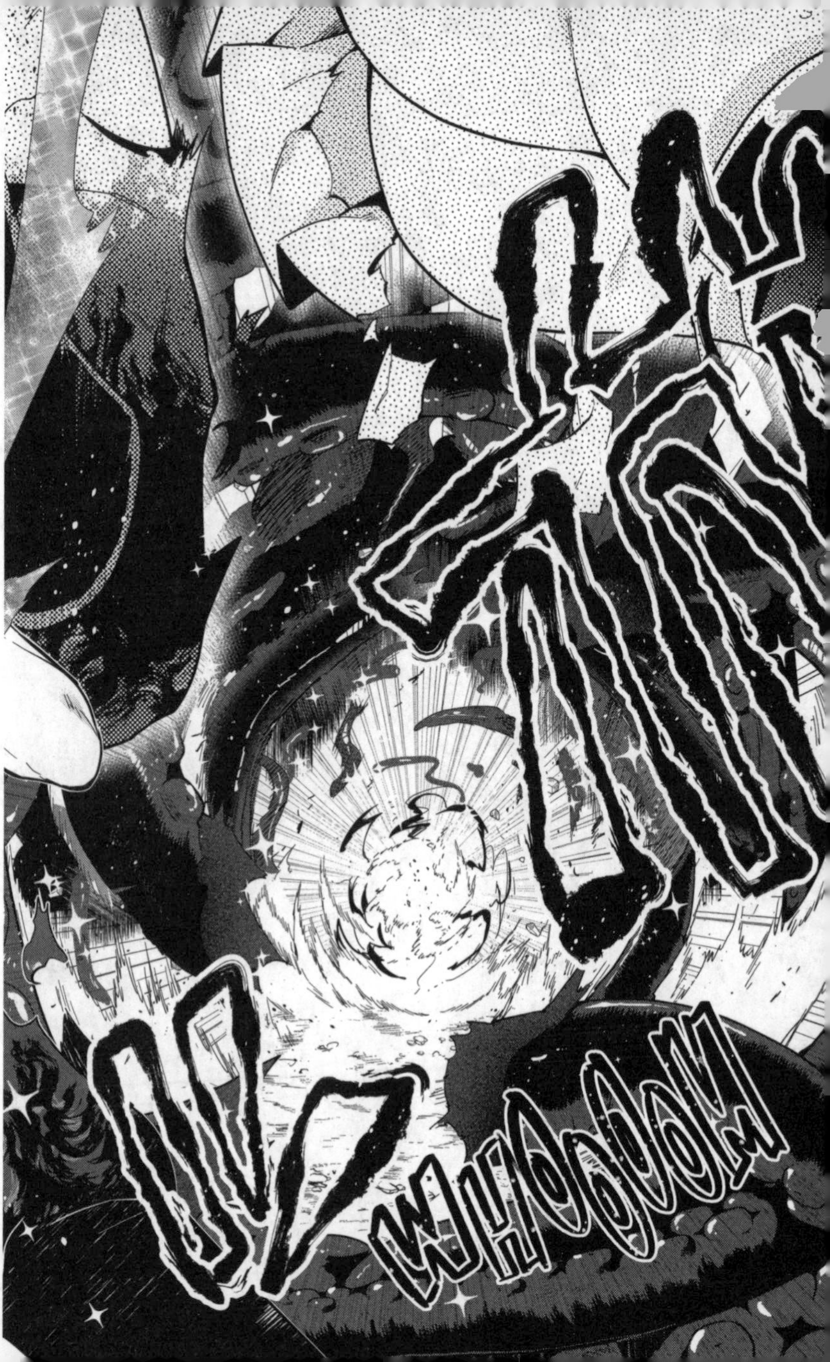
WHOOOOOM

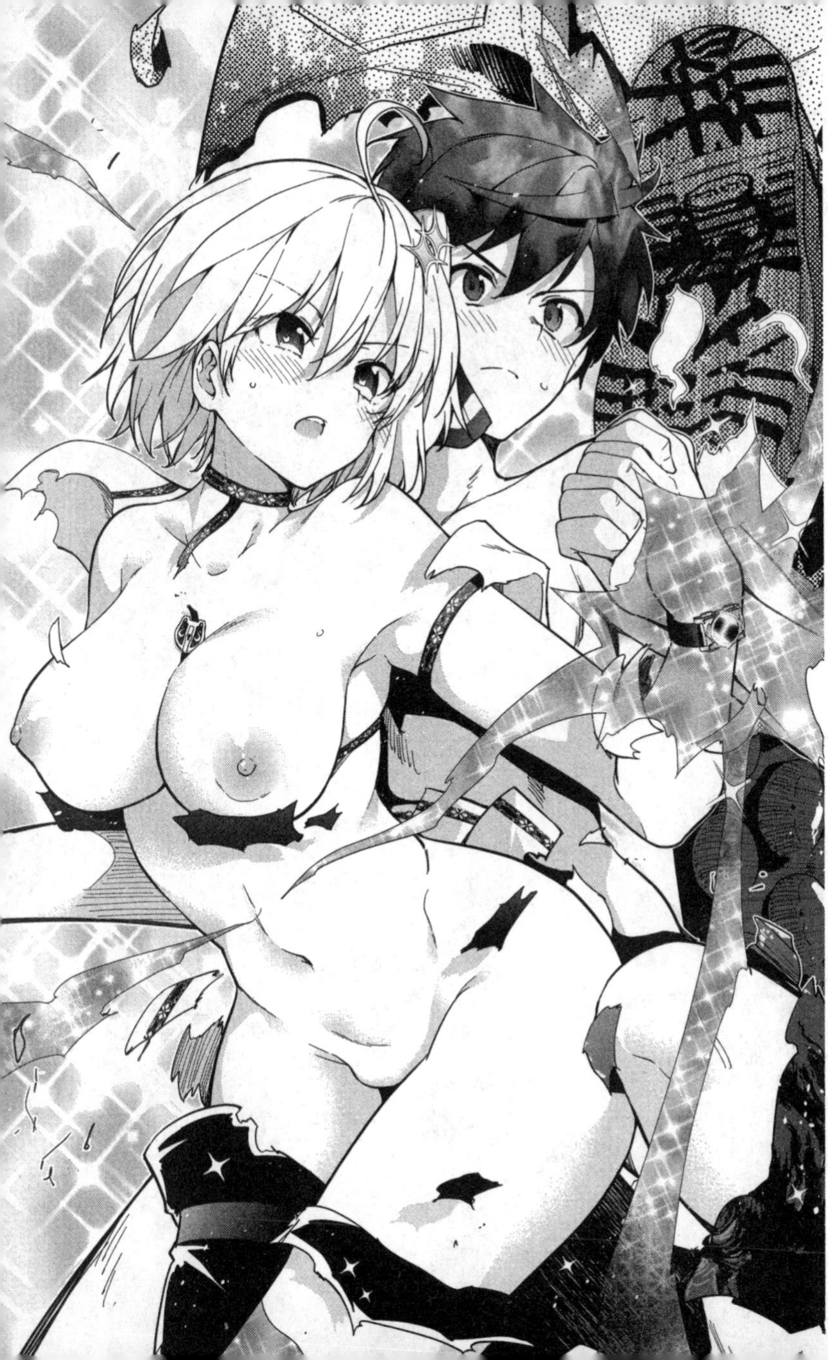

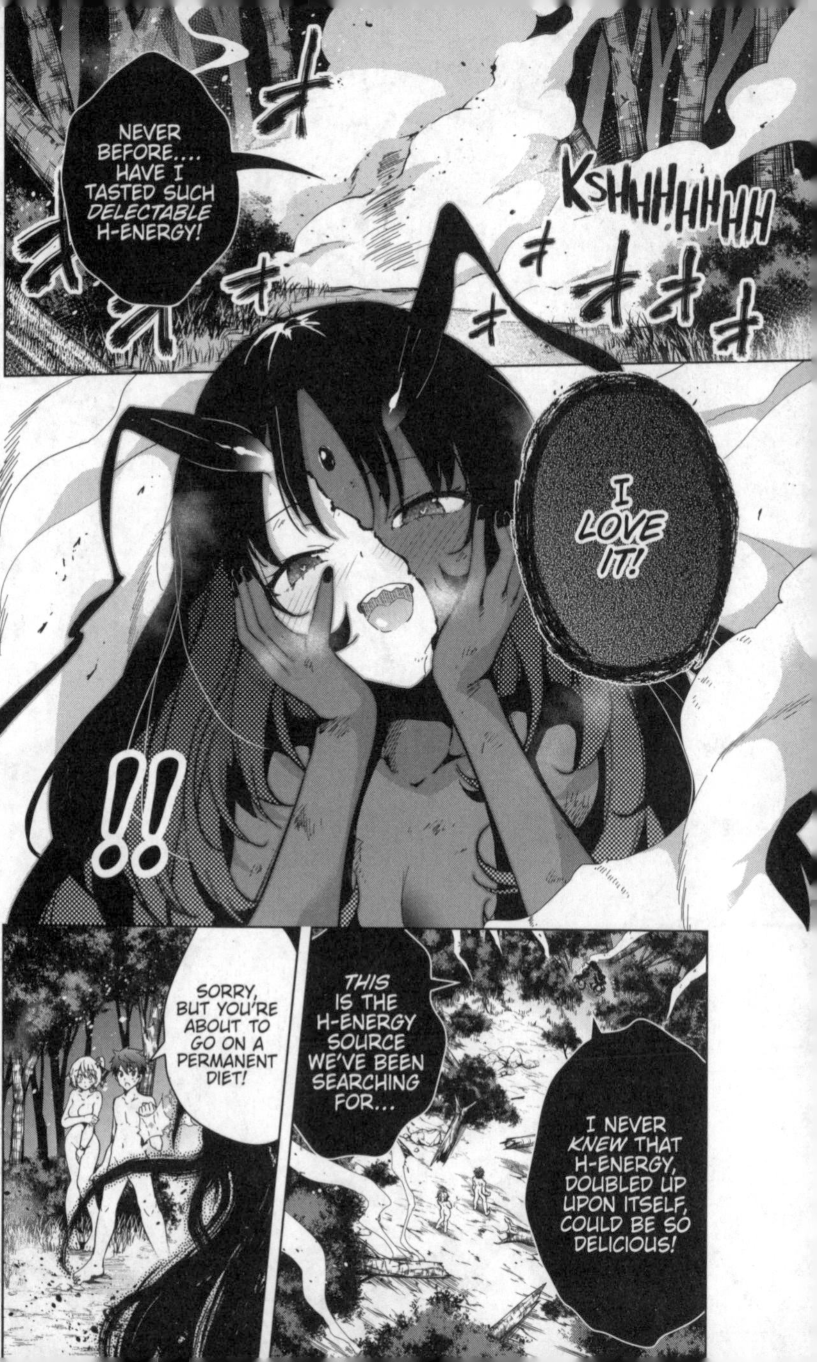

NEVER BEFORE.... HAVE I TASTED SUCH *DELECTABLE* H-ENERGY!
KSHHHHHHHH
I *LOVE IT!*
!!
THIS IS THE H-ENERGY SOURCE WE'VE BEEN SEARCHING FOR...
I NEVER *KNEW* THAT H-ENERGY, DOUBLED UP UPON ITSELF, COULD BE SO DELICIOUS!
SORRY, BUT YOU'RE ABOUT TO GO ON A PERMANENT DIET!

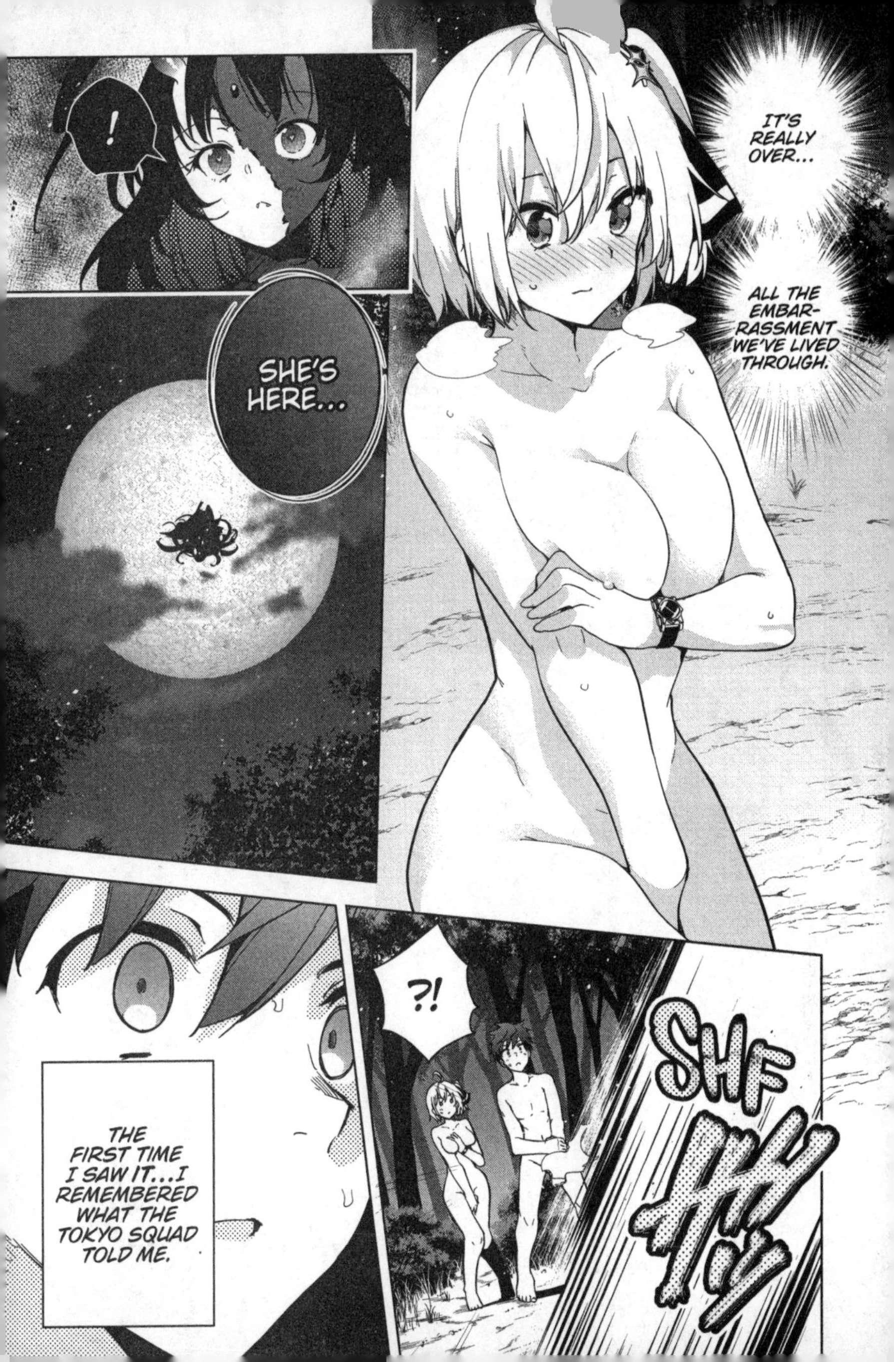
IT'S REALLY OVER...
ALL THE EMBAR-RASSMENT WE'VE LIVED THROUGH.
!
SHE'S HERE...
?!
SHF
THE FIRST TIME I SAW IT...I REMEMBERED WHAT THE TOKYO SQUAD TOLD ME.

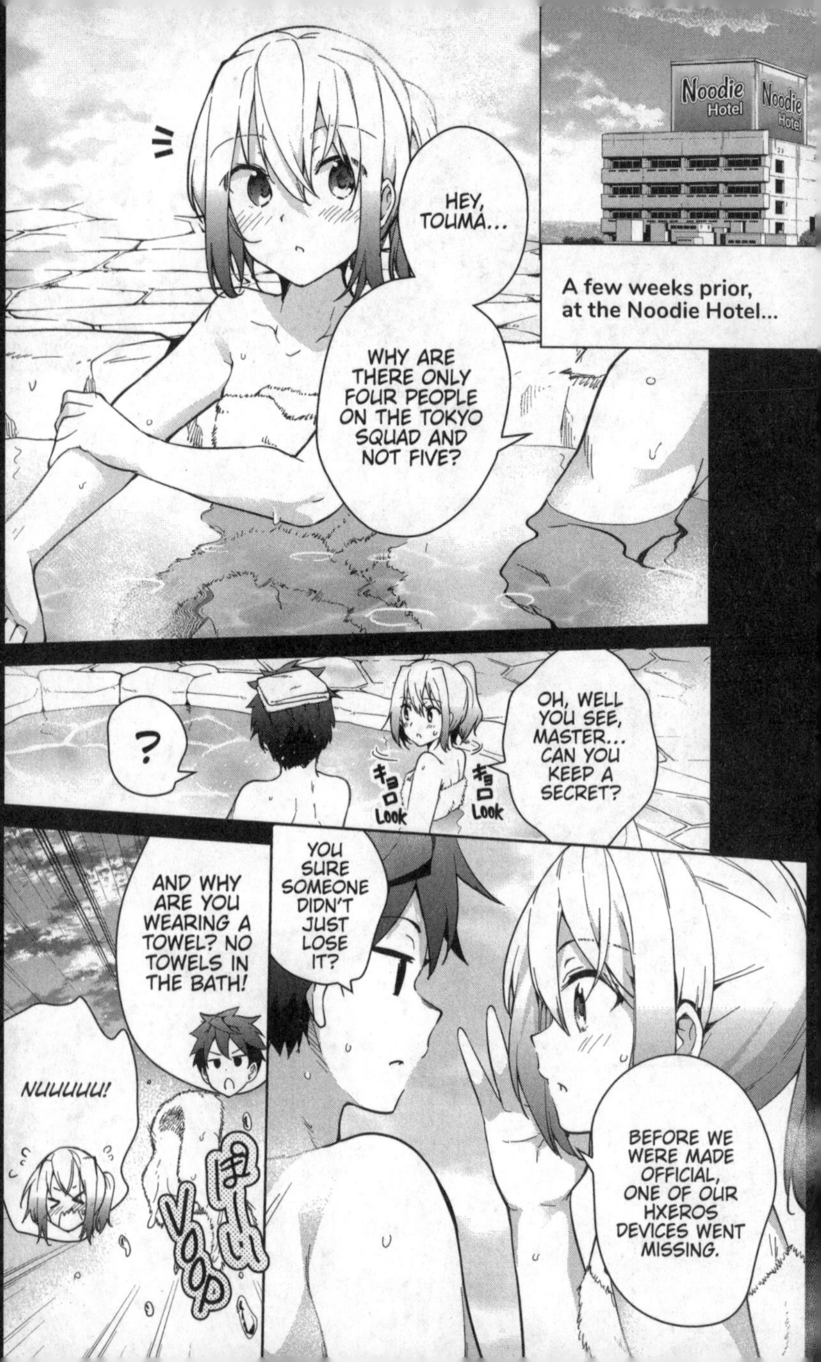

Noodie Hotel
Noodie Hotel
A few weeks prior, at the Noodie Hotel...
HEY, TOUMA...
WHY ARE THERE ONLY FOUR PEOPLE ON THE TOKYO SQUAD AND NOT FIVE?
OH, WELL YOU SEE, MASTER... CAN YOU KEEP A SECRET?
キョロ Look
キョロ Look
?
BEFORE WE WERE MADE OFFICIAL, ONE OF OUR HXEROS DEVICES WENT MISSING.
YOU SURE SOMEONE DIDN'T JUST LOSE IT?
AND WHY ARE YOU WEARING A TOWEL? NO TOWELS IN THE BATH!
NUUUUU!
ぽい VOOP

SEVEN SEAS ENTERTAINMENT PRESENTS

SUPER HXEROS

story and art by RYOMA KITADA

VOLUME 6

TRANSLATION
Katrina Leonoudakis

ADAPTATION
David Lumsdon

LETTERING AND RETOUCH
Joven Voon

COVER DESIGN
Nicky Lim

PROOFREADER
B. Lillian Martin

EDITOR
Elise Kelsey

PREPRESS TECHNICIAN
Melanie Ujimori

PRINT MANAGER
nnon Rasmussen-Silverstein

PRODUCTION MANAGER - GHOST SHIP
George Panella

PRODUCTION MANAGER
Lissa Pattillo

EDITOR-IN-CHIEF
Julie Davis

ASSOCIATE PUBLISHER
Adam Arnold

PUBLISHER
Jason DeAngelis

DEC 1 5 2022

SUPER HXEROS -"H"EROES SAVE THE WORLD
DOKYU HENTAI EGUZEROSU © 2017 by Ryoma Kitada
All rights reserved.
First published in Japan in 2017 by SHUEISHA Inc., Tokyo.
English translation rights arranged by SHUEISHA Inc.
through TOHAN CORPORATION, Tokyo.

No portion of this book may be reproduced or transmitted in any form without written
permission from the copyright holders. This is a work of fiction. Names, characters,
places, and incidents are the products of the author's imagination or are used
fictitiously. Any resemblance to actual events, locales, or persons, living or dead,
is entirely coincidental. Any information or opinions expressed by the creators of this
book belong to those individual creators and do not necessarily reflect the views of
Seven Seas Entertainment or its employees.

Seven Seas press and purchase enquiries can be sent to Marketing Manager Lianne
Sentar at press@gomanga.com. Information regarding the distribution and purchase of
digital editions is available from Digital Manager CK Russell at digital@gomanga.com.

Seven Seas and the Seven Seas logo are trademarks of
Seven Seas Entertainment. All rights reserved.

ISBN: 978-1-63858-173-4
Printed in Canada
First Printing: March 2022
10 9 8 7 6 5 4 3 2 1

//// READING DIRECTIONS ////

This book reads from *right to left*,
Japanese style. If this is your first time
reading manga, you start reading from
the top right panel on each page and
take it from there. If you get lost, just
follow the numbered diagram here.
It may seem backwards at first,
but you'll get the hang of it! Have fun!!

Follow us online: www.SevenSeasEntertainment.com

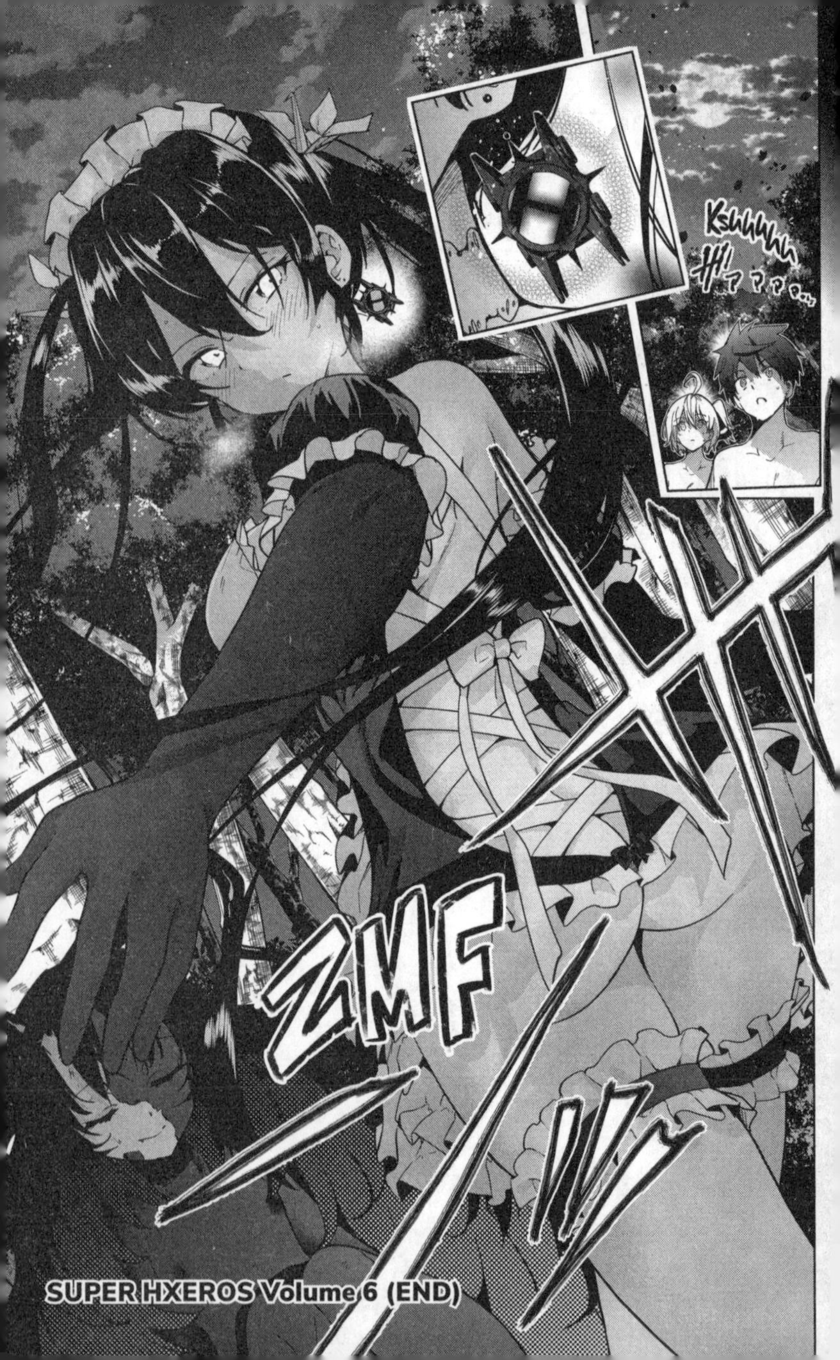
Kshuuuuu
ZMF

SUPER HXEROS Volume 6 (END)